'A timely and enriched revisit of the seminal and comprehensive manual for nations seeking to competitively and sustainably re-imagine their nation brands beyond the pandemic. It is a rich and valuable academic and pragmatic reference with insightful best practices for emerging and established nations alike.'

– Thebe Ikalafeng, Founder and Chairman, Brand Africa

'Not that it needed confirmation, but the fact that Keith Dinnie's masterpiece is now in its third edition proves that it is the go-to standard handbook on nation branding (and has been for a while).'

– Robert Govers, author of the award-winning book
Imaginative Communities (*2018*)

'The most comprehensive and updated book in this field. Dinnie's work is building a global brand for the study and practice of nation branding.'

– Koh Buck Song, author of Brand Singapore

'The 3rd Edition of *Nation Branding* is an essential read for those interested in branding places – it is a comprehensive book that covers all aspects of nation branding. Contributors include well-known researchers and practitioners from the field, which enriches the book from both a theoretical angle and a practical approach. The 3rd Edition of *Nation Branding* is the most important manual for students, researchers, professors and professionals who work in the area or have an interest in nation branding.'

– João Ricardo Freire, professor at Ipam and researcher at ICNOVA in
Lisbon, Portugal

T0313268

NATION BRANDING

Nation Branding: Concepts, Issues, Practice provides a theoretical framework, alongside insightful examples from the practice of nation branding, in which the principles of brand strategy and management are applied to countries globally. This new edition has been comprehensively updated and its influential original framework modified to reflect the very latest changes in the field. It remains an accessible blend of theory and practice rich with international examples and contributions.

Updates to this edition:

- New Academic Perspectives and Practitioner Insights in each chapter.
- Updated and new cases from a broad range of nations and cultures.
- Fresh coverage of online branding and social media.
- New material covering the critical and ethical issues of nation branding, including the limitations.
- Updated references and sources.
- Updated online resources, including PowerPoint slides, a test bank and a glossary.

This is an essential introduction to nation branding for students of Marketing, Brand Management, Communications, and Public and International Relations, as well as policy makers looking for a rigorous yet applied approach.

Keith Dinnie is Head of Management and Marketing at the University of Dundee School of Business, UK, and the founder of Brand Horizons (www.brandhorizons.com). Considered one of the world's leading experts on nation branding, he has published in several international journals and has delivered keynote speeches, workshops, seminars and conference presentations across the world.

3rd Edition

NATION BRANDING

CONCEPTS, ISSUES, PRACTICE

KEITH DINNIE

Routledge
Taylor & Francis Group

LONDON AND NEW YORK

Cover image: Getty

Third edition published 2022
by Routledge
4 Park Square, Milton Park, Abingdon, Oxon OX14 4RN

and by Routledge
605 Third Avenue, New York, NY 10158

Routledge is an imprint of the Taylor & Francis Group, an informa business

British Library Cataloguing-in-Publication Data
First edition published by Routledge 2007
A catalogue record for this book is available from the British Library

Library of Congress Cataloging-in-Publication Data
A catalog record for this book has been requested

ISBN: 978-0-367-56988-4 (hbk)
ISBN: 978-0-367-56989-1 (pbk)
ISBN: 978-1-003-10024-9 (ebk)

DOI: 10.4324/9781003100249

Access the Support Material: www.routledge.com/9780367569891

Contents

Preface

Interest in the field of nation branding has continued to grow since the time when the second edition of this book was published. It is therefore timely for this third edition to appear, reflecting the increasing attention focused on the topic by policy makers, business, students and academics.

The book is written for a number of audiences, each of whom will come to the field of nation branding with their own specific interests and agendas:

- MBA, master's, and upper-level undergraduates studying subjects including but not limited to marketing, branding, international business, public diplomacy, international relations, economic geography and tourism
- Governments and policy makers, particularly in the fields of economic development, trade and investment and tourism
- Individuals with an interest in how their country is perceived and the ways in which their country is (or is not) attempting to enhance its reputation

A key feature of the book is the provision of different perspectives on nation branding through the inclusion of contributions from a wide range of academics and practitioners. These contributions illuminate vividly the theories, concepts and frameworks that form the basis of the book. Case studies are provided on the nation branding activities and challenges of countries as diverse as the United States, China, Peru, Korea, India, Great Britain, Bosnia-Herzegovina, The Gambia, Chile, Sweden, Japan and many more. It is a key contention of this book that the principles of nation branding can be applied successfully by any nation whether small or large, rich or poor, developed or emerging. The case studies are designed to demonstrate this point.

Many people have contributed in different ways to this book. I hope that you will find it stimulating and thought-provoking to read. It is designed to act as a starting point for discussion and action, rather than as a final statement on the topic of nation branding.

Keith Dinnie
Dundee, Scotland

Acknowledgements

My thanks go to Emmie Shand and Sophia Levine at Routledge for all their hard work and commitment in bringing this third edition to fruition. Many thanks also to all of the contributors to this book, who have enriched it with their academic perspectives, practitioner insights and cases.

Disclaimer

Views and opinions expressed in this publication are solely those of the author and do not necessarily reflect the views of the author's organisations or the views of the other contributors and the publishers.

About the author

Keith Dinnie, PhD, is one of the world's leading experts on nation branding. He has published in several international journals including *International Marketing Review*, *Marketing Theory*, *Tourism Management*, *Journal of Brand Management*, *Place Branding and Public Diplomacy*, *Corporate Reputation Review*, *Journal of Consumer Marketing* and *Journal of Services Marketing*. He has delivered keynote speeches, workshops, seminars and conference presentations in the United States, United Kingdom, France, Germany, Netherlands, Russia, Iceland, Portugal, Greece, South Africa, Malaysia, China, South Korea and Japan. He is a faculty member at the University of Dundee School of Business (UDSB), Scotland. He is the founder of Brand Horizons (www.brandhorizons.com).

Contributors

Malcolm Allan, President, Bloom Consulting

Malcolm Allan is President of Bloom Consulting, an international place brand strategy consultancy with offices in London, Lisbon, Madrid and Sao Paulo. Previously Malcolm founded Placebrands (2002) and Placematters (2012) and has worked in this field since 2000. Recently he has worked for the following countries on their country or nation brand strategies – Australia, Costa Rica, Israel and Paraguay, and on city brand strategies for Cork, Riyad, Mississauga in Canada, Stockholm and St Petersburg in Florida, USA. He writes for *The Place Brand Observer*, most recently on place brand strategy and the climate emergency.

Simon Anholt

Simon Anholt is an independent policy advisor who has worked with the heads of state and heads of government of 58 nations to help improve their economic, political and cultural engagements with the international community. He is regarded as the world's leading expert on national image and the inventor of the term 'nation brand'. Anholt publishes the *Good Country Index*, a study measuring the impact of each of 163 countries on the rest of humanity and the planet. His TED talk launching the first edition of the GCI has passed 12 million views. He is the founder and publisher of the annual *Anholt-Ipsos Nation Brands Index* and *City Brands Index*, which since 2005 have used a panel of 20,000 people in 20 countries to monitor global perceptions of 50 countries and 50 cities. Anholt's latest book, *The Good Country Equation*, was published in 2020.

Daniel Valverde Bagnarello, Nation Brand Director, *essential* COSTA RICA

essential COSTA RICA is the country brand that showed the greatest annual growth in America according to the Bloom Consulting Country Brand Ranking 2017/2018. For over 20 years Daniel Valverde Bagnarello has built a career in the creative application of commercial management and the development of local brands for international audiences. He holds master's degrees in both Digital Marketing and Management from IE Business School in Madrid and is currently pursuing his PhD in Communication at Pompeu Fabra University in Barcelona. Along the way, Daniel has been appointed President of the Ibero American Country Brands Council, collected the Place Brand of the Year Award at the 2019 City Nation Place Global Conference in London and received the Branding Award at the 2020 Place Marketing Forum in Marseille.

Conrad Bird CBE, Director, Campaigns & Marketing, Cabinet Office
Conrad is Director of Campaigns & Marketing for the Cabinet Office, where he is responsible for Covid-19 communications, as well as major cross-government campaigns. Conrad was formerly at the Department for International Trade and before that, ran the GREAT Britain campaign, based at 10 Downing Street. He previously worked at the Foreign & Commonwealth Office as Head of Public Diplomacy and Strategic Campaigns and at the Cabinet Office. Before joining the Civil Service, Conrad spent 18 years in advertising, and during this time, set up his own award-winning communication consultancy.

Tom Buncle FTS, FTMI
Tom Buncle runs Yellow Railroad Ltd., an international destination consultancy specialising in destination branding, marketing, management planning and crisis recovery. His client list spans the United Kingdom, Europe, Africa, Asia, Middle East, North America and the Caribbean. Previously Tom was Chief Executive of Visit Scotland and worked for Visit Britain in the USA, Canada, Norway, London and Singapore. He is Honorary Professor at Edinburgh's Heriot-Watt University and lectures at international conferences, universities and business schools, on destination branding, tourism marketing, crisis recovery and global travel trends. He authored the definitive *Handbook on Tourism Destination Branding*, published by the United Nations World Tourism Organisation (UNWTO) and European Travel Commission (ETC). Tom has served as a non-executive director on Edinburgh International Festival Council, Cairngorm Partnership, Scotland the Brand and Contact Singapore's European Panel (former guardian of Singapore's international image). He is a Fellow of the UK Tourism Society and the UK Tourism Management Institute.

Andrew Burnett, Founder, helleau®
Andrew Burnett is a brand strategist based in Edinburgh, Scotland. He once read that a tagline should be short and simple; he agreed and trademarked Short and Simple® as his strapline. Andrew distills complex information into simple truths. He founded helleau® to help clients who care about how they are perceived. Andrew has over two decades of experience branding and marketing brands ranging from nations, blue chips and multinationals to owner operated start-ups. For 13 years his personal website, andrewburnett.com, was the top result on Google for the search term 'Social Media Scotland'. Andrew believes that his greatest piece of writing ever was his Tinder profile. After reading this bio, he is sure you will agree.

Félix Lossio Chávez, PhD, Former General Director of Cultural Industries and Arts at the Ministry of Culture in Peru (2020–2018, 2013–2012) and former consultant for the Ministry of Tourism and External Commerce in Peru
Félix Lossio Chávez has co-edited three books and published more than ten articles on subjects related to creative industries, cultural policies, nation branding and citizenship.

He was awarded a PhD in Latin American Studies by Newcastle University (2018), with a thesis entitled 'The construction of Latin America as a brand: designs, narrations and disputes in Peru and Cuba'. He obtained an MSc in Sociology – Culture and Society from London School of Economics and Political Science and a BA in Sociology from

Pontificia Universidad Católica del Perú. He currently gives lectures at Pontificia Universidad Católica del Perú and is consultant to international organisations in the fields mentioned above.

Nicholas J. Cull

Nicholas J. Cull is Professor of Public Diplomacy at the University of Southern California's Annenberg School for Communication and Journalism. He is a scholar of the interface between media and foreign policy and has written widely on the history of propaganda in international affairs. His recent books include *Public Diplomacy: Foundations for Global Engagement in the Digital Age* (2019) and (co-edited with Michael Hawes) *Canadian Public Diplomacy* (2021). He is a former editor of *Place Branding and Public Diplomacy* and, with Simon Anholt, is co-host of the podcast People, Places, Power.

Luke Devereux, PhD, Middlesex University London

Luke Devereux, PhD is a lecturer in Marketing at Middlesex University London. His research interests include corporate identity, complex systems and social enterprise. His research has been published in *International Studies of Management and Organisation* and *Journal of Business Research*. Before joining academia, he worked as a journalist, editor and market researcher.

Clare Dewhirst, Founder and Director, City Nation Place

Clare's interest in the complex area of place branding was sparked whilst working on a series of Nation Branding Masterclass events, led by Simon Anholt, one of the first thought-leaders to speak about and promote the concept of place branding. Having listened to Simon address audiences around the world on how policy, governance and symbolic actions need to combine with branding and marketing to create a competitive identity and drive economic growth, she continued to follow the growth in this sector. As Global Conference Director for *The International Herald Tribune*, now the *New York Times*, Clare also saw growth in advertising and storytelling around tourism and investment promotion strategy. Clare launched the first City Nation Place Global conference in London in 2015, and has since established annual events for the Americas (USA and Canada), LatAm & Caribbean, and the UK, as well as events for the Asia region. The citynationplace.com website has steadily built an audience for its articles, interviews and research. The CNP Connections membership hub was launched at the start of 2021 to provide a platform for off the record, peer-to-peer conversations between place brand leaders. Clare manages the small team at City Nation Place alongside providing event consultancy and management for a number of clients in the publishing and trade association sector.

Vana Dimitropoulou

Vana Dimitropoulou is a tourism and hospitality marketing expert. She obtained an MSc in Marketing with Brand Management at the University of Stirling where she won the award for the Best MSc Marketing Dissertation for the academic year 2017–2018. Her dissertation on country branding focused on the brand image of the Greek islands during the Syrian refugee crisis. Consequently, promoting Greece and exploring its hospitality scene has become her passion. Currently she works as Marketing Specialist at the H&P Hotels and Restaurants in Athens, a hospitality group company which owns hotels, summer houses and restaurants in Athens and the Greek islands. With a specialty of social media, she also works on projects which include clothing, jewelry and cosmetics companies operating within Greece. Outside of the office, she enjoys travelling and remains committed to her role as Scout Leader of her residential area.

Jeet Dogra, Indian Institute of Tourism and Travel Management (IITTM)

Dr Jeet Dogra is Assistant Professor at the Indian Institute of Tourism and Travel Management (IITTM), Gwalior, Madhya Pradesh, India (an autonomous body under Ministry of Tourism, Government of India). His research areas are destination marketing and branding. He has a PhD in Tourism Management and a Masters in Tourism Management (Gold Medallist) from University of Jammu, India as well as being University Grant Commission's Junior Research Fellow (JRF).

Hong Fan

Hong Fan is a professor in the School of Journalism and Communication, where she teaches Place Branding, Global Communication and Strategic Communication for PhD and MA programmes, and a professor of Corporate Communication for the EMBA Programme in the School of Economics and Management at Tsinghua University, Beijing. Professor Fan obtained her PhD in Cross-Cultural Communication from University of Oxford, United Kingdom. She worked as a diplomat at the Chinese Embassy in New Zealand in the 1990s. Currently she is director of the National Image Research Centre (NIRC) and director of the City Branding Studio, Tsinghua University, Beijing. She is also a board member of the International Place Branding Association (IPBA). Professor Fan's research areas include national image, city branding, reputation management and corporate communication. She is editor-in-chief of the *National Image Research* book series, with six books published over the past decade by Tsinghua University Press.

Haiyan Feng

Dr Haiyan Feng is Assistant Professor at the School of Journalism and Communication, Xiamen University. She achieved her doctoral degree at the School of Journalism and Communication, Tsinghua University (THU) in 2020, and then joined Xiamen University in the same year. During her PhD studies at THU, she worked as a sessional academic and research assistant. Her research interests include nation image studies, cross-cultural communication and visual communication. Recent publications include peer-reviewed journal articles in *Modern Communication* and *Chinese Journal of Journalism & Communication*.

Una FitzGibbon

Una FitzGibbon is the Director of Marketing of Bord Bia – The Irish Food Board, which exists to bring Ireland's outstanding produce to world markets, in turn bringing growth and sustainability to producers. Una's role, together with her teams, is to create lasting impact and brand value by leading the development of Ireland's reputation as a source of natural, sustainable food, through world-class global brand marketing. Una does this by leading the development and evaluation of marketing and brand strategies, optimising and scaling marketing activities across integrated channels and acting with the consumer in mind at all times to build brand positioning nationally and globally. Her leadership in developing and building Ireland's association with sustainable food through Origin Green is recognised by sustainability, agri-food business experts and academics around the world and is shaping modern nation food branding.

João Ricardo Freire, PhD

Dr João Ricardo Freire is a professor at Ipam and a researcher at ICNOVA in Lisbon, Portugal. Joao's background in economics initially led him to work in the fields of finance and then marketing for several multinational companies in Brazil, Portugal and the United Kingdom. Joao Ricardo Freire is also the co-founder of two companies, Ecoterra and Epicuspicy, which specialis in marketing and branding food products. João's greatest interest is in branding and, more specifically, place branding. After years of quantitative and qualitative research, Dr Freire has developed new ideas and unique methodologies for place brand identity construction. He has developed several branding projects for different places around the world. Joao is also an author and frequent speaker on branding topics. His research has been published in articles and book chapters in several international publications. He is currently the Regional Editor for Europe, Middle East and Africa for the journal *Place Branding and Public Diplomacy*.

Robert Govers

Robert Govers is an independent international adviser, scholar, speaker and author on the reputation of cities, regions and countries and is chairman of the International Place Branding Association. Since 2009 Robert has co-edited and authored four books with Palgrave Macmillan publishers. *Imaginative Communities: Admired cities, regions and countries* (2018) is his first award-winning book published under his own imprint. In addition, he is co-editor of the quarterly journal, *Place Branding and Public Diplomacy*, and a contributor to Apolitical, the World Economic Forum Agenda and The Economist Intelligence Unit Perspectives. He has also been an adjunct or visiting scholar at Tsinghua University, Beijing; the Indian School of Business, Hyderabad; the University of Leuven, Belgium; Rotterdam School of Management, the Netherlands; Loughborough University London Campus; IULM University Milano, Italy; and several institutes in Dubai, UAE. He also teaches place branding in the UNESCO World Heritage at Work master's programme in Torino, Italy.

Natasha Grand, Co-Founder, INSTID (Institute for Identity)

Natasha took on place branding after studying modern national ideologies at LSE following a natural fascination with the sense of home and belonging. She co-founded INSTID (Institute for Identity) in London in 2009 and has worked in regions and cities with a total population of over 20 million people since. Dr Grand established herself as a 'therapist for nations', with a specialty in finding purpose and common values for residents at any place. She speaks and interviews extensively on the subjects of place identity, popular engagement and communication, and the creation of modern lifestyles, traditions and experiences.

David Haigh, Chairman and CEO, Brand Finance

David is the Chairman and CEO of Brand Finance Plc – the world's leading brand valuation consultancy. He has worked in the area of branded business, brand and intangible asset valuation since 1991. He specialised entirely in the field after becoming the Director of Brand Valuation for Interbrand in 1995. He subsequently left Interbrand in 1996 to launch Brand Finance which is celebrating 25 years in business this year. David represented the British Standards Institution in the working parties responsible for crafting international industry standards: ISO 10668 on Brand Valuation in 2010 and ISO 20671 on Brand Evaluation in 2019. David is a passionate writer and has authored many articles on brand valuation, published in numerous marketing and finance newspapers and magazines, such as: *Financial Times*, *Accountancy Age* and *Marketing Week*. He has also lectured on the topic of brand valuation for Harvard, Chicago and London Business Schools. David graduated from Bristol University with an English degree, qualified as a Chartered Accountant with Price Waterhouse in London, and obtained a postgraduate diploma in Marketing from the Chartered Institute of Marketing (CIM). He is a Fellow of The Royal Institution of Chartered Surveyors (RICS) and has a practising certificate with the Institute of Chartered Accountants in England and Wales (ICAEW).

Lucy Hall, Independent Researcher

Lucy Hall is an independent researcher based in the north of England. She has a particular interest in place branding, particularly the branding and projected image of destinations.

Rosemarijn Hoefte

Rosemarijn Hoefte is a professor of the history of Suriname after 1873 at the University of Amsterdam and a senior researcher at KITLV/Royal Netherlands Institute of Southeast Asian Studies in Leiden, the Netherlands. In her monograph *Suriname in the Long Twentieth Century: Domination, Contestation, Globalization* (Palgrave Macmillan, 2014) she discusses the socioeconomic history of this Caribbean country. One of her research interests is the interlinkage between nation building and nation branding in post-colonial states.

Thebe Ikalafeng, Founder, Brand Africa, Brand Leadership, Africa Brand Leadership Academy

Thebe Ikalafeng is a global African thought leader in branding and reputation management. He is the founder of Brand Africa (www.brand.africa), an Africa-focused brand-led movement to inspire the African renaissance, Brand Leadership (www.brandleadership. africa), a pan-african branding and reputation advisory firm, and the Africa Brand Leadership Academy (www.abla.academy), an Africa-focused postgraduate academy of brand leadership. He has been to every country in Africa and every continent in the world, and has summitted the highest mountains in Africa and Europe.

Florian Kaefer, PhD, Founder and Editor of PlaceBrandObserver.com (The Place Brand Observer)

Florian Kaefer, PhD is the Founder and Editor of PlaceBrandObserver.com (The Place Brand Observer), the leading knowledge hub on place branding and location reputation. Dr Kaefer obtained his PhD from the Waikato University Management School in New Zealand, for which he researched the country's perceived brand credibility. He holds a master's degree in sustainable development (Exeter University, United Kingdom) and a bachelor's in tourism management (Brighton University, United Kingdom). He is the author of *An Insider's Guide to Place Branding* (Springer, 2021) and *Sustainability Leadership in Tourism: Interviews, Insights and Knowledge from Practice* (Springer, forthcoming). Based in St Gallen, Switzerland, Florian is also the Founder of the Sustainability Leaders Project (Sutainability-Leaders.com) and is an accredited member of the German Journalist Association DFJV.

Nadia Kaneva, Associate Professor, Department of Media, Film and Journalism Studies, University of Denver, United States

Nadia Kaneva's research draws on critical theories of culture, power and communication to examine the intersections of media, ideologies and markets. Her publications explore nation branding as a strategic instrument for the advancement of various actors' claims to power, with an emphasis on post-communist and post-conflict societies. She is the editor of three books: *Mediating Post-Socialist Femininities* (Routledge, 2015), *Branding Post-Communist Nations: Marketizing National Identities in the "New" Europe* (Routledge, 2011), and, with Stewart Hoover, *Fundamentalisms and the Media* (Bloomsbury, 2009). Her research appears in numerous academic journals and edited collections, and she is a member of the editorial boards of the *Journal of Communication, Place Branding and Public Diplomacy,* and the *Public Diplomacy Journal.*

Venkata Rohan Sharma Karri, Independent Researcher

Venkata Rohan Sharma Karri is an independent researcher based in Hyderabad, Telangana, India. His research work focuses on luxury tourism, consumer behaviour, tourist experiences, destination branding and management with a special emphasis on developing regions.

Mihalis Kavaratzis

Dr Mihalis Kavaratzis is Associate Professor of Marketing (University of Leicester School of Business) and holds a PhD in City Marketing. Mihalis is a founding board member of the International Place Branding Association and Senior Fellow of the Institute of Place Management. He is one of the most cited authors in the field of place marketing and place branding. Mihalis is co-editor of *Inclusive Place Branding* (with M. Giovanardi and M. Lichrou, 2017), *Rethinking Place Branding* (with G. Warnaby and G.J. Ashworth, 2015) and *Towards Effective Place Brand Management* (with G.J. Ashworth, 2010).

Kim, You Kyung, PhD, Professor, Hankuk University of Foreign Studies (HUFS), Korea

Kim, You Kyung is a professor at Hankuk University of Foreign Studies (HUFS) where he teaches Media Communication and currently serves as Director of the Public Brand Research Center. He served as Vice President at HUFS and as Chairman of the Seoul City Brand Council. He was formerly a senior member of the Presidential Council on Nation Branding in Korea. He is a member of the executive committee of UNESCO's Korean Committee and a vice chairman of the Culture and Communications Division. He holds a PhD in Mass Communication from Syracuse University. His research interests include nation branding, city branding, corporate brand management, culture and consumer behaviour, and global branding. He is currently a regional editor of the journal *Place Branding and Public Diplomacy* and served as an editor at the *Korean Journal of Advertising*. He served as President of the Korean Advertising Society. He has worked widely as an advisor, lecturer and consultant in both the public and private sectors in Korea.

Koh Buck Song

Koh Buck Song is a Singaporean country brand adviser, and author and editor of more than 30 books, including *Brand Singapore* (third edition, with a Chinese edition in China) and the place branding-themed travel memoir *Around the World in 68 Days*. A member of the Marketing Advisory Panel of Singapore's current country brand, he worked on brand Singapore for over 20 years, including as head, communications and strategic planning, Economic Development Board; and head, public affairs (Southeast Asia) at Hill & Knowlton, with branding projects including the global launch of Gardens by the Bay and National Gallery. Overseas, he has spoken on brand Singapore including in London (keynote speaker, City Nation Place global forum), Tokyo, Bhutan and Tahiti, and the universities of Harvard, MIT, Chicago, Oxford, Fudan and Melbourne. A graduate of Harvard Kennedy School, he has taught at Lee Kuan Yew School of Public Policy and Singapore Management University.

Cat Leaver, Head of Brand & Content, VisitScotland

Cat is a strategic marketing leader with experience across traditional and digital channels, complex stakeholder management and a track record of delivering results in both agency and client-side environments. She heads up global brand and content for VisitScotland and holds a non-executive board position for CodeClan – Scotland's national digital skills academy – and an advisory board position for City Nation Place. In 2018, Cat was brought in to lead on the cross-agency initiative Brand Scotland, setting out a bold new strategy for Scotland and worked across national organisations to establish a team of talent, a digital infrastructure and a platform which set out to build Scotland's international profile and reputation as a choice destination in which to live, work, study, visit and do business. Over her tenure, this team delivered the multi award-winning *Scotland Is Now* platform, establishing Scotland as one of the top five most admired place brands in the world by the Anholt-Ipsos City Nation Place Survey in April 2020.

Patrick Lennon, Content Coordinator, Tourism Ireland

Patrick has worked for Tourism Ireland for 19 years and has been Content Coordinator for the last seven years. Patrick holds an MA in Marketing and has specialised in online and offline publishing. In past years, Patrick has led successful print and social media projects in marketing the island of Ireland as a holiday destination including the development of a book published in 2019 highlighting ten years of the Tourism Ireland Global Greenings initiative around the world on St Patrick's Day. As early as 2003 Patrick lobbied for the adoption of an image bank within Tourism Ireland and has led the efforts from 2011 to embrace Digital Marketing Asset Management Systems within Tourism Ireland and partner organisations.

Daniela Montiel, Director of Strategic Partnerships at Fundación Imagen de Chile

Daniela Montiel holds a master's degree in Public Diplomacy from the University of Southern California and a bachelor's degree in Literature from Loyola Marymount University. She is currently the Director of Strategic Partnerships at Fundación Imagen de Chile, the public–private foundation that manages Chile's country brand, where she leads a partnership strategy which aims to position Chile internationally and provide support in target markets for international efforts carried out by members of both the public and private sectors. She started her career in international relations at the United Nations' Economic Commission for Latin America and the Caribbean where she spent six years working on economic development projects in Latin America on topics including open data, telecommunications and transportation. Originally from Los Angeles, California, she is currently based in Santiago, Chile.

Dan Nunan, Professor, Warwick University, United Kingdom

Dan Nunan is a professor at Warwick University, UK. He previously held positions at the University of Reading, University of London and University of Portsmouth. He has published more than 50 journal articles and conference papers and is author of Europe's leading marketing research methods textbook (*Marketing Research: Applied Insight*) now in its sixth edition. His research interests are focused on macro-level phenomena relating to the digital economy and public policy. Recent projects have focused on customer privacy and big data, the ethical implications of artificial intelligence as well as the role of social media in spreading misinformation. Dan is currently Editor-in-Chief of the *International Journal of Market Research*.

James Pamment

James Pamment, PhD, is Associate Professor of Strategic Communication at Lund University and a non-resident scholar at the Carnegie Endowment for International Peace. In addition, he is co-editor-in-chief of the journal *Place Branding and Public Diplomacy*.

Theresa Regli

Theresa Regli is a 26-year veteran of the information technology industry, with a particular focus on Media and Marketing Asset Management (aka Digital Asset Management or DAM) for the last 17 years. As a consultant or fractional chief digital officer, she advises executives and technology project leads on Martech, DAM and broader digital strategy, data design, technology business cases and vendor selection, and subsequently supports the sustainment of digital stewardship and best practices. She has led and developed marketing technology strategies for over 20 per cent of the Fortune 500, including Unilever, Coca-Cola, General Mills, Shell and Nestlé. Over the course of her career Theresa has authored over 1000 pages of in-depth research on DAM, CMS (content management system) and MarTech vendors and tools, and she is the author of the definitive book on managing media and digital marketing assets, *Digital & Marketing Asset Management: The Real Story of DAM Technology & Practice* (Digital Reality Checks, 2016). She has presented keynotes in 18 countries over the last ten years, and is DAM industry liaison and guest lecturer in the digital media master's programme at King's College, London. She also serves on several advisory boards.

Dr Victoria Rodner, Lecturer in Marketing, University of Edinburgh
Originally from Venezuela, Victoria has worked in the United Kingdom and Brazil and much of her research has centred on the Global South. Her main areas of interest include value creation and management in the visual arts market, branding narratives, institutional theory and the role of actors in legitimising discourse and practice. Her more recent research – funded by the British Academy – is in the field of consumer culture theory and explores the phenomenon of spirit possession within a religious context. She is fiercely qualitative in her approach to research and has a keen interest in Grounded Theory, embodied research and introspective methodologies, including autoethnography and the poetic method. She has published her work in international marketing, management and sociology journals. She is a Fellow of the Higher Education Academy (UK).

Efe Sevin, PhD, Assistant Professor of Public Relations, Department of Mass Communication, Towson University, Maryland, United States
Efe Sevin's current research focuses on identifying and measuring the impacts of social networks on place branding and public diplomacy campaigns. His works have been published in several academic journals and books including *American Behavioral Scientist*, *Public Relations Review* and *Cities*. His most recent co-edited volume, *City Diplomacy Current Trends and Future Prospects*, was published by Palgrave MacMillan in 2020.

Neil H. Simon
Neil H. Simon is a partner at US-based Bighorn Communications. He has worked at the nexus of diplomacy, journalism and business communications in the United States, Europe, Asia and the Middle East and North Africa. He has been a spokesperson for the US Helsinki Commission and the Organization for Security and Cooperation in Europe, where he helped pass human rights legislation and produced the 57-country region's first interactive guide to digital open government practices. As a journalist, he covered the White House, Congress and state legislatures. He has produced award-winning documentary films on human rights on the US–Mexico border and US mistreatment of Japanese-Americans in WWII and bipartisanship. Mr. Simon has published dozens of op-eds on the virtues of soft power, human rights, inclusion and social justice. He is a graduate of the Medill School of Journalism at Northwestern University.

Heather Skinner, PhD
Dr Heather Skinner is Senior Fellow of the Institute of Place Management (IPM), a widely published author on place marketing, branding and tourism and Associate Editor of the IPM's official journal, the *Journal of Place Management and Development*. Now retired, she is founding chair of the Corfu Symposium on Managing and Marketing Places (2014–2019) and has been Chair of the IPM's *Visiting Places Special Interest Group*, and Co-Chair of the Academy of Marketing's *Place Marketing and Branding Special Interest Group*. Following a highly successful 15-year academic career in the United Kingdom at the University of South Wales (formerly the University of Glamorgan) Heather now lives on the Greek island of Corfu where she has continued to research and write about place management, marketing and branding issues that are related to responsible tourism.

Nancy Snow

Nancy Snow is Professor Emeritus of Communications at California State University, Fullerton and Pax Mundi ('Distinguished') Professor of Public Diplomacy at Kyoto University of Foreign Studies, the first public diplomacy professor in Japan. A two-time Fulbright Scholar and Social Science Research Council Abe Fellow, she has taught at two of the world's leading public diplomacy masters programmes, Syracuse University and the University of Southern California, and as visiting professor at IDC-Herzliya in Israel and UiTM in Malaysia. She is author, editor or co-editor of 13 books, including the *SAGE Handbook of Propaganda* and the second edition of the *Routledge Handbook of Public Diplomacy*. In 2020 Snow was Walt Disney Chair in Global Media at Schwarzman College, Tsinghua University.

Jan-Benedict E.M. Steenkamp

Jan-Benedict E.M. Steenkamp is the Massey Distinguished Professor of Marketing at the University of North Carolina. He has published over 100 articles in academic journals. His work has received over 54,000 citations. He is ranked fifth in marketing on career-long impact, and in the 0.1 per cent of scientists across all sciences. He has written five managerial books *Private Label Strategy: How to Beat the Store Brand Challenge* (Harvard Business School Press, 2007), *Brand Breakout: How Emerging Market Brands Will Go Global* (Palgrave Macmillan, 2013), *Global Brand Strategy: World-wise Marketing in the Age of Branding* (Palgrave MacMillan, 2017), *Retail Disruptors: The Spectacular Rise and Impact of the Hard Discounters* (Kogan Page, 2019) and *Time to Lead: Lessons for Today's Leaders from Bold Decisions that Changed History* (Fast Company Press, 2020). He has received lifetime achievement honours from the American Marketing Association and the European Marketing Academy.

Jose Filipe Torres, CEO, Bloom Consulting

Jose Filipe Torres advises place leaders such as heads of state, directors of national tourism organisations and investment promotion agencies on strategy and branding. Beyond Mr Torres' work across five continents, he has collaborated directly with the Organisation for Economic Co-operation and Development (OECD) and the World Economic Forum (WEF). Mr Torres has been a guest speaker at universities including Harvard and the London Business School. His publications include the Bloom Consulting Country Ranking, his latest book, *Nation Brand Builders*, and the Digital Country Index derived from Bloom Consulting analytical software, Digital Demand (D2©). Mr Torres is trilingual in English, Portuguese and Spanish.

Wouter Veenendaal, Associate Professor, Institute of Political Science, Leiden University, The Netherlands

Wouter Veenendaal's research examines the effects of population size on politics, with a particular focus on politics in small (island) states. He is the (co)author of *Politics and Democracy in Microstates* (Routledge, 2014), *Democracy in Small States: Persisting Against All Odds* (Oxford University Press, 2018) and *Population and Politics: The Impact of Scale* (Cambridge University Press, 2020), as well as numerous journal articles. His new research project focuses on the effects of decentralisation on democratic participation and competition in European subnational administrations.

Giannina Warren, Middlesex University London

Dr Giannina Warren is Senior Lecturer and Programme Leader of the BA Advertising PR and Branding at Middlesex University, London, United Kingdom. Prior to shifting to academic studies and research in the UK, her career spanned nearly two decades in Toronto, Canada as a specialist in visual identity, branding, advertising and public relations in high impact sectors such as finance, energy, legal, tourism, festivals/events and urban economic development. Her research focuses on the work of cultural intermediaries in place branding, applying a promotional culture lens to place. She has been published in *Tourism Management, Annals of Tourism Research* and *International Journal of Tourism Cities*.

Elsa G. Wilkin-Armbrister

Elsa G. Wilkin-Armbrister is a diplomat currently serving as Minister Counsellor at the St Kitts and Nevis High Commission in London and Commissioner General St Kitts and Nevis for Expo 2020 Dubai. Mrs Wilkin-Armbrister holds two master's degrees in Contemporary Diplomacy and International Marketing, and is known for her aptitude in cultural, art and public diplomacy. Matters of nation branding are a favourite pastime. She is a global citizen who has lived and worked in eight countries, with a penchant for travel, experiencing and embracing new cultures, cuisine and art. Mrs Wilkin-Armbrister lives in the United Kingdom with her daughter and husband.

FIGURES

TABLES

Glossary

ADIA	=	Abu Dhabi Investment Authority
AgriTech	=	agricultural technology
AMCL	=	Australian Made Campaign Limited
ANRET	=	Associação Nacional das Regiões de Turismo
ASEAN	=	Association of Southeast Asian Nations
BBG	=	Broadcasting Board of Governors
BRICS	=	Brazil, Russia, India, China, South Africa
CABE	=	Commission for Architecture and the Built Environment
CBBE	=	customer-based brand equity
CBD	=	country brand delegation
CETSCALE	=	consumer ethnocentric tendency scale
COO	=	country-of-origin
CPPI	=	contextualised product-place image
CRM	=	customer relationship management
CSA	=	country-specific advantage
CSR	=	corporate social responsibility
DAM	=	digital asset management
DCMS	=	Department for Culture, Media and Sport
DFA	=	design, fashion and architecture
DIT	=	Department for International Trade
ECA	=	Bureau of Educational and Cultural Affairs
ECLAL	=	explore Canada like a local
EFI	=	Environmental Footprint Index
EPI	=	Environmental Performance Index
ESI	=	Environmental Sustainability Index
EU	=	European Union
EVI	=	Environmental Vulnerability Index
FATF	=	Financial Action Task Force
FCO	=	Foreign & Commonwealth Office
FDI	=	foreign direct investment
FICH	=	Fundación Imagen de Chile

FIFA	=	Fédération Internationale de Football Association
FinTech	=	financial technology
FMCG	=	fast-moving consumer goods
FOSS	=	Forum of Small States
FTZ	=	free trade zone
GCC	=	Gulf Cooperation Council
GDP	=	Gross Domestic Product
GIPC	=	Ghana Investment Promotion Centre
GVA	=	gross value added
IBB	=	International Broadcasting Bureau
ICAIC	=	Instituto Cubano del Arte e Industria Cinematográficos
IIAG	=	Ibrahim Index of African Governance
IMC	=	integrated marketing communications
IPBA	=	International Place Branding Association
Kea	=	Kiwi Expatriates Association
MarTech	=	marketing technology
METI	=	Ministry of Economy, Trade and Industry
MIME	=	Multipurpose Internet Mail Extensions
MNE	=	multinational enterprise
NATO	=	North Atlantic Treaty Organization
NBAR	=	nation brand architecture
NBEQ	=	nation brand equity
NBI	=	Nation Brands Index
NBTC	=	Netherlands Board of Tourism & Conventions
NFC	=	need for cognition
NFIA	=	Netherlands Foreign Investment Agency
NHK	=	Japan Broadcasting Corporation
NTO	=	National Tourism Organization
NUFFIC	=	Netherlands Organization for Internationalization of Higher Education
OECD	=	Organisation for Economic Cooperation and Development
OOH	=	out-of-home advertising
OPEC	=	Organization of the Petroleum Exporting Countries
PCI	=	product-country image
PCNB	=	Presidential Council on Nation Branding
PDO	=	Protected Designation of Origin
PLC	=	product life cycle
PR	=	public relations
PROMPERÚ	=	Comisión de Promoción del Perú para la Exportación y el Turismo
ROI	=	return on investment
SCORE	=	Sarawak Corridor of Renewable Energy

SDI	=	Scottish Development International
SERI	=	Samsung Economic Research Institute
SWA	=	Scotch Whisky Association
SWF	=	sovereign wealth fund
TLA	=	technologically less advanced (countries)
TMA	=	technologically more advanced (countries)
UAE	=	United Arab Emirates
UNCTAD	=	United Nations Conference on Trade and Development
UNDP	=	United Nations Development Programme
UKTI	=	UK Trade & Investment
USAGM	=	United States Agency for Global Media
USAID	=	United States Agency for International Development
USP	=	unique selling proposition
UX	=	user experience
VAT	=	value added tax
VOA	=	Voice of America
WEF	=	World Economic Forum
WFK	=	World Friends Korea
WHO	=	World Health Organization
WISCOMP	=	Women in Security, Conflict Management and Peace
YoY	=	year on year

PART 1

SCOPE AND SCALE OF NATION BRANDING

1 The relevance, scope and evolution of nation branding

Key points

- Nations are making increasing efforts to hone their country branding in recognition of the need to fulfil nationally important trade, investment and tourism objectives
- Research in the fields of national identity and country of origin contribute to our understanding of the evolution of nation branding
- The branding of nations, and other places such as cities and regions, is more complex and multidimensional than the branding of a physical product or of a corporation owing to factors such as the multitude of stakeholders and the infinite range of brand touchpoints associated with the branding of places

DOI: 10.4324/9781003100249-2

Introduction

Nation branding is a complex phenomenon. Its complexity is reflected in the many disciplines that now feature research into the theory and practice of nation branding. As a formal discipline, nation branding is still relatively young (Koh, 2021) and new conceptual models are still being developed (Steenkamp, 2021; Torelli, 2021). Whilst the majority of studies into nation branding are rooted in the marketing and branding literature (Freire, 2021; Hao et al., 2021; Kaefer, 2021; Zeineddine, 2017), increasing attention is being paid to the phenomenon in other fields such as management (Yalkin, 2018), history (Gienow-Hecht, 2019; Viktorin et al., 2018), cultural studies (Cormack, 2008; Kaneva, 2018), media studies (Christensen, 2013; Miazhevich, 2018), public relations (Rasmussen and Merkelsen, 2012), public administration (Eshuis et al., 2013), political geography (Hymans, 2010) and postcolonial studies (Holmes and Buscaglia, 2019; Roy, 2019). Merkelsen and Rasmussen (2016) provide an institutionalist perspective on the field of nation branding. Interest in nation branding has thus spread rapidly beyond the limited realm of conventional brand strategy. The growth of interest in the field has also been accompanied by critical perspectives that challenge the practices of nation branding (Aronczyk, 2013; Browning, 2014; Kaneva, 2011, 2021).

As well as attracting increasing interest from academic researchers, in recent years nation branding has steadily gained prominence in practice as more and more countries around the world commit resources to the development of their nation brand. This chapter investigates the relevance of nation branding in terms of what value a nation brand strategy can deliver to a country, as well as tracing the evolution of nation branding and outlining the prominence which it has achieved in recent years.

The first case in this chapter focuses on public diplomacy and the United States brand. The second case discusses China's promotional videos for national image building. In an academic perspective, Jan-Benedict E.M. Steenkamp outlines a six-step process to build strong nation brands, whilst Simon Anholt provides a practitioner insight into the creation of the Good Country Index.

Defining 'brand' and 'nation brand'

Before looking in detail at the concept of treating a nation as a brand, it is worthwhile to look at some definitions of what is meant by a 'brand'. Such definitions tend to fall into two camps. On the one hand are those definitions which focus upon the visual manifestation of a brand. On the other hand there are deeper definitions which go beyond the visual aspects of a brand and attempt to capture the essence of a brand.

Doyle (1992) defines a successful brand as having differential advantage through visible identifiers such as a name, symbol or design. A slightly richer definition of a brand, which incorporates a consumer perspective as well as a producer perspective, is given by Macrae et al. (1995), who state that a brand represents a unique combination of characteristics and added values, both functional and non-functional, which have taken on a relevant meaning that is inextricably linked to the brand, awareness of which might be conscious or intuitive. A similar perspective is taken by Lynch and de Chernatony (2004), who define brands as clusters of functional and emotional values that promise a unique and welcome experience between a buyer and a seller.

Brands do not exist in a vacuum and to be successful they must co-exist effectively with the prevailing zeitgeist. Popular culture and trends in society drive and influence strong brands (Roll, 2006). This theme is amplified and theorised by Holt (2004), who analyses how brands become icons through creative interaction with their environment in a process that he terms 'cultural branding', a process that he considers particularly suitable for applying to nations. A similar culturally aware vision of brands is proposed by Grant (2006), who suggests that a brand is 'a cluster of strategic cultural ideas'. Through the foundations of their national identity, nation brands possess far richer and deeper cultural resources than any other types of brands, such as product brands or corporate brands. These cultural resources are explored in Chapter 5.

The practice of branding has been defined as the process by which companies distinguish their product offerings from those of the competition (Jobber and Fahy, 2003). In an increasingly globalised economy, the challenge of distinguishing their product offerings from those of the competition has assumed critical importance for nations competing for both domestic and foreign consumers. Keller (2012) suggests that the strategic brand management process involves the design and implementation of marketing programmes and activities to build, measure and manage brand equity. The concept of brand equity is explored in detail in Chapter 3.

A clarification regarding the role of branding is provided by de Chernatony and McDonald (2003), who warn that it is imperative to recognise that while marketers instigate the branding process (branding as an input), it is the buyer or the user who forms a mental vision of the brand (branding as an output), which may be different from the intended marketing thrust. This point is particularly relevant to the branding of nations, where pre-existing national stereotypes may be entrenched in consumers' minds and therefore difficult to change. The notion that a brand is something that resides in the minds of consumers has been noted by Kotler and Keller (2011) and Temporal (2010). The brand-building process requires long-term commitment over a period of several years and in the short term only a small payoff may occur (Aaker and Joachimsthaler, 2009). Nations need to acknowledge this reality and adopt a long-term strategic view when building their nation brand, rather than aiming for a quick fix short-term advertising campaign whose effects may be ephemeral.

When applying the concept of a brand to nations rather than to mere products, there is an ethical obligation to do so in an honest, respectful manner and to acknowledge the limits of how appropriate it is to treat nations as brands. A nation brand should derive from the culture of the country, rather than merely taking the form of a superficial advertising logo or campaign. Nations do not belong to brand managers or corporations. Indeed, if they 'belong' to anyone, it is to the nation's entire citizenry. This and other ethical considerations related to nation branding are examined in detail in Chapter 7.

In this book the nation brand is defined as *the unique, multidimensional blend of elements that provide the nation with culturally grounded differentiation and relevance for all of its target audiences*. This definition acknowledges the multifaceted nature of the nation brand, together with the need to integrate national identity dimensions as discussed in Chapter 5. Moreover, the proposed definition of the nation brand also recognises the contention that brands exist in consumers' minds rather than being a controllable creation of the marketing function. The definition therefore acknowledges the importance of perceptual attributes and target markets.

Why countries engage in nation branding

The application of branding techniques and terminology to nations is a relatively new phenomenon, one which is growing in frequency given the increasingly global competition which nations now face in both their domestic and external markets. Nations are making increasingly conscious efforts to hone their country branding in recognition of the need to fulfil nationally important objectives in terms of trade, investment and tourism. A further objective for many nations is talent attraction, whereby countries compete to attract higher education students (Herrero-Crespo et al., 2016) and skilled workers. Much of nation branding strategy constitutes an effort to embrace both the past heritage and present living culture, so that outdated images do not obscure consumer perceptions from what may be vibrant modern societies. Transitional countries such as those in Central and Eastern Europe may turn to nation branding to distance their countries from the old economic and political system which existed before transition (Szondi, 2007).

The achievement of such goals requires countries to adopt conscious branding if they are to compete effectively on the global stage (Kotler and Gertner, 2002), a view also expressed by Olins (1999), who asserts that within a few years, identity management will be seen as a key way of contributing to the nation's brand. It has also been suggested (van Ham, 2001) that the unbranded state has a difficult time attracting economic and political attention, and that image and reputation are becoming essential parts of the state's strategic equity. A powerful and positive nation brand can provide crucial competitive advantage in today's globalised economy. In his landmark text, *The Competitive Advantage of Nations*, Michael Porter (1998) emphasises that nations and national character remain of prime importance, even in the age of globalisation.

The realm of competitive advantage encompasses many sectors, including attracting tourists, investors, entrepreneurs and foreign consumers of a country's products and services. Nation branding can also help erase misconceptions about a country and allow the country to reposition itself more favourably with regard to target audiences. For example, the development of a strong nation brand by Estonia was driven by key objectives including attracting investment, expanding the country's tourist base beyond Sweden and Finland and broadening European markets for its exports (Interbrand, 2008).

Some central themes and issues in treating the nation as a brand are summarised in Table 1.1.

It has been argued that thoughtful brand positioning gives a country a competitive advantage (Anholt, 1998; Gilmore, 2002; Konecnik Ruzzier and de Chernatony, 2013; Yousaf, 2014) and that active repositioning of a country through branding can be done successfully and holds great potential for countries, particularly in cases where a country's stereotype lags behind reality. In such cases there exists great scope for country branding.

A further incentive for countries to embrace branding lies in the capacity of branding techniques to create meaningful differentiation. The nation brand can play a role

Table 1.1 Key issues in treating nations as brands

Author	Themes and issues
Aldersey-Williams (1998)	The branding or rebranding of a nation is a controversial and highly politicised activity
Wolff Olins (2003)	Although historically brands are associated with products and corporations, the techniques of branding are applicable to every area of mass communications; political leaders, for example, to inspire, need to become brand managers of their parties and preferably of the nation
O'Shaughnessy and Jackson (2000)	The image of a nation is so complex and fluid as to deny the clarity implicit in a term such as brand image; different parts of a nation's identity come into focus on the international stage at different times, affected by current political events and even by the latest movie or news bulletin
Gilmore (2002)	The importance of truthfulness when constructing the nation brand; what is required is amplification of the existing values of the national culture rather than the fabrication of a false promise
Mihailovich (2006)	The simplistic strapline approach to nation branding could be counter-productive; altruistic goals such as sustainable long-term employment and prosperity are objectives that may be met through emphasising all forms of cluster and kinship alliances
Anholt (2007)	The vocabulary of branding can appear cynical and arrogant; therefore to some extent, politicians need to avoid the explicit use of such terminology

in attracting foreign direct investment (Lee and Lee, 2021), although the role of nation branding has not been researched as extensively in the field of FDI attraction as it has in the field of tourism. In the tourism sector, most destinations make similar claims regarding the beauty of their scenery, the purity of their beaches, the hospitable nature of the locals and so on. Therefore the need for destinations to create a unique identity, to find a niche and differentiate themselves from their competitors, is more critical than ever (Morgan et al., 2002). This needs to be done on a long-term strategic basis rather than in an ad hoc manner if positive outcomes are to be sustained. A note of caution is struck in this regard by Lodge (2002), who cites the so-called 'Dallas experiment', where what was then called the New Zealand Market Development Board saturated the city of Dallas with New Zealand events, promotions and trade fairs. This intensive burst of marketing activity was sustained for six months during which sales increased sharply, but one year after the experiment had ended the levels of awareness and purchase returned to the same levels as they had been before the experiment started. This kind of activity must be seen as a promotional exercise, and not as a substitute for a long-term strategic branding strategy.

The evolution of nation branding

The evolution of nation branding is traced in Figure 1.1. The figure shows how the academic fields of national identity and country-of-origin interact within the context of economic globalisation. The contradictory effects of globalisation consist of homogenisation of markets and at the same time an increasing sense of national identity. In recent years resistance to globalisation has led to the emergence of the concept of deglobalisation, reflecting a reduced interdependence between countries and a reduction in the flow of people and goods between countries (Dandolov, 2021).

The streams of knowledge embodied within the national identity literature on the one hand and within the country-of-origin literature on the other, have only recently converged. The publication of a special issue devoted to nation branding by the *Journal of Brand Management* (2002) was an early manifestation of this convergence. Although sporadic individual articles on nation branding had appeared in other publications in previous years, the *Journal of Brand Management* special issue for the first time provided a focused forum for the topic and contained papers from scholars including Philip Kotler and David Gertner (2002), Nicolas Papadopoulos and Louise Heslop (2002), as well as papers from consultants in the field such as Wally Olins (2002), Fiona Gilmore (2002) and Creenagh Lodge (2002). Such was the level of interest generated by the special issue that the journal publishers went on to launch a new journal in November 2004 entitled *Place Branding*, dedicated to the branding of nations, cities and regions. That journal was subsequently renamed *Place Branding and Public Diplomacy* to reflect the subject matter's broad and interdisciplinary scope.

A significant earlier work in what has now become known as the emerging field of nation branding is *Marketing Places: Attracting Investment, Industry, and Tourism to Cities, States and Nations* (Kotler et al., 1993). Although that text takes a broad economic and marketing perspective rather than an explicit brand perspective, it sets the scene for much of the work that has followed in the field. To put the evolution of nation branding into yet wider historical perspective, it could be claimed that nations have always branded themselves – through their symbols, currency, anthems, names and so on – and that it is just the terminology of nation branding that is new, rather than the practice itself (Olins, 2002).

The use of branding techniques is now highly pervasive. From the most basic physical product to the most diverse nation, branding has steadily increased its scope of application. It could be argued that corporate branding is the closest type of branding to nation branding. The parallels between corporate branding and nation branding lie in the complex, multidimensional nature of the corporate/nation entity and also in the multiple stakeholder groups which must be acknowledged by both corporations and nations. Balmer and Gray (2003), for example, note that there is an increasing realisation at organisational level that corporate brands serve as a powerful navigational tool to a variety of stakeholders for a miscellany of purposes including employment, investment and, most importantly, consumer behaviour. The scope of branding has thus increased incrementally from its original application to simple products through to services, companies and organisations, and now nations. The product-nation brand continuum is depicted in Figure 1.2.

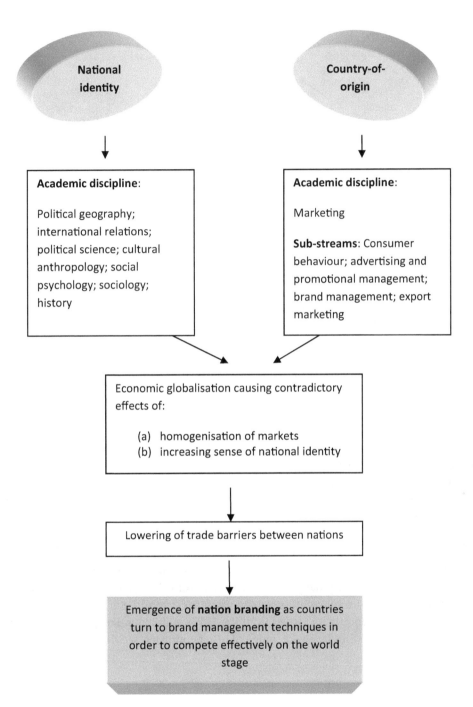

Figure 1.1
The evolution of nation branding

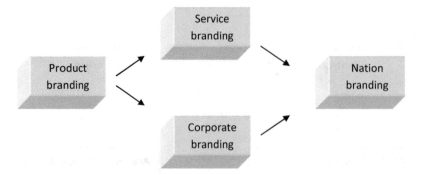

Figure 1.2
Evolution of the scope of branding: The product-nation brand continuum

The branding of nations, and other places such as cities and regions, is more complex and multidimensional than the branding of a physical product or of a corporation owing to factors such as the multitude of stakeholders and the infinite range of brand touchpoints associated with the branding of places. However, it has been argued that the differences between place marketing and more mainstream marketing may have been overstated, and that place marketing resembles mainstream marketing more closely than much of the place marketing literature has implied (Warnaby, 2009).

Nation branding issues and initiatives

Different countries have adopted different strategies in order to confront the specific challenges they face. More and more countries around the world are embracing nation branding in order to differentiate themselves on the world stage and to strengthen their economic performance, primarily in terms of exporting, inward investment and tourism. Countries as culturally and geographically diverse as Germany, South Korea, New Zealand, Scotland and Spain have judged it worthwhile to develop nation branding strategies. We will now provide an overview of the issues impacting upon such countries and some of the initiatives they have taken as they confront the challenges of branding their respective nations. The following overview provides a retrospective summary of some countries' nation branding initiatives from the 1990s and 2000s. For current examples of nation branding activities by a wide range of other countries, see the case studies in each chapter.

Germany

Jaffe and Nebenzahl (2001) describe how in 1999 ZDF, the German television network, approached identity consultants Wolff Olins to create a national brand for Germany. Although this was not an official campaign, the brand strategy suggested for Germany generated much public interest and debate within Germany. The campaign's main objective was to change consumer perceptions of Germany from what was found to be a nation of 'mechanical perfection', which lacks creativity, to a country that is also 'exciting and surprising'. The perception of Germany as cold and unemotional was attributed partly to German manufacturers such as Audi, whose famous slogan 'Vorsprung durch Technik' extolled German engineering prowess but lacked warmth and emotional depth.

The website of identity consultants Wolff Olins (www.wolff-olins.com/germany) gives details of the approach taken to fashioning a brand for Germany. The basis of their approach was founded upon the belief that Germany is the economic dynamo of Europe, but for historical reasons it is often perceived in ways that are negative, even hostile. Wolff Olins suggested six practical steps to the German government and its agencies should they wish to address the issue of branding Germany: (1) Set up a national brand steering committee under the leadership of the Chancellor or President of the Republic; (2) Create a research and development team responsible for reporting to the steering committee; (3) Begin a process of national consultation involving representatives of all the Lander as well as national figures in industry, commerce, education, media, culture and the arts; (4) Commission extensive research into perceptions of Germany overseas, benchmarking these studies against data on perceptions of other nations; (5) Carry out a thorough review of how and where the national brand could appropriately be utilised; (6) Draw up and submit for Bundestag approval a programme of implementation for the brand options adopted by the national steering committee.

Although Germany ranks highly in various nation brand indexes and has implemented campaigns such as 'Germany works' to promote the country as a business location and 'German accelerator' to network German startups with international companies and investors, it has been argued that the country could do more to align federal and state governments in its nation branding strategy (Schwan, 2021). This illustrates the challenge of stakeholder management inherent in any nation branding activity.

Scotland

In Scotland, the organisation Scotland the Brand was set up in 1994 in order to promote Scottish tourism, culture and trade. The organisation's initial credo was as follows:

> As more and more countries focus and promote their national strengths, Scotland too must collectivise and synthesize its considerable virtues into appropriate persuasive messages. With Devolution, the European Union and the globalisation of world markets, now is a key time for Scotland to build its identity and to exploit its history and heritage and contemporary values as a marketing tool to generate increased awareness of Scotland and drive commercial benefits for Scottish trade.
>
> (www.scotbrand.com/about-branding.asp)

A driving force behind the creation of the Scotland the Brand organisation was the growing conviction, based on empirical research, that Scotland has distinctive brand values that are recognised internationally. However, there was also concern that as a nation Scotland had not harnessed these values in its marketing efforts as effectively as it could have in order to derive commercial advantage. Consequently, Scotland the Brand was established in 1994 to promote the distinctive brand values of Scotland.

The organisation aimed to provide a collective voice in the promotion of Scottish excellence in both domestic and international markets by combining the marketing efforts of Scottish business. Scotland the Brand Chairman Nick Kuenssberg (Sunday Herald, 2003) summed up the organisation's goals as including the promotion of Scotland as a place to visit, a place to study, a place to invest in and a place to source knowledge from. This echoed the views expressed by the Scottish Executive (2001) in their document 'A Smart, Successful Scotland', which emphasises the need to promote Scotland as a world class business location for the globalisation programmes of overseas and domestic companies.

In order to help achieve its objectives, Scotland the Brand commissioned a large-scale piece of international research into the brand equity of 'Scottishness'. The study comprised a survey of opinion inside Scotland and in the key export markets of England, France, Germany, Spain, Japan and the United States, and a comprehensive review of existing data. The outcome was used as the basis of efforts to construct a competitive positioning for Scotland, a persuasive proposition to buy Scottish products, services and facilities, and a strategy to help Scotland achieve long-term sustainable competitive advantage. An events/promotions plan covering the period 2002–4 was drawn up, consisting of what the organisers termed an ambitious and expanding range of happenings in the form of a series of creative, effective and targeted campaigns. The events and promotions all had the common theme of identifying and fostering the core values of spirit, tenacity, integrity and inventiveness that had been elicited through the Scottish brand equity research referred to earlier.

Scotland the Brand's events/promotions plan 2002–4 possessed both an internal and an external focus. Within Scotland, the organisation intended to focus upon capitalising on existing major events and calendar dates including Saint Andrew's Day, Burns Celebrations and regional events, as well as sporting events such as established golf, rugby and football occasions. An annual Scotland the Brand conference and awards dinner was also being developed as well as a series of monthly networking events. Externally, the most high profile event engaged in by Scotland the Brand was the Tartan Week celebrations held in Chicago, United States. The Chicago celebrations included tourism events, the finale of an international fashion competition, a ministerial event and a tartan ball. In addition to events in Chicago, a three-month series of lectures on Scotland and a Scottish Folklife Festival were organised in Washington D.C. in participation with the Smithsonian Associates and Institute. Although open to criticism on the grounds that such events rely overly much on old-fashioned imagery such as tartan, kilts and bagpipes, there is no doubt that these events represented a major opportunity to raise Scotland's profile within the United States, the most lucrative consumer market in the world.

The visual aspect of Scotland's brand identity, as promoted by the Scotland the Brand organisation, consisted of a logo known as the 'Scotland mark'. This logo was developed as a definitive mark for Scotland that would not only uniquely identify and authenticate Scottish products, but would offer a guarantee of product quality. Although the creation of such a visual identity can be challenged as being purely superficial and cosmetic, the research process and design solution involved in this type of activity can help to articulate strategy with regard to corporate branding and communication (Baker and Balmer, 1997). The 'Scotland mark' could be found on a wide range of Scottish products, from the traditional such as food, drink, textiles and hotels, to more modern products/services such as electronics, software, financial services and transport. Research in the United Kingdom software sector has demonstrated that a quality assurance certificate benefits users by adding value to and confidence in a software product (Jobber et al., 1989), and the logo provided by Scotland the Brand was intended to perform the same value-adding and confidence-providing role for consumers when purchasing products and services made in Scotland.

Ironically, however, there has been a trend away from explicitly using Scottishness in the branding of financial services. As part of a rebranding operation in 2003, Abbey National shortened its name to 'abbey' and simultaneously closed two famous Scottish names to new business – Scottish Mutual and Scottish Provident. Products for these two companies would henceforth be offered under the abbey brand. Scottish Amicable and Scottish Equitable are two other leading Scottish brands that have disappeared during the last decade (Flanagan, 2003). The strategic imperatives inherent in merger and takeover activity had thus taken precedence over the use of country-of-origin as a marketing cue in the area of Scottish financial services.

Scotland the Brand's intention was for the Scotland mark to become an instantly recognisable symbol, conveying strong positive Scottish values and imagery that would add real value to Scottish products and services around the world. In 2003, the Scotland the Brand organisation moved from the public to the private sector. Had the organisation continued to exist, it would have been interesting to observe whether the organisation could maintain its quality criteria for companies wishing to use the Scotland mark when public subsidy ceased and the organisation was obliged to sustain itself from membership subscriptions. If quality criteria had been lowered in order to boost short-term subscriptions, that could have resulted in devaluation of the Scotland mark with consequent defection of current members who would not wish to be associated with products, services and brands of inferior quality to their own.

Events in 2003–4 led to the demise of the Scotland the Brand organisation. On Friday, 28 March 2004, Scotland the Brand Chairman Nick Kuenssberg told an extraordinary general meeting that the board had voted to wind down the organisation's operations (Sunday Herald, 2004). Kuenssberg explained that this step was being taken in light of the Scottish Executive's decision to set up its own unit for the promotion of Scotland. The board of Scotland the Brand felt that this duplication of effort in promoting the nation undermined the very existence of the Scotland the Brand organisation and therefore the vote was taken to wind up the organisation's operations.

In 2018, a new strategy for Scotland's nation branding was established as a joint undertaking between the Scottish Government, VisitScotland, Scottish Development International and Universities Scotland. These stakeholders collaborated to develop the 'Scotland is Now' marketing initiative. The campaign was launched in New York, San Francisco and London, targeting a global audience with a focus on four pillars: live and work, invest, study and visit (VisitScotland, 2021).

New Zealand

As Chairman of Corporate Edge consultancy, Creenagh Lodge was involved in a brand definition and strategy exercise for New Zealand, a task which she defines as the identification of competitive positioning and a collectivised reason to buy across an economic spectrum comprising inward investment, culture, education, tourism and the export of produce and products. The process adopted in order to achieve a brand definition and strategy comprised the following series of steps. The first step was the gathering of data and opinion to produce a hypothesis as to how best the country can persuade the rest of the world to buy its collective offer. The data sought were information on the competitive set; the brand equity as ascertained through market research studies carried out by government bodies and exporting commercial bodies; the facts which constitute actual and potential 'pluses'; performance data and objectives on exports, tourism, inward investment and other relevant economic interests like education; and the views of influential people about the internal issues which could make or break adoption and subsequent delivery of the strategy.

Existing perceptions of New Zealand were found to be negative amongst British consumers but more positive amongst French and German consumers. British consumers tended to believe that New Zealand was essentially an English suburb, mostly bungalows, and populated by rather sleepy people; whereas the French and Germans knew of fine wine, dramatic landscape and a fascinating Maori culture. In order to reverse British perceptions of New Zealand as the land of the bungalow, a proposition was developed to recast New Zealand as a dramatically exotic destination and source of produce, utilising imagery based on the spectacular Southern Alps, the extraordinary birds and flowers, the live volcanoes and exotic fruits. Lodge emphasises that a major factor in the success of the New Zealand nation branding strategy was that the brand resonated as strongly for the people of New Zealand as it had been seen to motivate its prospective buyers. Further success factors included the fact that in New Zealand the nation branding project was initiated and driven by acknowledged vested interest; by people with the authority and responsibility to make it work; who had clear economic goals from the outset which could be used to guide and measure the work; who were unified in their goals and objectives; and who had committed monies for implementation before the work began.

In order to diversify New Zealand's brand beyond natural beauty, the New Zealand Story initiative has been developed, emphasising attributes such as creativity and problem-solving (New Zealand Story, 2021). New Zealand Story has run awareness campaigns in key international markets such as the USA, China, Japan and Australia, amplifying earlier campaigns such as 'Made with Care' by New Zealand Trade and Enterprise and 'Messages from New Zealand' by Tourism New Zealand (Scoop Independent News, 2020).

South Korea

A huge amount of attention was focused upon South Korea through its co-hosting of the 2002 FIFA World Cup. Anholt (2003) describes how, in an attempt to cash in on the publicity that would be generated by the co-hosting of the World Cup, the Ministry of Commerce, Industry and Energy announced an ambitious plan to raise the international recognition (and thereby boost the exports) of Korean brand-name products. Five strategies were worked out by the government – to internationalise Korean brand names; strengthen corporate brand management; reinforce electronic brand marketing; expand the infrastructure for brand marketing; and raise the nation's image abroad. In order to achieve the strategic objectives, a well-funded and coherent approach was adopted. The government announced that it would create a 100 billion won venture fund to help exporters improve the designs of their products, and that it would also open 'industrial design renovation centres' in ten cities nationwide to help small and medium-sized companies improve the design of their products as part of an integrated effort to boost the value and recognition of Korean brands.

Perhaps most visionary in the long term, according to Anholt, was the Korean government's plan to build up the nation's brand infrastructure by opening a 'Brand Academy' to train about 500 specialists every year in brand management, character design and industrial packaging. The internal education aspect of nation branding thus appears to have been grasped exceptionally well by Korea compared to the efforts of other nations.

In order to strengthen Korea's branding, in 2009 the Presidential Council on Nation Branding was established, comprising 47 members from the public and private sectors. The role of the Council was to improve the nation brand substance, enhance the country's brand image, and systematise the brand management system (Kim, 2016). Public diplomacy has played an increasing role in Korea's international communications as the country shifts from its previous focus on security-centred diplomacy (Park, 2020).

Spain

Spain is often held up as an example of successful nation branding. Preston (1999), for instance, claims that Spain is among the best examples of modern, successful nation branding because it keeps on building on what truly exists and its branding efforts incorporate, absorb and embrace a wide variety of activities under one graphic identity to form and project a multifaceted yet coherent, interlocking and mutually supportive whole. The repositioning of Spain as a vibrant modern democracy throwing off the negative connotations of its recent past is also hailed as an exemplar in nation branding by Gilmore (2002), who states that the core of a country's brand must capture the spirit of its people and how it can be developed into a brand positioning after consideration of four essential factors – macrotrends, target groups, competitors and core competencies. The positioning derived from such considerations should, according to Gilmore, be rich enough to translate into sub-positionings to target diverse groups and it should also be substantiated in terms of what the country can actually offer.

An important point made by Gilmore is that exceptional individuals and their exceptional stories have the potential to bring a country's brand alive and make it more real to audiences worldwide for the simple fact that people relate to people. Long-distance runners from Kenya, gymnasts from Romania, musicians from Cuba or past explorers from Scotland represent the kind of exceptional individuals that may contribute to a nation's brand strategy. This issue is further examined in the context of nation brand ambassadors (Chapter 9).

The challenge of place brand architecture is felt particularly acutely by Spain, whose nation branding efforts need to address powerful regional identities within the country whilst also acknowledging the supranational brand of the EU (Seisdedos, 2021).

Britain

The branding, or rebranding, of Britain in the late 1990s is perhaps the most controversial nation branding campaign that has been seen to date. A report by the Demos public policy think tank, 'Britain™: Renewing Our Identity' (Leonard, 1997), formed the basis of the attempted rebranding of Britain instituted by the incoming Labour government under Prime Minister Tony Blair. The renewal of identity was deemed urgent because, although Britain had enjoyed many successes in creative industries and steady economic growth, a major problem was that around the world Britain continued to be seen as backward-looking and aloof. British businesses had become wary of overtly marketing their national identity for fear of the more negative connotations associated with Britain – businesses did not want to be thought of as insular, old-fashioned and resistant to change.

The solution to this problem was considered by the New Labour government to be a modernisation of Britain's image. 'Cool Britannia' replaced 'Rule Britannia', although it should be noted that it was the media and not the government who attached the 'Cool Britannia' label to the rebranding of Britain that was attempted in the late 1990s. From the outset of the branding of Britain campaign, there was an overwhelmingly hostile reaction. Concerns were voiced about the viability and desirability of rebranding something as complex as national identity, as if the nation were just another supermarket product. Critics also asserted that it would not be so easy to airbrush out the myths, memories and rituals that underpinned the 'imagined community' of Britain. The concept of a nation as an 'imagined community' is well established in the national identity literature (Chapter 5).

The rebranding of Britain campaign could be viewed as a salutary lesson for those engaged in nation branding campaigns in the United Kingdom and elsewhere. Media reaction was hostile. The potential benefits of a nation branding strategy did not appear to be communicated effectively to target audiences. There seemed to be insufficient integration of all the stakeholders in the nation brand, and the perception arose of an exaggerated emphasis on the modern and cutting edge to the detriment of the traditional and established.

A more recent attempt to brand Britain has taken shape in the form of the GREAT campaign initiated by then Prime Minister David Cameron, bringing together the Department for International Trade, VisitBritain, British Council, the Foreign and Commonwealth Office as well as other government departments and private sector companies. Owen (2018) provided a review of the campaign on its seventh anniversary. The campaign appears to have gained significantly more traction than previous attempts to brand Britain, although it has been argued that the United Kingdom lacks a nation brand strategy due to the devolution of central government powers to Scotland, Wales and Northern Ireland, each of whom develops their own branding strategies (Allan, 2021).

ACADEMIC PERSPECTIVE: A SIX-STEP PROCESS TO BUILD STRONG NATION BRANDS

Jan-Benedict E.M. Steenkamp, C. Knox Massey Distinguished Professor of Marketing, University of North Carolina at Chapel Hill

A nation brand refers to a network of meanings in people's minds based on the visual, verbal, and behavioral expressions of a nation. When these meanings are a result of active management of these perceptions and strategic efforts to advance specific meanings by policy makers in the country in question, this is called nation branding (Kotler and Gertner, 2002). Nation branding has captured the attention of policy makers (politicians, government officials, industry organizations, tourist boards, and other stakeholder groups) around the world. They believe that a strong nation brand helps attract tourists, foreign direct investment, and skilled labor, increases exports and creates jobs, and enhances soft power. They are aware of the importance of company ("commercial") brands in consumer-decision making (Aaker and Joachimsthaler, 2000; Steenkamp, 2014, 2017, 2019; Steenkamp et al., 2003) and the enormous value that is captured in strong brand names. Policy makers also point to the benefits the nation brand bestows through country-of-origin image on products from their country (Verlegh and Steenkamp, 1999; Verlegh et al., 2005). But how can one build a strong nation brand? For this, policy makers can employ a six-step process (Steenkamp, 2021).

Step 1: Strategic nation brand analysis

The starting point of any nation branding strategy should be a comprehensive strategic nation brand analysis, including 1) assessment of trends and motivations in key target markets (customer analysis), 2) analysis of the image, strengths, weaknesses, and vulnerabilities of competing nation brands (competitor analysis), and 3) a *realistic* assessment of the nation's existing image (if any), its strengths, capabilities, weaknesses, heritage, and values (self-analysis).

Step 2: Select country meanings

The strategic nation brand analysis sets the context for the selection of specific globally recognized meanings with which the nation is to be associated. To help brand marketers develop specific meanings, Aaker's brand identity system (Aaker and Joachimsthaler, 2000) can be used, which distinguishes between four meta-categories of meanings – brand as product, brand as organization, brand as person, and brand as symbol. Each of these meta-categories is further subdivided into more fine-grained categories of meanings.

Step 3: Develop nation branding marketing strategy to convey these meanings

Nation-brand marketers transfer country meanings that have been selected to their nation brand through three interrelated activities: nation brand development (brand name, logo, and slogan), nation brand communication (building awareness and knowledge structures), and nation brand reinforcement (working closely with policy makers to deliver on the promises implied by these meanings).

Step 4: Country meanings in nation brand

The result of a successful nation branding marketing campaign will be that the nation brand is imbued with specific meanings. To assess whether this is indeed the case, the nation brand marketer should conduct surveys among the target segment in key foreign countries. This survey should be administered twice – at the beginning of the campaign to obtain a benchmark and at the end of the campaign to evaluate the statistical and substantive significance of the shift in perceptions on the intended meanings.

Step 5: Measure and monitor nation equity

Successful transfer of the chosen recognizable, credible, relevant, and differentiating country meanings should have a positive effect of nation equity. I define nation equity as *the differential preference and response to marketing and other efforts by home country actors in foreign countries by virtue of them hailing from that nation*. Nation equity is operationalized along five dimensions: differentiation, relevance, energy, esteem, and knowledge. Country scores on these dimensions can be used in a nation equity power grid, a tool to locate the nation versus other nations on nation equity, and to track its trajectory over time.

Step 6: Quantify outcomes of nation branding efforts

The improvement of a country's equity should lead to tangible and intangible outcomes, which can be economic (e.g., tourism, exports, price premium, foreign direct investment), social (e.g., attracting skilled immigrants), or political (increased soft power). It depends on the goals of the nation branding campaign, what the relevant outcomes are. Regardless of the aims of the campaign, it is important to establish that the resources invested in the nation branding efforts lead to intended outcomes. Because these campaigns are often funded with taxpayers' money, accountability for nation brand managers is at least as important as accountability for brand managers.

References

Aaker, D.A. and Joachimsthaler, E. (2000) *Brand Leadership*, New York: Free Press.

Kotler, P. and Gertner, D. (2002) 'Country as brand, product, and beyond: A place marketing and brand management perspective', *Journal of Brand Management*, 9 (4), 249–261.

Steenkamp, J.B.E.M. (2014) 'How global brands create firm value: The 4V model', *International Marketing Review*, 31 (1), 5–29.

Steenkamp, J.B.E.M. (2017) *Global Brand Strategy: World-Wise Marketing in the Age of Branding*, New York: Palgrave Macmillan.

Steenkamp, J.B.E.M. (2019) 'Global versus local consumer culture: Theory, measurement, and future research directions', *Journal of International Marketing*, 27 (1), 1–19.

Steenkamp, J.B.E.M. (2021) 'Building strong nation brands', *International Marketing Review*, 38 (1), 6–18.

Steenkamp, J.B.E.M., Batra, R. and Alden, D.L. (2003) 'How perceived brand globalness creates brand value', *Journal of International Business Studies*, 34 (1), 53–65.

Verlegh, P.W.J. and Steenkamp, J.B.E.M. (1999) 'A review and meta-analysis of country-of-origin research', *Journal of Economic Psychology*, 20 (5), 521–546.

Verlegh, P.W.J., Steenkamp, J.B.E.M. and Meulenberg, M.T.G. (2005) 'Country of origin effects in consumer processing of advertising claims', *International Journal of Research in Marketing*, 22 (2), 127–139.

PRACTITIONER INSIGHT: THE GOOD COUNTRY INDEX

Simon Anholt, Independent Policy Advisor

There are many surveys that rank countries according to the quality of life, prosperity, equality, freedom and happiness which they offer their own citizens, visitors or investors. But domestic performance is only half the story in our interconnected, interdependent world; countries don't exist in isolation, and yet somehow, nobody had ever thought of measuring their impact on the world outside their own borders.

In this age defined by big, borderless challenges, each country should surely be able to show its balance sheet. The idea of the Good Country Index was that it would rank each country's overall contribution – or its overall debt – to the rest of humanity, to the planet and to our shared resources.

So in 2012, with the help of Dr Robert Govers and others, we started work on preparing the first edition of the Good Country Index. We calculated the rankings by combining 35 indicators produced by the UN system and other international agencies. We grouped the indicators, some of which were positive and some negative, into seven sub-rankings: Contributions to Science and Technology, Contributions to International Peace and Security, Contributions to World Order, Contributions to Planet and Climate, Contributions to Prosperity and Equality and Contributions to Health and Wellbeing. Each sub-ranking contains five indicators.

Obviously, some of the behaviors we included had more impact than others. But we decided that we could not reflect this by weighting the different sub-indicators, as it is largely a matter of personal opinion whether, for example, emitting carbon dioxide does more harm to humanity than turning away migrants or invading another country. We also decided that, for most indicators, each country's score in the Good Country Index would be divided by its GDP so that smaller and poorer countries were not unduly penalized for their limited ability to 'make a difference' in the world.

One pleasant surprise in the first edition was that Kenya ranked in 26th place overall. This was an encouraging example to show that it is by no means the exclusive province of rich, 'first-world' nations to make a meaningful contribution to humanity.

The Good Country Index cannot claim to provide a complete account of how much each country contributes to humanity and the planet, but the exercise was more about encouraging people to think about countries in a new way. Instead of constantly asking 'how well is this country doing?', I wanted people to start asking 'how *much* is this country doing?'

According to Robert Govers' analysis (Govers, 2018), the correlation coefficient between the third edition of the Good Country Index (based on 2014 data) and the 2014 edition of the Anholt-GfK Roper Nation Brands Index, is greater than 80%.

The fact that principled national behavior is so strongly associated with a better national image – which in turn is associated with improved tourism, foreign investment and trade – points towards interesting ways of encouraging governments to work harder to tackle the grand challenges of the 21st century.

Reference

Govers, R. (2018) *Imaginative Communities: Admired Cities, Regions and Countries*, Antwerp: Reputo Press.

CASE: PUBLIC DIPLOMACY AND THE US BRAND

Neil H. Simon, Bighorn Communications

Americans may talk a little loud and eat a little much and generally throw their weight around on the world stage more than many like, but there is no debating the universal appeal of the USA brand. And a lot of that stems from generations of personal experience with the American people, through educational and cultural exchanges, international aid, and mass media.

For 80 years, US public diplomacy has strategically and organically buoyed America's global brand at times it otherwise may have sunk.

The United States is a global top destination for students seeking to study abroad.

The United States is still a global leader in sending volunteers and international aid to developing nations.

And, while struggling at times to connect to younger audiences in the digital age, the US has a history of leading public engagement around the world through broadcasting and journalism.

These actions have been critical to preserving a positive reputation for the global superpower. The US systems of separation of powers and the relatively siloed nature of the country's marquee public diplomacy functions combine to create a system that ultimately protects the US brand despite periods of setbacks.

Education and cultural exchanges

The United States takes a holistic approach to bolstering its image and creating citizen-based cultural, educational, economic, and informational ties with other nations. Through academic exchanges, the work of the volunteer Peace Corps, and numerous connections fostered by the Department of State, the United States Government directly arranges exchanges for more than 55,000 people every year, including 15,000 Americans who travel abroad. That does not even count the more than one million international students who enroll in US higher education institutions each year and the countless tourist exchanges which help foster cross-cultural ties.

Among the most well-known of US exchange programs is the Fulbright program, established in 1945 by the US Congress thanks to the leadership of Senator William Fulbright, who had studied abroad at Oxford University. More than 3,000 students and educators each year receive Fulbright scholarships to study abroad, ensuring that the prestigious program continues to serve the goal of increasing understanding and strengthening friendly relations between the U.S. and more than 155 countries.

The Fulbright program is one of 120 exchange programs created by the State Department and managed by the Bureau of Educational and Cultural Affairs (ECA) that takes US civilians abroad and encourages foreign civilian engagement in the US.

ECA provides opportunities for athletes and artists to practice and hone their craft around the world. ECA's Private Sector Exchange Programs welcomed over 308,000 exchange visitors to the United States in 2018 from 200 countries and territories. ECA also supports more than 400 EducationUSA advising centers to help international students find the best US program to fit their academic goals.

These popular programs that rely on in-person travel, in-person connection and immersive in-country experiences all serve to build future leaders and a strong foundation of friendly relations with the United States for years to come. Survey data consistently shows these experiences have a positive impact on the US brand abroad. Eighty-nine percent of foreign exchange participants surveyed after their exchange programs in 2018 reported a more favorable view of the American people.

While much of the educational and private sector exchanges are founded on peer-to-peer opportunities, one of the most long-standing exchange programs within the US Government is more service-oriented. Established by President John F. Kennedy in 1961, the Peace Corps provides Americans with an opportunity to work anywhere in the world, representing America as a volunteer in a service program. The Peace Corps has sent over 220,000 Americans to work abroad in over 140 countries since its inception. Volunteers gain knowledge of global affairs from a personal and professional view, and those in the host nations see a positive representation of America.

From improving water quality in Peru, educating pharmacy students in Malawi, or growing gardens in Cambodia, the Peace Corps allows Americans to use their knowledge to better the world while representing American values. The same Peace Corps values of service and international development are seen at a larger scale within the government's international aid body, USAID.

USAID

Amid the COVID-19 pandemic, as US hospitalizations soared, the US government continued to work on its global brand. In its own time of need, and amid a globally criticized White House response to the virus, the US Agency for International Development (USAID) delivered more than 8,000 ventilators to 37 countries and the NATO stockpile.

Images of large pallets emblazoned with the agency's logo – a seal, handshake and slogan 'FROM THE AMERICAN PEOPLE' – assured recipients would see the US brand when receiving the aid.

That logo – whether on a truck of clean water or the uniform of a search and rescue team after an earthquake – is among the most recognizable US Government brands. The USAID emphasis on the

American people underscores the highest value connections in public diplomacy are just that: human connections.

That moment of delivery is the diplomatic connection point that turns a general donation into a direct connection. USAID turns product delivery into public diplomacy.

USAID functions as its own agency within the State Department, spending more than $16 billion around the world on direct assistance. The agency's mission emphasizes people. 'On behalf of the American people,' the mission starts, 'we promote and demonstrate democratic values abroad, and advance a free, peaceful, and prosperous world' (USAID, 2021). USAID leads the US Government's international development and disaster assistance through partnerships and investments that 'save lives, reduce poverty, strengthen democratic governance, and help people emerge from humanitarian crises and progress beyond assistance' (USAID, 2021).

With its 790,000 followers on Twitter (the largest of any nation's international aid organization), @USAID used the #AmericaActs hashtag to highlight the $1.6 billion US State Department Covid-19 response that went beyond the ventilator donations. Through highly visual storytelling, direct quotes from experts delivering aid and recipients in country, USAID's global story always comes back to people. America's broader values are thus always reflected in USAID's work. Expanding access to education, strengthening laws to protect open markets and free societies, and advancing agricultural techniques, public health and sanitation services help developing communities survive and ultimately thrive.

Journalism and broadcasting

Aside from direct aid and international exchanges, government-funded international broadcasting has been a hallmark of US public diplomacy.

These broadcast initiatives are independent from, and do not function in anyway as, US Government mouthpieces.

For example, the State Department's main Twitter feed has 5.3 million followers and another 1.9 million on Facebook. Those channels share key messages of the moment, just as US Embassies and regional media hubs do around the world. The US-funded international news outlets are different.

Since 1940, the US has established more than 70 broadcast services around the world, originally under the Voice of America (VOA) brand. These are essentially newsrooms of journalists putting on objective newscasts in local languages that adhere to journalist ethics.

As the VOA code of ethics states, 'Accuracy, balance, comprehensiveness, and objectivity are the qualities audiences around the world expect of VOA,' and 'because of them, VOA is a vital information lifeline to nations and peoples around the world' (VOA Journalistic Code, 2009).

In countries lacking traditions of a free press, these broadcast programs are often the only place for the general public to hear views from internal opposition parties or minority groups that would otherwise be censored by their state-owned media channels.

VOA was expanded in 1994 with the creation of the Broadcasting Board of Governors (BBG) and International Broadcasting Bureau (IBB) to oversee international non-military government broadcasting, like VOA. The oversight bodies also created a layer of independent oversight further protecting international journalists from US policymakers' influence. In 1998, the BBG became the United States Agency for Global Media (USAGM).

Today, the USAGM broadcasts in over 60 languages and has a weekly audience of over 278 million people worldwide.

While the State Department continues to modernize these legacy broadcast programs to reach the wider world on new platforms each year, VOA remains a trusted a tool for public diplomacy. Sixty-four percent of VOA listeners say the VOA is helpful when deciding where they stand on important issues, a slight uptick from 2019, according to a USAGM report (USAGM, 2020).

In the battle for hearts and minds at the center of all public diplomacy, numbers like that show the US continuing to succeed.

Whether it is a college student who studies for an exchange year in the US, a rural farmer trained by USAID to increase his crop yield, or a VOA listener, US public diplomacy works through trust. Student-to-student, farmer-to-farmer and journalist-to-audience. At the core of this public diplomacy is the removal of officialdom, the general absence of a government voice. When global issues can be brought down the personal level, they became local connections. That is why for decades the US brand continues to be strong in the face of global challenges.

References

USAGM (2020) 'FY 2020 performance and accountability report', available at: www.usagm.gov/wp-content/uploads/2020/11/USAGM-FY2020-PAR.pdf (accessed 2/1/2021).

USAID (2021) 'Mission, vision and values', available at: www.usaid.gov/who-we-are/mission-vision-values (accessed 2/1/2021).

VOA Journalistic Code (2009) available at: www.voanews.com/archive/voa-journalistic-code (accessed 2/1/2021).

CASE: REFLECTING ON CHINA'S PROMOTIONAL VIDEOS FOR NATIONAL IMAGE BUILDING

Hong Fan, Professor, School of Journalism and Communication of Tsinghua University and Director of National Image Research Centre, Tsinghua University, Beijing, China
Haiyan Feng, Assistant Professor, School of Journalism and Communication of Xiamen University, Xiamen, China

Driven by globalization, the level of interest for nation branding continues to grow as countries compete with one another on the global stage. In the rush to stake a claim in the global arena, more countries are beginning to manage their international reputations through nation image building. China, following the success of the 2008 Beijing Olympics, places a particular emphasis on the shaping of its global image. Despite the money that China puts into various branding practices, there is only limited evidence showing China's reputation as being in pace with its political and economic power (Ramo,

2007; Li and Jing, 2010; Zhang and Zhang, 2019; Xu, 2015). One might ask where China went wrong when it comes to national image building.

In the past decades, the Chinese government has actively engaged in various image building practices, such as hosting overseas cultural exchanges and international mega-events as well as releasing national image promotional videos on media platforms. These serve as the main channels through which China communicates its image to the world. In particular, China's promotional videos are a critical tool in managing its international reputation. Ever since the release of Beijing Olympics' promotional video series in 2001, the Chinese government has been regular in launching one to two promotional videos in English every year for its global audience. An enormous amount of money is being put into this sector; yet, not much is being used wisely and efficiently (Wu et al., 2013). In this article, we want to discuss the existing problems in China's global branding strategies, focusing particularly on the topic of national promotion videos.

In our study, a content analysis of more than 20 image promotional videos released by China in the last two decades was conducted. Two indicators, 'content' and 'image', can help us examine why certain videos lack appeal. 'Content' can be illustrated in terms of three dimensions: theme, narrative, and symbol. In terms of theme, all videos sampled were dedicated to 'positive publicity', that is, they all attempt to depict the picture of a 'good China' through various aspects. In terms of narrative, there is a strong emphasis on achievement. The explicit showcasing of China's economic achievements is recurrent in sampled videos. The style of a grand narrative is frequently paired with an emotional voiceover, inciting feelings of grandeur, thrill, and inspiration. The videos sampled are full of symbolism, especially political ones; the Chinese national flag, Tiananmen Square, and the national emblem all frequently appear. With titles like 'Experience China', 'My China', 'China Steps into a New Era', 'Made in China', and 'Quick Facts About Chinese Enterprises', the titles of promotional videos are loosely connected to a common theme. Notably, there are no slogans in these videos, nor any signs of effort to set out a clear national identity. It seems that as much as possible is being jammed into the minute-long videos. Iconic cultural symbols like the Beijing National Stadium, Peking Opera, calligraphy, and city landscapes are followed one after one after another like they do in slide shows.

A closer look at 'Experience China' reveals more details. This image promotion video was released at New York City's Times Square in 2011, and it is by far the one most discussed by the media and international scholars. Professor Jian Wang from the University of Southern California offered an in-depth discussion on 'Experience China' in the second edition of this book (Dinnie, 2016). The one-minute video showcased the achievements of China through a portrait of 50 renowned celebrities. They are household names in China, yet most are unheard of for the international audience. To add on, the English subtitles provided were obscure – filled with self-promoting and generic words like 'enchanting', 'thrilling', and 'inspiring'. As it turned out, the release of this video brought out more negative feedback than positive. Comments expressing skepticism like 'publicity or propaganda?' and 'carefully monitored' flooded social media platforms.

In terms of 'image,' a longitudinal examination of the sampled videos reveals China's attempt to build itself as strong, rich, and beautiful through visual languages. These images evoked resonate with 'a harmonious China', which is the key narrative advocated by China's political leaders. Such efforts, however, are much misinterpreted. Prominent media outlets such as *The New York Times*, *Washington Post*, *Wall Street Journal*, CNN, *The Economist*, *Financial Times*, Fox News, and Bloomberg, frequently use words like 'propaganda' and 'brainwashed' to describe China's effort to communicate itself globally. Comments from media platforms like Twitter, Facebook, and YouTube indicate similar contention. A content analysis of these media comments reveals three key codes generated by the public in describing China: 'a stranger from a distant land', 'a disrupter of present world order', and 'a nation of rich culture and history'. The sharp contrast between China's self-depicted image and the image received by its audiences is evident. In fact, some scholars argue that the videos have deteriorated China's image by adding to existing stereotypes (Wang, 2012; Zhou, 2011). This leads to the question: why do these videos lack in appeal?

First, when branding practice is politically driven, it often neglects its target audience. It becomes top-down communication that centers around the political orders. Knowing the audience becomes an inferior task. Second, the 'achievement narrative' is not always a wise choice when communicating to foreign audiences. Claims like 'I am great', 'I am successful', 'I am beautiful' are hardly likeable and relevant to foreign audiences. Further, cultural differences also play a role in undermining the attractiveness of these promotional videos. China favors the traditional mindset of 'Quan', meaning to include all, which explains why these videos are overwhelmed with bits and pieces of information that are only loosely connected. Nation branding, however, is prone to fail without a core message (Fan, 2015). The top-down communication style, grand 'achievement narrative', and loosely connected themes can all be attributed to the absence of a clear national identity in China's branding practices.

We propose that it is necessary to adopt the 4D brand work model based on Discover, Define, Design, and Deliver (Fan, 2014) in order to improve China's international reputation. First, to discover, in-depth research should be carried out to uncover China's rich and diverse national elements. Following that, it is essential to define, refine, and determine the core competitiveness of China's national image. Third, a systematic architecture must be designed based on China's national image branding elements. Finally, the contents must be effectively delivered to audiences of different cultural backgrounds.

As Dinnie (2004) and Anholt (2008) have discussed, the process of national image building requires long-term commitment, perhaps over a period of several years. It is therefore necessary to establish a competitive identity upon which a variety of publicity related activities may follow and look toward. This will help communicate an authentic China to an international audience, allowing the world to have a better understanding of the real China and its culture. Only with genuine acceptance will audiences worldwide support the continuous growth and development of China.

References

Anholt, S. (2008) ''Nation branding' in Asia', *Place Branding and Public Diplomacy*, 4 (4), 265–269.

Dinnie, K. (2004) 'Place branding: Overview of an emerging literature', *Place Branding*, 1 (1), 106–110.

Dinnie, K. (2016) *Nation Branding: Concepts, Issues, Practice*, 2nd edn, London: Routledge.

Fan, H. (2014) 'Branding a place through its historical and cultural heritage: The branding project of Tofu Village in China', *Place Branding and Public Diplomacy*, 10 (4), 279–287.

Fan, H. (2015) 'Nation image building and the communication strategies', in Fan, H. and Zheng, C.Y. (eds.), *Nation Image Research*, Beijing: Tsinghua University Press.

Li, Y.B. and Jing, X.M. (2010) 'A study on the existing problems in the research of nation image communication', *Chinese Journal of International Communication*, 32 (6), 118–122.

Ramo, J.C. (2007) *Brand China*, London: The Foreign Policy Centre.

Wang, R. (2012) 'Hey, "Red China is brand new": A case study of China's self-depicted national identity on its promotional video "experience China"', *Quarterly Journal of Chinese Studies*, 2 (1), 33–66.

Wu, G.H., Lin, S.D. and Xu, L. (2013) 'American college students watching Chinese nation image promotion ads – the hopes on the young', *Journalism & Communication*, 20 (6), 57–64, 126.

Xu, Y.Y. (2015) 'The international perception gap of China's national image and an analysis of the reasons', *Journal of Shenzhen University (Humanities & Social Sciences)*, 32 (5), 98–102, 149.

Zhang, K. and Zhang, T.Y. (2019) 'The "consensus" and the "consensus degree": An alternative dimension of perceiving nation image', *Modern Communication (Journal of Communication University of China)*, 41 (6), 68–72.

Zhou, Q.A. (2011) 'The historical laws and realistic challenges of national image promotion videos', *International Communication*, 3, 18–19.

Summary

This chapter has provided an overview of the relevance, scope and evolution of nation branding. We have looked at the nature of brands and also at the way in which nations may be viewed as brands, however limited and imperfect the concept of nation-as-brand may be. The key objectives to be attained by nation branding include the stimulation of inward investment, the promotion of a country's branded exports and the attraction of tourists. The next chapter delves more deeply into brand theory, with a particular focus upon the concepts of nation brand identity, image and positioning.

Discussion points

1   Identify three countries and compare their nation branding strategies in terms of promoting trade, investment and tourism. Discuss the similarities and differences between the approaches employed by the three countries.

2   How useful is the 'brand' concept when applied to nations? Could other approaches from different disciplines be more helpful in enabling countries to manage their reputations on the global stage?

References

Aaker, D.A. and Joachimsthaler, E. (2009) *Brand Leadership: Building Assets in an Information Economy*, New York: The Free Press.

Aldersey-Williams, H. (1998) 'Cool Britannia's big chill', *New Statesman*, 10 April, 12–13.

Allan, M. (2021) 'United Kingdom', in Freire, J.R. (ed.), *Nation Branding in Europe*, chapter 4. London and New York: Routledge.

Anholt, S. (1998) 'Nation-brands of the twenty-first century', *Journal of Brand Management*, 5 (6), 395–406.

Anholt, S. (2003) *Brand New Justice: The Upside of Global Branding*, London: Butterworth-Heinemann.

Anholt, S. (2007) *Competitive Identity: The New Brand Management for Nations, Cities and Regions*, London: Palgrave Macmillan.

Aronczyk, M. (2013) *Branding the Nation: The Global Business of National Identity*, Oxford: Oxford University Press.

Baker, M.J. and Balmer, J.M.T. (1997) 'Visual identity: Trappings or substance?', *European Journal of Marketing*, 31 (5–6), 366–375.

Balmer, J.M.T. and Gray, E.R. (2003) 'Corporate brands: What are they? What of them?', *European Journal of Marketing*, 37 (7–8), 972–997.

Browning, C.S. (2014) 'Nation branding and development: Poverty panacea or business as usual?', *Journal of International Relations and Development*, advance online publication 22 August, doi:10.1057/jird.2014.14.

de Chernatony, L. and McDonald, M. (2003) *Creating Powerful Brands*, 3rd edn, London: Butterworth-Heinemann.

Christensen, C. (2013) '@Sweden: Curating a nation on Twitter', *Popular Communication: The International Journal of Media and Culture*, 11 (1), 30–46.

Cormack, P. (2008) ' "True stories" of Canada: Tim Hortons and the branding of national identity', *Cultural Sociology*, 2 (3), 369–384.

Dandolov, P. (2021) 'COVID-19: The deglobalization amplifier', *Geopolitical Monitor*, 28 May, available at: www.geopoliticalmonitor.com/covid-19-the-deglobalization-amplifier/ (accessed 29/5/2021).

Doyle, P. (1992) 'Branding', in Baker, M.J. (ed.), *The Marketing Book*, 2nd edn, London: Butterworth-Heinemann.

Eshuis, J., Braun, E. and Klijn, E.H. (2013) 'Place marketing as governance strategy: An assessment of obstacles in place marketing and their effects on attracting target groups', *Public Administration Review*, 73 (3), 507–516.

Flanagan, M. (2003) 'Abbey rebrand sees Scottish names consigned to history', *The Scotsman*, 25 September, 27.

Freire, J. (ed.) (2021) *Nation Branding in Europe*, London and New York: Routledge.

Gienow-Hecht, J. (2019) 'Nation branding: A useful category for international history', *Diplomacy & Statecraft*, 30 (4), 755–779.

Gilmore, F. (2002) 'A country – can it be repositioned? Spain – the success story of country branding', *Journal of Brand Management*, 9 (4–5), 281–293.

Grant, J. (2006) *The Brand Innovation Manifesto*, London: John Wiley & Sons.

Hao, A.W., Paul, J., Trott, S., Guo, C. and Wu, H.-H. (2021) 'Two decades of research on nation branding: A review and future research agenda', *International Marketing Review*, 38 (1), 46–69.

Herrero-Crespo, A., Gutiérrez, H.S.M. and Garcia-Salmones, M.del M. (2016) 'Influence of country image on country brand equity: Application to higher education services', *International Marketing Review*, 33 (5), 691–714.

Holmes, G. and Buscaglia, I. (2019) 'Rebranding Rwanda's peacekeeping identity during post-conflict transition', in Grayson, H. and Hitchcott, N. (eds.), *Rwanda Since 1994: Stories of Change*, Francophone Postcolonial Studies 10, 104–124, Liverpool: Liverpool University Press.

Holt, D.B. (2004) *How Brands Become Icons: The Principles of Cultural Branding*, Cambridge, MA: Harvard Business School Press.

Hymans, J.E.C. (2010) 'East is East, and West is West? Currency iconography as nation-branding in the wider Europe', *Political Geography*, 29, 97–108.

Interbrand (2008) 'Country case insight – Estonia', in Dinnie, K. (ed.), *Nation Branding – Concepts, Issues, Practice*, 1st edn, 230–235, London: Butterworth-Heinemann.

Jaffe, E.D. and Nebenzahl, I.D. (2001) *National Image & Competitive Advantage: The Theory and Practice of Country-of-Origin Effect*, Denmark: Copenhagen Business School Press.

Jobber, D. and Fahy, J. (2003) *Foundations of Marketing*, London: McGraw-Hill Education.

Jobber, D., Saunders, J., Gilding, B., Hooley, G. and Hatton-Smooker, J. (1989) 'Assessing the value of a quality assurance certificate for software: An exploratory investigation', *MIS Quarterly*, 13 (1), 19–31.

Journal of Brand Management (2002) 'Special issue: Nation branding', *Journal of Brand Management*, 9 (4–5).

Kaefer, F. (2021) *An Insider's Guide to Place Branding: Shaping the Identity and Reputation of Cities, Regions and Countries*, New York: Springer International Publishing.

Kaneva, N. (2011) 'Nation branding: Toward an agenda for critical research', *International Journal of Communication*, 5, 117–141.

Kaneva, N. (2018) 'Simulation nations: Nation brands and Baudrillard's theory of media', *European Journal of Cultural Studies*, 21 (5), 631–648.

Kaneva, N. (2021) 'Nation branding in the post-communist world: Assessing the field of critical research', *Nationalities Papers*, First View, 1–11.

Keller, K.L. (2012) *Strategic Brand Management: Building, Measuring, and Managing Brand Equity*, 4th edn, Upper Saddle River, NJ: Prentice Hall.

Kim, Y.-K. (2016) 'Case: Branding Korea', *Nation Branding: Concepts, Issues, Practice*, 233–238.

Koh, B.S. (2021) *Brand Singapore: Nation Branding in a World Disrupted by Covid-19*, 3rd edn, Singapore: Marshall Cavendish Business.

Konecnik Ruzzier, M. and de Chernatony, L. (2013) 'Developing and applying a place brand identity model: The case of Slovenia', *Journal of Business Research*, 66 (1), 45–52.

Kotler, P. and Gertner, D. (2002) 'Country as brand, product, and beyond: A place marketing and brand management perspective', *Journal of Brand Management*, 9 (4–5), 249–261.

Kotler, P., Haider, D.H. and Rein, I. (1993) *Marketing Places: Attracting Investment, Industry, and Tourism to Cities, States and Nations*, New York: Free Press.

Kotler, P. and Keller, K.L. (2011) *Marketing Management*, 14th edn, Upper Saddle River, NJ: Prentice Hall.

Lee, R. and Lee, Y.-I. (2021) 'The role of nation brand in attracting foreign direct investments: A case study of Korea', *International Marketing Review*, 38 (1), 124–140.

Leonard, M. (1997) *Britain™: Renewing Our Identity*, London: Demos.

Lodge, C. (2002) 'Success and failure: The brand stories of two countries', *Journal of Brand Management*, 9 (4–5), 372–384.

Lynch, J. and de Chernatony, L. (2004) 'The power of emotion: Brand communication in business-to-business markets', *Journal of Brand Management*, 11 (5), 403–419.

Macrae, C., Parkinson, S. and Sheerman, J. (1995) 'Managing marketing's DNA: The role of branding', *Irish Marketing Review*, 18, 13–20.

Merkelsen, H. and Rasmussen, R.K. (2016) 'Nation branding as an emerging field – an institutionalist perspective', *Place Branding and Public Diplomacy*, 12 (2–3), 99–109.

Miazhevich, G. (2018) 'Nation branding in the post-broadcast era: The case of RT', *European Journal of Cultural Studies*, 21 (5), 575–93.

Mihailovich, P. (2006) 'Kinship branding: A concept of holism and evolution for the nation brand', *Place Branding*, 2 (3), 229–247.

Morgan, N., Pritchard, A. and Piggott, R. (2002) 'New Zealand, 100% pure: The creation of a powerful niche destination brand', *Journal of Brand Management*, 9 (4–5), 335–354.

New Zealand Story (2021) available at: www.nzstory.govt.nz/ (accessed 16/7/2021).

Olins, W. (1999) *Trading Identities: Why Countries and Companies Are Taking Each Others' Roles*, London: The Foreign Policy Centre.

Olins, W. (2002) 'Branding the nation – the historical context', *Journal of Brand Management*, 9 (4–5), 241–248.

O'Shaughnessy, J. and Jackson, N. (2000) 'Treating the nation as a brand: Some neglected issues', *Journal of Macromarketing*, 20 (1), 56–64.

Owen, J. (2018) 'Seventh anniversary of the great campaign: Three billion reasons to be cheerful', *PR Week*, 28 September, available at: www.prweek.com/article/1494006/seventh-anniversary-great-campaign-three-billion-reasons-cheerful (accessed 16/7/2021).

Papadopoulos, N. and Heslop, L. (2002) 'Country equity and country branding: Problems and prospects', *Journal of Brand Management*, 9 (4–5), 294–314.

Park, E. (2020) 'Korea's public diplomacy', in Snow, N. and Cull, N.J. (eds.), *Routledge Handbook of Public Diplomacy*, 2nd edn, chapter 32, 323–330, New York and London: Routledge.

Porter, M. (1998) *The Competitive Advantage of Nations*, London: Palgrave Macmillan.

Preston, P. (1999) 'Branding is cool', *The Guardian*, 15 November, 22.

Rasmussen, R.K. and Merkelsen, H. (2012) 'The new PR of states: How nation branding practices affect the security function of public diplomacy', *Public Relations Review*, 38, 810–818.

Roll, M. (2006) *Asian Brand Strategy: How Asia Builds Strong Brands*, London: Palgrave Macmillan.

Roy, I.S. (2019) *Manufacturing Indianness: Nation-Branding and Postcolonial Identity*, New York: Peter Lang.

Schwan, A. (2021) 'Germany', in Freire, J.R. (ed.), *Nation Branding in Europe*, chapter 2, London and New York: Routledge.

Scoop Independent News (2020) 'New Zealand's ingenuity story hits key offshore markets as innovation scores see post-Covid uplift', 16 November, available at: www.scoop.co.nz/stories/BU2011/S00272/new-zealands-ingenuity-story-hits-key-offshore-markets-as-innovation-scores-see-post-covid-uplift.htm (accessed 16/7/2021).

Scottish Executive (2001) 'A smart successful Scotland', 30 January, www.scotland.gov.uk/publications.

Seisdedos, G. (2021) 'Spain', in Freire, J.R. (ed.), *Nation Branding in Europe*, chapter 6, London and New York: Routledge.

Steenkamp, J.-B. (2021) 'Building strong nation brands', *International Marketing Review*, 38 (1), 6–18.

Sunday Herald (2003) 'Scotland the brand ready to go private', *Sunday Herald*, 9 March, 8.

Sunday Herald (2004) 'Scotland the brand votes to wind up', *Sunday Herald*, 30 May, 1.

Szondi, G. (2007) 'The role and challenges of country branding in transition countries: The Central European and Eastern European experience', *Place Branding and Public Diplomacy*, 3 (1), 8–20.

Temporal, P. (2010) *Advanced Brand Management: Managing Brands in a Changing World*, 2nd edn, New York: John Wiley & Sons.

Torelli, C.J. (2021) 'Dissemination and consensual perceptions of nation brands: A framework for future research', *International Marketing Review*, 38 (1), 36–45.

van Ham, P. (2001) 'The rise of the brand state: The postmodern politics of image and reputation', *Foreign Affairs*, 80 (5), 2–6.

Viktorin, C., Gienow-Hecht, J., Estner, A. and Will, M. (eds.) (2018) *Nation Branding in Modern History*, New York: Berghan.

VisitScotland (2021) 'Scotland is now', available at: www.visitscotland.org/about-us/what-we-do/marketing/scotland-is-now (accessed 17/7/2021).

Warnaby, G. (2009) 'Towards a service-dominant place marketing logic', *Marketing Theory*, 9 (4), 403–423.

Wolff Olins (2003) 'Branding Germany', available at: www.wolff-olins.com/germany (accessed 16/5/2003).

Yalkin, C. (2018) 'A brand culture approach to managing nation-brands', *European Management Review*, 15 (1), 137–149.

Yousaf, S. (2014) 'Branding Pakistan as a "Sufi" country: The role of religion in developing a nation's brand', *Journal of Place Management and Development*, 7 (1), 90–104.

Zeineddine, C. (2017) 'Employing nation branding in the Middle East – United Arab Emirates (UAE) and Qatar', *Management & Marketing*, 12 (2), 208–221.

2 Nation brand identity, image and positioning

Key points

- Identity and image are key concepts in nation branding; the identity–image gap can be damaging and is frequently in urgent need of addressing
- Positioning the nation brand relates to identifying the desired associations of the brand in the minds of target audiences
- Establishing coherent brand positioning is challenging for highly diverse nations

Introduction

This chapter explores three key elements of branding theory – brand identity, brand image and brand positioning – and looks at ways in which these concepts apply in the context of nation branding. This chapter's first case focuses on the historical context, brand creation process and renewed challenges and opportunities for Brand Peru. The second case discusses the global branding of Korea. The academic perspective by Mihalis Kavaratzis considers the complexity of image and identity, whilst Andrew Burnett's practitioner insight discusses the MITS Framework and its applicability to nation branding.

DOI: 10.4324/9781003100249-3

Identity versus image

In discussions of the concept of *identity* there often arises confusion regarding the related but distinct concept of *image*. Therefore it is worth spending some time clarifying these terms and assessing their relevance to nation branding.

Identity is defined by the Concise Oxford English Dictionary (2009) as 'the fact of being who or what a person or thing is', with a sub-sense definition 'the characteristics determining this'. On the other hand, image is defined by the same dictionary in various ways including 'the general impression that a person, organization, or product presents to the public' and 'a mental representation'. There are other dictionaries that could be consulted for alternative definitions, and there will never be universal consensus on the precise meanings of the terms. For our purposes, we shall take the following simple but robust perspective – *identity* refers to what something truly is, its essence; whereas *image* refers to how something is perceived. There is frequently a gap between these two states. The identity–image gap tends to be a negative factor. Many nations struggle with the frustration of not being perceived by the rest of the world for what they truly are. Stereotypes, clichés and racist caricatures can dominate perceptions of certain nations. It is a prime objective of nation branding to identify such prejudices and negative perceptions and provide nations with the means to challenge the negative forces that might otherwise hold back the nation's economic development and standing in the world.

The nature and importance of brand identity and brand image has been highlighted by many writers on brand management and strategy. Frequently this has been done in the context of products, services or corporations rather than nations. However, the core concepts of brand identity and brand image are transferable to the context of nation branding and place branding more widely (Kavaratzis and Hatch, 2013).

An analysis of the components of brand identity and brand image represents a useful starting point to develop an understanding of nation brand identity and image. Roll (2006) proposes the following five factors that companies should consider when developing a brand identity. First, brand vision – an internal document clearly describing the future direction for the brand and the desired role and status that the brand hopes to achieve in the stated time. Second, brand scope – a subset of the brand vision document, outlining the market segments and product categories the brand can enter into. Third, brand positioning – the place that the brand strives to occupy in customers' minds. Fourth, brand personality – a brand can take on a personality that helps the customer connect emotionally with the brand. Fifth, brand essence – the heart and soul of the brand, what it stands for and what makes it unique.

Roll's analysis of the key factors underpinning brand identity development requires only minor modification to be effectively applied to nation brand identity development. Brand vision, brand scope, brand positioning and brand personality are as applicable to nation brands as to product brands. However, when it comes to brand essence, Roll contends that this can be stated in two or three words. Whilst this may be valid for many product or service brands, it would be rash to apply such a minimalist approach to nation brands. The multidimensional nature of nation brands defies such brisk categorisation. This is a central challenge in nation branding – the dilemma of encapsulation. How can the infinite cultural richness of nations be reduced to the soundbite-sized chunks of high impact brandspeak favoured by fast-moving consumer goods (FMCG) marketers? Nations transcend such efforts at encapsulation. This is a theme that we will revisit in later chapters, as it represents one of the fundamental issues that those engaged in nation branding must address.

Whereas Roll suggests five key factors in developing a brand identity, Lehu (2006) suggests that brand identity comprises 12 components, all of which need to be taken into consideration when planning branding activities. The 12 components identified by Lehu are as follows: the name of the brand – without which no clear and unambiguous clear and unambiguous identification is possible; heritage – every brand has a past, a narration of former events; codes of expression – graphical characteristics such as a logo, font size and type, colours, etc.; positioning – the space occupied by the product in the minds of its target market; status – the necessity of making a clear statement of status, e.g., market leader, challenger brand and so on; personality – the brand's character, creativity, dynamism, independence, etc.; everyday behaviour – brands are much more in the public eye now than in previous times; beliefs – the emotional, descriptive and qualitative components an individual will associate with the brand; values – the increasing importance of social awareness credentials; projected image – the image that the brand desires and that it presents to consumers; attitude of the brand's consumers towards it – the relationship between brand and consumer is now an interactive one; and finally, attitude of the brand towards its consumers – the need for brands to study, include and respect their consumers.

Lehu's detailed and insightful deconstruction offers multiple opportunities for analysis of brand identity. It could be argued that 'projected image' should not appear as a component of identity on the grounds that image resides in the mind of the consumer and is thus beyond the control of the brand owners. As Nandan (2005) has pointed out, brand identity originates from the company whereas brand image refers to consumer perceptions, and identity and image are thus distinct but related concepts. However, the remaining 11 components are manipulable by brand managers and capable of application to nation brands. Ways in which existing concepts of brand identity may be transferred to the context of nation branding are illustrated in Table 2.1.

The notion of identity is central to stakeholder management. A sense of identity and the core values that underpin it provide an anchor around which all activities and communications can be structured and carried out. Additionally, inside an organisation a strong sense of identity can help raise motivation and morale among employees by allowing people to identify with their organisations (Cornelissen, 2004). This latter point relates to the field of internal branding, which represents another key challenge in nation branding, namely: how do you generate buy-in to the nation brand from a country's own population? The notion of identity as an anchor around which brand communications may be planned, as outlined earlier, is also addressed by Madhavaram et al. (2005) who describe how brand identity plays a key role in informing, guiding, and helping to develop, nurture and implement a firm's integrated marketing communications (IMC) strategy. A coordinated approach needs to be taken so that countries understand how they are perceived by other publics around the world and to ascertain how the country's achievements, people, products and so on are reflected in their brand images.

Table 2.1 Brand identity components and nation brand manifestation

Brand identity component	Nation brand manifestation
Brand vision	Strategy document agreed upon by the various members of the nation brand development team – the team should comprise representatives of the government, public and private sectors and civil society
Brand scope	Outline of the industry sectors and target markets in which the nation brand can effectively compete. Will include segmentation strategies for sectors such as tourism, inward investment, education, etc.
Name of the brand	Some countries are known by more than one name – Holland/ Netherlands, Greece/Hellas, etc. Nations should evaluate whether such a duality in naming represents a potential asset or liability
Codes of expression	National flags, language, icons
Everyday behaviour	Political/military behaviour, diplomatic initiatives, conduct of international relations
What makes the brand different?	The uniqueness of the nation – embodied in its culture, history, people
Narrative identity	National myths and heroes, stories of emerging independence
Advocate an ideology	Human rights, sustainable development, the pursuit of happiness, etc.

Adapted from Roll (2006), Lehu (2006), Kapferer (2004), Elliot and Percy (2007), Buchholz and Wordemann (2000)

Kapferer (2004) states that the following questions have to be answered in order to define brand identity clearly: What is the brand's particular vision and aim? What makes it different? What need is the brand fulfilling? What is its permanent nature? What are its value or values? What is its field of competence? Of legitimacy? What are the signs which make the brand recognisable? This perspective on brand identity encompasses both the internal elements of the brand (its permanent nature, values and so on) as well as the external elements of the brand (the visual signs of the brand). Such a blend of internal and external brand components is also advanced by Aaker (1996) who contrasts a brand's core identity – the central, timeless essence of the brand – with a brand's extended identity where various brand identity elements may be combined when the brand enters new markets. Nation brand development teams should draw inspiration from existing national iconography as regards the visual manifestation of the nation brand.

Identity-building activities for brands need not be limited to merely ticking boxes on identity criteria lists. There is considerable scope for imaginative and creative input in brand identity development. Narrative identity theory, for example, suggests that in order to make time human and socially shared, we require a narrative identity for our self and this is done by the stories we can or cannot tell (Elliott and Percy, 2007). Nations are clearly in an excellent position to construct such identity-building narratives, given the historical and cultural foundations upon which nations are built. Branding and marketing professionals are not generally renowned for their narrative skills. Therefore it would make sense for nations to invite their 'real' writers to be involved in constructing the nation's narrative. Poets, playwrights, novelists and other creative writers could potentially play a significant role in enhancing their nation's reputation. This already happens in an organic unplanned way, but nation brand strategy can benefit from a planned approach to integrating the country's creative community.

A further creative approach to identity-building lies in the possibility for brands to advocate an ideology by standing up for what the consumer believes in and visibly sharing their convictions (Buchholz and Wordemann, 2000). Human rights, sustainable development and respect for the environment potentially represent some ideologies that nation brands could advocate, although the political nature of such ideologies throws into doubt whether such a tactic could withstand a change of political regime within a country. An incoming government, for example, may be less favourable to sustainable development policies than the outgoing government and therefore would not embrace or advocate the same ideology. Changes in political leadership can thus affect the direction of a nation brand in the same way that the arrival of a new chief executive officer or marketing director can affect the direction of a corporate brand.

The facets of nation brand identity

Nation brand identity is a multifaceted concept. The principles of brand identity explored in the previous section provide a useful grounding for understanding the complex nature of nation brand identity. In order to navigate from the infinite and irreducible concept of national identity towards the more limited concept of nation brand identity, it is necessary to acknowledge that nation brand identity is built upon a limited range of all the constituent parts of national identity. It would be impossible to effectively develop a nation brand identity that drew upon every strand of a country's national identity. External audiences – whether potential tourists, investors, students, workers, etc. – are not going to be willing to receive gargantuan amounts of information about a country's history, culture and people. Therefore a key task of those engaged in constructing a nation brand identity is to be selective in identifying which elements of national identity can usefully serve the stated objectives of the nation branding strategy. In Chapter 5 we analyse in more detail the rich and fascinating area of national identity. In this section, we look at some ways in which nation brand identity may be constructed.

In a study on the creation of a country brand for Poland, Florek (2005) describes the development of a potential core brand identity for Brand Poland and the possibilities over which the brand could be extended. The core value proposed by Florek for Poland's brand is 'nature', based on the country's relatively low level of industrialisation. This core value is extended to relevant areas such as nature reserves, agrotourism, nature trails, natural foods, resorts and spas, extreme sports and so on. A later study by Konecnik Ruzzier and de Chernatony (2013) in the context of Slovenia further developed the theoretical foundations of nation branding by proposing a place brand identity model with roots in marketing, tourism and sociological theory. In terms of the relationship between nation branding and identity, Ståhlberg and Bolin (2016) caution against simplistic solutions that may have superficial appeal but lack substance.

In addition to the natural environment, which for many nations is a key element of nation brand identity, there are many other facets of nation brand identity. The commercial brands produced by a country, for example, can represent an important facet of nation brand identity. Damjan (2005) highlights this point by expressing the hope that Slovenian brands can conquer a niche in the global market and thereby stand as symbols of the strength of the Slovenian economy. A similar point is made by Jaworski and Fosher (2003) who describe how the nation brand identity of Germany has been largely built upon the global success of brands such as BMW, Mercedes and Daimler. The implication of this for nation brand identity development is that the country's exporters need to be included in, or at least consulted on, the export brand facet of the country's nation brand identity.

Deconstructing nation brand image

So far we have looked mainly at brand identity and by extension, nation brand identity. We now turn to the issue of nation brand image and examine how this complex concept may be deconstructed. The mental representations that individuals may have of different countries can derive from various influencing factors. First-hand, personal experience of a country through working or holidaying there can play a key role in the image an individual holds of a country. When one does not have any first-hand experience of a country, word-of-mouth can influence country image as can numerous other inputs in the image-formation process. Other such inputs include pre-existing national stereotypes, the performance of national sporting teams, political events, portrayals of the country in film, television or other media, the quality of brands emanating from the country, the behaviour of individuals associated with a certain country and so on. Natural disasters can have a powerful influence on a country's image (Wu and Shimuzu, 2020). The naming of Covid-19 variants after their place of origin resulted in a negative country image effect through the stigmatisation of countries such as the UK, South Africa and Brazil (Ng, 2021), which led the World Health Organization (WHO) to advocate renaming variants with Greek letters rather than with the variant's place of origin (BBC, 2021). For example, the B.1.617.2 Covid variant first detected in India was initially widely referred to as 'the Indian variant' but following the WHO's intervention most media outlets ceased using that term and instead referred to it as 'the Delta variant'.

These inputs can all determine to a greater or lesser extent a country's nation brand image, even before one considers the potential effects of a planned nation brand strategy. It could be argued, for example, that the international success of the TV series *Fauda* has had a greater impact on Israel's image than could have been achieved by any official, government-led nation branding activities.

Nation branding strategies aspire to positively influence country image perceptions amongst target audiences. Country image has attracted much attention in the literature (Alvarez and Campo, 2014; Hynes et al., 2014; Lopez et al., 2011; Lu et al., 2019; Roth and Diamantopoulos, 2009). Jaffe and Nebenzahl (2001) consider country image to influence evaluations of the country's products and brands. Usunier and Lee (2005) demonstrate how confusion regarding national images can arise due to the multiple levels on which such images operate, particularly relating to the combined influence of brand name and country-of-origin on product image where factors to be taken into consideration include the national image of the generic product; national image of the manufacturer; country evoked by the brand name label; and, country image diffused by the 'Made In' label. An example of the importance attached to the national image of the generic product can be seen in the strenuous and unrelenting efforts of the Scotch Whisky Association to pursue and prosecute any companies which attempt to pass off as 'Scotch' whisky any product which does not meet the rigorous criteria for Scotch whisky as a generic product.

When examining the concept of brand image and nation brand image, it becomes clear that segmentation analysis needs to be carried out in order to monitor and influence the image that is held by different target audiences. As Riezebos (2003) explains, groups of consumers will share similar subjective mental pictures. In the same way that product brands segment their consumer base by whatever segmentation variables are appropriate to their specific context, nation brands must also segment their different audiences in order to understand existing nation brand images and to develop targeted communications to counter negative perceptions and to reinforce positive perceptions. A deconstruction of the corporate image of Egypt, for example, reveals three components of the country's corporate image: first, institutional and political image; second, image of Egyptian products; and third, image of Egyptian business contacts (ZAD Group, 2008). Country image may also influence perceptions of acquiring companies' corporate reputation in cross-border acquisitions (Matarazzo et al., 2018). Papadopoulos et al. (2018) have investigated the wide range of effects that place brand image may have on product/brand associations.

A commonly used technique by brand marketers who wish to assess their brand's image is brand personification. Brand personification is a qualitative research technique that invites consumers (and non-consumers) of a brand to treat the brand as if it were a person. At its simplest, the technique consists of asking consumers a question along the lines of 'If brand X were a person, what kind of person would it be?' Product brands have been using this technique for years and there is no reason why it could not be applied to nation brands. Because brand personification is such an open-ended qualitative technique, the results can be surprising and illuminating, and at times disconcerting. As with any qualitative technique, the objective is not to provide statistically valid data but rather to produce insight and understanding into the mental associations that consumers hold regarding the brand. In the context of nation branding, the brand personification research technique can be used to gain insight into the degree to which the nation's image is bound up with its political leader or head of state. The image of Russia, for example, may be closely associated with the image of Russian President Vladimir Putin. Wike et al. (2021) reported that the image of the United States amongst international audiences improved markedly with the transition of the presidency from Donald Trump to Joe Biden. On the other hand, the leaders of some countries may play little or no role in perceptions of their country image. It is unlikely, for example, that the image of Dutch Prime Minister Mark Rutte plays a significant role in country image perceptions of the Netherlands.

The findings from brand personification research can provide useful pointers for areas in which the brand personality is weak, strong, desirable or undesirable. It has been suggested that when a brand has a well-defined personality, consumers interact with it and develop a relationship in much the same way as people do in life (de Chernatony and McDonald, 2003). With ever increasing use of the internet, the consumer–brand relationship now frequently occurs online as well as offline (Okazaki, 2006). In nation branding terms, particularly for smaller or emerging nations with limited promotional budgets, online offers a relatively affordable means to attempt to establish a clearly defined nation brand personality.

As with any type of brand, nation brand image may decay over time. If a nation brand finds itself in such a situation then a brand revitalisation programme will need to be put in place. Product brands that have gone into decline need to display certain characteristics if a brand revitalisation programme is to succeed. These characteristics include a long-held heritage; a distinct point-of-differentiation; and to be under-advertised and under-promoted (Wansink and Huffman, 2001). All nation brands can fulfil the first two criteria, and given the varying degrees of commitment to nation branding by governments around the world, it could be argued that the majority of nations are also under-advertised and under-promoted, and thus capable of undergoing successful revitalisation programmes.

Sjodin and Torn (2006) describe how consumers react when a piece of brand communication is incongruent with established brand associations, and the authors go on to maintain that sometimes it may be essential to challenge consumer perceptions if the brand is to remain relevant and vigorous. However, challenging consumer perceptions can be a high-risk strategy. Existing consumers may be alienated or alarmed by brand communications that are incongruent with their mental associations of the brand. Additionally, as Ries and Trout (2001) have noted, most people do not like being told they are wrong, and therefore attempting to change minds is a risky undertaking.

Whilst advertising may be limited in its mind-changing power, this does not imply that nation brands should passively accept the status quo, particularly if negative perceptions are dominant.

Conceptual model of nation brand identity and image

The conceptual model of nation brand identity and image shown in Figure 2.1 displays the multidimensional nature of the identity and image constructs in a nation brand context. In the construction of their nation brands, different nations will selectively focus upon those components and communicators of identity that are most appropriate for attaining their specific nation brand objectives. For example, some countries may benefit from a range of successful branded exports and therefore seek to integrate branded exports as a communicator of their nation brand identity. Other countries may focus more on notable sporting achievements, their tourism offering, the activation of their diaspora and so on. Whatever route is chosen, countries are becoming increasingly aware that in today's globalised economy, the sphere of country image is assuming great importance.

The conceptual model of the nation brand demonstrates and acknowledges the multifaceted nature of the nation brand construct. Key components of nation brand identity

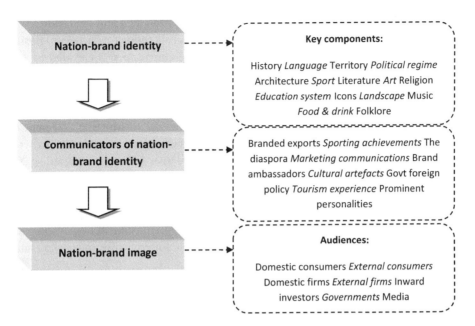

Figure 2.1
Conceptual model of nation brand identity and image

such as history, territory, sport, icons and folklore represent the enduring essence of the nation. From these enduring characteristics are derived the communicators of nation brand identity. These may be tangible or intangible. The model shows how nation brand image is derived as a consequence of nation brand identity as communicated through means such as cultural artefacts, the diaspora, brand ambassadors, marketing communications and so on. For example, branded exports may play an important role in the nation brand image held by external consumers. Cultural artefacts such as TV series may also influence nation brand image (Jacobsen, 2018). The conceptual model illustrates the diverse range of audiences that the nation brand must address.

Positioning the nation brand

The concept of positioning is a key issue in brand management and strategy. The literature on the topic is copious (see for example Blankson et al., 2014; Fuchs and Diamantopoulos, 2010; Jakubanecs and Supphellen, 2010). A good understanding of what positioning entails is a key requisite for anyone involved in nation brand development. This is particularly so when it comes to dealing with advertising agencies or branding consultancies, whose work rests largely on establishing effective positioning platforms and then designing appropriate creative executions to achieve successful implementation of the desired positioning.

Kotler and Keller (2006) view positioning as the designing of a distinctive image in target markets' minds. Jobber (2004) builds on this definition and suggests that the keys to successful positioning are clarity, consistency, competitiveness and credibility. Whilst clarity, competitiveness and credibility are evidently useful criteria for successful positioning, the notion of consistency needs to be nuanced. If consistency is elevated to a high status in brand positioning it could lead to excessively predictable and uninspiring brand communications.

Establishing points of difference is a key task in brand positioning. From a consumer perspective, a brand's points of difference must be relevant, distinctive and believable (Keller, 2003). National tourism advertising campaigns can often be criticised for scoring very poorly on the 'distinctive' criteria regarding effective points of difference. Many tourism campaigns make generic, undifferentiated claims for their sandy beaches, sunny climate, laidback lifestyle, friendly people and so on. Competing in this unimaginative way represents a step on the slippery slope towards commoditisation. Hence the recent efforts of many countries to refocus on more precise segmentation strategies to promote higher-end cultural tourism, where it is indeed possible for countries to stake a claim to utterly distinctive and unique points of difference.

Meeting the criteria of distinctiveness does, however, bring with it one notable drawback or challenge. In order to make a strong and compelling appeal to any one particular consumer segment, the brand is likely to alienate other consumer segments; however, an acceptance of such a sacrifice is a characteristic of highly distinctive brands (Bauer et al., 2006). This kind of sacrifice may be relatively easy for a commercial brand to accept. The company behind Bacardi Breezers, for example, are unlikely to be overly troubled by their brand's lack of acceptance from the 65 years and older male demographic. But for nation brands it is a different matter. It is much more daunting for a nation brand to actively consider alienating a potential consumer segment or audience, given that the nation brand's remit extends to all areas of the nation's economic life. Therefore the potential pitfall for nation brands is that they select bland, inoffensive positioning platforms that offend nobody but at the same time are relatively meaningless and thus inspire nobody either. Table 2.2 illustrates some positioning platforms that have been used by nations across the world in recent years.

An ever-present complicating factor in nation branding in general, and in nation brand positioning specifically, resides in the political sensitivities of the various stakeholders

Table 2.2 Nation brand positioning platforms

Nation brand	Positioning platform
South Africa	'Alive with possibility'
Bolivia	'The authentic still exists'
Scotland	'The best small country in the world'
India	'India Shining'
Thailand	'Amazing Thailand'
Malaysia	'Truly Asia'

that must be accommodated. How, for example, should a highly diverse Britain be cohesively positioned (Hall, 2004)? This is not merely an abstract question, as some of the constituent parts of the United Kingdom are already establishing their own, distinct nation brands. Scotland, for instance, developed a nation brand positioning based on the key values of integrity, inventiveness, quality and independence of spirit (Lodge, 2002). This positioning platform is quite distinct from any United Kingdom umbrella branding. On the other hand, a clear political statement may be used as the basis for a clear, positive positioning platform as can be seen in the case of Costa Rica, whose commitment to democracy and rejection of a standing army has allowed the country to position itself as a peaceful ecotourism destination (Quelch and Jocz, 2005). Achieving a positive brand positioning is particularly challenging for countries embroiled in long-term conflict, as Bassols (2016) explores in the case of Colombia.

Liberation through modularity

We have previously argued that when it comes to brand positioning and brand communications, consistency may be an over-rated virtue. Clearly, wild and random fluctuations in brand positioning will lead to consumer confusion and erode brand equity and are not to be recommended. However, an imaginative approach to the consistency dilemma is advocated by Grant (2006), who suggests that brands should be coherent rather than consistent.

There may be lessons to be learnt in this regard from *modularity*, a technique practised in the field of innovation and new product development. Modularity has been described as building a complex product from smaller subsystems that can be designed independently yet function together as a whole (Baldwin and Clark, 1997). Transferring this concept to the domain of nation branding, the overarching umbrella nation brand may be viewed as the 'complex product' whilst entities such as inward investment agencies, tourism boards, and export promotion agencies may be viewed as the 'smaller subsystems that can be designed independently yet function together as a whole'. When utilising the technique of modularity, different companies take responsibility for each of the modules in the knowledge that their collective efforts will create value for customers (Mohr et al., 2005). By adopting a modularity approach, nation brands may be able to liberate themselves from the straitjacket of consistent but bland, indistinct positioning and communications. The nation brand development team will need to act as the architect company, ensuring that brand design rules are clearly set out to the different national agencies, each of whom are tasked with creating their own 'module' or sub-system to be integrated into the overarching nation brand.

Nation branding and tourism promotion

For many countries, the national tourism organisation has been the traditional custodian of the nation brand. Destination branding activities by national tourism organisations may have been implemented over a significantly longer time period than more

Table 2.3 Nation branding tourism campaigns

Country	Branding campaign
Canada	'Canada. Keep Exploring.'
China	'Beautiful China'
Egypt	'Where it all begins'
Ireland	'The Wild Atlantic Way'
Mexico	'The Place You Thought You Knew'
Spain	'I Need Spain'
Wales	'Have you packed for Wales?'

recent nation brand strategies in the domains of trade and investment, for example. The relationship between nation branding, tourism promotion and identity construction has been examined in the context of Estonia by Pawlusz and Polese (2017). Some examples of nation branding tourism campaigns can be seen in Table 2.3.

Regarding the effectiveness of a tourism destination's brand communications, an interesting insight is provided by Nikolova and Hassan (2013) who suggest that consumers' retrospective global evaluation of past leisure trips can be positively influenced by brand communications. An implication of this finding is that NTOs need to communicate effectively to past visitors rather than focusing solely on attempting to attract first-time visitors.

Nation branding and investment attraction

Foreign direct investment has been extensively studied in the international business (IB) literature, but less so in the marketing and branding literature. The IB literature provides an understanding of key issues such as firms' international location decisions (Boeh and Beamish, 2012; Cantwell, 2009; Dunning and Gugler, 2008; Galan et al., 2007), MNE-host government relationships (Lee and Rugman, 2009), the work of investment promotion agencies (Anderson and Sutherland, 2015) and the tactical instruments that can be used to attract FDI (Wilkinson and Brouthers, 2000; Paniagua et al., 2017). The IB literature also highlights the influence of country-specific advantages (CSAs) on FDI attraction (Cho et al., 2009; Rugman and Verbeke, 1992). In one of the small number of studies that adopts a place branding perspective on FDI attraction, Capik (2007) investigates FDI promotion in the Czech Republic, Poland and the Slovak Republic and concludes that a more systematic approach to FDI promotion is required by the actors in that domain. Later studies by Papadopoulos et al. (2016), Pasquinelli and Vuignier (2020), and Lee and Lee (2021) have added to knowledge about the role of nation branding in attracting FDI. The EY Attractiveness Surveys, based on the views of panels of opinion leaders and decision-makers, provide an annual report on the attractiveness of different countries as investment destinations (EY Attractiveness Surveys, 2021).

National government investment agencies are now communicating their country-specific advantages using similar promotional techniques as are used in other dimensions of the nation brand. Invest in Argentina, for example, has produced a promotional brochure featuring a tango-dancing couple on the front cover, accompanied by the message, 'Embrace your Passion. Invest in Argentina'. This is an unusual example of a country using an emotional appeal for investment attraction purposes rather than the more conventional appeals based on sound economic policies, a favourable legal and business environment, well-developed infrastructure and so on. A promotional brochure from Brand South Africa, with 'South Africa: An investor's dream' as the front-cover text, takes the more conventional approach by promoting the country's strengths in industrial capability, competitiveness, trade reform, sound economic policies and access to other African markets.

Sometimes countries take a cooperative rather than competitive approach to branding their territories for investment attraction. Invest in France and Invest in Germany cooperated on such a joint initiative in 2007 by launching The European Attractiveness Scoreboard, designed to inform investors about the benefits of doing business in the European Union. The factors in the scoreboard include market and business vitality, human resources, research and innovation, infrastructure, administrative environment, costs and taxation, energy and sustainable development and internet and ICT-readiness.

ACADEMIC PERSPECTIVE: THE COMPLEXITY OF IMAGE AND IDENTITY

Mihalis Kavaratzis Associate Professor of Marketing, University of Leicester School of Business, United Kingdom

Identity and image are fascinating topics to examine. Their relationship to place brands in general and nation brands in particular is not as straightforward as one might think.

Two common assumptions can be observed within place branding. First, that identity is thought to be internal to the place: it is 'what we are' or 'how we see ourselves'. Second, that image is the opposite of identity and it is external to the place: it is 'how others see us'. Place branding then is often tasked with distilling a complex place identity into a simple, desired, manageable claim or expression that will be communicated and will have a positive effect on the image. However, it is clear that the relationships involved are more nuanced.

In earlier work (Kavaratzis and Hatch, 2013), we propose that identity and image are inseparable; they are the two sides of the same coin. That is something of paramount importance when dealing with these two concepts in the effort to brand a place or a nation. Image might have a first layer of place perceptions held by outsiders and these are certainly important considerations for tourism, exports, public diplomacy and so on. Along with this externality, the other crucial aspect is how the image influences and helps shape the identity. As Jaffe and Nebenzahl (2001) also argue, image is not simply the perceptions that people hold, but the impact that perceptions have on behaviour. This impact extends to identity. In order to examine this effect, we used a third, closely connected concept: culture. To put it simply – if not a little simplistically – it might be useful to think of 'what we are' as culture, 'what we think we are' as identity and 'what others think we are' as image. What others think we are, affects what we think we are, which in turn affects what we really are, or, more precisely, what we can and will become.

The interaction between image, identity and culture is where branding is called to play a role. That brings us to the branding effort and its aim to achieve a certain brand position in peoples' minds. Contemporary thinking rejects that brand positioning is a simple managerial exercise and posits that brand positioning is achieved through brand narratives, through 'storytelling'. Those who write and tell place or nation brand stories are the place brand authors, the list of which is long and varies from place to place, from nation to nation. It always includes cultural institutions, educational institutions, the tourism industry, media (local, national and international), place branding organisations and other public sector organisations. Very importantly, the list is incomplete if we do not include residents and visitors, especially in our times of online interconnectedness. To use a single term for the various brand authors, they are the place brand stakeholders. That brings us to a crucial final point. Branding is about stakeholders. They all make their own small contribution to the wider 'story' and its meaning. In this sense, as the author of this book points out, the notion of modularity is indeed relevant as it helps understand how the small parts contributed by stakeholders are different and have different requirements but come together and function as one.

References

Jaffe, E.D. and Nebenzahl, I.D. (2001) *National Image & Competitive Advantage: The Theory and Practice of Country-of-Origin Effect*, Denmark: Copenhagen Business School Press.

Kavaratzis, M. and Hatch, M.J. (2013) 'The dynamics of place brands: An identity-based approach to place branding theory', *Marketing Theory*, 13 (2), 69–86.

PRACTITIONER INSIGHT: THE MITS FRAMEWORK AND ITS APPLICABILITY TO NATION BRANDING

Andrew Burnett, Founder, helleau®

helleau® developed the MITS framework to facilitate strategic brand intelligence, to be flexible across sectors and scalable from personal brands to nation brands.

What is the MITS framework?

The MITS framework is a method for working with clients to identify and distil the core of a brand identity. We use the framework to turn complex inputs into simple outputs, by:

- Mining
- Interrogating

- Testing
- Simplifying

We start by **mining** which is the process of collating all relevant and tangentially relevant information from stakeholders, both internal and external.

We then **interrogate** our data by analysing what we have for patterns and repeating potential truths. This is done from a viewpoint of inquisitive ignorance – we do not bring our own assumptions to the material and stay open and receptive to what the data tells us.

We follow up by **testing**: presenting what we have found back to stakeholders, often framed as questions designed to encourage exploration and elicit confirmation.

We conclude by **simplifying** what we have tested and confirmed: we distil concepts to their simplest form and take soundings again with stakeholders.

Case study: Brand Scotland

Brand Scotland approached helleau® to compile a strategic brand report on the nation of Scotland, that would work across five key pillars: live, work, study, business and visit.

We facilitated stakeholder workshops in four cities across Scotland, for over 60 sector leaders across industry, academia and tourism.

These workshops were based on the MITS framework and invited participants to share their perceptions of how Scotland could be – through a series of fun and engaging group and individual tasks.

We experimented with concepts like imagining Scotland were run by another brand, such as IKEA, Apple, Lego, Coca-Cola or Microsoft. We explored how we would describe Scotland, how we think others see Scotland, how Scotland sounds and feels. We created positioning statements to give the workshop participants an appreciation of how their work may be used.

In our half-day workshops, we mined, interrogated, tested and simplified core brand concepts for the nation of Scotland.

After running the series of workshops, we took all the data we had mined, and again interrogated, tested and further simplified – delivering our distilled strategic recommendations to the nation of Scotland.

CASE: BRAND PERU: HISTORICAL CONTEXT, BRAND CREATION PROCESS, AND RENEWED CHALLENGES AND OPPORTUNITIES[1]

Félix Lossio Chávez, Lecturer at Pontificia Universidad Católica del Perú and Former General Director of Cultural Industries and Arts at the Ministry of Culture in Peru

A nation brand determined by its historical context

Brand Peru was first conceived in 2006 and officially launched in 2011. It was, therefore, born and raised during the first decades of the 21st century, which are of major relevance to understand contemporary Peru – and from this, to identify the need, opportunities and perhaps threats regarding the brand.

As mentioned elsewhere (Lossio, 2018), three processes characterize the historical context which frames Brand Peru. The first one is political and has to do with the post-conflict period in the aftermath of the systematic crisis experienced between 1980 and the early 2000s. During the 1980s, known as the 'lost decade', Peru went through political, economic, and social instability which consolidated not only a poor reputation, but marginalized the country from global trade and tourism routes and even challenged the sustainability of the nation state. In economic terms, high rates of inflation, money depreciation, and scarcity of basic everyday products characterized the end of the millennium. In addition, the country experienced an internal armed conflict that caused the death and disappearance of almost 70,000 people, the majority being rural native language-speaking indigenous people.[2] Finally, during the 1990s, Peru witnessed a political dictatorship which weakened the national institutions, boosted corruption, and provoked constant social unrest.

The second process concerns the economy and the continuity of the neoliberal model from which Peru has implemented its public policies for the last thirty years. These policies contributed, in macro-economic terms, to a constant and sustained economic growth since 2002, an expansion of the middle class and its consumption capacity, and the reduction of poverty and extreme poverty. Simultaneously, this growth widened internal economic inequality.

The third process regards a sociocultural phenomenon. Over the last fifteen years, national cultural referents, mainly related to the Peruvian popular knowledge and culture, gained more presence in the media and in everyday conversations. Particularly relevant in this process was local gastronomy, which won enormous notoriety during those years and since then has become, to some extent, a novel social glue for national identity. To a lesser extent, areas such as music, literature, sports, and film gained more relevance, based upon the international success of local representatives. In the wake of growing international recognition, Peruvian personalities, products, and services were no longer, as in previous years, thought of as low-quality and of bad reputation; but became associated with innovation and entrepreneurial success.

Finally, in the fields of tourism, commerce, and branding, those same years saw an extensive promotion to 'consume local' through public campaigns such as 'Cómprale al Perú' ('Buy from Peru', 2004), 'El Perú está de moda' ('Peru is on trend', 2007), and 'El Perú es Super' ('Peru is Super', 2008). These campaigns showed to the public that there was something interesting called 'Peru' which deserved more attention. In all, these processes can be understood as the historical substratum that framed Brand Peru. The post-conflict, post-crisis scenario became an opportunity to produce a new national narrative, internally and externally.

The Brand Peru creation process, values, mission, and strategies

Considering favourable national macro-economic indicators, the need for renewed national referents and the aggressive promotion of nation brand strategies in Latin American countries such as Colombia, Mexico, and Brazil, in 2006 the Peruvian government sought to create a nation brand that could strengthen the country's reputation on the global stage.

In 2007, as mentioned in Lossio (2018), PROMPERÚ, the agency in charge of promoting the country externally, was given the responsibility 'to carry out pertinent actions that lead to the formulation, implementation and administration of the "Nation Brand"'.[3] In 2008, the 'Country Brand Project' was created, aimed at contesting the stereotypes in the global media and public opinion about Peru such as poverty, instability, natural disasters – a major earthquake had occurred in 2007 – and bad news.

To make this happen, a Country Brand Work Group was installed, and its first task was to create Peru's nation brand 'core idea'.[4] Throughout a consultation process that involved stakeholders in the areas of tourism, commerce, and investment, the final concept of the Peruvian nation brand was defined, highlighting three national dimensions:

- *Multifaceted Peru*, referring to the varied cultures, geographies, and products.
- *Specialist Peru*, referring to history, legends, and ancestral knowledge.
- *Captivating Peru*, referring to the emotional effect that the visitor gets by visiting Peru.

With the core idea established, the logo – a reference to Peru's ancient cultures blended with its current insertion into the global digital world, all part of the Peruvian unique identity – and the slogan 'There is a Peru for each one of us', were created.

In 2010, the implementation and dissemination of Brand Peru began. It was decided that an office exclusively in charge of the brand management was needed and the 'Country Image and Promotion Directorate' was established. The specific objectives of this office were the following:[5]

(i)   Contribute to improving perceptions of Peru around the world.
(ii)   Increase positive exposure of Peru in the international media of the targeted markets.
(iii)   Contribute to strengthening the self-esteem and pride of Peruvian citizens.
(iv)   Contribute to strengthening relationships between Peruvian citizens.

The Country Image and Promotion Directorate was tasked with managing the brand in the technical, legal, administrative, and communicative dimensions. This was in the context of three targeted sectors: tourism, export, and investment; nine targeted markets: Latin America, Brazil, the United States, Germany, the United Kingdom, France, Spain, China, and Peru; and eight prioritized fields: gastronomy, fashion, film, arts and culture, sports, music, self-esteem, and values. In March 2011, Brand Peru was officially launched.

From 2011 to 2016, strategies such as the 'Brand Peru ambassadors' and 'Brand Peru licensees' were carried out. In the former, as happens in several nation brand strategies, the goal was/is to reach a wider audience and to emotionally engage citizens with the brand through charismatic local personalities-celebrities or familiar 'national' brands, avoiding the idea of a 'top-down' strategy. In the case of Brand Peru, the brand ambassadors included well-known celebrities and entrepreneurs – 'celepreneurs' – mainly from the fields of gastronomy, arts, television, and sports, who had accomplished significant achievements and represented the renewed national identity the country aspired to.

Regarding the licensees' strategy, the goal was to engage small and medium businesses and regulate the proper uses of the brand. To achieve this, PROMPERÚ encouraged local companies to apply for the use of the brand logo on their products/services and to become 'licenciatarios' (licensees). By being granted a licence to use the logo, the licensees won prestige by associating their products with an already well-known and respected brand, whilst Brand Peru engaged the key stakeholders and expanded its messages and visual identity in all possible spaces.

Finally, the Brand Peru team produced and disseminated two videos in the form of 'mockumentaries', in which the nation brand ambassadors visited and interacted with the locals of the state of Peru in Nebraska (United States) and of Loreto (the same name as the largest Amazon region in Peru) in Italy by announcing to them their 'Peruvian rights'. These were a group of national values associated with the country's distinctiveness: gastronomy, music, nature. In short, 'real' Peruvian representatives (brand ambassadors) taught the 'fake' Peruvian people (local inhabitants) how to become proper Peruvian citizens. This campaign won several prizes nationally and internationally and for many, it encapsulates the narrative at the heart of Brand Peru.

Renewed challenges and opportunities

Brand Peru has achieved enormous awareness both nationally and globally during its first decade of existence. Nonetheless, new challenges have appeared since recent years. Perhaps the most important one is to think beyond gastronomy. With this field still the most important in terms of external reputation, distinctiveness and competitiveness, Brand Peru needs to explore – and has been doing so – novel territories from where to diversify the basis of Peru's reputation, identity, and distinctiveness.

In this scenario, the cultural industries and arts have been taken more into consideration than during the 'first wave' of Brand Peru. Strategies such as 'Film in Peru' – a film commission programme which aims to attract external film and TV productions to shoot in different locations in Peru, or the participation in world arts and innovation exhibitions and fairs such as the Arcomadrid International Contemporary Art Fair in 2019, where Peru was the guest country, or Expo 2020 Dubai (rescheduled to October 2021–March 2022 due to the Covid-19 pandemic) have been gaining a more significant role in the Brand Peru portfolio of activities.

Additionally, the promotion of sustainable uses and conservation of natural resources, which emphasizes the role of the different actors involved in the agriculture ecosystem, beyond the ones involved in the more visible gastronomy field, appears to be a key dimension of contemporary Brand Peru. A clear example of this is the campaign for promoting Peruvian 'superfoods': natural products cultivated for thousands of years through ancient techniques in biodiverse lands and rich in nutrition and flavour. In it, Peru is presented as 'the planet's super pantry', comprising its rich fruits (e.g., blueberries), grains (e.g., quinoa) and vegetables (e.g., asparagus), all of them 'ideal for a healthy lifestyle' and which can also become global genetic resources. From this, Brand Peru has renewed its pillars which are now: (i) talent, (ii) agriculture/gastronomy (iii) investment, (iv) external commerce, and (v) tourism.[6]

Beyond this, Brand Peru will need to constantly rethink its strategies in the near future, amid the context of Covid-19. Far away from campaigns that exclusively celebrate the country's success in different fields, the branding strategies will probably need to pay closer attention to the role they play in the nation's current institutional weakness, evidenced in the midst of the pandemic. With Peru being one of the countries with the higher number of deaths per million inhabitants in the Latin American region, and where the economy has suffered the most significant negative impact, perhaps a further challenge for Brand Peru is to look back to our recent history and current internal social fractures and crisis, while continuing to work on consolidating a reputation based upon those areas where Peru has demonstrated leadership, innovation, and constant talent for hundreds of years.

Reference

Lossio, F, (2018) 'The counter-narratives of nation branding: The case of Peru', in Fehimović, D. and Ogden, R. (eds.), *Branding Latin America: Strategies, Aims, Resistance*, chapter 2, 59–77, London: Lexington Books.

CASE: BRANDING KOREA GLOBALLY

You Kyung Kim, Professor, Division of Media Communication,
Hankuk University of Foreign Studies, Seoul, South Korea

In the modern world, Korea is almost the only nation that has been able to rise from the ashes of war and poverty, and succeed in industrialization while realizing democracy. However, there has been virtually no time to invest in Korea's national image throughout the short history of modernization. As a result, the national image has not been able to keep up with the rapid growth in the nation's economic status. While the formation of an image that adequately represents the nation requires substantial investments and time, there has been a lack of interest in such activities.

Since the 2002 Korea–Japan FIFA World Cup, several attempts have been made to enhance Korea's national image. The Korean government established the 'Council for National Image Enhancement' with civilian partners to remove negative information such as Korea being a divided nation, while systematically and continuously improving the national image. All public relations which have been relying heavily on PR agencies and mass media prior to 2002, was focused on the brand 'Dynamic Korea'. However, the Council for National Image Enhancement was unable to deal with national image related issues in a systematic manner due to insufficient budget and authority. This was a time when the concept of nation brand management was not fully understood, and experience in the field was scarce. Nevertheless, the Council for National Image Enhancement has succeeded in developing a new and innovative nation brand which was 'Dynamic Korea' and its conceptual manual.

Korea, which is proud of its long history (5,000 years), has been famous to most foreigners as the land of the morning calm. For the past 5,000 years, Korea used to be invaded by neighboring countries such as China and Japan nearly once every five years, ended up being invaded as many as 1,000 times in total. Forced division of the nation into two parts was also made by these countries, including the United States and Russia. As such, Korea and its people could not help being defensive and quiet. At the beginning of the 21st century, a new movement has finally risen throughout the nation. Korea wanted to escape from the image of quietness and calmness, heading toward more aggressive, energetic, and challenging entities. It is called 'Dynamic Korea'. This is the nation brand identity that signifies the core spirit of Korea. It denotes the strength Koreans have drawn on throughout history to overcome many difficulties and the creativity and innovation they call upon when exploring the future.

As such, 'Dynamic Korea' has been derived from a characteristic of national identity which is dynamism. From the cultural perspective, Korea and its people have shown a variety of different dynamisms: functional/physical dynamism, emotional dynamism, intellectual dynamism, Confucius dynamism, and spiritual dynamism. These dimensions were generally found in Korea's history, tradition, and daily life, etc. For the most part, such a variety of dynamic aspects have been recognized as an actual and realistic identity discovered around the world.

As a more systematic endeavor for pushing forward the nation branding, the Nation Brand Council was established as an institution directly responsible to the president in order to improve the status and class of Korea by implementing an integrated strategy. Such efforts made by the government aimed to resolve disadvantages caused by a low perceived level of nation brand value. In 2009, Korea's economy was 13th in the world in terms of scale, but its brand status ranked in 33rd place. Korea's nation brand value was greatly undervalued at lower than 30% of its GDP, while the United States and Japan had their nation brands valued at 143% and 224% of their GDP respectively. Such undervaluation affected the price of Korean-made products resulting in a 'Korea Discount' effect, which caused the prices of Korean products to be 66%–67% lower than identical products made in the United States. To alleviate the 'Korea Discount' problem, all nation brand related activities which had been scattered across various departments were incorporated under a single central management system.

The Nation Brand Council defined the nation brand as the generic concept of desirability and reliability, which includes the political, economic, and cultural competence, and also the vision and values of a nation and established Korea's nation brand vision as being reliable, and having dignity. The objective was to reinforce soft power, such as culture and image, by harnessing hard power, which includes economy and technology. The council, in concert with the public and private stakeholders, made many efforts to distill universal values such as communication and harmony in Korea's brand, and create cultural content by discovering values within its cultural heritage.

The government defined improving the nation brand substance, enhancing the brand image, and systemizing the management system as the three axes and started nation brand value-enhancing activities focused on the following critical areas: expanding international participation, tolerating multiple cultures and caring for foreigners, advanced technology and product promotion, participation in society, and reinforcing competence, and diffusing cultural asset values.

Considering the scale of Korea's economy, it has played a relatively small role in development assistance in developing nations, global climate issues, and peacekeeping. It would be more appropriate for Korea as a responsible member of international society to expand personal exchange and cooperation in development. In this context, the Korean government has integrated overseas volunteer efforts into a single brand to better represent the nation and has shared its experience in economic policies with other countries in order to spread the Korean Wave into economic areas.

The purpose of diffusing cultural assets is to reinforce Korea's soft power by creating and sharing attractive cultural content based on cultural and historic values, such as communication, harmony, sharing, and caring, and also by establishing a strong cultural tourism infrastructure.

Because the amount of interaction between Korea and the rest of the world has increased significantly, it has become necessary to integrate society in a forward-looking manner. When people interact with foreigners while keeping in mind that they are themselves, global citizens, it is possible to enhance Korea's image. The government built an environment where the younger generation can feel proud of their nation brand image, and actively participate in improving it further. The global etiquette of understanding other cultures has been introduced in everyday life to cultivate global citizenship. Also, efforts to enhance the nation brand image have been made in the field of overseas tourism, and activities such as the 'smile campaign' have spread the culture of politeness, cleanness, and order. The importance of pan-national participation has been emphasized by affiliating with companies and Korean nationals in other countries. Also, the council endeavored to improve the perception of cultural diversity by launching campaigns, such as the campaign for the social integration of culturally diverse families, and improved the living standards of foreigners in terms of education, medical care, housing, and language. Furthermore, the council offered increased access to foreign media and communication to increase communication with the rest of the world, and also offered various content.

With the aim to escape from the Korea Discount, which was a long-term and chronic problem, the council attempted to create a 'Korea Premium' by designating Korean products with world-leading quality as 'Advanced Technology & Design Korea (AT&D Korea)' products. The council pursued a nation brand development plan associated with corporate marketing and enabled corporate brands to proudly mark products as 'Made in Korea'.

Also, it should be noted that Korea's nation brand activities not only engaged in image-oriented management, but also included discovering the fundamental national identity and applied modern reinterpretation to solidify the core concept and factors of national identity, which lead to social discussion and consensus. The government, working with academia, derived six dimensions, which are cultural uniqueness, global citizenship, national heritage, social value system, global leadership, and emotional attachment, and applied the competitive advantages and differentiation factors to the nation brand management process.

Along with the publicity efforts for branding the nation, the value of the nation brand continued to grow rapidly. And it seemed that this phenomenon kindled the advent of the time of the Korean Wave (*Hallyu*), led by K-pop. With the emergence of BTS, K-pop activities culminated. They have made many albums number one on the Billboard chart. They also served as cultural ambassadors for Korea's public diplomacy. K-pop has been regarded as a form of soft power that has built up Korea's image as a nation brand at home and abroad. Furthermore, Korean films have been considered some of the best in the world, with the film *Parasite*, for example, winning the Best Picture award at the 2020 Oscars.

As a result, the nation brand value of our country has recently gradually returned to its original position. Foreign audiences feel more favorable about Korea and its products as they encounter the Korean Wave culture. Above all, the popularity of *Hallyu* has boosted the popularity of purchases of its economic derivatives, including Korea's general merchandise. This has led to a more positive assessment of Korea's image. All in all, *Hallyu* has played a pivotal role in transforming the 'Korea Discount' into the 'Korea Premium'.

It seems clear that the Korean Wave has established itself as the symbolic agent of cultural exchange that enhances the overall image and reputation of the nation, such as its national status and dignity. Korea's nation brand in the 21st century will eventually become a culture and its relevant activities, and *Hallyu* is certainly at the center of the trend.

As Covid-19 began to be in full swing around the world, Korea's successful quarantine has been positively reported abroad. Korea's advanced medical system has been in the spotlight recently, contributing to the rise of the nation brand. More important is that progress in inter-Korean and North Korea–US relations have been visible since 2017. As the leaders of each country have been meeting quickly and frequently, it began to attract profound attention from all of the world, sending another positive signal to the management of Korea's nation brand. This is what we call 'peninsular branding' rather than just nation branding.

Summary

This chapter has discussed the key branding concepts of brand identity, brand image and brand positioning. A distinction has been made between the two frequently confused concepts of identity and image. The components of nation brand identity and nation brand image have been analysed and the issues involved in positioning the nation brand have been discussed. Basic principles of branding have been shown to apply to nations, despite the increased complexity inherent in a nation brand as compared to commercial brands.

Discussion points

1   Identify three countries that suffer from an identity–image gap. Explain why their identity–image gap exists, and suggest measures those countries could take to address the problem.
2   Evaluate the brand positioning of a country of your choice. How clear is the brand positioning? How appropriate is the positioning for the relevant target audiences?

Notes

1   The present contribution is partially based upon my PhD thesis entitled 'The Construction of Latin America as a brand: designs, narrations and disputes in Peru and Cuba', submitted to the Faculty of Humanities and Social Sciences, Newcastle University, 2018.
2   'Hatun Willakuy', Short Report of the Truth and Reconciliation Commission Report, IDE-HPUCP, 2008.
3   PromPerú (2017) 'Decreto Supremo' N°009–2007 MINCETUR.
4   W. Olins (2002) 'Branding the nation – the historical context', *Journal of Brand Management*, 9 (4), 241–248.
5   *El Peruano* (2010) Decreto Supremo N°014–2010 – MINCETUR' September.
6   Brand Peru web page, available at: https://peru.info/es-pe/#.

References

Aaker, D.A. (1996) *Building Strong Brands*, New York: Free Press.

Alvarez, M.D. and Campo, S. (2014) 'The influence of political conflicts on country image and intention to visit: A study of Israel's image', *Tourism Management*, 40, February, 70–78.

Anderson, J. and Sutherland, D. (2015) 'Developed economy investment promotion agencies and emerging market foreign direct investment: The case of Chinese FDI in Canada', *Journal of World Business*, 50, 815–825.

Baldwin, C.Y. and Clark, K.B. (1997) 'Managing in an age of modularity', *Harvard Business Review*, September–October, 84–93.

Bassols, N. (2016) 'Branding and promoting a country amidst a long-term conflict: The case of Colombia', *Journal of Destination Marketing & Management*, 5 (4), 314–324.

Bauer, A., Bloching, B., Howaldt, K. and Mitchell, A. (2006) *Moment of Truth: Redefining the CEO's Brand Management Agenda*, London: Palgrave Macmillan.

BBC (2021) 'Covid: WHO renames UK and other variants with Greek letters', 31 May, available at: www.bbc.co.uk/news/world-57308592 (accessed 16/7/2021).

Blankson, C., Kalafatis, S.P., Coffie, S. and Tsogas, M.H. (2014) 'Comparisons of media types and congruence in positioning of service brands', *Journal of Product & Brand Management*, 23 (3), 162–179.

Boeh, K.K. and Beamish, P.W. (2012) 'Travel time and the liability of distance in foreign direct investment: Location choice and entry mode', *Journal of International Business Studies*, 43, 525–535.

Buchholz, A. and Wordemann, W. (2000) *What Makes Winning Brands Different: The Hidden Method Behind The World's Most Successful Brands*, London: Wiley.

Cantwell, J. (2009) 'Location and the multinational enterprise', *Journal of International Business Studies*, 40, 35–41.

Capik, P. (2007) 'Organising FDI promotion in Central-Eastern European regions', *Place Branding and Public Diplomacy*, 3 (2), 152–163.

Cho, D.-S., Moon, H.-C. and Kim, M.-Y. (2009) 'Does one size fit all? A dual double diamond approach to country-specific advantages', *Asian Business & Management*, 8 (1), 83–102.

Concise Oxford English Dictionary (2009) *Concise Oxford English Dictionary*, 11th rev. edn, Oxford: Oxford University Press.

Cornelissen, J. (2004) *Corporate Communications: Theory and Practice*, London: Sage Publications.

Damjan, J. (2005) 'Development of Slovenian brands: Oldest are the best', *Place Branding*, 1 (4), 363–372.

de Chernatony, L. and McDonald, M. (2003) *Creating Powerful Brands in Consumer, Service and Industrial Markets*, 3rd edn, London: Butterworth-Heinemann.

Dunning, J. and Gugler, P. (2008) *Foreign Direct Investments, Location and Competitiveness*, Oxford: Elsevier.

Elliott, R. and Percy, L. (2007) *Strategic Brand Management*, Oxford: Oxford University Press.

EY Attractiveness Surveys (2021) 'Attractiveness surveys', available at: www.ey.com/en_uk/attractiveness (accessed 17/7/2021).

Florek, M. (2005) 'The country brand as a new challenge for Poland', *Place Branding*, 1 (2), 205–214.

Fuchs, C. and Diamantopoulos, A. (2010) 'Evaluating the effectiveness of brand-positioning strategies from a consumer perspective', *European Journal of Marketing*, 44 (11–12), 1763–1786.

Galan, J.I., González-Benito, J. and Zuñiga-Vicente, J.A. (2007) 'Factors determining the location decisions of Spanish MNEs: An analysis based on the investment development path', *Journal of International Business Studies*, 38, 975–997.

Grant, J. (2006) *The Brand Innovation Manifesto: How to Build Brands, Redefine Markets & Defy Conventions*, London: Wiley.

Hall, J. (2004) 'Branding Britain', *Journal of Vacation Marketing*, 10 (2), 171–185.

Hynes, N., Caemmerer, B., Martin, E. and Masters, E. (2014) 'Use, abuse or contribute!: A framework for classifying how companies engage with country image', *International Marketing Review*, 31 (1), 79–97.

Jacobsen, U.C. (2018) 'Does subtitled television drama brand the nation? Danish television drama and its language(s) in Japan', *European Journal of Cultural Studies*, 21 (5), 614–630.

Jaffe, E.D. and Nebenzahl, I.D. (2001) *National Image & Competitive Advantage: The Theory and Practice of Country-of-Origin Effect*, Denmark: Copenhagen Business School Press.

Jakubanecs, A. and Supphellen, M. (2010) 'Brand positioning strategies in Russia: Regional differences in the importance of corporate endorsement and symbolic brand attributes', *Journal of East-West Business*, 16 (4), 286–302.

Jaworski, S.P. and Fosher, D. (2003) 'National brand identity & its effect on corporate brands: The nation brand effect (NBE)', *Multinational Business Review*, 11 (2), 99–113.

Jobber, D. (2004) *Principles and Practice of Marketing*, 4th edn, London: McGraw-Hill.

Kapferer, J.-K. (2004) *The New Strategic Brand Management: Creating and Sustaining Brand Equity Long Term*, London: Kogan Page.

Kavaratzis, M. and Hatch, M.J. (2013) 'The dynamics of place brands: An identity-based approach to place branding theory', *Marketing Theory*, 13 (1), 69–86.

Keller, K.L. (2003) *Strategic Brand Management: Building, Measuring, and Managing Brand Equity*, 2nd edn, Upper Saddle River, NJ: Prentice Hall.

Konecnik Ruzzier, M. and de Chernatony, L. (2013) 'Developing and applying a place brand identity model: The case of Slovenia', *Journal of Business Research*, 66, 45–52.

Kotler, P. and Keller, K.L. (2006) *Marketing Management*, 12th edn, Upper Saddle River, NJ: Pearson Prentice Hall.

Lee, I.H. and Rugman, A.M. (2009) 'Multinationals and public policy in Korea', *Asian Business & Management*, 8 (1), 59–82.

Lee, R. and Lee, Y.-I. (2021) 'The role of nation brand in attracting foreign direct investments: A case study of Korea', *International Marketing Review*, 38 (1), 124–140.

Lehu, J.-M. (2006) *Brand Rejuvenation: How to Protect, Strengthen and Add Value to Your Brand to Prevent It from Ageing*, London: Kogan Page.

Lodge, C. (2002) 'Branding countries: A new field for branding or an ancient truth?', *Journal of the Chartered Institute of Marketing*, February, 21–25.

Lopez, C., Gotsi, M. and Andriopoulos, C. (2011) 'Conceptualising the influence of corporate image on country image', *European Journal of Marketing*, 45 (11–12), 1601–1641.

Lu, I.R.R., Kwan, E., Heslop, L.A., Thomas, D.R. and Cedzynski, M. (2019) 'The ivory tower and the street: How researchers defined country image over four decades and what consumers think it means', *Journal of Business Research*, 105, 80–97.

Madhavaram, S., Badrinarayanan, V. and McDonald, R.E. (2005) 'Integrated marketing communication (IMC) and brand identity as critical components of brand equity strategy: A conceptual framework and research propositions', *Journal of Advertising*, 34 (4), 69–80.

Matarazzo, M., Lanzilli, G. and Resciniti, R. (2018) 'Acquirer's corporate reputation in cross-border acquisitions: The moderating effect of country image', *Journal of Product & Brand Management*, 27 (7), 858–870.

Mohr, J., Sengupta, S. and Slater, S. (2005) *Marketing of High-Technology Products and Innovations*, 2nd edn, Upper Saddle River, NJ: Pearson Prentice Hall.

Nandan, S. (2005) 'An exploration of the brand identity-brand image linkage: A communications perspective', *Journal of Brand Management*, 12 (4), 264–278.

Ng, K. (2021) 'Naming Covid variants after place of origin "stigmatises" countries, says WHO', *The Independent*, 7 April, available at: www.msn.com/en-gb/news/world/naming-covid-variants-after-place-of-origin-stigmatises-countries-says-who/ar-BB1fnLJ6?ocid=mail signout&li=AAnZ9Ug (accessed 16/7/2021).

Nikolova, M.S. and Hassan, S.S. (2013) 'Nation branding effects on retrospective global evaluation of past travel experiences', *Journal of Business Research*, 66 (6), 752–758.

Okazaki, S. (2006) 'Excitement or sophistication? A preliminary exploration of online brand personality', *International Marketing Review*, 23 (3), 279–303.

Paniagua, J., Korzynski, P. and Mas-Tur, A. (2017) 'Crossing borders with social media: Online social networks and FDI', *European Management Journal*, 35 (3), 314–326.

Papadopoulos, N., Cleveland, M., Bartikowski, B. and Yaprak, A. (2018) 'Of countries, places and product/brand place associations: An inventory of dispositions and issues relating to place image and its effects', *Journal of Product & Brand Management*, 27 (7), 735–753.

Papadopoulos, N., Hamzaoui-Essoussi, L. and El-Banna, A. (2016) 'Nation branding for foreign direct investment: An integrative review and directions for research and strategy', *Journal of Product & Brand Management*, 25 (7), 615–628.

Pasquinelli, C. and Vuignier, R. (2020) 'Place marketing, policy integration and governance complexity: An analytical framework for FDI promotion', *European Planning Studies*, 28 (7), 1413–1430.

Pawlusz, E. and Polese, A. (2017) ' "Scandinavia's best-kept secret": Tourism promotion, nation branding and identity construction in Estonia (with a free guided tour of Tallin airport)', *Nationalities Papers*, 45 (5), 873–892.

Quelch, J. and Jocz, K. (2005) 'Positioning the nation-state', *Place Branding*, 1 (3), 229–237.

Ries, A. and Trout, J. (2001) *Positioning: How to Be Seen and Heard in the Overcrowded Marketplace*, New York: McGraw-Hill.

Riezebos, R. (2003) *Brand Management: A Theoretical and Practical Approach*, London: FT Prentice Hall.

Roll, M. (2006) *Asian Brand Strategy: How Asia Builds Strong Brands*, London: Palgrave Macmillan.

Roth, K.P. and Diamantopoulos, A. (2009) 'Advancing the country image construct', *Journal of Business Research*, 7 (62), 726–740.

Rugman, A.M. and Verbeke, A. (1992) 'A note on the transnational solution and the transaction cost theory of multinational strategic management', *Journal of International Business Studies*, 23, 761–771.

Sjodin, H. and Torn, F. (2006) 'When communication challenges brand associations: A framework for understanding consumer responses to brand image incongruity', *Journal of Consumer Behaviour*, 5 (1), 32–42.

Ståhlberg, P. and Bolin, G. (2016) 'Having a soul or choosing a face? Nation branding, identity and cosmopolitan imagination', *Social Identities*, 22 (3), 274–290.

Usunier, J.-C. and Lee, J.A. (2005) *Marketing Across Cultures*, 4th edn, Upper Saddle River, NJ: FT Prentice Hall.

Wansink, B. and Huffman, C. (2001) 'Revitalizing mature packaged goods', *Journal of Product & Brand Management*, 10 (4), 228–242.

Wike, R., Poushter, J., Silver, L., Fetterolf, H. and Mordecai, M. (2021) 'America's image abroad rebounds with transition from Trump to Biden', *Pew Research Center*, available at: www.pewresearch.org/global/2021/06/10/americas-image-abroad-rebounds-with-transition-from-trump-to-biden/ (accessed 15/6/2021).

Wilkinson, T.J. and Brouthers, L.E. (2000) 'Trade shows, trade missions and state governments: Increasing FDI and high-tech exports', *Journal of International Business Studies*, 31, 725–734.

Wu, L. and Shimuzu, T. (2020) 'Analyzing dynamic change of tourism destination image under the occurrence of a natural disaster: Evidence from Japan', *Current Issues in Tourism*, 23 (16), 2042–2058.

ZAD Group (2008) 'Egypt – an aspiring modern state', in Dinnie, K. (ed.), *Nation Branding – Concepts, Issues, Practice*, 1st edn, 37–41, London: Butterworth-Heinemann.

3 Nation brand equity

Key points

- There are two main approaches to considering brand equity: the consumer perspective and the financial perspective
- Nation brand equity comprises internal and external assets
- Internal assets include iconography, landscape, and culture
- External assets include country image perceptions and external portrayals in popular culture

Introduction

This chapter focuses on the concept of brand equity. We first look at the two major perspectives on brand equity: the consumer perspective and the financial perspective. We then apply the brand equity concept to nation brands and examine the range of potential sources and dimensions of nation brand equity. The first case in this chapter discusses a sustainable nation brand for The Gambia. The second case considers the role of culture, heritage and tourism in the development of India's soft power. The third case investigates a potential future path for Brand Africa. The academic perspective by Dan Nunan addresses the theme of building a nation brand through a diaspora, whilst José Filipe

DOI: 10.4324/9781003100249-4

Torres' practitioner insight elaborates a nation branding approach built on research, strategy, implementation and measurement.

Alternative perspectives on brand equity

The term *brand equity* is a prominent one in the theory and practice of branding. Brand equity refers to the value of a brand. The notion of equity is borrowed from the field of finance, although when the term is transposed to the field of branding it loses any precise, universally accepted meaning. There has been increasing interest in recent years in applying the concept of brand equity to places (Jacobsen, 2012; Lucarelli, 2012; Mariutti and Giraldi, 2019; Zenker, 2014) and the ways in which nation equity may be embedded into commercial brands (He et al., 2021).

There are two distinct approaches to considering the concept of brand equity. One approach is the consumer perspective, whereby brand equity is evaluated in terms of consumer awareness of the brand in question, consumer judgements regarding brand quality, uniqueness, prestige and so on. The alternative approach to viewing brand equity is the financial perspective, which involves attempts of various kinds to attach a financial value to specific brands. Within both the consumer perspective and the financial perspective there exist several different viewpoints with regard to what brand equity means. These different viewpoints will now be examined.

Consumer perspective

One of the leading proponents of the consumer perspective on brand equity (Keller, 2003) uses the term customer-based brand equity (CBBE) to refer to the awareness, familiarity and associations held by consumers with regard to a brand. In a study by Pappu et al. (2005), the following four dimensions of CBBE were proposed: brand awareness, brand associations, perceived quality and brand loyalty. It is important for nations to conduct research to gain insight into such dimensions of their nation brand equity, rather than relying on gut instinct. Many nations might assume, for example, that they are suffering from negative brand associations when in reality there might be an almost complete lack of awareness of their nation brand in the minds of external audiences. A standard CBBE instrument is advocated by Pike et al. (2010) to track any strengthening or weakening of brand equity over time. Chekalina et al. (2018) have applied the concept of customer-based brand equity to destination brands, identifying the key roles played by destination resources, value for money and value in use.

Still grounded in the consumer perspective on brand equity, although utilising the vocabulary of accounting, Aaker (1991) views brand equity in terms of assets and liabilities that enhance or decrease the value of the brand. The idea of adding value is also referred to by Farquhar (1989), who considers brand equity as added value relevant to the firm, the consumer or the trade.

Farquhar's inclusion of 'the trade' is a useful indication that the consumer perspective on brand equity should take a broad-based view of who the 'consumer' or the 'customer' is. Stakeholder models suggest that a brand must appeal to and communicate with multiple constituencies, rather than take a myopic uni-dimensional view of the customer. The stakeholder theory of brand equity is articulated by Jones (2005), who argues that brand value is co-created through interaction with multiple strategic stakeholders and therefore it would be erroneous to focus only on the customer when assessing brand equity.

Temporal (2002) describes how the term brand equity is often used in referring to the descriptive aspects of a brand, whether symbols, imagery or consumer associations, and to reflect the strength of a brand in terms of consumer perceptions. Nations are particularly rich in terms of symbols and imagery. Every nation possesses its own unique and distinctive iconography. These, and other components of national identity, underpin nation brand development and ensure that nation branding remains an encapsulation and expression of a nation's true essence rather than a mere public relations or advertising exercise.

Brand equity can create a relationship and a strong bond between brand and consumer which grows over time, involving trust and an emotional connection (VanAuken, 2002). Baker (2002) defines brand equity as the value imputed to a brand which recognises its worth as an asset; this value reflects the market share held by the brand, the degree of loyalty and recognition it enjoys, its perceived quality and any other attributes which distinguish it positively from competitive offerings, e.g., patent protection, trademark and so on. Baker's perspective on brand equity is echoed by Riezebos (2003) who identifies four sources of brand equity: the size of the market share; the stability of the market share; the price margin of the brand for the organisation; and the rights of ownership (patents, trademarks) linked to the brand. In his discussion of brand equity, Kapferer (2004) also proposes four indicators of brand assets: aided brand awareness; spontaneous brand awareness; membership of the consumer's evoked set; and, has the brand been already consumed or not. A similar view is taken by de Chernatony and McDonald (2003), whose view is that brand equity describes the perceptions consumers have about a brand, and this in turn leads to the value of a brand.

Consumer loyalty is a key element in brand equity. Brand-building efforts typically focus on creating differentiation and value for consumers and achieving high levels of customer loyalty is a useful metric for assessing the success of a brand's strategy. Whereas commercial brands have for many years dedicated considerable resources to developing loyalty programmes, nation brands have taken relatively few initiatives in this area. Loyalty programmes must aim to build consumers' emotional attachment to the brand rather than aiming solely at engendering repeat buying, since the correlation between emotional loyalty and brand purchase is exponential rather than linear – at the highest level of emotional loyalty to a brand, consumers will buy at least twice as much as consumers just slightly less attached to the brand, and often three to four times more (Hallberg, 2004). As rich repositories of cultural meanings, possessing deep emotional and experiential qualities, nation brands should be well-placed to develop powerful emotional attachment to their brands.

In the context of product brands, it has been shown that regular permission-based email marketing can have various positive effects on brand loyalty: email-activated consumers go on to visit retail stores, recommend the brand to their friends and loyal customers appear to appreciate regular communication and various other information content from the brand more than mere offers (Merisavo and Raulas, 2004). If a brand fails to develop customer loyalty then there is the risk of what Perrin-Martinenq (2004) has termed *brand detachment*, where the affective or emotional bond between a brand and a consumer dissolves in a similar way to the dissolution of other types of relationships. One way in which nation brands can avoid the negative consequences of brand detachment is through the application of customer relationship management (CRM) principles to the nation's full range of audiences and stakeholders (Buttle, 2008).

The visual manifestations of a brand play an important role in contributing to overall brand equity. For many consumers, a brand's logo, name, symbols, typeface and colour scheme represent a prime contributor to brand awareness. It has been claimed that there is a significant relationship between visual design and positive brand responses in terms of positive affect, perceptions of quality, recognition and consensus of meaning (Henderson et al., 2003). Nations need to actively manage their visual identity to ensure maximum impact and synergy across different target audiences and stakeholders.

Financial perspective

As we have seen, the consumer perspective on brand equity has clear relevance to nation brands, particularly in light of the stakeholder theory concept of multiple audiences which for nation brands include potential tourists, investors, employees, students and consumers both domestic and international. The relevance to nation branding of the financial perspective on brand equity is less obvious. In this section we briefly overview the financial perspective on brand equity before discussing one specific attempt that has been made to place a financial valuation upon nation brands.

To date, there is no universal consensus on accounting methods and procedures for the financial valuation of brands. There are, however, certain techniques available to companies and analysts who wish to make an estimate of a brand's financial value. Such techniques include valuation by historic costs, valuation by replacement costs, and valuation by future earnings. Valuation by historic costs treats a brand as an asset whose value is derived from investments over a period of time; valuation by replacement costs centres upon estimating how much it would cost to create an equivalent brand; and, valuation by future earnings aims to estimate future cash flows associated with the brand (Kapferer, 2004).

A well-established, high-profile exercise in brand valuation is the annual Best Global Brands report by branding consultancy Interbrand. To qualify for inclusion in the Best Global Brands report a brand must meet the following criteria: derive at least 30% of revenue from outside its home region; have publicly available data on the brand's financial performance; have a significant presence in Asia, Europe and North America as well as broad coverage in emerging markets; economic profit must be expected to be positive over the longer term, delivering a return above the brand's cost of capital; and the brand must have a public profile and awareness across the major economies of the world (www. bestglobalbrands.com/2014/methodology/). Interbrand's top two global brands in 2014, along with their estimated financial valuations, were Apple Inc. valued at $118.9bn and Google Inc. valued at $107.43bn. From a corporate point of view, brand valuation can be a useful tool in that it can allow a company to use a brand to raise credits; determine potential revenue streams from licencing agreements; and gain an insight into the value of a possible future brand acquisition (Riezebos, 2003). The rationale for conducting brand valuation for commercial brands is clear. The potential relevance of financial valuation for nation brands is discussed by Roger Sinclair in his Practitioner insight in this chapter.

Sources and dimensions of nation brand equity

In this section, we identify the major sources of nation brand equity (NBEQ) which potentially form the basis for developing nation branding strategy. These sources are presented in the form of an asset-based model of nation brand equity in which the internal and external assets comprising nation brand equity are conceptualised in terms of innate, nurtured, vicarious and disseminated assets. We build on the preceding discussion and definitions of brand equity and apply them to the context of nation branding. We define nation brand equity (NBEQ) as *the tangible and intangible, internal and external assets (or liabilities) of the nation.* These internal and external assets (or liabilities) represent the sources of nation brand equity. Internal assets are conceptualised as innate (iconography, landscape and culture) or nurtured (internal buy-in, support for the arts). External assets are conceptualised as vicarious (country image perceptions, external portrayal in popular culture) or disseminated (brand ambassadors, the diaspora, branded exports). These sources will now be discussed in terms of their contribution to overall nation brand equity.

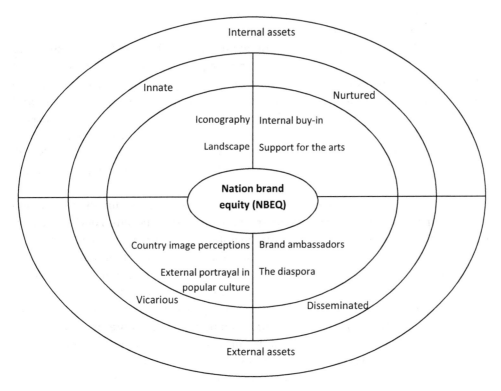

Figure 3.1
Model of asset-based nation brand equity

Internal assets

We view a nation brand's internal assets as being either innate or nurtured. Innate assets are enduring elements of national identity, those aspects of the essence of the nation that can be viewed as assets in attempts to build nation brand equity. Such assets include a nation's iconography, landscape and culture. Nurtured assets, on the other hand, derive from conscious contemporary efforts to create a healthy environment for nation brand equity development. Internal buy-in and support for the arts represent such nurtured assets.

Innate assets: Iconography, landscape, culture

The distinguishing features of a nation include its iconography, landscape and culture. These provide a powerful and authentic means of differentiation for the nation brand. A nation's iconography comprises visual images, symbols and other unique representational elements associated with the nation. National flags are the most obvious element of a nation's iconography, although the modern meaning of the word 'icon' now extends to cover places, individuals and even products that have attained the status of symbolically representing something with wider connotations in society. In this light, for example, Nelson Mandela may be regarded as an icon of South Africa, the Acropolis as an icon of Greece and whisky as an icon of Scotland. As with the other innate assets possessed by nations, these elements are unique and cannot be copied. They are the kind of distinctive attributes that any type of brand is built upon.

Landscape, including cities, plays a prominent role in helping define the essence of a nation and is a key component of nation brand equity. Landscape is one of the great equalisers in nation branding. Even if a nation is economically poor or disadvantaged in other ways, it may possess landscape that is sufficiently distinctive to represent a powerful asset. The coloured lagoons, exotic rock formations and volcanic craters that surround the Uyuni Salt Flats in Bolivia, for instance, represent a key asset for that nation. Another nation that is economically deprived yet rich in unique and dramatic landscape is Nepal, where the beauty of the landscape has contributed to that country's image as one of the most exciting destinations in the world.

As with iconography and landscape, a nation's culture represents a unique and authentic facet of national identity. These assets are not contrived artificialities devised by marketers. On the contrary, they are authentic manifestations of what the nation truly is. Culture, in particular, offers an infinitely rich source for nations attempting to fashion their nation brand. Russia, for example, has been increasingly active in modernising its cultural centres abroad as part of a wider attempt to develop a more positive image for its nation (Lebedenko, 2008). For smaller or emerging nations with limited financial resources, highlighting their national culture via music, film, literature, art and food and drink represents a more attractive and feasible means to build nation brand equity rather than resorting to potentially expensive and superficial advertising campaigns.

Traditional forms of culture may play a critical role in terms of external recognition of the nation, but these must not be allowed to position the country as backward-looking as this would act counter to attempts to portray the country as a vibrant modern economy.

The fast-growing sector of ecotourism provides a contemporary context within which a focus on the past, in terms of promoting a nation's traditional culture, represents a potentially key aspect of sustainable development. The true identity of Bolivia, for example, lies largely in its ancestral cultures manifested in folklore, clothing, food and ancestral traditions and these aspects of culture form a core part of the country's 'The authentic still exists' positioning.

Music, film, literature, language and sport are expressions of contemporary culture that can play a significant role in determining country image perceptions and which therefore should be integrated into nation branding strategy. Negative perceptions connected with a country's political regime or military profile may be offset by more positive associations with the same country's contemporary culture. The worldwide appetite for American films, for example, to some extent counterbalances the hostility in many parts of the world to perceived American dominance of world affairs. Organisations such as the British Council are charged with the task of actively promoting British culture abroad, thus implicitly acknowledging the economic importance of culture. For smaller countries with a low or invisible political profile, culture can compensate through enabling a perceptual niche to be occupied on the global stage via association with the nation's unique and distinctive cultural figures.

Nurtured assets: Internal buy-in, support for the arts, loyalty levels

Securing internal buy-in to the nation brand is an important component of nation brand equity. This represents a challenge in developing nation brand strategy. If the domestic population and other domestic stakeholders are not aware of or do not support the images and narratives that are being projected of their own country, they cannot be expected to 'live the brand'. The result can be a gap between reality and the projected image, which will create dissonance when tourists, foreign investors and so on discover that the nation's projected image is not rooted in reality. There needs to be internal buy-in to the nation brand by both the public and private sectors. As an example of generating internal buy-in from the country's citizens, Taiwan invited the public to vote online to choose the set of iconic images that would be used in the country's future branding. It may therefore be argued that rather than expecting the population of a country to 'live the brand', the nation brand should be reflective of the people and the culture.

Another key nurtured asset is support for the arts. Support may come from the state through organisations tasked with fostering the nation's cultural life. Alternatively, support may be more overtly commercially driven via sponsorship of the arts by private companies. Management of the commerce–culture interface can be challenging. Traditionally, suspicion abounds between the worlds of commerce and culture. Although patronage of the arts by wealthy business people dates back several centuries and continues in varied forms in the present day, many individuals and organisations from the cultural sector harbour serious reservations about using culture as part of a branding strategy. The word *brand* in particular alienates many people. On the other hand, business people often appear to lack a sense of cultural awareness and reject any initiative that is not easily financially quantifiable, a common view being that culture is either a luxury or an irrelevance.

Loyalty is an important component of brand equity. In the context of nation brands, programmes need to be put in place to enhance loyalty levels amongst a very diverse range of audiences, including the country's own citizens, trading partners, foreign consumers of the nation's goods and services, international organisations, political allies, tourists and inward investors.

External assets

The external assets that constitute nation brand equity are either vicarious, in that they are experienced second-hand rather than through direct personal contact, or they are disseminated, tangible projections of the nation brand existing beyond the nation's homeland and throughout the wider world. As with the nation brand's internal assets, these external assets need to be strategically managed if they are to deliver maximum benefits to the nation.

Vicarious assets: Country image perceptions, external portrayal in popular culture

Country image perceptions may not always accord with reality. When this occurs, a conscious strategy needs to be implemented in order to ensure that negative or outdated perceptions do not damage overall nation brand equity. On the other hand, a negative image may be an accurate reflection of underlying problems such as high crime levels, government corruption and so on. In such cases, remedial action to tackle the real problems needs to occur before any branding work can be undertaken.

It is important to monitor and evaluate existing country image perceptions and to manage these effectively. Such perceptions can be a powerful asset or a severe liability. If image tracking is not done, then historically skewed and stereotypical imagery may obscure the present-day reality of the nation. This issue is addressed further in Chapter 9. Sometimes a country's image is strongly positive but only in one dimension, and this can be a problem if it limits that nation's potential scope of activity. Such a challenge has been successfully addressed by the Brazilian information technology sector, where a lack of knowledge about the existence of Brazil's IT sector was hampering the country's efforts to compete effectively on the global stage (Sanches and Sekles, 2008).

There are many sources of nation brand equity that are beyond the control of those responsible for developing nation branding strategy. For example, national sporting teams may perform poorly, government may prove to be blatantly corrupt and companies producing branded exports may be caught behaving in an unethical and anti-social way. In the same way, little control can be exerted over external portrayals of a country in popular culture. Positive or negative national stereotypes may be endlessly repeated in books and on film. For example, when recounting his arrival in Ireland in September 1841 the English author Anthony Trollope acknowledged the stereotype he had of Ireland: 'I had learned to think that Ireland was a land flowing with fun and whisky, in which irregularity was the rule of life, and where broken heads were looked upon as honourable badges' (Trollope, 2014, p. 44). Although such expressions of stereotypes cannot be controlled, it is important to manage their effects and consequences by highlighting positive associations that are helpful to the nation brand, and downplaying more negative portrayals. The film *Braveheart*, whilst of questionable historical accuracy, has raised the profile of Scotland and contributed to the country's positioning as heroic underdog. Other small countries which do not receive the same external portrayal in popular culture may struggle to establish themselves in the minds of consumers.

Cinema is not the only medium through which powerful images of contemporary culture can be expressed. Music can play a similarly powerful role. This is acknowledged through the public funding of musicians to tour abroad, enhancing a country's reputation in a non-military, non-imperialistic way. Cultural relations of this type can build bridges between the peoples of different countries, and should play an important part in a country's nation brand strategy.

Disseminated assets: Brand ambassadors, the diaspora, branded exports

A potentially cost-effective strategy for countries that lack the resources to undertake expensive promotional campaigns is to appoint a network of brand ambassadors whose role is to advance the nation brand at every opportunity. In Scotland, the internationally known golfer Colin Montgomerie was appointed as such a brand ambassador. Individual companies within Scotland, such as Scotch whisky company William Grant & Sons, employ brand ambassadors in order to enhance their corporate reputations and it is likely that nations will in future also use view the concept of brand ambassadors as an integral component of their nation brand equity. A key issue when appointing brand ambassadors is to ensure that as far as possible, the individuals selected truly reflect the personality of the country and the positive attributes that the nation wishes to project. Many sporting figures are *de facto* nation brand ambassadors, even if they have not officially been appointed to such a role. For certain audiences, individuals such as tennis player Roger Federer could be regarded as a brand ambassador for Switzerland, footballer Ronaldo as a brand ambassador for Brazil, and so on.

Closely linked to the concept of brand ambassadors is the diaspora that a nation may possess. The diaspora may be viewed as a pre-existing network of potential nation brand ambassadors awaiting activation. Leautier (2006) has stated that the people within diaspora networks can be important links between their homeland and cutting edge expertise in policy, technology and management, a view that is shared by Kuznetsov and Sabel (2006) who identify policy expertise and managerial and marketing knowledge as the most significant resources of diaspora networks. However, this intangible benefit of diaspora networks is complemented by the more tangible financial benefit offered by diaspora networks through the provision of FDI and individual remittances. China, for instance, has benefited from its diaspora in terms of FDI – the Chinese diaspora has provided an estimated 70% of recent foreign investment (Devane, 2006). For other countries, remittances play an equally crucial role in the home country's economy. Haiti and Jordan, for example, both receive about the equivalent of 20%of GDP from remittances (Torres and Kuznetsov, 2006).

The third type of disseminated asset is branded exports. Branded exports can play an important role in establishing a country's reputation abroad. Chilean wine producers, for example, now export more than 50%of their produce to 90 countries in five continents around the world (Felzensztein, 2008). For many consumers, their only personal experience of Chile will be through consuming a brand of Chilean wine. Branded exports may be viewed as a key asset in a nation's brand equity; therefore, countries engaged in nation branding need to ensure that the nation's export promotion agency is adequately resourced.

ACADEMIC PERSPECTIVE: BUILDING A NATION BRAND THROUGH A DIASPORA

Dan Nunan, Professor of Management, University of Portsmouth

A core challenge with nation branding is in understanding how to apply concepts borrowed from mainstream marketing thought into the complex multifaceted concept of 'the nation'. There are limits to the roles that traditional branding strategies can play, particularly when taking into account pre-existing relationships that drive perceptions of country image. One example of this is the way in which nation branding strategies leverage diaspora communities through nation days.

For many countries forming relationships with diasporas is an important part of the national fabric. For places that are less well endowed with cultural attractions or scenery, a diaspora can provide a ready route toward building a relationship with a potential market. Additionally, within the nation branding literature diaspora communities are often characterised as potential 'brand ambassadors'. With an appropriate relationship built, diasporas can leverage their experience and knowledge of a country and be an effective 'word of mouth' communication tool. Whilst these approaches can be effective they mask sometimes complex and conflicting identities of place held by diaspora communities.

Two countries that have made particularly strong efforts to leverage their extensive diasporas are Scotland and Ireland. On the surface, Ireland and Scotland both have similar heritages on which to build linkages to diaspora groups, and large diasporas that far outnumber the actual number of citizens in their home countries. One particular approach adopted by these countries is showcasing national identities during events such as national day celebrations, which reach out to diaspora groups. For example, the 'St Patrick's Day' and less well known 'St Andrew's Day' events that each country supports. St. Patrick's Day events in cities such as New York have been criticised for their commercialism and increasing stereotyping of contemporary Irish culture. However, despite the controversies, they also provide a high-profile outlet for displays of the Irish 'brand'. St. Andrew's Day events have been more closely tied into contemporary Scottish identity and sought to avoid many of the stereotypes that are a feature of St. Patrick's Day events.

The challenge that tourism agencies in both Ireland and Scotland face is managing the extent to which these external identities reflect the contemporary attributes of a country. Building nation brands is about generating stories and weaving myths that appeal to the needs of prospective visitors. The fact that the images portrayed in nation day events may not represent the reality of the modern nations works as long as visitors are willing to buy into the myth. By leveraging a diaspora community to build a nation brand it provides an opportunity for anyone to feel part of that diaspora community. For example, a slogan that often accompanies St. Patrick's Day events is 'anyone can be Irish for the day'. Where the nation brand becomes separated from the citizenship of the country it becomes a global brand with which anyone can identify if they accept the authenticity of its attributes. Yet, regardless of how global the diaspora becomes, the brand is still rooted in the local culture and heritage of the home country. In turn, this makes the brand attributes difficult to copy. How many countries would be able to successfully copy the 'St. Patrick's Day' events on such a global scale?

Nation days can strip down the complexities of a place identity into a simple national story. However, the ability to run from the reality of what a country stands for has its limits. In the long run perhaps what is important is not whether the images reflect national realities, but whether they are ones that are accepted by their country's population.

PRACTITIONER INSIGHT: A NATION BRANDING APPROACH BUILT ON RESEARCH, STRATEGY, IMPLEMENTATION AND MEASUREMENT

José Filipe Torres, CEO and Founding Partner, Bloom Consulting

Bloom Consulting's carefully curated and practical approach to nation branding is built on the foundation of research, strategy, implementation and measurement. The methodology of Bloom Consulting is driven by the **Bloom Consulting Nation Brand Wheel©**, made up of five dimensions, each measurable in their own regard in terms of attraction and appeal and influenced by the nation brand. The five dimensions are:

Investment
Tourism
Talent
Prominence
Exports

Each dimension caters to a specific *target audience*: investors, tourists, workforce, general public and companies (respectively). Nation branding strategies are furthermore implemented to work on their behalf with consideration for the unique needs of each target audience: advantages, experience, lifestyle, admiration and uniqueness (respectively).

Our course of action follows the **20 Steps to Nation Branding**, a practical guide to building and managing a nation brand. The first step, Lay the Foundation. Taking us right into the nation branding process, we begin by building a strong base; identifying advisors and creating the preliminary team structure comprised of brand builders, those who will do the heavy lifting and generate the necessary momentum to succeed. In looking more closely at the organizational development, it is our recommendation that nation brand building teams are autonomous, removed from political interests and unaffected by changes in government which often come with their own agenda. With that said, we see this challenge as an opportunity. We have had the pleasure of working with Vibe Israel, a not-for-profit organization working independently to '[energize] and inspire the next generation about Israel (*https://vibeisrael. com/*). Faced with the challenge of moving from a general lack of knowledge about Israel around the globe, to a well-known and prominent destination for tourism, talent and foreign direct investment was, and still is, no easy task.

Understanding perceptions – gathering a diverse range of domestic and international perceptions of the national situation will paint a clear picture of what constituents and our global community think of a nation as well as determine whether there is a misalignment between perceptions and reality. Perceptions also work to define strategic benchmarks, competitors, target markets and which dimensions (if not all) the Nation Brand Strategy will address.

A part of understanding perceptions is the analysis of Digital Identity and making the move from Nation Branding 1.0 to Nation Branding 2.0. Places no longer can afford to ignore the age of information and online reputation, and to manage one's Digital Identity means to address how a place is being perceived via online searches and moreover, how they *could* be perceived. In doing so, the nation brand strategy will simultaneously tackle *offline* place brand touchpoints which include:

Actions
Activities
Policies
Marketing

Diverse in nature, place brand touchpoints are the platforms through which a brand is experienced, each with the power to influence individual image and overall reputation of a country, region or city and validate the Central Idea of a place for better or worse through the eyes of their target audience.

Central Ideas are silent, simple, not a slogan, and the differentiator behind a successful nation brand strategy. It should come from a place's essence and purpose, an emotion which can be felt without being spoken. The Central Idea must be regularly validated through brand behaviour and proof points without external communication or marketing. Having a look at an example of a nation brand, Australia defines its Central Idea as *optimism*. The Central Idea acts as the reference point which determines whether place brand touchpoints are ON or OFF Brand. ON and OFF Brand Filters are key to brand stabilization and acceptance, they are a measure of defense to avoid going *off brand* and creating confusion in the minds of target audiences whether domestic or abroad who are misled by weakly branded material or touchpoints.

The unique position that nation brand building teams are in allow for, and require, strategic partnerships with both the private and public sector. Working on behalf of the people, for the people, necessitates listening to the people. Ninety-nine per cent of all reasons related to place brand strategy failure are related to low stakeholder engagement. Ensuring that all relevant stakeholders are in support and understand your nation brand's purpose and Central Idea is critical as they hold a vast amount of influence over the greater reputation of the nation. Listen, respect and respond to your stakeholders' criticisms and concerns. Understanding their perspectives are often driven by different motivations, it would be wise to collectively assess and act accordingly.

As brand builders push forward, the odds will always be against them while misconceptions of nation branding exist, and objectives are not satisfactory for certain stakeholders. As the field develops, different methods have emerged. There is no telling which is the *truest* approach, but often times this is beneficial as we all learn to adapt from a practitioner standpoint and recognize that each place (country, region or city) is different and requires its own unique strategy. It is important to remain resilient and resist the temptation to change the modus operandi. Staying true to objectives, staying true to the Central Idea, and staying true to the nation brand.

Monitor, measure, build supply and demand, stay relevant and repeat. The final steps are easier said than done but speak to our single most important piece of advice for all nation brand builders, nation brands cannot be *launched*. The idea that the culmination of strategic objectives results in a one and done reveal of work thus far is an ineffective falsehood of *real* nation branding. The brand can be developed, nurtured and monitored but must be done so on a continual basis. Returning to the organizational structure, it is critical to build a qualified and committed team who understand the importance of sustainable and ongoing management of the brand.

CASE: A SUSTAINABLE NATION BRAND FOR THE GAMBIA

Lucy Hall, Independent Researcher

Nation branding involves active image building and management strategies pursued by policy makers and organisations of the country in question (Steenkamp, 2021). For many African countries, a key challenge in enhancing their image lies in overcoming negative stereotyping of the whole continent, which can obscure the unique attributes of individual countries. Such stereotyping poses a particular challenge in attracting tourists, who may be put off by stigmatising coverage of Africa in the global media. In this case, we discuss some nation branding issues pertaining to The Gambia, the smallest, most densely populated non-island country in Africa.

Key competitors for The Gambia as a tourist destination are the clearly defined safari destinations that are so popular in Africa. Eastern and Southern Africa are known as the world's top destinations for viewing the so-called 'big five': African elephant, Cape buffalo, leopard, lion and rhinoceros (UNWTO, 2015). The fascination is very lucrative and the safari industry generated $12.4 billion in 2018 (Hashemi, 2020). While The Gambia is not typically home to these 'big five' species, The Gambia does offer some of the most accessible and prolific bird-watching opportunities in West Africa (naturalist.co.uk, 2020) which acts as a distinctive competitive edge within this competitive set. The country also has other plentiful, diverse wildlife (The Gambia Experience, 2020), which helps in positioning The Gambia as an attractive ecotourism destination.

The image often peddled by (typically Western) media channels implying that Africa is simply one huge monolithic poverty-stricken nation, leads to a misperception of the continent of Africa as one body, rather than individual nations. This increases the challenge of changing people's perceptions and increasing awareness of the rich diversity and appeal of The Gambia as a destination brand. It is critical to challenge existing misperceptions in order to create and build sustainable nation brand policies and practices to ensure the safeguarding of The Gambia's nation brand for citizens now and in the future.

The development of a nation brand strategy should focus on a systematic examination of the country's attributes as a destination, presenting a unique comparative advantage to attract investors, tourists and other resources such as technology and talent (Hassan and Mahrous, 2019). Ashworth and Kavaratzis (2010) suggest that a place must first decide on what kind of brand the place wants to become, how it can create the mental, psychological and emotional ties that are necessary for place brands to be created and managed, and the functional, physical attributes that the place needs to create, improve, emphasise or even avoid. In this light we can view the key attributes highlighted on the Gambian Tourism Board website, as follows:

- Five to six hours flight from Europe
- An English-speaking country
- Over 550 species of birds for birdwatching enthusiasts
- Breathtaking and captivating eco-tourism products
- Three world-acclaimed UNESCO heritage sites
- Water sporting and fishing activities made possible by the Atlantic Ocean and River Gambia
- Unspoiled beaches with 80 kilometers of pristine coastline
- Pleasant sub-tropical climate with average daytime temperature of 27 degrees Celsius or 80 degrees Fahrenheit
- Eco-friendly parks such as the Abuko Nature Reserve, River Gambia National Park, and Kiang West National Park

    (*www.visitthegambia.gm/quick-facts*, 2020)

The Gambia has a rich, diverse landscape and as such, a multitude of place brand strategy development opportunities. The UNESCO world heritages sites are especially worthy of discussion as one of them is Kunta Kinteh Island, famous for its history as it was once a major waypoint of the transatlantic slave trade. Victims of note included the famous rebel, Kunta Kinte, whose story inspired Alex Haley's 1976 novel *Roots* and the hit TV series of the same name. His legacy has been kept alive in popular culture by artists such as Kendrick Lamar (Monks, 2017). Because of this dissemination into popular culture the demand of tourists wanting to visit the island has increased; the trips to the island provide a regular source of visitors, enjoying boat excursion and experiences.

A key goal of the country's brand strategy is to highlight the natural landscapes that can be found within The Gambia. The Gambian place brand features the slogan, 'The Smiling Coast of Africa' (Gambian Tourism Board, 2021). This is due in part to its position appearing like that of a smile on the map of the continent (Janko, 2018). However it is not only the geography that creates this image; the people of The Gambia are friendly and hospitable, and life is taken at a very relaxed pace (gambia.co.uk, 2020).

The use of the River Gambia as a tool for facilitating responsible tourism objectives can be seen in tourism experiences such as the 'Ninki Nanka trail', a five-day river excursion along the River Gambia. The trail enables visitors to discover The Gambia's rich natural and cultural heritage whilst experiencing the legend of the mythical Ninki Nanka dragon said to reside in the creeks of the River Gambia

(GamReality, 2020). This initiative aims to provide youth employment opportunities whilst at the same time promoting responsible tourism. Practices like these are of upmost importance when developing a place brand strategy as they represent a responsible approach to community-based tourism (McCombes, 2020) as well as contributing to an authentic and sustainable nation brand for The Gambia.

References

Ashworth, G. and Kavaratzis, M. (2010) *Towards Effective Place Brand Management*, Cheltenham: Edward Elgar.

The Gambia Experience (2020) 'The Gambia guide', available at www.gambia.co.uk (accessed 11/5/2021).

Gambian Tourism Board (2021) available at: www.visitthegambia.gm/ (accessed 11/5/2021).

GamReality (2020) 'How the Gambia is reshaping tourism after the lockdown', available at: https://gambiarealestatenews.com/how-the-gambia-is-reshaping-tourism-after-the-lockdown/ (accessed 3/12/2020).

Hashemi, G. (2020) 'Maintaining tourism in Africa through virtual safari tours', available at: www.borgenmagazine.com/tourism-in-africa/ (accessed 30/11/2020).

Hassan, S. and Mahrous, A. (2019) 'Nation branding: The strategic imperative for sustainable market competitiveness', *Journal of Humanities and Applied Social Sciences*, 1 (2), 146–158.

Janko, S. (2018) 'Why the Gambia is known as "the smiling coast"', available at: https://theculturetrip.com/africa/the-gambia/articles/why-the-gambia-is-known-as-the-smiling-coast/ (accessed 28/11/2020).

McCombes, L. (2020) 'Responsible development of the Nink Nanka trail in the Gambia', available at: https://ecoclub.com/blogs/responsible-development-of-the-ninki-nanka-trail-in-the-gambia (accessed 11/5/2021).

Monks, K. (2017) 'Gambia fights to stop Kunta Kinteh returning to sea', available at: https://edition.cnn.com/2017/05/03/africa/kunta-kinteh-island/index.html (accessed 3/12/2020).

Steenkamp, J.B.E.M. (2021) 'Building strong nation brands', *International Marketing Review*, 38 (1), 6–18.

UNWTO (2015) 'Towards measuring the economic value of wildlife watching tourism in Africa', available at: https://sustainabledevelopment.un.org/content/documents/1882unwtowildlifepaper.pdf (accessed 30/11/2020).

CASE: INDIA: SOFT POWER SUPREMACY THROUGH CULTURE, HERITAGE AND TOURISM

Jeet Dogra, Indian Institute of Tourism and Travel Management (IITTM) and Venkata Rohan Sharma Karri, Independent Researcher

India emphasises Buddhism for its nonviolent co-existence and widespread pan-Asian occurrence, so as to construct a religious bridge that would foster its international affairs. For the long-lasting success of India's 'Look East' policy, the government has been actively promoting and protecting Buddhist sites in the country. The pan-Asian presence of Buddhism makes it a potent means to enhance collaboration and transnational network. Counter to China's efforts, the Indian government is utilising Buddhist heritage and tourism as a channel for successful communication. In addition to that, it is also drawing upon the Buddhist ancestry as a vital tool in the soft power battle between India and China. Being the cradle of four major religions, India possesses enormous potential for religious and spiritual tourism. In other words, India is a 'great network of pilgrimage places – referential, inter-referential, ancient and modern, complex and ever-changing. It constitutes what would have to be called "sacred geography", as vast and complex as the whole of the subcontinent' (Eck, 2012, p. 2). Among these, the Buddhist circuit is considered to be the most powerful on the country's tourism and political levels. It is 'a key symbol of India's national historiography that plays into ongoing diplomatic exchanges with neighbouring countries where the cultural influence of Buddhism remains prominent' (Geary, 2018, p. 50).

India is widely admired and respected by Buddhists across the world, as it was the birthplace as well as the nexus for the worldwide spread of Buddhism (Agrawal et al., 2010). Buddhist sites in India attract international tourists from countries where Buddhism is predominantly followed such as Sri Lanka, Thailand, Japan, Myanmar, China, South Korea, Laos, Cambodia, Malaysia and Singapore (Agrawal et al., 2010; Koldowski and Martin, 2008). The Federation of Indian Chambers of Commerce and Industry (FICCI) estimated 2,00,000 annual Buddhist tourist visits in India with a prospective growth rate of 400% if the Buddhist circuits were properly developed (Singh, 2010). Dr. A.P.J. Abdul Kalam, the then president of India and the 14th Dalai Lama along with tourism ministers and Buddhist dignitaries from 12 different countries attended the *International Conclave on Buddhism and Spiritual Tourism* at New Delhi in 2004. The deliberations were concluded by the Government of India, adopting a resolution to rehabilitate and restore the ancient places of Buddhist interest in India (Geary, 2008, 2014; Singh, 2010). In fact, tourism bodies are actively engaged in innovative developments with Buddhist sites across the country (Agrawal et al., 2010). Similar to other religious sites, Buddhists sites have also been categorised based on their religious significance. The hierarchy of Buddhist sites organised by Hall (2006) include (a) core pilgrimage sites which are places that have been emphasised by the godhead and are pious locations of faith; (b) sites that are associated with the stories and experiences mentioned in scriptures, and in the case of Buddhism had been visited by Buddha; (c) sites that are associated with different traditions of Buddhism across the world and (d) routine sites such as community temples and sites of religious festivals. With regard to India's heritage, it has benefitted through the inheritance of all the four types of Buddhist sites.

In order to disseminate the economic benefits of tourism, state tourism bodies in India were asked to identify sites of historical and cultural significance for infrastructural development. The concept of regional circuits for the promotion of spiritual tourism around the Buddhist sites led to the launch of an action plan for the development of the Buddhist circuit in 1986 (Geary, 2014, 2018). This was followed by projects of foreign investments, notably by countries with strong Buddhist influence for the preservation of Buddhist sites (Singh, 2010; Koldowski and Martin, 2008).

Tourism can strengthen the relationships between countries (Roy and Tisdell, 1998) and so has been the case with India and Japan. It has been noted that 'The expansion of Buddhist spiritual tourism can also be seen as part of a larger range of interactions between India and East Asia, particularly Japan, especially about the conservation and promotion of India's Buddhist heritage' (Singh, 2010, p. 204). India tourism websites and brochures emphasise the country's connections to Buddha, trying to promote the nation as the land of Buddha. Interestingly, these strategies explore more landscapes of India's rich heritage, which is indeed a channel of communicating India's tourism potential.

The number of tourists and pilgrims increased with the completion of Gaya International Airport that brought tourists directly from Bhutan, Thailand, Sri Lanka, Nepal, Singapore and Myanmar (Geary, 2008, 2014) to Bihar, India. Similarly in the year 2007, Indian Railway Catering and Tourism Corporation (IRCTC) launched a luxury Buddhist circuit tourist train – the Mahaparinirvan Express that enables tourists to go on a spiritual tour of the core Buddhist destinations in India and Nepal (Koldowski and Martin, 2008). The journey includes destinations such as Lumbini, Kushinagar, Rajgir, Nalanda, Gaya, Sravasti, Varanasi, Sarnath and Agra (Geary, 2013). Moreover, the train is equipped with world-class facilities and offers a wide range of cuisines on board. Often taken as an example of dedicated brand infrastructure for communicating India's identity as the land of Buddha, the Mahaparinirvan Express has been attracting international as well as domestic tourists.

India's Ministry of Tourism, the gtate Governments of Uttar Pradesh and Bihar and the International Finance Corporation (a member of World Bank Group) collaborated for the first time to develop a framework for private and public sector investments that would enhance the tourist experience while unleashing the job creation potential of tourism around the Buddhist. The *'Investing in the Buddhist circuit'* document (International Finance Corporation, 2014) emphasises the need for keen involvement in planning, skill development, market access and access to finance in order to enhance the tourist experience beyond the tangible aspects of the circuit. Intangible aspects of tourism that contribute to the tourists' overall experience at a destination are as important as the tangible aspects of a destination. Despite having the most preserved and unique Buddhist attractions, 'locations have been neglected from a tourism and visitor perspective, and there are very few attractive opportunities on the Circuit to leverage and enhance visitor enjoyment, experience, and value beyond the monuments and temples' (International Finance Corporation, 2014, p. 48). With the vision of transforming and positioning the Buddhist circuit from a mere collection of sites to a holistic tourism experience, three experience pillars were proposed: 'pilgrimage', 'ancient heritage' and 'mind, body, spirit'. The first experience pillar, 'pilgrimage', includes an opportunity to get a deeper understanding of life by visiting four of the holiest sites in Buddhism. The second experience pillar, 'ancient heritage', includes stupas, temples, local traditions and culture, while the third experience pillar, 'mind, body, spirit', includes wellness activities such as meditation, yoga and healthy eating (International Finance Corporation, 2014).

Extensive data collection, consultations and analysis conducted by the International Finance Corporation (2014) identified four major types of visitors on the Buddhist circuit: Budget Pilgrims, Comfort Pilgrims, Budget Explorers and High-end Explorers. Budget Pilgrims are Buddhists who travel in large groups by road or rail and prefer basic facilities. They usually visit all the sites that Buddha once visited. Comfort Pilgrims are Buddhists who prefer to travel independently and need better comforts than budget pilgrims. Budget Explorers are usually non-Buddhist backpackers who visit a few sites on the circuit while High-end Explorers are foreigners who visit only a few selected sites on the circuit and require exceptional levels of comfort (International Finance Corporation, 2014). Taking inspiration from the primary Buddhist circuit in the northern states of Uttar Pradesh and Bihar, several other states in India have come up with individual Buddhist circuits that include Buddhist heritage of their state, such as the Himalayan circuit of Buddhist monasteries (Jammu and Kashmir), Andhra Pradesh Buddhist Circuit, Odisha Buddhist circuit and the Maharashtra Buddhist circuit (Geary, 2018). In conclusion, these strategies may help the country in becoming the land of Buddha as it falls behind other Asian countries in terms of Buddhist followers. As stated by Kishwar (2018, p. 4) 'successfully leveraging the associations with other Buddhist countries could have an impact beyond the realm of cultural diplomacy, and aid in other areas of foreign policy as well'. Deepening ties with nations on the basis of Buddhism could potentially feed into the government's broader policy objectives, for instance, the 'Neighbourhood First' policy, and the 'Act East' policy.

References

Agrawal, M., Choudhary, H. and Tripathi, G. (2010) 'Enhancing Buddhist tourism in India: An exploratory study', *Worldwide Hospitality and Tourism Themes*, 2 (5), 477–493.

Eck, D.L. (2012) *India: A Sacred Geography*, New York: Harmony Books.

Geary, D. (2008) 'Destination enlightenment: Branding Buddhism and spiritual tourism in Bodhgaya, Bihar', *Anthropology Today*, 24 (3), 11–14.

Geary, D. (2013) 'Incredible India in a global age: The cultural politics of image branding in tourism', *Tourist Studies*, 13 (1), 36–61.

Geary, D. (2014) 'Buddhist circuits and worlding practices in North India', in del Marmol, C., Morell, M. and Chalcraft, J. (eds.), *The Making of Heritage: Seduction and Disenchantment*, 44–58. New York: Routledge.

Geary, D. (2018) 'India's Buddhist circuit(s): A growing investment market for a "rising" Asia', *International Journal of Religious Tourism and Pilgrimage*, 6 (1), 47–57.

Hall, C.M. (2006) 'Buddhism, tourism and the middle way', in Timothy, D.J. and Olsen, D.H. (eds.), *Tourism, Religion and Spiritual Journeys*, 172–185, New York: Routledge.

International Finance Corporation (2014) 'Investing in the Buddhist circuit', available at: www.ifc.org/wps/wcm/connect/2bdd4697-6d7f-4f78-bca0-269aa100b25a/Buddhist+Circuit+Tourism+Strategy+Final.pdf?MOD=AJPERES&CVID=kC1uny1 (accessed 25/6/2021).

Kishwar, S. (2018) *The Rising Role of Buddhism in India's Soft Power Strategy*, New Delhi: Observer Research Foundation, available at: www.orfonline.org/wp-content/uploads/2018/02/ORF_Issue Brief_228_Buddhism.pdf (accessed 25/6/2021).

Koldowski, J. and Martin, O. (2008) 'Emerging market segments: Religious and medical tourism in India', in Conrady, R. and Buck, M. (eds.), *Trends and Issues in Global Tourism 2008*, 121–129, Heidelberg: Springer.

Roy, K.C. and Tisdell, A.C. (eds.) (1998) *Tourism in India and India's Economic Development*, New York: Nova Publishers.

Singh, U. (2010) 'Exile and return: The reinvention of Buddhism and Buddhist sites in modern India', *South Asian Studies*, 26 (2), 193–217.

CASE: INSPIRING A BRAND-LED AFRICAN REVOLUTION

Thebe Ikalafeng, Founder, Brand Africa, Brand Leadership,
and the Africa Brand Leadership Academy

A recent survey by Africa No Filter, an organization focused on championing a world where the prevailing narrative within and about Africa is reflective of a progressive and dynamic continent, established that 63% of outlets that report on Africa do not have correspondents in Africa (Africa No Filter, 2021). More than 80% of coverage was hard news and largely political in nature – politics and elections (26%), conflict (13%) and economics, trade and business (13%), and few offered a counter-narrative with limited coverage of human interest, arts, culture, celebrity. Alarmingly, only 1% of the content was generated by African correspondents. While Africa has changed much over the past decade or so – and more than 60 years since the first independence in Sub-Sahara Africa in Ghana in 1957, with fewer and isolated wars and conflicts, the imbalance in Africa-focused news has created a generally negative narrative and brand image of Africa.

While nations such as Germany have been shaped around their engineering ingenuity, the United States around entrepreneurship leadership, and Brazil around culture, African nations – which are individually distinctive – are rather collectively branded around conflict, famine, and aid. As well as addressing other impediments such as creating and broadcasting its own content and strengthening some governance issues, among others, it is important for Africa to re-imagine its brand.

In essence, Africa, historically branded a supplier of raw materials to the world and net importer of finished goods and services, can reverse its economic course by creating made-in-Africa goods and services that will ultimately become a vector of its image and identity – and most importantly, its economic independence. Many studies and experience have shown that brands can be an effective vehicle nations can leverage to shape their image, while a nation's image can also significantly influence purchase decisions. As Simon Anholt argued in his book *Brand New Justice: How Branding Places and Products Can Help the Developing World* (Anholt, 2016), branding can be a powerful tool for economic development, and can contribute to the growth of places. A similar argument was made by Wally Olins, who stated that countries can develop their national brands to compete for investment, trade, and tourism (Olins, 2000).

In their recent 'Lions (still) on the move: Growth in Africa's consumer sector' research, McKinsey & Co projects that African consumer spending will reach $2.1 trillion by 2025 driven by the continent's

> young and growing population – projected to grow by 20 percent, with Africa's youth making up 40 percent of the total; rapid urbanization to a projected 45 percent of the population urbanized by then; rising household incomes which will shift the profile of goods and services that Africans purchase from basic necessities toward more discretionary products, and widespread technology adoption with more than half of Africans expected to own a smartphone, which they can use for e-commerce that is projected to account for 10 percent of retail sales in Africa's largest economies by 2025.
>
> (Hattingh et al., 2017)

Branding Africa

The blueprint to develop 'brand Africa' could possibly be traced to the seminal speech by Ghana's founding President and arguably the father of pan-Africanism, Kwame Nkrumah's 'Africa Must Unite

Now or Perish' speech on the eve of the founding of the Organisation of African Unity (OAU) on 24 May 1963. In this speech, he laid out a challenge to set up (1) A constitution for a Union Government of African States, and (2) A unified or common economic and industrial programme for Africa, encompassing (a) a common market for Africa, (b) an African currency, (c) an African monetary zone, (d) an African central bank, (e) a continental communication system, (f) common foreign policy and diplomacy, (g) a common system of defence, and (h) common African citizenship.

Engaged mostly with governance and peace matters, much of this agenda had not been accomplished in the first 50 years of the OAU, rebranded to the African Union (AU) on July 9 2002 in Durban, South Africa, symbolically the last colonized African nation. Fifty years later in Ethiopia on 25 May 2013, the AU revisited this bold plan in its *Agenda 2063*, which envisions an 'integrated continent, politically united and based on the ideals of Pan-Africanism and the vision of Africa's Renaissance' (African Union Commission, 2015, p. 2). Consequently, Nkrumah's 'common passport' and 'common market' vision has resulted in the launch of the African Union Passport in 2016 and the African Continental Free Trade Area (AfCFTA) in 2018. The AfCFTA has introduced an urgency to the African economic agenda, with its stated goal to accelerate intra-African trade from 15% to 50% by 2030.

At an individual level, some African nations, in particular South Africa, Kenya, Botswana, Ghana, Nigeria, Rwanda, and Mauritius have established initiatives and/or agencies to proactively establish a compelling, coordinated, and harmonized nation brand to stimulate and grow foreign direct investment (FDI), tourism, trade, and export – and grow their nation brands. Kenya launched 'Make it Kenya', a campaign to promote international tourism, commerce, and investment in Kenya. Rwanda partnered with English football club, Arsenal with a call to 'Visit Rwanda' on players' sleeves which lifted overall tourism numbers by 8%. Similarly, the Mauritius Tourism Promotion Authority signed a three-year deal with English Premier League football team Liverpool in a drive to become a leading global tourist destination and business hub. South Africa has leveraged global mega events such as the FIFA World Cup 2010 and other events in rugby, cricket, and continental football to position itself as a place for tourism and investment.

The implementation of the African Continental Free Trade Area (AfCFTA) Agreement which came into effect in 2021 – in the midst of the Covid-19 pandemic – will create a single free trade area of 55 African Union member countries with a market opportunity of 1.2 billion citizens and $2.5 trillion combined GDP. This creates an enviable opportunity for Africa to re-imagine its brand and future.

Leveraging made in Africa brands to inspire the African brand

Beyond being a vector of a nation's image and identity, brands reflect the industrial capacity of nations, create jobs and contribute to the tax base to fund development agendas. Therefore, there is no doubt that brands will play a pivotal role in the differentiation, development, and competitiveness of Africa.

An analysis of the Top 100 most admired brands since inception in 2011 of the *Brand Africa 100: Africa's Best Brands*, which yields over 180,000 brand mentions and over 3,500 unique brand mentions annually, shows an unabated dominance of non-African brands in Africa (Brand Africa, 2021). Non-African brands have on average maintained an 80% share of the Top 100 most admired brands relative to African brands at 20%. The list has been dominated by European brands (37.12%) led by Germany's Adidas and Finland's Nokia, followed by North American brands (29%) with Nike and Coca-Cola,

African brands (20.5%) led by South Africa's MTN and Nigeria's Dangote, and Asian brands (17.25%) led by South Korea's Samsung and Japan's Toyota.

Non-African brands have carved their place in African hearts and wallets through their sustained investment in brand-building over decades, partnerships with record-breaking African athletes such as Kenyan Eliud Kipchoge, the first athlete to achieve a sub-two-hour marathon, collaborations such as the ones with South African designer Karabo Poppy and Nigeria's music sensation Wizkid and his Starboy brand.

Shaping the African brand narrative

The media category continues to reflect a bias towards non-African media which represent more than 75% of most admired media in Africa. With Covid-19 limiting entertainment options beyond the house, while most businesses faltered, digital businesses such as Netflix and Showtime streaming services have thrived at the expense of global legacy brands such as BBC, CNN, and Al Jazeera which have dominated the Brand Africa media rankings over the past decade. Consequently, as a content aggregator, South Africa's DStv has been propelled to the #1 media brand. Africa's story and perceptions continue to be shaped outside its borders.

Conclusion

Despite improved telecommunications, rising internet connectivity, improved ease of doing business, and an emerging confidence in made in Africa by Africans for Africa, to compete and build competitive nation brands individually and the African brand collectively – and achieve the AfCFTA vision – Africa will have to drive, grow, and support African private sector champions, and ultimately the emergence and rise of individual African brands which will shape the overarching African brand.

References

Africa No Filter (2021) 'How African media covers Africa', available at: https://africanofilter.org/uploads/files/How-African-Media-Covers-Africa_Report.pdf (accessed 13/6/2021).

African Union Commission (2015) 'Agenda 2063', available at: https://au.int/sites/default/files/documents/36204-doc-agenda2063_popular_version_en.pdf (accessed 13/6/2021).

Anholt, S. (2016) *Brand New Justice: How Branding Places and Products Can Help the Developing World*, rev. edn, London: Routledge.

Brand Africa (2021) 'Brand Africa 100™: Most valued brands in Africa', available at: www.brandafrica.net/BrandAfrica100Awards.aspx (accessed 13/6/2021).

Chekalina, T., Fuchs, M. and Lexhagen, M. (2018) 'Customer-based destination brand equity modelling: The role of destination resources, value for money and value in use', *Journal of Travel Research*, 57 (1), 31–51.

Hattingh, D., Leke, A. and Russo, B. (2017) 'Lions (still) on the move: Growth in Africa's consumer sector', available at: www.mckinsey.com/industries/consumer-packaged-goods/our-insights/lions-still-on-the-move-growth-in-africas-consumer-sector# (accessed 13/6/2021).

Olins, W. (2000) *Trading Identities: Why Countries and Companies are Taking on Each Others' Roles*, London: The Foreign Policy Centre.

Summary

In this chapter the concept of brand equity has been applied to the context of nation branding through a focus upon the sources and dimensions of nation brand equity. Differing, though complementary, perspectives on brand equity have been analysed in terms of the consumer perspective and the financial perspective on brand equity. Taking an asset-based perspective on nation brand equity, we have seen how NBEQ comprises internal and external assets which can be considered as being innate, nurtured, vicarious, or disseminated.

Discussion points

1   How useful is the financial perspective on brand equity when applied to nation brands? What benefits can policy makers gain from insights into financial evaluations of nation brand equity?
2   Apply the model of asset-based nation brand equity (Figure 3.1) to a country of your choice. Is the country's nation brand equity well balanced, or is it strong in some areas and weak in others?

References

Aaker, D. (1991) *Managing Brand Equity*, New York: The Free Press.

Baker, M.J. (2002) *The Westburn Dictionary of Marketing*, Westburn Publishers Ltd., available at: www.themarketingdictionary.com.

Buttle, F. (2008) 'A CRM perspective on nation branding', in Dinnie, K. (ed.), *Nation Branding – Concepts, Issues, Practice*, 1st edn, 66–67, London: Butterworth-Heinemann.

de Chernatony, L. and McDonald, M. (2003) *Creating Powerful Brands*, 3rd edn, London: Butterworth-Heinemann.

Devane, R. (2006) 'The dynamics of diaspora networks: Lessons of experience', in Kuznetsov, Y. (ed.), *Diaspora Networks and the International Migration of Skills: How Countries Can Draw on Their Talent Abroad*, 59–67, Washington, DC: WBI Development Studies, The World Bank.

Farquhar, P. (1989) 'Managing brand equity', *Marketing Research*, September, 1–11.

Felzensztein, C. (2008) 'Chile – "all ways surprising"', in Dinnie, K. (ed.), *Nation Branding – Concepts, Issues, Practice*, 1st edn, 59–61, London: Butterworth-Heinemann.

Hallberg, G. (2004) 'Is your loyalty programme really building loyalty? Why increasing emotional attachment, not just repeat buying, is key to maximising programme success', *Journal of Targeting, Measurement and Analysis for Marketing*, 12 (3), 231–241.

He, J., Wang, C.L. and Wu, Y. (2021) 'Building the connection between nation and commercial brand: An integrative review and future research directions', *International Marketing Review*, 38 (1), 19–35.

Henderson, P.W., Cote, J.A., Leong, S.M. and Schmitt, B. (2003) 'Building strong brands in Asia: Selecting the visual components of image to maximize brand strength', *International Journal of Research in Marketing*, 20 (4), 297–313.

Jacobsen, B.P. (2012) 'Place brand equity: A model for establishing the effectiveness of place brands', *Journal of Place Management and Development*, 5 (3), 253–271.

Jones, R. (2005) 'Finding sources of brand value: Developing a stakeholder model of brand equity', *Journal of Brand Management*, 13 (1), 10–32.

Kapferer, J.-N. (2004) *The New Strategic Brand Management: Creating and Sustaining Brand Equity Long Term*, London: Kogan Page.

Keller, K.L. (2003) *Strategic Brand Management: Building, Measuring, and Managing Brand Equity*, 2nd edn, Upper Saddle River, NJ: Prentice Hall.

Kuznetsov, Y. and Sabel, C. (2006) 'International migration of talent, diaspora networks, and development: Overview of main issues', in Kuznetsov, Y. (ed.), *Diaspora Networks and the International Migration of Skills: How Countries Can Draw on Their Talent Abroad*, 3–19, Washington, DC: WBI Development Studies, The World Bank.

Leautier, F.A. (2006) 'Foreword', in Kuznetsov, Y. (ed.), *Diaspora Networks and the International Migration of Skills: How Countries Can Draw on Their Talent Abroad*, Washington, DC: WBI Development Studies, The World Bank.

Lebedenko, V. (2008) 'On national identity and the building of Russia's image', in Dinnie, K. (ed.), *Nation Branding – Concepts, Issues, Practice*, 1st edn, 107–111, London: Butterworth-Heinemann.

Lucarelli, A. (2012) 'Unraveling the complexity of "city brand equity": A three-dimensional framework', *Journal of Place Management and Development*, 5 (3), 231–252.

Mariutti, F.G. and Giraldi, J. de M.E. (2019) 'How does a brand reputation-driven construct impact on country brand equity? A cross-national study of Brazil and China', *Journal of International Consumer Marketing*, 31 (5), 408–428.

Merisavo, M. and Raulas, M. (2004) 'The impact of e-mail marketing on brand loyalty', *Journal of Product and Brand Management*, 13 (7), 498–505.

Pappu, R., Quester, P.G. and Cooksey, R.W. (2005) 'Consumer-based brand equity: Improving the measurement – empirical evidence', *Journal of Product and Brand Management*, 14 (2–3), 143–154.

Perrin-Martinenq, D. (2004) 'The role of brand detachment on the dissolution of the relationship between the consumer and the brand', *Journal of Marketing Management*, 20 (9–10), 1001–1023.

Pike, S., Bianchi, C., Kerr, G. and Patti, C. (2010) 'Consumer-based brand equity for Australia as a long-haul tourism destination in an emerging market', *International Marketing Review*, 27 (4), 434–449.

Riezebos, R. (2003) *Brand Management: A Theoretical and Practical Approach*, London: FT Prentice Hall.

Sanches, R. and Sekles, F. (2008) 'Brazil IT: Taking Brazil's successful domestic IT industry abroad', in Dinnie, K. (ed.), *Nation Branding – Concepts, Issues, Practice*, 1st edn, 133–136, London: Butterworth-Heinemann.

Temporal, P. (2002) *Advanced Brand Management: From Vision to Valuation*, Singapore: John Wiley & Sons.

Torres, F. and Kuznetsov, Y. (2006) 'Mexico: Leveraging migrants' capital to develop hometown communities', in Kuznetsov, Y. (ed.), *Diaspora Networks and the International Migration of Skills: How Countries Can Draw on Their Talent Abroad*, 99–128, Washington, DC: WBI Development Studies, The World Bank.

Trollope, A. (2014) *Anthony Trollope: An Autobiography and Other Writings*, Oxford: Oxford University Press.

VanAuken, B. (2002) *The Brand Management Checklist: Proven Tools and Techniques for Creating Winning Brands*, London: Kogan Page.

Zenker, S. (2014) 'Measuring place brand equity with the advanced brand concept map (aBCM) method', *Place Branding and Public Diplomacy*, 10, 158–166.

PART 2

CONCEPTUAL ROOTS OF NATION BRANDING

Nation branding and the country-of-origin effect

Key points

- The country-of-origin effect refers to the effect that a product or service's origin has on consumer attitudes and behaviour towards that product or service
- The consumer behaviour literature offers many insights into the country-of-origin effect
- 'Made in' campaigns are strategic tools used by governments to attempt to positively influence country-of-origin perceptions

Introduction

This chapter examines the country-of-origin effect and places it in the context of nation branding. The chapter focuses on issues including country-of-origin and brands, country-of-origin and demographics, country-of-origin and semiotic theory, as well as noting that country-of-origin perceptions are not necessarily static but can change over time. The first case in this chapter discusses the general purpose and strategy of the Fundación

DOI: 10.4324/9781003100249-6

Imagen de Chile. The second case focuses on the GREAT Britain campaign and debates whether this is a national marketing campaign, a nation brand, or a national soft power play. In this chapter's practitioner insight, Florian Kaefer provides insights into the creation of The Place Brand Observer, whilst Efe Sevin's academic perspective considers whether 'COO' should include *city*-of-origin as well as the more established concept of *country*-of-origin.

Consumer behaviour

The country-of-origin effect has been extensively studied within the domain of consumer behaviour (Andéhn and L'espoir Decosta, 2018; Kim et al., 2017; Usunier, 2006). However, surprisingly few links have been made between the field of country-of-origin and the field of nation branding, despite these being two highly related fields. A major contribution to bridging this gap between place branding and country-of-origin has been made by Papadopoulos and Cleveland (2021), who provide a wide-ranging synthesis of research concerning places and the products associated with them.

Recent contributions to the country-of-origin literature have deepened our understanding of concepts such as brand attachment (Park et al., 2013), consumer affinity for foreign countries (Nes et al., 2014) and the potential influence of a country's ecological image (Dekhili and Achabou, 2015). The impact of consumers' emotional bonds with foreign countries on buying intentions (Oberecker and Diamantopoulos, 2011) is an important issue in the context of nation branding attempts to manage country-of-origin perceptions.

Overview of country-of-origin research

The country-of-origin effect refers to the effect that a product or service's origin has on consumer attitudes and behaviour towards that product or service. There are many product categories where country-of-origin plays an important role as a differentiator that is valued by consumers. French perfume, Scotch whisky, Swiss watches, Italian fashion, Japanese technology and Colombian coffee represent some of the best known product categories where a perceived fit between the product and its country-of-origin confers consumer value. In such cases, there is a positive association between the product and its country-of-origin, although it may not always be clear in which direction the positive perceptions flow. For example, does a prestigious brand such as Sony enhance the nation brand image of Japan, or does the credibility of Japan as a source country for high-tech products enhance the Sony brand?

The symbiotic relationship between a nation brand and the commercial brands that highlight (or downplay) their country-of-origin deserves attention because the nation branding activities of a country may impact upon country-of-origin perceptions for that country's product and corporate brands.

Criticism has been levelled at some of the country-of-origin literature on the grounds that the methodology employed in the research to date has tended to exaggerate the influence of country-of-origin because of the use of single cue designs (where the only attribute of the product given to respondents is its country-of-origin, rather than a multi-cue design where country-of-origin would be just one attribute alongside other relevant criteria such as price, brand name, design, etc.) and also because of the use of verbal descriptions rather than real, tangible products (Peterson and Jolibert, 1995). Other reviews of the country-of-origin literature have identified further weaknesses as being the small number of studies which have examined the impact of country-of-origin effects on the consumption and evaluation of services, and the tendency of those few studies on services and country-of-origin to focus upon services in the West rather than in the rest of the world (Al-Sulaiti and Baker, 1998); an over-reliance on student samples which limits the generalisability of research findings to a wider population (Dinnie, 2004); and, it has also been suggested that there is a need for more research on the symbolic and emotional aspects of country-of-origin (Verlegh and Steenkamp, 1999).

Country-of-origin and brands

When Icelandic vodka brand Reyka launched in the United Kingdom market in 2005, it did so with advertising which proclaimed that 'In Iceland, vodka is a natural resource . . . Reyka vodka is made with arctic spring water in one of the purest countries in the world. We make Reyka in small batches and we use geothermal energy to make sure that our country stays as pure as our vodka'. This claim led to the brand being described by one journalist as being a leader amongst environmentally friendly drinks (Lyons, 2005). The match, or fit, between the product and its country-of-origin is seamless. The Reyka brand benefits from Iceland's association with environmental purity, whilst Iceland the nation benefits from the emergence of a new high quality brand that should add to the nation's existing brand equity. Such win-win scenarios testify to the potential power of country-of-origin as a brand-building tool. The Reyka brand is not actually owned by an Icelandic company. Its owners are Scotch whisky firm William Grant and Sons. Yet the discreet foreign ownership is unlikely to impact upon consumer perceptions of the brand as being Icelandic.

There has been increasing interest in how brands can better utilise country-of-origin in their marketing efforts (Aichner, 2014; Magnusson et al., 2019; Suter et al., 2018), whilst the matching of product category and country image perceptions has been widely researched (Papadopoulos and Heslop, 1993; Zafar et al., 2004; Verlegh et al., 2005). One such study (Roth and Romeo, 1992) concluded that product–country match information should be used by managers to assess consumers' purchase intentions and to assist them in managing their product's country-of-origin. The term 'brand origin' has been coined in order to conceptualise cases where consumer perceptions of a brand's origin may not coincide with reality – in such cases, brand origin is the place where target groups perceive the brand to come from (Thakor and Kohli, 1996). Consumers may hold misperceptions of a brand's country-of-origin simply through ignorance or through branding activity by companies designed to suggest a more positive country-of-origin than is actually the case. Table 4.1 shows some brands whose names may lead to consumer confusion regarding their country-of-origin.

The emergence of China as a global economic superpower, together with the opening up of the Chinese market to foreign firms, has created considerable interest in how

Table 4.1 Brand origin: Potentially perceived origin versus actual origin

Brand	Product category	Potentially perceived origin	Actual origin
Haagen-Dazs	Ice cream	Scandinavia	United States
Matsui	Consumer electronics	Japan	United Kingdom
Lexus	Automotive	United States	Japan
Klarbrunn	Bottled water	Switzerland, Austria, Germany	United States

Chinese consumers view domestic Chinese brands compared to imported foreign brands. Within Asia, Japanese brands such as Toshiba, Mitsubishi and Sony have for many years established premium quality perceptions. More recently, South Korean brands such as Samsung and LG have done the same. Now Chinese brands such as Haier and Lenovo are joining their Asian neighbours in the set of positively perceived brand names.

Traditionally, emerging nations have suffered from low quality perceptions for their products but the increasing confidence of the BRICS nations (Brazil, Russia, India, China, South Africa) is set to galvanise those and other emerging nations to make the change from commodity suppliers to producers of sought-after branded goods. An investigation into country-of-origin effects and how these affect the attitudes and behaviour of urban Chinese consumers, conducted amongst a sample of 432 Shanghai consumers, produced results which support the growing view that Chinese consumers are not necessarily attracted to foreign brands; an implication drawn by the researchers involved in that study is that in order to capitalise on the stated preference for local brands, managers should highlight the Chinese origin of their brands and use this in their brand positioning strategies (Kwok et al., 2006). The shoes, sportswear and sports accessories brand Li Ning is an example of a local Chinese brand that has successfully competed against the global might of brands such as Nike, Adidas and Reebok in the Chinese market, with a positioning based largely upon the brand's eponymous founder, the Olympic gold medal-winner Li Ning (Roll, 2006).

Some countries find that their brands are disadvantaged due to an overpowering image of the nation as just a tourism destination and nothing more. Other countries may enjoy more favourable country-of-origin associations for their products but find themselves in fiercely competitive sectors, forcing the countries in question to redouble their nation branding activities. Chile, for example, has sought to enhance its country-of-origin effect for the benefit of its wine sector.

Country-of-origin and services

Compared to the copious attention that has been devoted to the effects of country-of-origin on physical products, there have been far fewer studies on how country-of-origin effects can impact upon services. One review of the country-of-origin literature, covering a 20-year period and 24 marketing and general business journals, found only 19 studies in which country-of-origin was specifically applied to services; the rapid growth in service economies argues for far more research in this area (Javalgi et al., 2001). Given the predominance of the service sector over the manufacturing sector in most developed economies, such a paucity of research into how country-of-origin affects services is surprising. One of the few studies on country-of-origin and services measured the country-level images of ski resorts in Switzerland, France and Austria by asking 269 skiers attending a ski show in New York to rate each country on a five-point scale for ten attributes; the images of the three countries were found to be relatively homogeneous, with the American skiers unable to differentiate between the countries (Ofir and Lehmann, 1986). Another country-of-origin and services study examined the relative effects of national stereotype and advertising information on the selection of a service provider in the ophthalmology sector. The results from the study indicated that there existed a same-nationality bias in service provider selection, although different-nationality service providers could overcome this bias to some extent by providing consumers with more information in their advertising (Harrison-Walker, 1995). Aruan et al. (2018) examined the influence of country of service delivery, country of person and country of brand on service evaluations, concluding that firms need to understand that the country-of-origin construct is multidimensional for services.

Many international service brands have adopted acronyms as their brand names, perhaps in an attempt to minimise any possible negative country-of-origin biases against their place of origin. Table 4.2 illustrates some such cases from a range of international service sectors.

It is perhaps not surprising that international financial service brands seek to position themselves as global rather than parochial. HSBC's positioning as 'the world's local bank' combines the prestige and credibility of globalness with the reassuring impression that the brand is conscious of the specific needs of local communities. Consumers may make the assumption that since a financial service brand is global, it must be successful, well run and reliable. On the other hand, the bland, not-from-anywhere-in-particular positioning of the major financial services brands may leave a niche open for other brands to occupy with a more explicit country-of-origin positioning.

Being too closely associated with one specific country-of-origin can leave brands vulnerable to political or military events beyond their control. This potential vulnerability

Table 4.2 Service brand acronyms downplaying country-of-origin

Acronym	Full name	Service sector
HSBC	Hong Kong and Shanghai Banking Corporation	Finance
RBS	Royal Bank of Scotland	Finance
UBS	Union Bank of Switzerland	Finance
KFC	Kentucky Fried Chicken	Restaurants
BP	British Petroleum	Energy

has been acknowledged by American Express, who conducted research when the 2003 war in Iraq started because they were very concerned about a possible backlash against their brand, given its US-centric name; the company found, however, that in most places in the world people associated the brand with being a global business rather than being American (Mortimer, 2007).

The international airline sector is an interesting industry with regard to the use of brand management in general, and the country-of-origin effect in particular. Due to the heritage of national carriers, the use of country-of-origin in the international airline sector is often explicit. Singapore Airlines, for instance, highlights its country-of-origin to strengthen its positioning as a widely admired global service brand. British Airways, however, attracted criticism when it attempted to downplay its country-of-origin by repositioning itself as BA in an attempt to distance itself from some negative connotations of Britain's imperialistic past. This was perceived to be unpatriotic and caused a political storm in which the then Prime Minister Margaret Thatcher publicly berated the company for its apparent slight against 'Britishness'.

Country-of-origin and the product life cycle

The product life cycle is a well-established concept in marketing. The concept's premise is that products, like other living organisms, undergo a series of life stages. For products, these stages have been characterised as introduction, growth, maturity and decline. In the first two stages, products experience growth; in the third phase (maturity) they reach a plateau in terms of sales and market share; and in the final phase the product approaches the end of its commercially viable life, perhaps left behind by changing consumer needs or the arrival of new technology that renders the product obsolete. The usefulness of the product life cycle concept lies in its ability to let marketers assess the current status of the product and to tailor appropriate marketing strategies according to which stage of the life cycle the product finds itself in. For instance, a new product at the introduction stage of the product life cycle will require a launch strategy whose marketing communications will be radically different from a well-established product which has reached its maturity phase.

However, the product life cycle concept's inherent flaw is the assumption that products do indeed resemble living organisms and thus follow a similar birth–growth–maturity–death trajectory. The model lacks a measurable temporal dimension that would allow marketers to accurately assess the product's stage on the life cycle. The model also carries the implication that decline, sooner or later, is inevitable. This assumption would be challenged by many managers who see their job as being to ensure that their product remains at the top of its life cycle indefinitely.

There have been attempts to view the product life cycle concept in the context of country-of-origin. One study examined country-of-origin marketing over the product life cycle and found that the use of country-of-origin references varied, with country-of-origin references used more in the introduction stage than in the growth and maturity stages (Niss, 1996). The explanation advanced for this finding was that when a product is launched into a foreign market there will be little or no awareness of the specific product brand, but there may be reasonably high levels of awareness of the country from which the product originates – in such cases, it makes sense to capitalise on the existing country image perceptions in order to establish the product in its new foreign market. The same study found that as the product life cycle progresses, the tendency is for firms to lessen their use of country-of-origin and simultaneously increase their use of brand name marketing. Other studies appear to support the view that country-of-origin is used prominently in the product's introduction phase, in order to benefit from the country-of-origin halo effect (Lampert and Jaffe, 1998) and that the use of country-of-origin is highly contextual and evolves over time (Beverland and Lindgreen, 2002). When developing export promotion campaigns as a component of overall nation brand strategy, governments, trade councils and export promotion agencies should therefore carefully evaluate which of their country's brands will most significantly benefit from initiatives highlighting their country-of-origin.

Country-of-origin and demographics

A product's country-of-origin may matter to some consumers and be irrelevant to others. Demographic segmentation is one technique that can be used to categorise consumer groups for whom country-of-origin is a relevant product cue. Several country-of-origin studies have examined the effect that the major demographic variables can have upon product or service perceptions. For example, an early study in the country-of-origin field found significant differences towards products of foreign origin amongst different demographic groups – consumers with a high level of education were found to be more favourable towards foreign products than consumers with a lower level of education; female consumers evaluated foreign products more highly than males; and younger consumers evaluated foreign products more highly than did older consumers (Schooler, 1971).

However, there is little consensus on the impact of country-of-origin on different demographic groups. Other studies have supported the contention that the higher the level of a person's education, the more favourable they are to foreign products but have not found evidence of any difference in perception of foreign products between males and females (Dornoff et al., 1974). Brand managers need to conduct their own, contextualised and brand-specific research in order to ascertain which demographic segments of their targeted markets are influenced by the brand's country-of-origin.

Country-of-origin and ethnocentrism

Ethnocentrism is considered to be home-country bias (Shimp and Sharma, 1987). It refers to consumers' predisposition to favour products from their own country over products from foreign countries. Hamin and Elliott (2006), for example, investigate the phenomenon of consumer ethnocentrism amongst Indonesian consumers. Scales have been devised to measure consumer ethnocentrism, the most widely known of which is the consumer ethnocentric tendency scale (CETSCALE). The CETSCALE comprises 17 items based on a seven-point scale which allow an individual's ethnocentrism to be measured (Shimp and Sharma, 1987). Consumer demographics such as education, income and social class are believed to affect an individual's ethnocentrism (Jaffe and Nebenzahl, 2001). Brands of foreign origin need to know about prevailing levels of consumer ethnocentrism within specific markets, so that appropriate marketing strategies can be developed and strategic mistakes avoided. It has been found, for example, that the use of a foreign celebrity and an English brand name can be a liability in a country (Austria) with a different cultural heritage and language (Chao et al., 2005).

Country-of-origin and social identity

One study in the country-of-origin field examined the link between social identity and brand preference in South Africa (Burgess and Harris, 1999). One of the interesting aspects of this study was its focus on South Africa rather than the usual Western nations. Another interesting aspect was its consideration of the concept of national identity, and more specifically 'within-country diversity', a previously neglected issue in country-of-origin research. The study drew attention to the need to be wary of using nationality as a segmentation variable in contexts where other ethnic or religious affiliations may be more powerful than nationality. This idea was amplified in a later study which placed an emphasis on identifying the various subcultures that exist within any society in order to avoid making unsubstantiated generalised claims regarding consumers from a certain country when in reality the subcultural groupings within one country will often display greatly differing characteristics (Lenartowicz and Roth, 2001). It has been argued that most cross-cultural studies on country-of-origin or product country image effects have implicitly assumed that national markets are composed of homogeneous consumers and such studies are in reality cross-national rather than cross-cultural (Laroche et al., 2003).

Country-of-origin and semiotic theory

Semiotics is concerned with the study of signs. In semiotics, the concept of the sign is more wide-ranging than it is in normal daily usage. From a semiotic perspective, a sign can take the form of a word or image or anything else that the receiver may infer meaning from (Shimp, 2003; Fiske, 1990). One of the benefits of adopting a semiotic perspective in the brand management process is that it emphasises the primacy of context. Signs used in a brand's communications may be interpreted in very different ways according to the identity characteristics of the consumer (or interpreter, to use the semiotic vocabulary). In terms of the country-of-origin effect, there is considerable scope for brands of all types – whether simple tangible physical products brand at one end of the spectrum, or complex multifaceted nation-brands at the other – to make creative use of signs.

A semiotic approach to the study of country-of-origin and product country image effects has been advocated by Askegaard and Ger (1998) who argue that a rich set of connotations needs to be used in the analysis of images attached to a product and its place of origin. Taking a semiotic approach, Askegaard and Ger propose a conceptual model of contextualised product-place images (CPPI) containing four dimensions: place, product, market context and usage context. This approach may be considered to be a form of applied semiotics, the utilisation of knowledge about signs for the accomplishment of various goals (Morris, 1946). The acknowledgement of context is central to semiotic theory (Mick, 1986). This has important implications for branding. Within Arab culture, for example, calligraphy, colour, pattern and symbols represent visual elements that provide coded references to cultural, national and religious identity and as such need to be taken into consideration when constructing the visual manifestation of brands (Acton, 2007).

Country-of-origin perceptions in flux over time

Country-of-origin perceptions are not necessarily static over time (Darling and Puetz, 2002). Positive country-of-origin perceptions can degrade over time due to numerous factors, including political–military events beyond the control of any company. On the other hand, country-of-origin perceptions can also improve over time as Japan, South Korea and Taiwan can all happily testify to (Usunier, 2006). Taiwan has run a concerted nation branding campaign for a number of years and appears to have reaped benefits from it in terms of enhanced country-of-origin perceptions.

The global country image advertising campaign conducted by Taiwan's Ministry of Economic Affairs over the period 1990–2004 comprised a sequence of advertisements placed in publications such as *The Economist*, with key themes introduced in each new campaign (Amine and Chao, 2005). The development of the campaign is illustrated in Table 4.3.

There are a number of observations to be drawn from Taiwan's country image advertising campaign. First, it has a coherent long-term structure; second, it displays consistent commitment by the government; third, it shows close collaboration between public and private sectors; fourth, it evolves from basic awareness-building into more specific brand-related claims; and fifth, after firmly establishing product technology quality attributes, it adds another dimension to the country image by promoting its spectacular natural beauty. Taiwan's efforts are an illustration of the capacity of a country to seek to manage its image rather than merely remaining as a passive victim of existing external perceptions.

Country-of-origin perceptions may also change over time in relation to domestic products. For example, Chinese brands have become increasingly popular within China in recent years. In a mobile-based ethnography study amongst female consumers of luxury products in Shanghai, insight agency Spark 'found signs of more pride and interest in local brands and references to a cultural renaissance' (McQuater, 2020, p. 15).

Combatting a negative country-of-origin bias

A negative country-of-origin bias causes numerous problems for a nation's product and corporate brands. Consumers may not wish to be associated with brands that come from nations whose country-of-origin effects are damaged by poor quality perceptions, animosity towards that nation's political regime, unflattering portrayals in the media, or a multitude of other social, cultural, economic or historical associations.

Lotz and Hu (2001) propose a social stereotype approach in order to dilute negative country-of-origin stereotypes, whilst Kotler and Gertner (2002) suggest that in order to improve a country's image, creating new positive associations may be easier than refuting old negative associations. Khazakstan has, for example, sought to improve its *Borat*-battered image by promoting positive yet hitherto unknown aspects of its nation rather than

Table 4.3 Taiwan's government-sponsored country image advertising campaign 1990–2004

Year	Slogan	Key theme
1990	Not cited	Build basic knowledge about Taiwan's relative advantage of geographic location in the heart of Asia
1992	'It's very well made in Taiwan'	Strengthen perceptions of products associated with Taiwan
1993	'Taiwan: Your source for innovalue'	Present two new attributes about Taiwanese manufacturing (innovation and value), inviting the reader to consider more than just the price-based competitive advantage of the past
1994	'Excellence, made in Taiwan'	Message of excellence linked directly to specific company names and product classes, e.g., Kunnan (golf clubs), Feeler (computer-controlled machinery for heavy industry) and Startek (security systems)
1996	'Today's Taiwan: More and more an important part of our world'	Link Taiwan to a global perspective and position it as an active member of the world business community
1997	'Taiwan: Your source for innovalue'	Previously used slogan now applied to specific Taiwanese brands. Objectives and themes of past ad executions reinforced as salient beliefs.
2001	'Taiwan: Your partner for innovalue'	Promote preference, in line with theoretical hierarchy of advertising effects leading from awareness, to interest, knowledge, liking and then preference
2003	'Taiwan: Helping leading companies reach targets'	Strengthen positive linkages already made to the word 'Taiwan', reinforcing salient beliefs in established knowledge networks
Late 2003	'Taiwan stands tall: Reaching out to the world, soaring toward the future'	The use of new and striking attributes of Taiwan, linked to modern architecture and traditional culture. Convey sense of pride and achievement that Taiwan has enjoyed as an 'Asian tiger' over the last 40 years. Advanced technology promoted together with the spectacular natural beauty of Taiwan
2004	'Today's Taiwan'	Position Taiwan as an attractive tourist destination. An emotive appeal quite different from the low-key, objective reasoning of ads from ten years earlier

Adapted from Amine and Chao, 2005 (47)

attempting to refute the unflattering depiction it received in the 2006 film. Saunders (2017) has investigated the challenges and opportunities presented to the government of Kazakhstan by the *Borat* film.

All kinds of brands – whether product, service or corporate – may suffer from a negative country-of-origin bias. According to the Edelman Trust Barometer, which surveys the opinions of 3,100 people in 18 countries, Europeans place most trust in companies from Sweden, Canada and Germany, whereas they place least trust in companies from the emerging BRIC countries and Mexico (Smith, 2007). The poll's sample has the following demographic characteristics – college-educated, between 36 and 64 years old, reporting a household income in the upper quartile for their country; and showing a significant interest in and engagement with the media and current affairs. In other words, a demographic profile that would suggest high receptiveness to brands of foreign origin and a low level of consumer ethnocentrism. Even with such a presumably relatively cosmopolitan demographic segment, the BRIC nations clearly still have work to do in order to combat a negative country-of-origin bias amongst European consumers that could hinder future attempts by BRIC nation companies to enter European markets. Nations need to conduct rigorous research to form the basis of promotional activities aimed at mitigating negative country image perceptions (Pasquier, 2008).

Nation branding and export promotion

Exports can play an important role in building the nation brand (Florek and Conejo, 2007). 'Made in' campaigns are a key nation branding tool for aiding export promotion. Vietrade, for example, is a nation branding programme conducted by the Government of Vietnam to promote the national image through product brands. One of the best established and longest-running campaigns is 'Australian Made', administered by Australian Made Campaign Limited (AMCL). AMCL is a not-for-profit company which licenses companies to use the now famous Australian Made, Australian Grown logo. The credibility of the logo and the campaign is enhanced by the strict compliance programme for participating companies. The logo's green and gold colours and outline of a kangaroo make a clear and distinctive contribution to Australia's overall nation brand.

ACADEMIC PERSPECTIVE: CAN THE 'C' IN COO STAND FOR 'CITIES'?

Efe Sevin, Assistant Professor, Towson University

Nation branding and country-of-origin (COO) effect are closely related – while the former concept is not centered on any product, there is still a 'product-country image link' that influences consumer behavior (Fan, 2006). Recent research provide empirical evidence that the link is indeed limited by product categories (Andéhn et al., 2016) – while consumers might have confidence in German engineering, they might not be equally excited about the German fashion industry. Yet even in these more nuanced studies that operationalize COO beyond generic stereotypes (Hakala et al., 2013), countries remain as the dominant unit of analysis. It is the nation brand or the experiences with the country that affect consumer behavior (Steenkamp, 2019). Diplomacy and international relations primed researchers – and individuals – to study everything outside the borders of a country at a national level. Since the concepts of COO and nation branding do not fall exclusively under these disciplines (Yalkin, 2018), is it time to move beyond the limitation of countries and include cities in COO arguments?

This question has two starting points. First, cities have been increasing their presence in the international arena, mainly through two practices: city diplomacy and city branding. The latter concept is the city equivalent of nation branding. Cities promote themselves to attract tourists, businesses, and residents (Anttiroiko, 2015; Dinnie, 2011). The former includes activities in which cities follow their own agendas in the international arena (see Amiri and Sevin, 2020 for further discussions), actively building global networks, collaborating with other cities and even countries to provide solutions to global challenges (Acuto et al., 2017). Moreover, with projections showing them as the future home for two-thirds of the world population by 2050 (United Nations, 2018), cities are at the heart of all our experiences. Tourists experience countries through cities, countries produce goods and services using the infrastructures of cities, cultural events take places in cities.

Second, this new agency and level of activity do not necessarily shatter the relationship between the perception of cities and of countries. This argument should not be seen as countries leading cities. On the contrary, city branding campaigns might not be in line with the overall nation brand (Ojo, 2019). Similarly, their diplomatic agendas do not have to mirror national priorities or discourse (Gambino, 2017). But, over time, the characteristics of cities will eventually transfer to their countries (Crilley and Manor, 2020). Dubai's progressive brand, for instance, has helped improve the reputation of the United Arab Emirates (Ojo, 2019). The interactions of Chinese mega-cities such as Chengdu and Chongqing with other international actors contributed to a new image of China in economic, cultural, and political terms (Björner, 2014,).

Cities are becoming integral parts of product and country images as they increase their visibility in the international arena and position themselves as economic, social, and cultural hubs. COO effect studies should not dismiss their substantial contribution to the perception of countries.

References

Acuto, M., Morissette, M. and Tsouros, A. (2017) 'City diplomacy: Towards morestrategic networking? Learning with WHO healthy cities', *Global Policy*, 8 (1), 14–22.

Amiri, S. and Sevin, E. (2020) *City Diplomacy: Current Trends and Future Prospects*, London: Palgrave Macmillan.

Andéhn, M., Nordin, F. and Nilsson, M.E. (2016) 'Facets of country image and brand equity: Revisiting the role of product categories in country-of-origin effect research', *Journal of Consumer Behaviour*, 15 (3), 225–238.

Anttiroiko, A.-V. (2015) 'City branding as a response to global intercity competition', *Growth and Change*, 46 (2), 233–252.

Björner, E. (2014) 'Imagineering Chinese mega-cities in the age of globalization', in Berg, P. and Björner, E. (eds.), *Branding Chinese Mega-Cities*, 106–120, Cheltenhamn: Edward Elgar Publishing.

Crilley, R. and Manor, I. (2020) 'Un-nation branding: The cities of Tel Aviv and Jerusalem in Israeli soft power', in Amiri, S. and Sevin, E. (eds.), *City Diplomacy Current Trends and Future Prospects*, 137–160. London: Palgrave Macmillan.

Dinnie, K. (2011) *City Branding Theory and Cases*, London: Palgrave Macmillan.

Fan, Y. (2006) 'Branding the nation: What is being branded?', *Journal of Vacation Marketing*, 12 (1), 5–14.

Gambino, L. (2017) 'Pittsburgh fires back at Trump: We stand with Paris, not you', *The Guardian*, 1, June, available at: www.theguardian.com/us-news/2017/jun/01/pittsburgh-fires-back-trump-paris-agreement.

Hakala, U., Lemmetyinen, A. and Kantola, S. (2013) 'Country image as a nation-branding tool', *Marketing Intelligence & Planning*, 31 (5), 538–556.

Ojo, S. (2019) 'Place consumption: Interrogating the relationship between nation brand and city brand', in Gbadamosi, A. (ed.), *Exploring the dynamics of consumerism in developing nations*, 218–242, Hershey, PA: IGI Global.

Steenkamp, J.-B. (2019) 'Building strong nation brands', *International Marketing Review*, ahead-of-print, doi:10.1108/IMR-10-2019-0253.

United Nations (2018) 'The world's cities in 2018', *UN*, available at: www.un.org/en/events/citiesday/assets/pdf/the_worlds_cities_in_2018_data_booklet.pdf.

Yalkin, C. (2018) 'A brand culture approach to managing nation-brands', *European Management Review*, 15 (1), 137–149.

PRACTITIONER INSIGHT: THE PLACE BRAND OBSERVER

An interview with Florian Kaefer, Founder of The Place Brand Observer

Why did you establish The Place Brand Observer?

I established TPBO in 2014 upon completion of my doctoral thesis at Waikato Management School in New Zealand, to fill a gap by facilitating access to latest research insights into place branding. I realized that there was no platform where practitioners could find out about academic work on the topic in a way which they would understand, and where academics could learn about the actual experiences and challenges of place brand managers and marketers 'on the ground'.

Since I had just completed a thorough review of academic literature on place branding for my PhD, I started by making summaries available, on the website PlaceBrandObserver.com. Most academic work is outdated by the time it is published (since it can take up to two–three years for academic work to be published), so I began to invite leading thinkers and practitioners to share their story and insights in the form of interviews. By now over 260 professionals have contributed to our series of interviews (which is still ongoing).

What role does The Place Brand Observer play in the field of place branding?

As a knowledge platform and global network of specialists, TPBO supports country and nation brand teams with insights, examples, and advice on how to strengthen community identity and location reputation. We highlight best practice examples and give locations – cities, regions, countries – the opportunity to present answers to the question 'why (visit, invest, live) here?'

TPBO facilitates dissemination of latest research insights (we have a knowledge partnership with the journal *Place Branding and Public Diplomacy*). Through our bi-monthly expert panel (around 60 participants around the world), we are able to facilitate timely advice on place branding issues and developments, trends, and challenges.

With our interview portraits of leading changemakers and influencers in the field of place branding, we illustrate how diverse this field of research and practice is and how place branding is approached around the world.

TPBO serves both place branding professionals and those on the lookout for their next business or investment location. We realized early on that many of our social media followers and website readers are senior level executives who are interested in how places – especially countries – position themselves, how they deal with challenges such as the coronavirus pandemic or the climate emergency, and what they have to offer. Whereas economic developers, foreign direct investment and talent attraction teams, country brand managers, and other professionals involved with place branding are still our key audience, discerning visitors, talents, and investors complement those as a growing audience segment for TPBO.

The Place Brand Leaders podcast complements what we offer through the website and is a great way to engage even more strongly with those in charge of developing or managing the identity and reputation of their country or nation.

What are the most inspiring nation branding cases you have come across in the past two–three years?

Costa Rica, Slovenia, and New Zealand are, to my mind, some of the best cases of successful nation branding right now. All three are very much engaged with country branding and are carrying it beyond marketing, backing brand propositions with policy and action. I find their strong focus on sustainability very appealing and convincing, especially since this is a topic which our panel of place brand experts identified as crucial for future place branding success.

Peru and Uruguay are two other countries which I had the opportunity to experience first-hand (and you'll find the country reports on PlaceBrandObserver.com). Both are great examples of how much is possible with the right policies and determination, which is what it takes nowadays to succeed with nation or country branding.

Can you give any examples of nation branding campaigns that were developed to promote export products, e.g., by enhancing the country-of-origin effect?

New Zealand is the example I know best, having benefited tremendously from its '100%Pure New Zealand' tourism marketing campaign, and the 'clean and green' image of its produce – for instance apples and other fruits, and dairy. This was also the topic of my PhD, and you will find more on the meaning and economic success of New Zealand's country of origin branding on PlaceBrandObserver.com.

What motivated you to publish *An Insider's Guide to Place Branding*?

Over the last seven years we collected and published hundreds of research and practitioner insights, case studies and interviews on PlaceBrandObserver.com. I wanted to make those more accessible, to bring it all together in one book, giving location managers and marketers an easy-to-understand introduction to place branding – what it means, how to succeed with it, the challenges and trends – in the eyes of leading professionals around the world whose work focuses on strengthening community identity and location reputation. So it is not an academic work or a consultant's reflection on own work experience. Rather, a snapshot of latest thinking on the topic. And a Who's Who of expert interviews, which can be found in the second part of the book.

CASE: FUNDACIÓN IMAGEN DE CHILE: GENERAL PURPOSE AND STRATEGY

Daniela Montiel, Director of Strategic Partnerships, Marca Chile

Soon after democracy was restored in Chile in the early 1990s, the government began to make a concerted effort to re-insert the country into the global market through the establishment of international trade agreements throughout the world. It thus made logical sense to complement that effort with active strategies aimed at increasing awareness for the country and what it has to offer.

In the early stages of this awareness-raising effort, the approach was almost entirely based on trade and commerce but marketing research on the matter pointed increasingly to the fact that a country's favorability and the increased willingness to trade with, visit and invest in that country (the country-of-origin effect) made room for an ample array of communication tools and strategies.

Who are the main stakeholders and what role do they play?

In its role as the main driver of Chile's nation branding strategy but not its sole executor, FICH takes a stakeholder approach to all branding and campaign efforts. Although some of our main stakeholders are ProChile (trade promotion), InvestChile (investment attraction), and the Undersecretariat of Tourism (tourism attraction), we also count the aforementioned network of partnerships with various ministries, public and private institutions, trade associations, and chambers of commerce with international presence among out main stakeholders as through these partnerships they commit to aligning themselves with us in terms of branding and messaging. The insights and participation we are able to secure by working in collaboration with these stakeholders allow us to build a nation brand that truly reflects Chile, align the key messages surrounding it and also secure reach and visibility for these messages as well as any related campaigns.

Chile and its country-of-origin effect

Listening

Research is the centerpiece of FICH's efforts and is regularly carried out to improve our understanding of Chile's country image abroad as it pertains to consumer attitudes and behavior toward Chilean products and services but also in international relations and policy contexts. Results are shared with stakeholders in Chile as well as its diplomatic missions abroad with the hope that these insights will help guide strategies and form part of the decision-making process of a broad range of Chilean institutions and industries.

How these findings should be incorporated into stakeholder strategies in target markets is a crucial part of our work. Some examples of the research we have developed in recent years includes:

The value of 'Marca Chile': A national study aimed at understanding the value national consumers place on the nation brand, understanding that it is equally important for a national audience to be familiar with Marca Chile and its attributes.

Longitudinal study of Chile's image abroad: Covering 12 major cities on 12 different topics. 100 participants per city monthly. Every month we publish a study on the month's findings and share the results with our stakeholders as well as the national media.

Perception studies in Brazil and the UK: Studies meant to gain detailed insights on how Chile, its products, people, and culture are perceived within those countries. The results are incorporated into our communication content and international campaigns and shared with our stakeholders through mailings and the Marca Chile toolkit.

Stakeholder engagement

As previously mentioned, securing stakeholder buy-in is a key aspect of FICH's work and making the most of the resources invested. This engagement is mainly geared toward the following networks:

FICH Network of Strategic Partnerships are generally formed with larger institutions and companies based on the relevance of their work and potential to help broaden visibility for Chile and its attributes. This space also allows us to collaborate with a significant number of cultural actors from both the public and private sectors which would not traditionally fall under trade, travel, or investment promotion efforts but absolutely contribute to them positively. Of the over 100 partnerships that we have formed over the years, roughly 75% are from the private sector and 25% represent the public sector. From this network, we are also able to draw inspiration for much of our nation branding content.

ChileOne is a public sector work group composed of export and tourism promotion and investment attraction agencies, an effective way we found in order to ensure relevant stakeholder input and priorities are incorporated into our various efforts and a way to gain credibility among them. The periodic group meetings also serve as a sounding board for initiatives and help ensure that messaging between institutions is aligned and as consistent as possible.

Our **Marca Chile Brand Licensing Program** is open to Chilean brands who export (or intend to).

There are currently over 750 goods and services using the Marca Chile which in turn secures nation brand presence in over 75 countries. The program currently consists of over 800 brands who have applied and been granted the right to use the nation brand on their goods or services. Roughly 70% of the brand licensees represent goods and the other 30% represent services. An important aspect of the evaluation process to become a Marca Chile licensee is the degree to which the brand represents Chile, its people, and its attributes. To further encourage representation within the program from as many of Chile's regions as possible, we regularly hold workshops with regional entities such as local startup networks, cultural and artisanal groups, and tourism organizations. We continue to grow the program each year as it is truly an opportunity for the nation brand to be extended to a broader portion of the population and also associate itself internationally with quality Chilean goods and services in over 78 countries.

Positioning international campaigns (national and international, sectoral and general)

In collaboration with the Treasury, and a series of public and private actors, in 2017 Imagen de Chile led its first attempt at a multi-stakeholder campaign aimed at diversifying Chile's image from a primarily natural resources and primary goods exporter to include global services. Although the campaign had modest results, mainly in Latin America, it provided the team a wealth of experience so that in 2020 it was well-equipped to once again attempt diversifying Chile's image abroad, this time putting its people, talent, and capacity to innovate at center stage.

The **#MadebyChileans** campaign aims to emphasize Chilean national talent and the country's capacity to innovate in order to help generate solutions to global problems ranging from climate change to malnutrition and relied entirely on FICH's network of partnership and licensees from our previously mentioned Brand Licensing Program to ensure that messaging is based on concrete examples rather than vague attributes and taglines.

Chile Keeps on Going is another international campaign driven by members of the meat, fruit, salmon, wine, and milk export industries and guided by ProChile and FICH. This effort to promote and drive the consumption of Chilean products is being co-financed by both public and private entities as a response to the global pandemic and its damaging effect on global exports. The campaign, primarily digital in this phase, is geared toward Brazil, China, and the U.S. and seeks to reinforce Chile's commitment and responsibility toward national exports and also takes the opportunity to associate these positive attributes as integral aspects of Chilean identity. An added bonus to this strategy is that it effectively creates an umbrella message for its stakeholders and serves as a base from which each industry develops more targeted messaging.

Marcas Sectoriales

ProChile's Sectoral Brands Program is an initiative carried out in close collaboration with key actors related to branding and international trade promotion, including FICH. The program seeks to promote specific productive sectors through the creation and implementation of brands meant to represent said sector.

This program accompanies brands from inception, helping them identify their distinguishing characteristics and generate their sector's narrative. Every sectoral brand proposal must present a strategy aimed toward at least one target market. This proposal must include public–private associative work with the potential to achieve economies of scale for brand positioning, all under the umbrella of the attributes associated with the nation brand. A panel of experts on the matter representing the aforementioned international trade promotion stakeholders then decides which sectoral brands to co-sponsor for a period of one to two years. In addition to the target market relevance of the sector, part of the selection criteria is also how much the sectoral brand itself will contribute to the construction of Chile's image abroad.

This program is an example of how Chile has managed to bring various sectors to work together in public–private collaboration to promote Chile's image as a reliable provider of products and services in the world. Over the years, the program has co-sponsored a broad range of sectoral brands from salmon, fruits and olive oil to music, cinema, and architecture.

Spotlight on wines of Chile

An example of a long-standing sectoral brand integral to both Chile's export industry as well as its identity is Wines of Chile. This sectoral brand, representing Chilean winemakers, predates Fundación Imagen de Chile and was one of the actors that drove and supported the creation of an entity to lead Chile's nation branding efforts. More than a brand, the Wines of Chile project started as an international marketing effort to promote the country's wine industry abroad geared toward opinion leaders and the general public in target markets with content meant to increase their awareness of Chile's wine offer.

Once Imagen de Chile was established in 2010, this and other similar international export efforts were channeled through the then newly launched nation brand. Wine bottles bearing the nation brand were some of the earliest and most broadly distributed products to do so. Since its early stages, the brand attributes that Wines of Chile sought to communicate were diversity, consistent quality, and sustainability. As a finished product that not only reaches importers but also final consumers, it represents a highly relevant vehicle for Chile's image abroad.

The primary objective of Wines of Chile's 2025 Strategy is to help the Chilean winemaking sector attain a greater market share and achieve the positioning of premium, diverse, and sustainable wines in an international context, with a focus on six priority markets: Brazil, Canada, Chile, China, the United States, and the United Kingdom.

As the entity in charge of leading Chile's nation branding strategy, it is highly motivating for us to see how even a long-standing sectoral brand like Wines of Chile within a highly competitive industry has progressively broadened its strategy over the years to include more elements such as geography and culture to buttress their promotion efforts, understanding that these elements are just as relevant to the Chilean wine industry's success as the price and quality of the wine itself.

CASE: THE GREAT BRITAIN CAMPAIGN – NATIONAL MARKETING CAMPAIGN? NATION BRAND? NATIONAL SOFT POWER PLAY?

Conrad Bird, CBE, Former Director, GREAT Britain Campaign

In September 2020, the GREAT Britain campaign passed its ninth year milestone. Compared with long-running campaigns from the private sector and, indeed, national tourism campaigns from the likes of India, Australia and New Zealand, the campaign is still in its infancy.

But in the sometimes turbulent world of government and especially in a time when Covid-19 has forced all organisations to take a dramatic root and branch rethinking of international activity, to sustain a long-term campaign of this nature can be considered as quite an achievement.

I believe part of the success of the campaign has been down to the fact that GREAT resolutely tries to avoid labelling or descriptions, especially the term 'nation branding'. This may seem a controversial statement in a book dedicated to the subject of nation branding, but allow me to expand.

First, a confession – I love and believe in the power of branding. I have worked in national and international advertising all my life, and I believe there is no more powerful concept than the brand. For me, brands are 'a promise of excellence, repeatedly delivered by first-class customer experience'. Brands are made in the mind, not the factory – they are owned by the customer, not the producer – and they deliver that most important of values: trust.

But can you truly 'brand' a nation? Can you define and project its unique essence, those values and strengths that represent (in the UK's case) the talents and aspirations of nearly 70 million, incredibly diverse people? Can you crystallise a country's long history and point to a compelling future? What 'national promise' can you make, that will be consistently delivered? Why should you embark on such an exercise in the first place – who can help you? Questions like these always come up when I hear the term 'nation branding' – and I always end up slightly daunted and defeated by the size and scale of the task. And the time needed to do it properly, paying true respect to the country one lives in.

So what then is the GREAT campaign? And how can it be defined? At its simplest, it is a long-term marketing campaign that promotes the UK to specific international audiences in order to deliver measurable increases in tourism, international trade and inward investment and education. We estimate it

Figure 4.1
Invest in Great

Figure 4.2
Innovation is Great

has delivered over £4 billion of benefit for the UK since 2017. At its heart is what I hope is a simple and inspiring message, 'GREAT aims to deliver jobs and growth for Britain'.

The campaign delivers this in a number of direct and indirect ways. Directly, for instance via our long-running tourism, education and FDI direct-response advertising campaigns which reach out to target audiences and encourage them to visit, study or invest in the UK.

'Ready to trade': Delivering FDI opportunities direct to UK experts

In February 2020, the UK Department of Trade's new 'Ready to Trade' GREAT campaign aimed to take advantage of the international attention and interest around Brexit to reposition UK trade and investment as a golden opportunity for global business as well as to reassure and inspire international buyers and investors in key markets that the UK is ready, willing and able to trade with them.

This campaign included high impact outdoor advertising in major global business cities, hub airports, financial and business press and specialist media partnerships, targeted LinkedIn and mobile lead-generation campaigns as well as leveraging the hundreds of events that the Department for International Trade DIT conducts around the world. Sectors focused on included Renewable Energy, Advanced Manufacturing, Automotive, Creative (gaming), Life Sciences, FinTech, Food and Drink, Artificial Intelligence (AI) and AgriTech.

Target cities for the campaign included New York, Los Angeles, Chicago, Toronto, Johannesburg, Seoul, Tokyo, Sydney, Singapore, Shanghai, Beijing, Hong Kong, Istanbul, Dubai and Mumbai. Although the campaign was curtailed due to the Covid-19 crisis, the campaign exceeded its original target of delivering 6,500 FDI enquiries, which at a conversion rate of 6%, gave our experts 390 qualified leads to follow up on. Previous FDI campaigns had delivered 3,000 business enquiries annually, £35m of landed or pipeline investment projects, and a trading GVA (gross value added) of £73m–£148m.

All these campaigns are based on strong customer insight and aim to present the UK's most compelling strengths to individuals, mindful of the competition they are considering, in order to elicit an actionable response. In other words, they are marketing campaigns – defined by their ability to deliver against a set of measurable and specific objectives.

But GREAT also works by more indirect means. It pulls together all these campaigns and many more messages and harnesses the power and reach of the UK government's international network of embassies and trade missions to deliver positive, wider messages about the UK in a consistent and high-quality fashion. For the last 9 years, from Shanghai to San Francisco – and 145 countries in between – the campaign has promoted the best the UK can offer.

From over 1,400 physical (pre-Covid) events and trade missions every year, to diplomatic receptions, to major festivals highlighting UK creativity and innovation, government officials and diplomats have used GREAT to good effect. From cultural activities, such as celebrating Shakespeare, to sporting occasions to LGBT+ Pride Marches around the world, where you find examples of the UK in action, you will very often find the GREAT campaign.

Some of this activity can be linked directly to return on investment while others promote British values, our soft power and cultural strengths. Possibly more importantly, GREAT has given the UK Government one overall consistent voice across the world (reducing the need for costs of new campaigns) as well as contributing to a measurable increase in familiarity towards and positive perceptions of the UK.

And, as all communicators know, there is a link between awareness, positive perceptions and action. In fact, for business, research shows that there is a very strong correlation between awareness of country's business opportunities and their propensity to do business. Recognisers of the GREAT campaign overseas are much more likely to say they would buy from UK companies in the next three years than non-recognisers (25% to 16%). In higher education, two-thirds of international students that were aware of the GREAT campaign took action, despite 72% of students considering studying in countries other than the UK.

GREAT also acts a galvanising force for UK companies, non-profit organisations and individuals. Over the years, the campaign has built up hundreds of strong relationships enabling the campaign to be used to promote iconic British products (from Mulberry and Burberry to Mini to Aston Martin, Jaguar and Land Rover) who in turn have been examples of great British ingenuity, creativity and quality. In fact, nearly £150m of cash and kind value has been contributed to the campaign to date.

In addition, hundreds of great British names (brands in their own right) – from almost every member of the British Royal Family, to fashion icons such as Victoria Beckham, famous actors such as Daniel Craig and sportsmen such as Lewis Hamilton and the current captain of the England football team, Harry Kane, have supported the campaign. These have all taken place on a pro-bono basis because the individuals involved believe strongly in promoting their country.

Finally, the campaign has acted as a huge source of pride and inspiration for the many thousands of British people and companies who have been involved in its creation – or who have seen it overseas. We never set out to measure this, but countless anecdotes from around the world have reinforced my view that many UK nationals who have seen the campaign actually feel better (greater, even?) for it. GREAT gives them confidence and a personal sense of pride in what they do every day and when our businesses and entrepreneurs are working overseas in the face of hard competition and tough conditions, a little slice of GREATness I hope, goes a long way!

As the UK emerges from the Covid-19 pandemic and renegotiates its relationship with the EU, there will be new challenges for the GREAT campaign to address – as well as new opportunities to promote. Our efforts will need to focus on Britain as a country of innovation and creativity, a country that is confident, outward-looking, opportunity-rich and cutting edge. Above all, a country that inspires scientific collaboration, shining a light on our credentials and focussing on the biggest challenges for the world today – whether these be developing Covid-19 vaccines, the road to net zero, internet security, harnessing the power of AI, big data, robotics and tech.

National marketing campaign? Nation brand? National soft power play? It may just be semantics, but when persuading peers (especially in the Ministry of Finance) that what is essentially a communications programme is a sound and sustainable investment, I hope the right choice of words can help practitioners overturn perceptions (and sometimes stereotypes) that impede nations to invest in their own international promotional efforts.

Summary

This chapter has reviewed the main themes in the field of country-of-origin and related these to the context of nation branding. The country-of-origin effect can influence attitude and behaviour towards brands, whether products, services or nations. Country-of-origin perceptions can change over time and it is the responsibility of nation branding strategists to ensure that such changes evolve in a favourable direction.

Discussion points

1   What can nation branding policy makers learn from the consumer behaviour literature?
2   Is it possible to combat a negative country-of-origin bias? Give examples of countries that have successfully overcome negative country-of-origin perceptions, and explain how these successes were achieved.

References

Acton, M. (2007) 'Fuel for thought', *Brand Strategy*, April, 54–55.

Aichner, T. (2014) 'Country-of-origin marketing: A list of typical strategies with examples', *Journal of Brand Management*, 21, 81–93.

Al-Sulaiti, K.I. and Baker, M.J. (1998) 'Country-of-origin effects: A literature review', *Marketing Intelligence & Planning*, 16 (3), 150–199.

Amine, L.S. and Chao, M.C.H. (2005) 'Managing country image to long-term advantage: The case of Taiwan and Acer', *Place Branding*, 1 (2), 187–204.

Andéhn, M. and L'espoir Decosta, J.-N.P. (2018) 'Re-imagining the country-of-origin effect: A promulgation approach', *Journal of Product & Brand Management*, 27 (7), 884–896.

Aruan, D.T.H., Crouch, R. and Quester, P. (2018) 'Relative importance of country of service delivery, country of person and country of brand in hybrid service evaluation: A conjoint analysis approach', *Journal of Product & Brand Management*, 27 (7), 819–831.

Askegaard, S. and Ger, G. (1998) 'Product-country images: Towards a contextualized approach', *European Advances in Consumer Research*, 3, 50–58.

Beverland, M. and Lindgreen, A. (2002) 'Using country of origin in strategy: The importance of context and strategic action', *Journal of Brand Management*, 10 (2), 147–167.

Burgess, S.M. and Harris, M. (1999) 'Social identity in an emerging consumer market: How you do the wash may say a lot about who you think you are', *Advances in Consumer Research*, 26, 170–175.

Chao, P., Wuhrer, G. and Werani, T. (2005) 'Celebrity and foreign brand name as moderators of country-of-origin effects', *International Journal of Advertising*, 24 (2), 173–192.

Darling, J.R. and Puetz, J.E. (2002) 'Analysis of changes in consumer attitudes towards the products of England, France, Germany and the USA, 1975–2000', *European Business Review*, 14 (3), 170–193.

Dekhili, S. and Achabou, M.A. (2015) 'The influence of the country-of-origin ecological image on ecolabelled product evaluation: An experimental approach to the case of the European ecolabel', *Journal of Business Ethics*, 131, 89–106.

Dinnie, K. (2004) 'Country-of-origin 1965–2004: A literature review', *Journal of Customer Behaviour*, 3 (2), 165–213.

Dornoff, R., Tankersley, C. and White, G. (1974) 'Consumers' perceptions of imports', *Akron Business and Economic Review*, 5, Summer, 26–29.

Fiske, J. (1990) *Introduction to Communication Studies*, New York: Routledge.

Florek, M. and Conejo, F. (2007) 'Export flagships in branding small developing countries: The cases of Costa Rica and Moldova', *Place Branding and Public Diplomacy*, 3 (1), 53–72.

Hamin and Elliott, G. (2006) 'A less-developed country perspective of consumer ethnocentrism and "country of origin" effects: Indonesian evidence', *Asia Pacific Journal of Marketing and Logistics*, 18 (2), 79–92.

Harrison-Walker, L.J. (1995) 'The relative effects of national stereotype and advertising information on the selection of a service provider: An empirical study', *Journal of Services Marketing*, 9 (1), 47–59.

Jaffe, E.D. and Nebenzahl, I.D. (2001) *National Image & Competitive Advantage: The Theory and Practice of Country-of-Origin Effect*, Denmark: Copenhagen Business School Press.

Javalgi, R.G., Cutler, B.D. and Winans, W.A. (2001) 'At your service! Does country of origin research apply to services?', *Journal of Services Marketing*, 15 (6–7), 565–582.

Kim, N., Chun, E. and Ko, E. (2017) 'Country of origin effects on brand image, brand evaluation, and purchase intention: A closer look at Seoul, New York, and Paris fashion collection', *International Marketing Review*, 34 (2), 254–271.

Kotler, P. and Gertner, D. (2002) 'Country as brand, product, and beyond: A place marketing and brand management perspective', *Journal of Brand Management*, 9 (4–5), 249–261.

Kwok, S., Uncles, M. and Huang, Y. (2006) 'Brand preferences and brand choices among urban Chinese consumers: An investigation into country-of-origin effects', *Asia Pacific Journal of Marketing and Logistics*, 18 (3), 163–172.

Lampert, S.I and Jaffe, E.D. (1998) 'A dynamic approach to country-of-origin effect', *European Journal of Marketing*, 32 (1–2), 61–78.

Laroche, M., Papadopoulos, N., Heslop, L. and Bergeron, J. (2003) 'Effects of subcultural differences on country and product evaluations', *Journal of Consumer Behaviour*, 2 (3), 232–247.

Lenartowicz, T. and Roth, K. (2001) 'Does subculture within a country matter? A cross-cultural study of motivational domains and business performance in Brazil', *Journal of International Business Studies*, 32 (2), 305–325.

Lotz, S.L. and Hu, M.Y. (2001) 'Diluting negative country of origin stereotypes: A social stereotype approach', *Journal of Marketing Management*, 17 (1–2), 105–120.

Lyons, W. (2005) 'Clear winner', *Scotland on Sunday, Food & Drink*, 30 October, 22.

Magnusson, P., Westjohn, S.A. and Sirianni, N.J. (2019) 'Beyond country image favorability: How brand positioning via country personality stereotypes enhances brand evaluations', *Journal of International Business Studies*, 50, 318–338.

McQuater, K. (2020) 'Made in China?, Impact', *The Market Research Society*, 31, October, 15.

Mick, D.G. (1986) 'Consumer research and semiotics: Exploring the morphology of signs, symbols, and significance', *Journal of Consumer Research*, 13 (2), 196–213.

Morris, C.W. (1946) *Signs, Language, and Behaviour*, New York: Prentice Hall.

Mortimer, R. (2007) 'Card of conscience', *Brand Strategy*, February, 20–23.

Nes, E.B., Yelkur, R. and Silkoset, R. (2014) 'Consumer affinity for foreign countries: Construct development, buying behaviour consequences and animosity contrasts', *International Business Review*, 23, 774–784.

Niss, H. (1996) 'Country-of-origin marketing over the product life cycle: A Danish case study', *European Journal of Marketing*, 30 (3), 6–22.

Oberecker, E.M. and Diamantopoulos, A. (2011) 'Consumers' emotional bonds with foreign countries: Does consumer affinity impact buying intentions?', *Journal of International Marketing*, 19 (3), 45–72.

Ofir, C. and Lehmann, D. (1986) 'Measuring images of foreign products', *The Columbia Journal of World Business*, 21 (2), 105–108.

Papadopoulos, N. and Cleveland, M. (eds.) (2021) *Marketing Countries, Places, and Place-Associated Brands*, Cheltenham: Edward Elgar Publishing.

Papadopoulos, N. and Heslop, L. (eds) (1993) *Product and Country Images: Research and Strategy*, New York: The Haworth Press.

Park, C.W., Eisingerich, A.B. and Park, J.W. (2013) 'Attachment-aversion (AA) model of customer-brand relationships', *Journal of Consumer Psychology*, 23 (2), 229–248.

Pasquier, M. (2008) 'The image of Switzerland: Between clichés and realities', in Dinnie, K. (ed.), *Nation Branding – Concepts, Issues, Practice*, 1st edn, 79–84, Upper Saddle River, NJ: Butterworth-Heinemann.

Peterson, R.A. and Jolibert, A.J.P. (1995) 'A meta-analysis of country-of-origin effects', *Journal of International Business Studies*, 26 (4), 883–900.

Roll, M. (2006) *Asian Brand Strategy: How Asia Builds Strong Brands*, New York: Palgrave Macmillan.

Roth, M.S. and Romeo, S.B. (1992) 'Matching product category and country image perceptions: A framework for managing country-of-origin effects', *Journal of International Business Studies*, 23 (3), 477–497.

Saunders, R.A. (2017) 'Buying into Brand Borat: Kazakhstan's cautious embrace of its unwanted "son"', *Slavic Review*, 67 (1), 63–80.

Schooler, R.D. (1971) 'Bias phenomena attendant to the marketing of foreign goods in the US', *Journal of International Business Studies*, 2 (1), 71–81.

Shimp, T.A. (2003) *Advertising, Promotion, & Supplemental Aspects of Integrated Marketing Communications*, 6th edn, Mason, OH: Thomson South-Western.

Shimp, T.A. and Sharma, S. (1987) 'Consumer ethnocentrism: Construction and validation of the CETSCALE', *Journal of Marketing Research*, 24 (3), 280–289.

Smith, S. (2007) 'Building the brands we love', *Brand Strategy*, March, 47–49.

Suter, M.B., Giraldi, J.M.E., Borini, F.M., MacLennan, M.L.F., Crescitelli, E. and Polo, E.F. (2018) 'In search of tools for the use of country image (CI) in the brand', *Journal of Brand Management*, 25, 119–132.

Thakor, M.V. and Kohli, C.S. (1996) 'Brand origin: Conceptualization and review', *Journal of Consumer Marketing*, 13 (3), 27–42.

Usunier, J.-C. (2006) 'Relevance in business research: The case of country-of-origin research in marketing', *European Management Review*, 3 (1), 60–73.

Verlegh, P.W.J. and Steenkamp, J.-B.E.M. (1999) 'A review and meta-analysis of country-of-origin research', *Journal of Economic Psychology*, 20 (5), 521–546.

Verlegh, P.W.J., Steenkamp, J.B.E.M. and Meulenberg, M.T.G. (2005) 'Country-of-origin effects in consumer processing of advertising claims', *International Journal of Research in Marketing*, 22 (2), 127–139.

Zafar, U.A., Johnson, J.P., Yang, X., Fatt, C.K., Teng, H.S. and Boon, L.C. (2004) 'Does country of origin matter for low-involvement products?', *International Marketing Review*, 21 (1), 102–120.

5 Nation branding and national identity

Key points

- Key concepts in the field of national identity include the nation as 'an imagined community' and 'invented tradition'
- Element of national identity such as language, literature, music, sport, architecture and so on embody the soul of a nation; this is one reason why nation branding is too large an undertaking to be left solely to marketing, branding or advertising professionals
- Public diplomacy involves governments reaching out to foreign populations; a key way in which this is done is through the promotion of cultural programmes that can be considered a form of 'soft power' projection

Introduction

National identity plays a key role in nation branding. An awareness and understanding of the core features of national identity is a prerequisite for developing nation branding

DOI: 10.4324/9781003100249-7

strategy, as the essence of any nation brand derives not only from the country's companies and brands, but also from its culture in the widest sense. Language, literature, music, sport, architecture and so on all embody the soul of a nation. This is one reason why nation branding is too large an undertaking to be left solely to marketing, branding or advertising professionals. In this chapter, the first case discusses Japan's nation brand in light of the three Gs of gender, generation and globalisation. The second case focuses on the role of food in branding Ireland. The academic perspective by Nadia Kaneva conceptualises the nation and its brand as a deeply contested relationship, whilst Natasha Grand's practitioner insight discusses how national identity has become a pursuit and a tool of place branders.

A deep and authentic nation brand must include the many elements and expressions of a nation's culture; if it fails to do so, it will rightly be perceived as shallow and super-ficial and not truly representative of the nation. Branding a nation is not the same as branding a simple product, where in many cases competing products with no real differ-ences are hyped and promoted on the basis of spurious differentiation. On the contrary, nation brands are rooted in the reality of the nation's culture, which is perhaps the truest, most authentic differentiator that any brand could wish to have.

The limited knowledge that people have with regard to nations other than their own gives rise to what can become a damaging identity–image gap, whereby a nation's true identity fails to be appreciated by external observers because of indifference or over-whelming negative stereotypes. The identity–image gap can be exacerbated by some-thing as apparently trivial as an unflattering portrayal in film. Khazakstan has been the most high-profile victim of this through the 2006 film *Borat*. To a lesser extent Slovakia received a gruesome and sinister depiction through the 2005 horror film *Hostel*. In such cases, a public relations damage limitation exercise may bring some short-term benefits. But in the longer term a more strategic promotion of the country's culture and identity will be necessary in order to close, or at least reduce, existing identity–image gaps. The importance of the relationship between the nation brand and national culture has been explored in studies such as Kubacki and Skinner (2006).

This chapter provides an overview of the key features of national identity that are rel-evant to the concept and practice of nation branding. Implications of national identity for nation branding are drawn and areas of particular relevance to nation brand devel-opment are discussed. It has been observed that at least nine academic disciplines have developed theories of nationalism and nation-states and it is therefore not surprising that authors in one discipline are unfamiliar with theory in another, or that there is overlap and duplication (Treanor, 1997). These disciplines include political geography, interna-tional relations, political science, cultural anthropology, social psychology, political phi-losophy, international law, sociology and history. We now address from some of these many disciplines the salient national identity issues for application in culturally informed nation brand development.

Fundamental features of national identity

The fundamental features of national identity include the following: an historic territory, or homeland; common myths and historical memories; a common, mass public culture;

common legal rights and duties for all members; and a common economy with territorial mobility for all members (Smith, 1991). Increasing levels of supranational legislation emanating from regional entities such as the European Union render the last two features less distinctively national than in the past. However, the notions of a historic homeland, common myths, historical memories and a common, mass public culture still prevail as key features of national identity. The lowering of international trade barriers and the border-transcending nature of the internet have made the world a more interconnected place, yet national identity retains its deep emotional and spiritual power as a source of identity for many people. The intense pride and emotion in national identity exhibited at international sporting events, for instance, demonstrates that even in our era of globalisation, national identity remains a relevant and powerful concept.

The visual manifestations of national identity are all around us. Flags, for example, are probably the most potent visual expression of national identity. Their recognition levels result in designs of a country's flag being used as a visual shorthand by products that wish to highlight their country-of-origin. One problem that can arise from this is that any brand from a given country is free to use a design of the flag in its packaging or other forms of marketing communications. This makes it difficult, if not impossible, for nations to ensure that only high quality products and brands use the flag in their branding. Countries can establish organisations to promote their country's products and services and create a logo or trademark that can only be used by member companies, and this is one means of protecting quality perceptions of a nation's brands.

Other visual manifestations of national identity include uniforms of the armed forces and other institutions, traditional dress and architectural styles. There also exist sonic manifestations of national identity, the most obvious of which is a country's national anthem, but which can also encompass language, regional accents and dialects, and specific voices of well known individuals who are closely associated with a particular country such as Nelson Mandela in the case of South Africa, Sean Connery in the case of Scotland and so on. Iconic individuals such as these constitute an element of the common, mass public culture identified earlier as a fundamental feature of national identity.

Landscape represents another powerful visual manifestation of national identity. For example, Mount Fuji, spectacular fjords and Ayers Rock dramatically symbolise Japan, Norway and Australia respectively. These types of unique, potent iconic landscapes have long been used by national tourism organisations. Consequently one of the key challenges in nation branding is how to position a country so that it is not perceived solely as a tourist destination but also as a credible location for inward investment, a source of high-technology products and so on. For emerging nations yet to fully exploit their tourism potential, the concept of 'cultivating poetic spaces' – the identification of a sacred territory that belonged historically to a particular community (Smith, 1991) – may be adopted as part of a sustainable development agenda centred on the fast-growing ecotourism sector.

One of the most critical issues in national identity is the tension that is frequently observable in many nations between cultural diversity and national unity (Burgess and Harris, 1999). It has been suggested that in the context of Russia, for example, the main problem in nation-building is how to reconcile inclusive civic identities on the one hand with exclusive ethnic identities on the other (Tolz, 1998). When cultural faultlines intersect within a nation, the social and political consequences can be devastating.

Table 5.1 Dimensions of national identity

Author	Dimensions of national identity
Smith (1991)	An historic territory, or homeland; common myths and historical memories; a common, mass public culture; common legal rights and duties for all members; a common economy with territorial mobility for members
Anderson (1991)	The nation as an imagined community, a deep horizontal comradeship
Tolz (1998)	The main problem of nation-building is how to reconcile civic identities based on inclusive citizenship and exclusive ethnic identities based on such common characteristics as culture, religion and language
Parekh (2000)	Identity is neither fixed and unalterable nor wholly fluid and amenable to unlimited reconstruction. It can be altered, but only within the constraints imposed by inherited constitution and necessarily inadequate self-knowledge
Thompson (2001)	Contrary to nationalist discourses and commonly held assumptions, the nation is not a unitary entity in which all members think, feel and act as one. Instead, each individual engages in many different ways in making sense of nations and national identities in the course of interactions with others
Bond, McCrone and Brown (2003)	Attempt to move beyond assumptions that nationalism is essentially cultural and/or narrowly political, primarily past-oriented and defensive. Examine evidence relating to the creative (re)construction of the nation from a contemporary economic perspective

Source: adapted from Dinnie (2002)

Alternatively, cultural diversity within a nation can be embraced, celebrated and treated as an asset rather than as a liability. This is a contentious political issue, and beyond the control of any individual or organisation engaged in nation brand strategy development. But nation brand teams must be sensitive to the political ramifications of including or excluding certain cultural groups or perspectives from nation branding campaigns. Derided from the political left for alleged cultural commodification and equally derided from the political right for alleged indifference to and disrespect for the nation's heritage and history, the short-lived 'Cool Britannia' campaign may still make politicians jittery about committing to a nation branding strategy. An inclusive, stakeholder approach represents the best means to overcome objections from either end of the political spectrum and to integrate a nation's cultural diversity into its nation branding. Campaigns crudely imposed from above, without prior consultation with a nation's diverse cultural groups, have little chance of resonating with a nation's citizens.

In order to facilitate comparative analysis and to contribute to effective decision-making, efforts have been made to construct scales that objectively measure national identity. One such scale is based on the view that national identity comprises the 'set of meanings' owned by a given culture which sets it apart from other cultures, and this scale identifies four major components of national identity – cultural homogeneity, belief structure, national heritage and ethnocentrism (Keillor and Hult, 1999). The scale was designed to allow national identity similarities and differences to be placed in a context that would allow enhanced international marketing decision-making. An alternative scale has been proposed by other researchers, who propose five subscales of national identity – membership (a person's worth for or contribution to the ingroup, in this case the nation); private (a person's view of the ingroup's value); public (other persons' view of this group); identity (contribution of ingroup membership to the self-concept of the person); and comparison (how the ingroup rates in comparison to relevant outgroups, i.e., other nations) (Lilli and Diehl, 1999). This scale draws upon the principles of social psychology theory and would therefore require adaptation if it were to be used in a branding context.

Although national identity scales can provide a degree of useful insight with regard to nation brand development and communication, it should be noted that national identity is only one form of identity upon which overall personal identity may be constructed. Individual self-categorisation can also be based on social, supra-national and personal sources of identity and the salience of each of these identity sources can vary according to the social context (Burgoyne and Routh, 1999). The concept of contingent self-categorisation may be extended from the individual and applied also at the level of the nation, whereby nations may highlight appropriate self-categorised aspects of their identity according to context. Northern Ireland, for example, has adopted such a strategy by marketing itself as 'Irish' in Irish-friendly markets and as 'British' in British-friendly markets (Gould and Skinner, 2007).

A country seeking to brand itself effectively in such a way that its nation brand covers a wide range of product/service sectors must 'customise' its identity according to the geographical and social environment in which it is competing. This view of identity sees identity not as static and fixed but as produced and fluid, although there are clearly limits to this fluidity given that the identity of a person or nation is not a blank slate (Macdonald, 1997; Higson, 1998).

Placing the concept of national identity as a fluid phenomenon in an economic context, Bond et al. (2003) note that the national past continues to have a strong influence upon the means by which economic agents mobilise national identity for contemporary economic ends. They suggest that the need to recognise the continuing importance of the historical influence of national identity, while at the same time constructing a contemporary identity, is achieved through four general processes: 'reiteration', which involves the mobilisation of a historically positive element of national identity; 'recapture', in which there is an ambition to revisit past success in an area of contemporary problems; 'reinterpretation', in which historically negative factors are presented as contemporary advantages or as largely neutral; and 'repudiation', where negative features that are not suitable for reinterpretation are omitted from contemporary constructions of identity. This concept, which proposes that identity is constructed rather than given, underpins the nation branding paradigm. Whilst not granting governments *carte blanche* to manipulate national identity for narrow party-political ends, the concept of identity as being both given and constantly reconstituted (Parekh, 2000) implies that governments can attempt to highlight certain aspects of national identity in order to shape national image perceptions.

The nation as an imagined community

A further key perspective on national identity is Anderson's (1991) conceptualisation of the nation as *an imagined community*. According to Anderson, the nation is 'imagined' as a community because although the members of even the smallest nation will never know most of their fellow members, the nation is conceived of as a deep, horizontal comradeship. The abstract nature of national identity is also examined by Cameron (1999), who focuses upon the role of myth in national identity. Cameron observes that myth is inextricably linked with the concept of national identity and many of the symbols which people seize upon to denote their national allegiance are shared with the people of other nations who do not attribute to them the same significance; although the value of such myths and symbols is in the mind more than in reality, the mind and our deep psychological reactions can govern our attitudes and therefore national myths and symbols have a real potency. Pittock (1999), however, offers a dissenting view on Anderson's concept of 'imagined community', maintaining that although the concept of 'imagining' the nation may be useful to some extent, adopting this concept without interrogation places too much power in the hands of creative writers and created narratives and too little on the lived experience and shared traditions of national communities. Again, in the context of developing nation branding strategy, such a perspective would argue in favour of an inclusive approach rather than a fabricated narrative handed down from on high. The issue of national identity-building narratives underpins debates on the teaching of history in a nation's schools, and leads to a consideration of one of the most intriguing themes in the national identity literature – the apparently paradoxical concept of 'invented tradition'.

Invented tradition

A landmark text in the national identity literature is *The Invention of Tradition* (Hobsbawm and Ranger, 1983), a collection of case studies written by various historians and anthropologists who argue that traditions which appear or claim to be ancient can be quite recent in origin and were sometimes literally invented in a single event or over a short time period. The book argues that there is probably no time or place which has not seen the 'invention' of tradition, although invented traditions occur more frequently at times of rapid social transformation when 'old' traditions are disappearing. A key aim of invented tradition is to establish or symbolise social cohesion and collective identities, and a key characteristic of invented tradition is that the continuity with a referenced historical past is largely fictitious. The fictitious nature of much invented tradition inevitably invites criticism on the grounds that such traditions lack authenticity or legitimacy, and are created in order to benefit the established social order. The invention of a Highland, tartan-clad tradition in Scotland has, for example, been vigorously contested:

> Tartanry, Highlandism and the rural representation of Scotland . . . were all indicative of the manufacture of a Scottish identity which had little to do with the reality of a rapidly urbanising and industrialising society, but everything to do with the appropriation of symbolic representations of Scotland which were located in a mythical past. . . . Because the bourgeoisie and aristocracy peddled such symbols as authentic,

it follows that their historical perception would have to be hazy and haphazard for such symbolism to acquire credibility. A rigorous and scientific historical tradition would have exposed this newly fashioned identity as bogus.

(Finlay, 1994)

Smith (1991) elaborates on the theme of invented tradition by stating that all those monuments to the fallen – ceremonies of remembrance, statues to heroes and celebrations of anniversaries – however newly created in their present form, take their meaning and their emotional power from a presumed and felt collective past. The risk of superficiality does however exist to some extent, and it has been claimed that national image can be a complete media creation when the media are the sole source of information (O'Shaughnessy and Jackson, 2000). This observation is echoed by Pittock (1999), who criticises the concept of inventing the nation, with its concomitant idea that a mass of people can accept a fraud perpetrated by a publicist or creative artist as part of their own identity. These well-founded concerns regarding manipulation of national identity need to be acknowledged in the development of nation branding strategy. In any country with a free press, the media would not allow any government-sponsored invention of tradition to pass uncontested; hence the importance of including a wide range of public and private sector stakeholders in the development of any nation brand strategy, particularly where the invention of tradition is being contemplated.

Cultural elements of national identity

Culture has been described as the most distinguishing but also the most intangible element of a country (Pant, 2005). As such, a nation's culture may be regarded as constituting the true essence of the nation brand. The integration of culture into the nation brand will also help elevate nation branding strategy above being merely trite, superficial advertising campaigns. Rodner et al. (2020) have, for example, discussed the ways in which nation branding can draw upon the arts, specifically museums, in order to position a country.

It has been argued that international business and especially marketing are a cultural as well as an economic phenomenon (Bradley, 2005), and that a perspective on what is important within national cultures is useful to international marketers in building marketing mixes which will appeal to customers belonging to a national culture (Muhlbacher et al., 1999; Torelli et al., 2021). This section therefore provides an overview of some key cultural elements of national identity. It is beyond the scope of this section to conduct an exhaustive, in-depth examination of these cultural elements. Rather, it is the relevance of these elements to the nation branding construct that is of prime interest for our purposes. A number of cultural perspectives on national identity are presented in Table 5.2.

High-context cultures and low-context cultures

A well known way of analysing cultures is Hall's distinction between high-context cultures and low-context cultures (Hall, 1976). Using Hall's terminology, in high-context cultures (such as Japanese, Arabic or Chinese cultures) indirect styles of communication and the ability to interpret non-verbal signals and indirect illusions are prized, whereas

Author	Cultural perspectives
Anderson (1991)	The cultural products of nationalism: poetry, prose fiction, music, plastic arts
McCreadie (1991)	The role of language in the formation of national identity
Hall (1976)	The contrast between 'high-context' and 'low-context' cultures
King (2000)	Through European club football, the outlines can be detected of a new Europe of competing cities and regions which are being disembedded from their national contexts into new transnational matrices.
Shulman (2002)	The main cultural components of national identity comprise language, religion and traditions
Tuck (2003)	The media evoke particularly strong invented traditions and well-established symbols of national identity in describing the exploits of the English national rugby team.

Table 5.2 Cultural perspectives on national identity

in low-context cultures (such as the United Kingdom and the United States) non-verbal behaviour is often ignored and therefore communicators have to provide more explicit information. Other differences between high-context and low-context cultures can also have an influence on cross-cultural communication and relationships. For example, in high-context cultures relationships tend to be relatively long-lasting; agreements tend to be spoken rather than written; insiders and outsiders are clearly distinguished; and cultural patterns are ingrained and slow to change. In low-context cultures the opposite characteristics prevail (Mead, 2005).

Individualism/collectivism

The link between elements of national identity and consumer behaviour was explored by Aaker and Williams (Aaker and Williams, 1998) in their study of the influence of emotional appeals across cultures. Cross-cultural persuasion effects are discussed by comparing the effects of emotional appeals across collectivist and individualist cultures. The authors found that appeals relying on other-focused emotions (e.g., empathy, peacefulness) versus ego-focused emotions (e.g., pride, happiness) led to more favourable attitudes for members of the individualist culture (United States), while appeals relying on ego-focused emotions, as opposed to other-focused emotions, led to more favourable attitudes for members of the collectivist culture (China). This perhaps surprising finding is explained by the authors as stemming from the notion that the novel types of thoughts generated by the persuasion appeals mediated attitudes, thereby driving the attitudinal and cognitive responses results. Aaker and Williams state, however, that further research is needed in order to understand the specific role of emotions in appeals across cultures.

The issue of individualism/collectivism is central to cross-cultural studies of decision-making and forms a major component of national identity, although opinion is divided as to whether the individualism/collectivism construct plays a dominant or merely contributory role in consumer decision-making (Takano and Osaka, 1999). Takano and Osaka report that proponents of the individualism/collectivism construct have arrayed a number of country difference findings, but others studying similar kinds of decisions have observed no country differences, and recent meta-analyses find no overall pattern of support for this construct's predictions. Similarly, the validity of highly abstract, general measures of cultural knowledge has been questioned on both methodological and conceptual grounds (Peng et al., 1997). Briley et al. (2000) share this view, declaring that cultural knowledge comprises a number of highly specific structures rather than a few monolithic structures, such as an individualist versus collectivist orientation. In terms of developing nation brand strategy, it is therefore clear that appeals to target markets displaying differing levels of individualism/collectivism will need to be framed accordingly. A monolithic nation brand will lack resonance if it is not adapted to fit its varying markets.

Ethnocentrism

According to Usunier and Lee (2005), the concept of ethnocentrism was first introduced in the early twentieth century by Sumner (1906) in order to distinguish between 'ingroups' (those groups with which an individual identifies) and 'outgroups' (those regarded as antithetical to the group). Keillor and Hult (1999) describe an ethnocentric tendency as one in which individuals, or societies, make cultural evaluations and attributions using their own cultural perspectives as the baseline criteria. Ethnocentrism is included in Keillor and Hult's national identity framework as a means of accounting for the importance placed on maintaining culturally centred values and behaviours. The relevance of ethnocentrism in economic terms is evident, in view of the globalisation of the world economy and the increasing competition that now exists in the provision of most products and services. Ethnocentrism may be treated as a potentially useful means of segmenting markets. For example, appeals to highly ethnocentric consumers will highlight the country-of-origin of domestic products in order to attempt to achieve favourable attitudes and behaviours towards those products as opposed to imported goods. An understanding of the baseline criteria cultural perspectives of ethnocentric consumers referred to earlier by Keillor and Hult may therefore be considered as a useful input to the design of nation branding strategy.

Language

It is important for policy makers to develop a heightened awareness of the importance of language when framing nation branding communications. The role and impact of language as a signifier of a brand's country-of-origin may be considerable. Furthermore, within any one language there exists a range of linguistic tones or registers which are used every day in social situations. This represents a rich and diverse range of communicative resources which marketing strategy in general and nation branding in particular could draw upon.

The flexibility and adaptability of language is examined by Macdonald (1997) from the theoretical standpoint of sociolinguistics, which posits that we cannot understand the meaning of any one term or inflection in isolation, and that analysis typically focuses upon linguistic practice, variation and change, for example, changes in accents, 'registers' and 'codes'. According to Macdonald, these practices generate a range of possibilities, of different idioms, with different degrees of overlap and spread, which may be variously drawn upon and realised. The author concludes that who the speakers and hearers are, their social positioning, and the manner of utterance and context becomes crucial. Macdonald's observations on the crucial nature of who the speakers and hearers are, their social positioning and the manner of utterance and context, are of direct relevance to marketing strategy. Although 'segmentation' is not a term used in the sociological approach taken by Macdonald, from a marketing perspective it could be argued that that is the phenomenon she is referring to, in that appropriate discourses must be used in addressing different audiences and stakeholders.

Another important linguistic issue concerns the nature of the relationship between language and reality. The linguist Edward Sapir contends that:

> No two languages are ever sufficiently similar as to be considered as representing the same social reality. The worlds in which different societies live are distinct worlds, not merely the same world with different labels attached.
>
> (1929)

An implication of this linguistic view that 'no two languages . . . represent the same social reality' is that nation branding communications related to cultural issues may need to be written and designed from scratch by professionals who are members of the target market, rather than merely translated.

Literature

Literature may be viewed as a determinant and also a manifestation of national identity. Novels, poetry, plays and other forms of literature can contribute to a sense of national identity and also occasionally act as state-of-the-nation pronouncements. The relevance of this to nation branding lies in the power of literature to establish in an unplanned way a certain image of the nation, which may or may not chime with the desired image of official bodies such as national tourist boards. Literary works such as the magical realism of Colombian writer Gabriel Garcia Marquez, the novels of Peruvian author Mario Vargas Llosa, or the hypnotically compelling stories of Japanese writer Haruki Murakami, all represent a deeper and richer route into a country's culture and psyche than could be obtained via any branding campaign, no matter how creative. The implications for nation branding are twofold. First, literature needs to be supported as part of the nation's cultural strategy. An example of this can be seen in the collaboration between the German Book Office New York, the Goethe Institut offices in New York and Chicago, and the magazine *New Books* in German to provide translation funding for a curated list of German literature. A further example can be seen in Publishing Scotland's Translation Fund, which has funded 15 international publishers to translate Scottish writing into German, Turkish, French, Danish, Italian, Arabic, Serbian, Macedonian, Hungarian and Portuguese (Graham, 2021). Second, a coordinating body needs to be established in order to ensure that when the nation's literary figures make an impact on the world stage, other sectors of the nation benefit from this through coordinated events to boost tourism, branded exports and so on. Without the existence of such a coordinating body, opportunities for synergy will be lost.

Music

Music as a core element of national identity has been underutilised in nation brand strategy. Some countries have been receptive to the potential power of music to communicate the nation's identity in a positive, celebratory way. Scottish folk music, for instance, is distinctive and has undergone fusion with more modern musical styles over the past decade and this represents a potentially powerful influence in the promotion of Scotland's reputation. This has been recognised by some of the relevant organisations which are stakeholders in the branding of Scottish products and services. For example, a trade mission by Scottish companies to the Far East was accompanied by the folk-fusion Scottish band Shooglenifty, whose music combines traditional Scottishness with an openness to innovation and world influences in a way that might serve as a source of inspiration for other Scottish sectors on the global stage. Devine (1999) observes that rock bands such as Deacon Blue, the Proclaimers and Runrig are emphatically Scottish in style but nevertheless able to convey their music to a much wider overseas audience. Runrig have celebrated Gaelic culture in particular and Scottishness in general to a younger generation of Scots increasingly confident in their own national identity. It would be squandering an opportunity not to incorporate the dynamic fusion of tradition and modernity evident in such music into a strategic nation branding strategy. Whether this would fall under the remit of a government-funded agency, or a private sector body or some other entity, is a key issue. Musicians, like other creative people, are generally loathe to be dragooned into any kind of formal structure. The rationale for a sonic branding strategy would need to be clearly articulated (in non-brandspeak) and a light-touch policy used.

Food and drink

Few components of national identity are more expressive of the nation than its food and drink. This is reflected in the proliferation of food and drink-related national promotions that have occurred over recent years. These promotions may be at a national or a regional level. Rockower (2020) has discussed the ability of 'gastrodiplomacy' to communicate culture, raise nation-brand status and enhance soft power. Rethy and Siriwat (2020) have reported on the role of food diplomacy in Cambodia's nation branding, framing food diplomacy as a type of cultural diplomacy which itself is a subset of public diplomacy.

Sport

Sport engenders high levels of passion and can be a significant contributing factor to a sense of national identity. For example, Bradley (1995) cites Spain as a country in which, although there are other important conduits of regional and ethnic identity, football remains symptomatic of the major diversities that exist within society. More than ever before, clubs such as Barcelona, Athletico Bilbao and Real Madrid are the symbols and the focus, as well as the open vehicles for the expression of ethnic, cultural and nationalistic identities and differences within Spanish society.

Whereas in some countries the dominant sport contributing to a sense of national identity is football, in other countries different sports fulfill the same function. In New Zealand, for instance, the All Blacks rugby team is a symbol of national pride. With the advent of professional rugby in the mid-1990s, the New Zealand Rugby Union (NZRU) employed Saatchi and Saatchi in order to identify a constellation of 'brand values' for the All Blacks, the national rugby team. Collectively, as a team, the All Blacks were deemed by Saatchi and Saatchi to represent the values of New Zealand, including values such as excellence, humility, teamwork and tradition (Motion et al., 2003). A similar study investigating the relationship between rugby union and national identity, in the context of England, was conducted by Tuck (2003). Tuck's study found that the English media employed numerous images to describe the exploits of the English national rugby team, evoking particularly strong invented traditions and well-established symbols of traditional Englishness such as bulldog spirit and Anglo-Saxon temperament. Another example of sport's role in identity-building comes from the Caribbean, where during the late 1950s and early 1960s cricket became a powerful expression of Caribbean progress and nationhood with links identified between cricket, black nationalism, Caribbean identity and the anti-colonial struggle (1963).

The hosting of international sports events such as the Olympic Games or the FIFA World Cup (Knott et al., 2017) have been effectively used to favourably publicise and re-image a place on a global scale (Jun and Lee, 2007). It has been suggested that incorporating sports into the nation branding mix is a relatively under-used positioning tool (Rein and Shields, 2007).

Architecture

The use of architecture in the creation of national identity is described by Hess (2000), who describes how the architecture and spatial organisation of Accra, Ghana reflects an identification between architecture and a consciously managed national ideal. In its embrace of architectural modernity and reconceptualisation of the urban environment, Hess suggests that the post-colonialist Ghanaian administration's reconfiguration of colonial architectural objectives has advanced a distinctive notion of the 'nation'. This use of architecture in pursuit of a consciously managed national ideal is examined by Hess in the context of post-colonial identity formation.

Art

The relationship between art and place is often strong and deep. Artists draw inspiration from their environment and in so doing produce work that may contribute to perceptions of place, as for example in John Constable's depictions of rural England or Horatio McCulloch's Scottish Highland landscapes. Art can play a significant role in expressing and shaping the nation brand (Rodner and Kerrigan, 2018) as well as strengthening society and elevating people's souls (Goudie, 2020).

Attitudes and national stereotypes

It is in the area of stereotyping that there is a clear conceptual overlap between the national identity literature on the one hand and the country-of-origin literature on the other. Nations are frequently stereotyped in a negative way. A major objective of developing a nation brand is to counter such potentially damaging national stereotypes.

When used in sociology, the word stereotype means a biased (usually prejudicial) view of a group or class of people, a view that is resistant to change or correction from countervailing evidence (O'Shaughnessy and Jackson, 2000). Nations too have stereotypes, which can be positive, negative or neutral, though the stereotypic attributes associated with a nation need have no carryover effect on a specific product (Elliott and Cameron, 1994). Avraham (2020) has discussed nation branding strategies that can help combat negative stereotypes suffered by destinations, whilst Bauer et al. (2018) have investigated whether stereotype-consistent messaging matters for place brands.

Cultural artefacts can be important determinants of national stereotype perceptions. In an examination of national stereotypes, Higson (1998) states that a nation's stereotype can be built up, planned or unplanned, in many ways. Cultural artefacts such as films, for example, can have a strong effect on how a nation is perceived. Higson explains how, because the domestic market for British films is not large enough to cover costs, films have to be made with the international market in mind and this inevitably has an impact on the ways in which national identities are represented in them. Such films will often resort to stereotyping as a means of readily establishing character and identity. Whether such glib stereotyping has an effect on consumer behaviour or on perceptions of national image is an area of obvious relevance to nation brand development.

The role of museums as a vehicle for the expression of national identity has been studied by McLean and Cooke (2000), who propose that museums, as sites of representation, are important discursive spaces where images of the nation are produced and consumed. Within a museum setting, suggest the authors, the narratives of nation are constructed through the relationship between the collection, interpretation and display of material culture and the interaction of visitors with the spaces of the museum. Anderson (1991) emphasises that the construction of such narratives of nation is not a neutral activity and that museums, and what he terms the museumising imagination, are both profoundly political. The important role played by museums in the projection of national identity therefore requires to be acknowledged in the development of nation branding strategy.

In a marketing context, the relationship between consumer attitudes and national stereotypes is a complex one. Papadopoulos et al. (1990) found that on the one hand, stereotypes about the people of a nation can arise from the association with their products (e.g., Hungarians viewed Japanese as trustworthy and likeable on the basis of their products) or, on the other hand, stereotypes may arise from an image of a people applied to their products (e.g., Hungarians rated Swedish products almost as highly as American products, even though few Swedish products at the time were sold in Hungary). This complexity is acknowledged by O'Shaughnessy and Jackson (2000), who observe that there is an inherent difficulty in having a coherent image of a nation as people edit out or rearrange certain attributes (we do not really connect Swiss chocolate with Swiss banking to be arranged into some coherent overall image of the nation). Nation branding strategy must include a significant investment in ongoing research in order to track which attributes people are editing out or rearranging when forming their country image perceptions.

Public diplomacy and soft power

The concept of *soft power* needs to infuse nation branding strategy. Soft power has been conceptualised as the power of attraction and persuasion as opposed to the intimidatory nature of hard power (Nye, 2003). Recent research has increasingly explored the relationship between nation branding and soft power (Bolin and Miazhevich, 2018; Hart, 2018; Li et al., 2021), with China having considerably intensified its soft power efforts in recent years (Edney et al., 2019). McClory (2021) has proposed a set of guiding principles for soft power and public diplomacy as the world emerges from the Covid-19 pandemic. A critical perspective on the potentially corporatising nature of nation branding and soft power in the context of Poland is provided by Surowiec (2017).

Internally, the relevance of soft power is that nation branding strategy can only succeed if it is voluntarily endorsed and agreed upon by a critical mass of stakeholders (Anholt, 2007). Coordinating bodies need to be established that do not impose obligations onto the nation brand's stakeholders, but which identify potential synergies between the different stakeholders and act as a catalyst to help realise these synergies. Simon (2020) has drawn attention to the need for foreign ministries to show progress on inclusiveness and the way in which they represent their minority populations to global audiences.

Public diplomacy is a practice that governments increasingly turn to in order to bolster the soft power dimension of their nation branding strategy. This involves an interplay between public diplomacy and marketing (Simonin, 2008; Dinnie and Sevin, 2020). In terms of operationalising public diplomacy, Leonard (2002) suggests that the practice comprises three dimensions: news management, strategic communications and relationship building. Spanning these three dimensions, public diplomacy involves governments reaching out to foreign populations (Rugh, 2011). A key way this is done is through the promotion of cultural programmes. It has been argued, for example, that culture is a vital element of the nation brand (Brown, 2005).

ACADEMIC PERSPECTIVE: THE NATION AND ITS BRAND – A DEEPLY CONTESTED RELATIONSHIP

Nadia Kaneva, PhD, Associate Professor, Department of Media, Film and Journalism Studies, University of Denver

In his seminal book, *Nations and Nationalism*, Ernest Gellner challenged the notion that nations and national identities are natural attributes of individuals and of communities. He formulated the problem of nationalism, with some flair, as follows:

A man must have a nationality as he must have a nose and two years; a deficiency in any of these particulars is not inconceivable and does from time to time occur, but only as a result of some disaster, and it is itself a disaster of a kind. All this seems obvious, though, alas, it is not true. But that it should have come to *seem* so very obviously true is indeed an aspect, or perhaps the very core, of the problem of nationalism. Having a nation is not an inherent attribute of humanity, but it has now come to appear as such.

(Gellner, 1983, p. 6)

While Gellner's arguments on the origins of nationalism has been challenged in subsequent decades, his constructivist approach to our understanding nationalism and his claim that, 'nations, like states, are a contingency, and not a universal necessity' (ibid., p. 6) have exerted an immense influence on the sociological study of nations and national identities.

Yet, his insights and their significant implications have been largely ignored by practitioners of nation branding and by much of the professional literature on the subject. A common theme in the marketing and public relations literature on nation branding is that a nation brand is an expression of the nation that aims to align the reality of the nation with its image in the world. This way of formulating the scope of nation branding is predicated on at least two implicit assumptions, which can be described as **originalism** and **essentialism**:

1   Originalism is the assumption that the existence of the nation precedes that of the brand – i.e., that a nation originates first and is only then 'branded'. Put differently, the nation is the original, while the brand is its reflection.
2   Essentialism is the assumption that a nation contains an identifiable 'essence' or 'soul' which can be distilled through marketing research and then faithfully represented to publics whose impressions of the nation must be managed.

These assumptions build upon each other and are grounded in a mode of thinking that refuses to see the constructed and contingent nature of national identities. In the past decade, critical communication and culture scholars have presented both theoretical and empirical arguments to challenge these assumptions (e.g., Aronczyk, 2013; Kaneva, 2018a), though it remains unclear how this critique may have influenced governments and place branding professionals. In what follows, I offer some brief examples in order to highlight the highly contested relationship between a nation and its brand and to illustrate the problematic nature of originalism and essentialism in nation branding.

To address the trouble with originalism, consider the example of post-war Kosovo, a small country that emerged from the former Yugoslavia after a protracted and violent conflict. Kosovo declared itself a sovereign nation in 2008, having never existed as a nation-state before. Among the many challenges it faced were a shattered post-war economy, a population scarred by ethnically motivated violence, and a lack of commonly accepted symbols and narratives of national identity. In this context, Kosovo's government called on nation branding experts – both domestic and international – to help it articulate a post-conflict, post-ethnic national identity, which could be presented to the world and also unite its population (Wählisch and Xharra, 2010; Kaneva, 2018b). Aside from drawing conclusions about the putative success of the various nation branding programs that followed, Kosovo's example illustrates that nation *branding* and nation *building* are not necessarily separate processes, nor do they occur in a neat temporal sequence in which the nation comes first and the brand follows later.

It may seem that Kosovo is a rare and unusual case – an exception to the general principle of original-ism, which may still hold in other cases. However, numerous countries with post-communist, post-colo-nial, post-imperial, or other post-conflict legacies are dealing with similar challenges, albeit to different extents. From post-apartheid South Africa, to post-civil war Peru, to post-invasion Iraq, nation building and nation branding cannot be neatly separated in time and space and they routinely influence and inflect each other, for better or worse.

Next, consider the claim of national essentialism – or the idea that each nation has a 'soul' which can be clearly identified and distilled to a handful of truthful and stable claims. If one follows Gellner's work, this assumption is problematic even on its face, but empirical corroboration sheds additional light. The case of Ukraine – a former Soviet republic, which has engaged in multiple rebranding efforts since the end of the Cold War (Bolin and Ståhlberg, 2015) – provides a helpful illustration. After months of protests and riots, and only days after the annexation of Crimea by Russia in 2014, Ukraine launched a new nation branding platform. Its brand strategy rested on the promotion of 'wholeness' and 'stability' as essential values held by the Ukrainian nation. As I have argued elsewhere, one might read in this an expression of national aspirations or a political stance towards the Russian aggressor. Yet one would be hard pressed to reconcile the alleged 'essence' of the Ukrainian nation with the realities of life on the ground (Kaneva, 2015).

While the Ukrainian example may also seem extreme, the flaws of essentialism in nation branding thought are evident even when nations are not under attack. In fact, many scholars have pointed out that, despite the focus on uncovering the national 'essence', there are many repeat-ing tropes and generic conventions across nation branding campaigns. Tourism and investment-oriented campaigns, for instance, often emphasizing generic 'product features' such as beautiful nature, low labor costs, or friendly locals, because that is what global travelers and corporations are looking to buy (Aronczyk, 2007; Kaneva, 2017). In other words, the narratives and symbols of nation branding often produce ahistorical, generic, and exclusionary versions of 'national identity *lite*' – closer to simulations than to any putative national soul (Kaneva and Popescu, 2011; Kaneva, 2018a).

The main examples presented here focused on countries who engaged in nation branding in the aftermath of major political turmoil. Because of this, they illustrate more vividly the relevance of Gell-ner's point about the contingency of nations for any consideration of nation branding. Yet the constantly contested nature of national identities can be witnessed in every nation and, thus, its complicated rela-tionship with nation branding efforts should not be dismissed.

References

Aronczyk, M. (2007) 'New and improved nations: Branding national identity', in Calhoun, C. and Sen-nett, R. (eds.), *Practicing Culture*, 105–128, New York: Routledge.

Aronczyk, M. (2013) *Branding the Nation: The Global Business of National Identity*, New York: Oxford University Press.

Bolin, G. and Ståhlberg, P. (2015) 'Mediating the nation-state: Agency and the media in nation-branding campaigns', *International Journal of Communication*, 9, 3065–3083.

Gellner, E. (1983) *Nations and Nationalism*, Ithaca, NY: Cornell University Press.

Kaneva, N. (2015) 'Nation branding and commercial nationalism: A critical perspective', in Volcic, Z. and Andrejevic, M. (eds.), *Commercial Nationalism: Selling the Nation and Nationalizing the Sell*, 175–190. New York: Palgrave Macmillan.

Kaneva, N. (2017) 'The branded national imagination and its limits: Insights from the post-socialist experience', *Strategic Review for Southern Africa*, 39 (1), 116–138.

Kaneva, N. (2018a) 'Simulation nations: Nation brands and Baudrillard's theory of media', *European Journal of Cultural Studies*, 21 (5), 631–648.

Kaneva, N. (2018b) 'Neoliberal development and nation branding: Lessons from post-war Kosovo', in, Pamment, J. and Wilkins, K. (eds.), *Communicating National Image Through Development and Diplomacy: The Politics of Foreign Aid*, 73–98. New York: Palgrave Macmillan.

Kaneva, N. and Popescu, D. (2011) 'National identity *lite*: Nation branding in post-communist Romania and Bulgaria', *International Journal of Cultural Studies*, 14 (2), 191–207.

Wählisch, M. and Xharra, B. (2010) *Public Diplomacy of Kosovo: Status Quo, Challenges and Options*, Prishtina: Friedrich-Ebert-Foundation.

PRACTITIONER INSIGHT: NATION BRANDING AND NATIONAL IDENTITY: A PRACTITIONER'S PERSPECTIVE

Dr Natasha Grand, Director, Institute for Identity (INSTID)

Ask anyone, in any part of the globe, what their nation is about, and you are likely to get a stumbled response. On the one hand, we tend to know clearly where we belong, nation-wise. On the other hand, our own view of our nation tends to be a chop-up of clichés, historical figures, events, and stereotypes, seasoned with our take on the current government and general mood of the day. National identity is a fundamental building block of our sense of self. Whole nations, whether old ones like France or Great Britain, or new like Rwanda or Kazakhstan, seem to perpetually ponder and evaluate their essence and aspirations, through rhetoric of politicians and musings of philosophers and trend-setters. National identity has also become a pursuit and a tool of place branders.

If in the 1980s and 1990s, place branding simply communicated tangible assets of any given place (e.g., historical sites or natural resource facilities), today it has to define, augment and communicate its meaning. The rapid development of social consciousness, especially among the younger generations, a heightened global competition for talent and visitors, and a relative levelling and uniformity of work and leisure infrastructure across the world has shifted competitiveness of a place from material objects onto its people, their culture and way of life. Today's hot topics in place branding are 'place making', 'community engagement' and 'ideas leadership' – a realization that a place brand is the outcome of a vibrant and flourishing local community, and people's choice to identify with it, whether by living there, visiting, or supporting its products and causes.

For nations that are well aware of their identity, branding is seemingly a breeze. Finland, for example, a country with 5.5 million residents, with average annual temperatures of less than 6 degrees Celsius, half of the territory practically empty,[1] and six hours of daylight for half a year,[2] attracted over

3.2 million foreign visitors in 2018[3] and consistently generated 14 billion Euro annually from tourism[4] – all from a simple and consistent offer to 'live like a Finn'.

Finland is an exception, however. The identity of the majority of nations and places remains contested or unarticulated, a matter of obvious and natural order of things. It takes informed outsiders to witness and highlight the nation's own uniqueness – and such experts, unwittingly, are place branders.

Defining national identity is surgical work: it requires precision, expertise and confidence. We distill a wealth of evidence: history, geography, folklore, culture – to a few core values that rule how people conduct their lives, see the world, success, love, family, money, honour, beauty. Here is place branding's holy grail: the archetypal personality of the nation: its strengths, character, way of life. From here derive the content, character and tonality of brand communication, the channels and manner of brand promotion and the nation's strategic priorities altogether. Tatarstan, a country of competitive achievers, focused on attracting and holding large-scale sports events and built its tourism offerings around extreme sports. The capital of Belarus, Minsk, a city with an engineering mind, offered grounds to professional conferences and intergovernmental negotiations. A quiet and peaceful Lipetsk region in Russia specialized in unhurried country lifestyle and its offerings; whereas a rebellious and powerful Siberian Irkutsk challenged visitors to epic experiences.

There are nations-achievers and nations-nurturers; nations-magicians and nations-soldiers. National identity is not informed by ethnicity, but rather by the accumulated wisdom of generations about how to live best on their land. Nation branding, conducted humbly and respectfully, is a homage to the ability of humans to find a way of living together in harmony in their particular part of the world, and to the ensuing beautiful diversity of humankind.

CASE: THE THREE GS OF NATION BRAND JAPAN

Nancy Snow, Pax Mundi Professor of Public Diplomacy,
Kyoto University of Foreign Studies

In summer 2013, half a year after Shinzo Abe returned triumphantly to office, I began a research investigation into Japan's nation brand image. I chose the immediate post-3/11 era as a starting point because it encompassed a nature/nurture combination of unavoidable disasters (earthquake/tsunami) with avoidable human error (Tepco's handling of the Fukushima-Daichi nuclear power plant meltdown). It also reignited domestic public citizen action in opposition to nuclear energy and government-industry collusion. Once Abe was reelected in December 2012 and Tokyo 2020 became a reality in September 2013, the lid was off: Japan was globally relevant again. But becoming relevant in the eyes of the world cuts both ways. Abe's 'nomics' led to unprecedented scrutiny and media criticism of public policies and embarrassing events in his administration. A quiver of arrows struck back on ministerial resignations, unpopular sales tax increases, lower consumer confidence, and executive fiats on secrecy and the military. Global campaigns against Japan's whaling and dolphin hunting policies (e.g., documentary film *The Cove*) suggested that Japan's post-3/11 relevance in the world would lead to efforts to align national policies with global standards. But that did not happen.

Japan has a number of demographic challenges that extend from the 1990s into the harsh realities of a global pandemic. These Three G challenges – gender, generation, and globalization – negatively impact the nation brand face of Japan in the world in contrast to the country's overall good image and reputation, e.g., The Soft Power 30 (2021). Abe had pledged to the nation and the world in 2013 that he would create a 'Japan in which women can shine'. The Womenomics' rhetoric promised far too much, that by 2020 women would fill 30% of leadership positions. The pace was so slow that two years later the government revised its goals to 7% women representation as national public servants and 15% for local government officials and private companies. Even with more modest goals, gender equality in Japan declined to its lowest level in 2020 before Covid-19. The World Economic Forum's *Global Gender Gap Report 2020*, released in December 2019, ranked Japan 121st out of 153 countries, a drop of 11 places in one year's time (World Economic Forum, 2019). In 2006, the first year of the index, Japan ranked 80th. Why the wrong way? So much attention has been paid to the empowerment of women in Japanese society, but cultural mores have not kept up. Many Japanese men and women are still not used to the image of a woman CEO or a woman serving in the national legislature. Political leadership is the worst for Japanese women – only one out of ten is female, but this is not a simple patriarchal cause. Women are less attracted to the rough and tumble arena of politics that gets oxygen from controversy and debate. The gender 'problem' for Japan will continue to plague its overall good image as it serves as a conundrum to an otherwise highly developed, extremely literate society of men and women.

Japan displays some unique outliers in generational gaps that make it stick out among its Asia Pacific neighbors. The Generation Gap in Japan is a common topic of concern, but not just in terms of younger Harajuku or *otaku*-loving teenagers versus their conservative elders. A 2004 report, 'A Global Generation Gap', by Pew Research Center's Global Attitudes Project, cited no major generation gaps in the Asian region, except in the outlier Japan, where 84% of older people thought that their culture was superior, compared with only 56% of those under age 30 who held the same view (Pew Research Center, 2004). The same report said that the Asian region had widespread agreement across all age groups about the importance of learning English, a sentiment shared in other regions like Latin America and Western Europe. The lone exception was Japan, where 75% of those ages 65 and older 'completely agreed' that it was important for children to learn English, while only 45% of ages 18–29 'completely agreed'. Today the generation gap intersects with the gender gap: more often than not, younger women in Japan express a more open attitude toward learning English and going abroad for travel or study. This feminine global mindset, what I call a new subnational brand of gender diplomats, can be explained in part due to traditional expectations put on the proverbial salaryman to stick to the home country for promotion from within. The more Japan's leaders emphasize women's empowerment, the more this is awakening women – and not men, to their global potential.

Globalization, or the lack thereof, is an ongoing challenge to Japan; it still has no global media center or global finance city to compete with the UK, US, Singapore, or Hong Kong models. In other measures, Japan stands tall. This is a country whose traditional cultural values have led to success in creating a relatively safe and secure society. Japan's proportional population in jail is one-tenth that of the United States. Japan's liberal democratic political structure, warts and all, is quite stable, though in dire need of more diversity and inclusiveness in ideology and political party representation. There is much for which the country can be proud – its science and innovation prowess, its rich food and service culture. On the weaker side, it is not entrepreneurial and risk-taking enough, both from the level of the individual and at the institutional level. To be even more blunt, it can be a red tape nightmare; just ask any returning foreigner after Japan gradually began to lift its foreign travel ban in September 2020.

Safe and nice Japan plays it safe, and it watched with chagrin in the 1990s and early 2000s as other countries in its neighborhood started to cast their economic and cultural prowess shadow far and wide. Japan's most egregious lag compared to its regional neighbors is in explaining and promoting its values and strengths to international society. Japan is a country where international third-party advisors with greater credibility than government spokespeople can be of enormous value in helping the country with its international communication.

When the World Health Organization (WHO) declared a global pandemic on March 11, 2020, it was nine years to the date since a 9.0 magnitude earthquake – the fifth largest in recorded history – triggered a deadly tsunami and radiation fallout from Fukushima Daiichi Nuclear Power Plant in Tohoku. The new 3/11 in 2020 had devastating consequences for Japan as it did for the world. Within two weeks, the Tokyo Summer Olympics, originally scheduled for July and August 2020, were postponed to the following year.

The first year of the *Reiwa* era ('Beautiful Harmony') coincided with the smooth installation of a new emperor and traveler numbers totaling 31.88 million (just 400,000 international visitors came to Japan in 1964, the year of Tokyo's first Olympics). During the first few months of 2020, the country was still inundated with tourists primarily from the Asia-Pacific region (China, Taiwan, South Korea) with several million foreign visitors per month visiting the country, but by August 2020 the number of international travelers to Japan had plummeted by over 97% compared to the previous year. Given the likelihood of a long recovery to Covid-19, it is doubtful that Japan's nation brand will ever fully depend on the country's inbound tourism economy that became a cornerstone of the Abe administration.

Another global outreach challenge for Japan in the region is that it has lagged with regional place branding competitors, the People's Republic of China and South Korea. China's Confucius Institutes, established in 2004, were expected to increase to 1,500 sites by 2020, but many have closed or not come to fruition. They are receiving pushback from some host countries, including the United States, that are questioning the propaganda nature of these language and culture centers. South Korea, a country of 51 million, has its own Korean-language centers known as King Sejong Institutes. As of 2018, there were 167 King Sejong Institutes in 55 countries, with no ideological pushback like that of the Confucius Institutes. Similarly, The Korea Center in Tokyo is one of 32 Korean Cultural Centers in 27 countries.

The Japan Foundation has fewer overseas offices (25) in 24 countries, not a large footprint for a country of 126 million with the third largest economy. Nation branding efforts improved when Abe came into office in December 2012, after he vowed to improve the image of 'beautiful' Japan in the world. The Ministry of Economy, Trade and Industry (known as METI) launched the Cool Japan Fund in late 2013 and in 2015 the Ministry of Foreign Affairs funded Japan House in three global hub cities: London, São Paulo, and Los Angeles. The purpose of both projects marks a more assertive outreach effort to promote appreciation for all things Japan in art, design, gastronomy, innovation, and technology. The challenge remains in the messaging and storytelling.

One of the ways to elevate Japan in the world is to identify its core strengths. Japan needs to tell a lot more stories about its work with international organizations, both officially from the Prime Minister's Office, but also unofficially at the grassroots. There are many globally active Japanese, and not all are business entrepreneurs. Japan needs to strengthen their ability to market what they do. Too many stories focus on security and economics. Abenomics and changes to Japan's security apparatus are big global media stories, but they can drown out stories about Japan's role in the United Nations (UN) and its multinational diplomacy efforts.

Japan's nation brand story is vibrant, centered in the realm of spiritual and humanistic moral values. Loyalty to commitments, a working will to serve, even at personal sacrifice is quite universal. It is based on a Japanese interpretation of Confucian values. Japanese values espouse social harmony, a public self that is mindful of how one's actions impact others. This has served Japan well during a pandemic. In terms of explaining Japan's global agenda to the world, this country needs improvement. In promoting Japanese products – particularly popular and trendy things, it has a better record.

Japan's main problem is its loss of global translators/synthesizers that can help carry the story of Japan to the rest of the world. Japan lost half of its foreign correspondents during the Lost Decades of the 1990s and 2000s. They were pulled out and moved to other Asian cities where important things seemed to be happening. Japan also sees itself as somewhat apart from Asia, and this is a mistake. It needs to be a global and Asian leader. As R. Taggart Murphy (2014, p. 375) writes in Japan and the Shackles of the Past, 'Japan's original sin lies in its attempts to separate itself from Asia'. The greatest ambassadors for Japan are the Japanese people. But as my NHK friend and special advisor for Japan International Broadcasting Hatsuhisa Takashima once said (2014), 'The greatest weakness of Japan lies in its citizens who do not realize that they are directly linked to global efforts to disseminate information about Japan.' Likewise, Kiyotaka Akasaka, President of the Foreign Press Center of Japan, said that if there are any active domestic discussions, people overseas are unaware of them, thus leading the world to assume that Japan does not have a global voice. He stressed the importance of Japan developing media tools with worldwide influence, together with a system to nurture talented individuals with a global perspective.

References

Murphy, R.T. (2014) *Japan and the Shackles of the Past*, Oxford: Oxford University Press.

Pew Research Center (2004) 'A global generation gap', available at: www.pewresearch.org/global/2004/02/24/a-global-generation-gap/ (accessed 3/1/2021).

The Soft Power 30 (2021) available at: https://softpower30.com/country/japan/?country_years=2019 (accessed 3/1/2021).

Takashima, H. (2014) Personal communication with author.

World Economic Forum (2019) 'Global gender gap report 2020', available at: http://www3.weforum.org/docs/WEF_GGGR_2020.pdf (accessed 3/1/2021).

CASE: FOOD BRAND IRELAND

Una Fitzgibbon, Director of Marketing, Bord Bia

Nation branding is uniquely important and achievable for a small country where moving parts can coordinate and carve out a place in the world.

And while the nation as a brand is a progressive notion from a marketing point of view, in truth all nations are already branded. Mention the country and people often jump to a conclusion based on their experience.

When we narrow nation down to food, the brand – whether that is Britain or Germany, France or Italy – and what that generates in people's minds and hearts is based on preconceived notions of what that nation and its food represents.

In 2010 Ireland's farmers, growers, fishermen and food processors came together to develop a plan for their future. The output of their deliberations focused on what they could sell strategically and over the long term. For the first time stakeholders called for a national brand for food, and drink – and they coined the term 'Food Brand Ireland', to capture that ambitious idea. Bord Bia, the Irish Food Board, was tasked with leading that brand's development.

We started by working to ensure a common stakeholder understanding of what was meant by 'Food Brand Ireland'.

We began with research, listening to our target audiences around the globe, to their needs and aspirations and to understand their perception of Ireland in a current and future food context.

Food Brand Ireland, we knew, would already have a default position in our prospects' minds.

In setting out to create Food Brand Ireland we faced the challenges of:

1   Unravelling any preconceived stereotype unless, of course the stereotype is very positive.
2   Developing a genuine brand based on reality.
3   Setting out a clear roadmap to success – ensuring the brand delivers real value for its stakeholders over the longer term.

1. Unravelling preconceptions

Consumer research in 2010 told us that while our national culinary capability or 'cuisine' was not a perceived strength, the ingredients we produced were. Consumers even went as far as saying that if Ireland did have a renowned cuisine, its closest cuisine in the world would be Japanese sushi. When we asked why they told us 'because Ireland's food is so pure, natural, clean, untainted, unadulterated that I could eat it raw'. The level of emotion displayed by consumers when pointing this strength out to us was palpable.

Our strategic starting point was clearly the essence of what we already have – natural, elemental food. Ireland's green grass, our rain, our Gulf Stream filtered clean air, our vast ocean to the west, our lack of heavy industry and our tradition of agriculture and fishing were the positive attributes that formed a very strong brand equity. This equity came from the nation brand features inherent in Ireland for thousands of years. The essence was a legacy of our geographic location, our long-held economic response through generations of agriculture, farming and fishing and the envy of nations who felt they had lost these traditions. In fact the plea to Ireland to preserve our natural food resources for the future was the single driver behind the emotional response from consumers in research groups at that time.

Uncovering why these renowned attributes that laddered up to natural food were so important to audiences is what would help us to develop an accurate brand positioning that would last for years to come.

And when we examined where food consumption was going and the macro trends at play for consumers over the longer term, two clearly stood out: the first was *health and wellness*, the second *responsible living*. Consumers wanted natural food, as the antidote to what they perceived as the over-industrialisation of food generally, for personal health and wellbeing. In addition, consumers wanted to live and consume responsibly and for them the consumption of natural and increasingly more sustainable food would deliver on this need. And it was clear to us that the emerging area of sustainability would ultimately encapsulate both these trends as the health of the environment would impact the health of people and as the social dimensions of sustainability were to evolve as much as their environmental dimensions into the years ahead.

Our stereotype was epitomised in the Ireland that people already knew:

- An island of green grass fed animals with plentiful rainfall, an island regarded for its excellent high quality and naturally produced food.
- A culture of agriculture and fishing and a growing population of progressive producers.
- A source that had no diluting factors that could impact on the credibility of our natural food – no heavy industry and no history of pollution.
- A country with no great urban–rural divide and with most people in Ireland no more than two generations away from the land.

And so by building on this positive stereotype our food nation brand would be built from our existing culture and traditions and *our strong unwavering image of green*.

Our business customers agreed that sustainability was the single biggest challenge in providing food for their consumers into the future.

In 2010 sustainability was seen as the pragmatic and business-led solution that would contribute to stable business growth. Business customers keen to optimise their investment potential were prioritising their sustainability agenda. As they did so their likely reliance on suppliers to help them would be prioritised too. The unwavering long-term commitment to sustainability was very apparent, and is carried through to this day.

Business customers also agreed that Ireland could uniquely serve this need if we could prove our industry's sustainability credentials.

Research clarified where a Food Brand Ireland might take us – by squaring the circle between our green image and the reality of our green behaviours.

2. Brand reality – the behavioural consequences of positioning

From the beginning brand reality was important for Food Brand Ireland. Our 2010 research pointed to the growing appetite for validating brand truth. This was seen as a particular challenge to nation brands compared to company-owned brands. Brand reality also has a disproportionate influence on target audiences (consumers and business customers) in a food context.

So, early on we defined brand as the *value* consumers and customers put on our products as a result of actual experiences of those products (brand reality) as well as the associations, thoughts and feelings they have about those products (brand reputation). The reality and reputation need to reinforce each other.

Continual reality and reputation reinforcement is essential to Food Brand Ireland's development and ensures a backbone to our authenticity. For us this brand definition also extends our responsibility to audiences to whom we owe our understanding of the actions to change our brand's behaviour as a consequence of their belief in Food Brand Ireland and to credibly shape it into the future.

It was imperative that the brand was credible and a major challenge we faced in Ireland was ensuring there was enough scale among industry to demonstrate that Ireland's food system is collectively sustainable. For this reason we created Origin Green, the groundbreaking national sustainability programme, rooted in evidence and proof, driving positive change across Ireland's food chain.

3. The roadmap in bringing Food Brand Ireland to life

Origin Green would be a programme of measurement and continuous improvement, and the underlying proof of Food Brand Ireland – our ability to produce world class, sustainable food like nowhere else in the world.

With a huge amount of effort, cooperation and coordination there was the potential through Origin Green to demonstrate the sustainability actions of an entire industry over time to credibly brand Ireland as a leading sustainable food and drink producer.

We agreed there were four things to do to be a credible leader in this space:

i   *That every farm and food manufacturer signs up to the sustainability agenda.*
ii   *That we measure what matters.*
iii *That the measurement system is accredited and independently verified (internationally).*
iv   *That performance is based on science, innovation and best practice.*

And so the Origin Green model was built around systems of audit, verification and reporting and was set to work across an entire value chain – farm to fork. Members would sign up to robust and stretching sustainability commitments that are independently measured and verified.

In 2012 a stakeholder and public advocacy marketing campaign (featuring the then 18-year-old Irish actress Saoirse Ronan) was launched to motivate and drive the entire industry to join Origin Green. From 2012 to 2016 stakeholder participation grew from zero to in excess of 90% of exports. From 2017 onwards that participation level was maintained and we worked since 2014 to build the narrative for the Food Brand Ireland proposition underpinned by Origin Green outwards in established and new markets. That proposition serves audiences' needs to be nurtured by nature to thrive, not only now, but for the future.

Our marketing is systemic with thousands of farmers, processors and distribution partners playing an active and working part in Food Brand Ireland. This gives people a comfort that the brand delivers on what the brand is promising.

Our communications for Food Brand Ireland externally by the end of 2020 drove targeted buyer awareness of Origin Green from zero to 67% in existing markets (Europe) and from zero to 37% in new markets (Asia). Propensity to purchase among the same audiences grew from zero to 66% in Europe and zero to 86% in Asia.

By focusing on brand relevance to consumers and customers lives we are successfully marrying the who-we-are with what the world needs now. Nation branding – or source branding for a nation's food in our case – can often be viewed as developing logos with straplines and executing annual promotional campaigns. However, nation branding is a discipline that should be deployed by leaders to aid communication and guide multiple stakeholder impressions and actions. By doing so, the brand extends its relevance beyond the world of marketing and takes its rightful place as an asset of government, utilised on behalf of its nations' citizens and industry, as an instrument of change.

The future

Research is important for the successful evolution of any brand and uniquely we have built a data model to measure the foundations, proofs and benefits of Food Brand Ireland that ladder up to our positioning.

One of the key resonating proofs of Ireland's Beef and Dairy is its grass fed system of production. This resonating reason to believe led to the development of our Grass Fed Standard providing a proven grass fed claim to our customers. A global campaign on the benefits of our verified Grass Fed Standard to our target business audience is in place. This campaign demonstrates the evolution of an Origin Green-backed Food Brand Ireland, allowing us to dial up the key proof points that matter most to customers for their consumers at a given point in time.

Ireland is a small country with a common production system and is a country which is agrifood-centric. Throughout our history agrifood has been an agile sector recognised for its central economic role in our island's prosperity.

Traditionally Ireland was agriculturally dominated until the 1960s when the country moved and shifted to more modern, high-tech and creative industries.

Right now though, agrifood is once again one of our most important economic sectors. It was central to the recovery needed in 2008 after the global banking collapse and is needed for future prosperity through Covid-19 and for a new post-Covid-19 world.

Arguably, driving a food nation brand as part of a broader nation brand agenda can be described as taking a functional approach. Importantly however, we do not take a functional stance of being product-led, shouting about the great functional benefits that our products offer. Instead we use research to establish our function's position in the prospect's mind (grounded in our behaviours) and work to shape our position to meet the needs and expectations of that prospect. In this way we ensure relevance and forge prospect relationships working together in an interdependent world for sustainable and differentiated growth.

Summary

This chapter has reviewed the fundamental features of national identity, showing the relevance of national identity concepts to the emerging field of nation branding. Key issues in national identity include viewing the nation as an 'imagined community', and the notion of 'invented tradition'. The cultural elements of national identity are wide-ranging, encompassing language, literature, food and drink, sport, architecture, and many other dimensions that nation branding strategists need to be aware of so that nation brand development is firmly rooted in the reality and essence of the nation, rather than being merely a creation of advertising, marketing and branding agencies.

Discussion points

1   Identify three countries that integrate support of their cultural sectors into their overall nation branding strategy. What are the common characteristics of such approaches?
2   It has been argued that music could be used more effectively to position nation brands. Give examples of countries that have successfully included their music in some form within their nation branding activities.

Notes

1   Population under ten people per sq km, available at: https://en.wikipedia.org/wiki/Finland.
2   Available at: https://finland.fi/life-society/finlands-weather-and-light/.
3   Available at: www.e-unwto.org/doi/pdf/10.18111/9789284421152, www.e-unwto.org/doi/abs/10.5555/unwtotfb0246191220142018201907.
4   Available at: https://tem.fi/en/finnish-tourism-in-numbers, www.statista.com/statistics/790995/travel-tourism-total-gdp-contribution-finland/.

References

Aaker, J.L. and Williams, P. (1998) 'Empathy versus pride: The influence of emotional appeals across cultures', *Journal of Consumer Research*, 25 (3), 241–273.

Anderson, B. (1991) *Imagined Communities*, London: Verso Books.

Anholt, S. (2007) *Competitive Identity: The New Brand Management for Nations, Cities and Regions*, London: Palgrave Macmillan.

Avraham, E. (2020) 'Nation branding and marketing strategies for combatting tourism crises and stereotypes toward destinations', *Journal of Business Research*, 116, 711–720.

Bauer, B.C., Johnson, C.D. and Singh, N. (2018) 'Place-brand stereotypes: Does stereotype-consistent messaging matter?', *Journal of Product & Brand Management*, 27 (7), 754–767.

Bolin, G. and Miazhevich, G. (2018) 'The soft power of commercialised nationalist symbols: Using media analysis to understand nation branding campaigns', *European Journal of Cultural Studies*, 21 (5), 527–542.

Bond, R., McCrone, D. and Brown, A. (2003) 'National identity and economic development: Reiteration, recapture, reinterpretation and repudiation', *Nations and Nationalism*, 9 (3), 371–391.

Bradley, F. (2005) *International Marketing Strategy*, 5th edn, Harlow: FT Prentice Hall.

Bradley, J.M. (1995) *Ethnic and Religious Identity in Modern Scotland: Culture, Politics and Football*, London: Avebury.

Briley, D.A., Morris, M.W. and Simonson, I. (2000) 'Reasons as carriers of culture: Dynamic versus dispositional models of cultural influence on decision making', *Journal of Consumer Research*, 27 (2), 157–192.

Brown, J. (2005) 'Should the piper be paid? Three schools of thought on culture and foreign policy during the cold war', *Place Branding*, 1 (4), 420–423.

Burgess, S.M. and Harris, M. (1999) 'Social identity in an emerging consumer market: How you do the wash may say a lot about who you think you are', *Advances in Consumer Research*, 26, 170–175.

Burgoyne, C.B. and Routh, D.A. (1999) 'National identity, European identity and the Euro', in Cameron, K. (ed.), *National Identity*, London: Intellect Books.

Cameron, K. (ed.) (1999) *National Identity*, London: Intellect Books.

Devine, T.M. (1999) *The Scottish Nation 1700–2000*, London: Penguin Books.

Dinnie, K. (2002) 'Implications of national identity for marketing strategy', *The Marketing Review*, 2, 285–300.

Dinnie, K. and Sevin, E. (2020) 'The changing nature of nation branding: Implications for public diplomacy', in Snow, N. and Cull, N.J. (eds.), *Routledge Handbook of Public Diplomacy*, 2nd edn, chapter 14, 137–144, New York and London: Routledge.

Edney, K., Rosen, S. and Zhu, Y. (2019) *Soft Power with Chinese Charactersistics: China's Campaign for Hearts and Minds*, New York: Routledge.

Elliott, G.R. and Cameron, R.S. (1994) 'Consumer perceptions of product quality and the country-of-origin effect', *Journal of International Marketing*, 2 (2), 49–62.

Finlay, R.J. (1994) 'Controlling the past: Scottish historiography and Scottish identity in the 19th and 20th centuries', *Scottish Affairs*, 9, Autumn, 127–142.

Goudie, L. (2020) *The Story of Scottish Art*, London: Thames & Hudson.

Gould, M. and Skinner, H. (2007) 'Branding on ambiguity? Place branding without a national identity: Marketing Northern Ireland as a post-conflict society in the USA', *Place Branding and Public Diplomacy*, 3 (1), 100–113.

Graham, H. (2021) 'Scots authors translated into 10 different languages', *The National*, 19 February, 19.

Hall, E.T. (1976) *Beyond Culture*, New York: Anchor Press, Doubleday.

Hart, J. (2018) 'Historicizing the relationship between nation branding and public diplomacy', in Viktorin, C., Gienow-Hecht, J.C.E., Estner, A. and Will, M.K. (eds.) *Nation Branding in Modern History*, New York: Berghahn.

Hess, J.B. (2000) 'Imagining architecture: The structure of nationalism in Accra, Ghana', *Africa Today*, 47 (2), 34–58.

Higson, A. (1998) 'Nationality: National identity and the media', in Briggs, A. and Golbey, P. (eds.), *The Media: An Introduction*, London: Longman.

Hobsbawm, E. and Ranger, T. (eds.) (1983) *The Invention of Tradition*, Cambridge: Cambridge University Press.

James, C.L.R. (1963) *Beyond a Boundary*, London: Stanley Paul.

Jun, J.W. and Lee, H.M. (2007) 'Enhancing global-scale visibility and familiarity: The impact of world baseball classic on participating countries', *Place Branding and Public Diplomacy*, 3 (1), 42–52.

Keillor, B.D. and Hult, G.T.M. (1999) 'A five-country study of national identity: Implications for international marketing research and practice', *International Marketing Review*, 16 (1), 65–82.

King, A. (2000) 'Football fandom and post-national identity in the New Europe', *British Journal of Sociology*, 51, 419–442.

Knott, B.K., Fyall, A. and Jones, I. (2017) 'Sports mega-events and nation branding: Unique characteristics of the 2010 FIFA world cup, South Africa', *International Journal of Contemporary Hospitality Management*, 29 (3), 900–923.

Kubacki, K. and Skinner, H. (2006) 'Poland: Exploring the relationship between national brand and national culture', *Journal of Brand Management*, 13 (4–5), 284–299.

Leonard, M. (2002) *Public Diplomacy*, London: The Foreign Policy Centre.

Li, E.P.H., Min, H.J. and Lee, S. (2021) 'Soft power and nation rebranding: The transformation of Korean national identity through cosmetic surgery tourism', *International Marketing Review*, 38 (1), 141–162.

Lilli, W. and Diehl, M. (1999) 'Measuring national identity', Working Paper, 10, Mannheimer Zentrum für Europäische Sozialforschung, Germany.

Macdonald, S. (1997) *Reimagining Culture: Histories, Identities and the Gaelic Renaissance*, Oxford: Berg Publishers.

McClory, J. (2021) 'Out of the pandemic: Guiding principles for soft power & public diplomacy going forward', *CPD Blog*, available at: https://uscpublicdiplomacy.org/blog/out-pandemic-guiding-principles-soft-power-public-diplomacy-going-forward (accessed 15/6/2021).

McCreadie, R. (1991) 'Scottish identity and the constitution', in Crick, B. (ed.), *National Identities: The Constitution of the United Kingdom*, Oxford: Blackwell.

McLean, F. and Cooke, S. (2000) 'From Oor Wullie to the Queen Mother's Tartan Sash: Representation and identity in the Museum of Scotland', Image into Identity Conference, University of Hull, Hull.

Mead, R. (2005) *International Management: Cross-Cultural Dimensions*, 3rd edn, New York: Blackwell Publishing.

Motion, J., Leitch, S. and Brodie, R.J. (2003) 'Equity in corporate co-branding: The case of adidas and the all blacks', *European Journal of Marketing*, 37 (7–8), 1080–1094.

Muhlbacher, H., Dahringer, L. and Leihs, H. (1999) *International Marketing: A Global Perspective*, 2nd edn, London: Thomson.

Nye, J.S. (2003) 'Propaganda isn't the way: Soft power', *The International Herald Tribune*, 10 January.

O'Shaughnessy, J. and Jackson, N. (2000) 'Treating the nation as a brand: Some neglected issues', *Journal of Macromarketing*, 20 (1), 56–64.

Pant, D.R. (2005) 'A place brand strategy for the Republic of Armenia: "Quality of context" and "sustainability" as competitive advantage', *Place Branding*, 1 (3), 273–282.

Papadopoulos, N., Heslop, L.A. and Beracs, I. (1990) 'National stereotypes and product evaluations in a socialist country', *International Marketing Review*, 7 (1), 32–47.

Parekh, B. (2000) 'Defining British national identity', *The Political Quarterly*, 71 (1), 4–14.

Peng, K., Nisbett, R.E. and Wong, N.Y.C. (1997) 'Validity problems comparing values across cultures and possible solutions', *Psychological Methods*, 2 (4), 329–344.

Pittock, M.G.H. (1999) *Celtic Identity and the British Image*, Manchester: Manchester University Press.

Rein, I. and Shields, B. (2007) 'Place branding sports: Strategies for differentiating emerging, transitional, negatively viewed and newly industrialised nations', *Place Branding and Public Diplomacy*, 3 (1), 73–85.

Rethy, C. and Siriwat, C. (2020) 'Food diplomacy for Cambodia's nation branding', *Khmer Times*, 23 December, available at: www.khmertimeskh.com/50796317/food-diplomacy-for-cambodias-nation-branding/ (accesed 17/7/2021).

Rockower, P. (2020) 'A guide to gastrodiplomacy', in Snow, N. and Cull, N.J. (eds.), *Routledge Handbook of Public Diplomacy*, 2nd edn, chapter 20, 205–212, New York and London: Routledge.

Rodner, V.L. and Kerrigan, F. (2018) 'From modernism to populism – art as a discursive mirror of the nation brand', *European Journal of Marketing*, 52 (3–4), 882–906.

Rodner, V.L., Preece, C. and Chang, Y.C. (2020) 'Country branding through the arts – the role of museums in positioning a nation on the global market', in Eckström, K. (ed.), *Marketization of Museums: Cultural Institutions in the Neoliberal Era*, 170–187, London: Routledge.

Rugh, W.A. (2011) *Preface, the Practice of Public Diplomacy: Confronting Challenges Abroad*, New York: Palgrave Macmillan Series in Global Public Diplomacy.

Sapir, E. (1929) 'The status of linguistics as a science', *Language*, 5 (4), 207–214.

Shulman, S. (2002) 'Challenging the civic/ethnic and West/East dichotomies in the study of nationalism', *Comparative Political Studies*, 35, 554–585.

Simon, N. (2020) 'How U.S. public diplomacy can reflect its public diversity', *CPD Blog, USC Center on Public Diplomacy*, 14 July, available at: https://uscpublicdiplomacy.org/blog/how-us-public-diplomacy-can-reflect-its-public-diversity (accessed 16/7/2021).

Simonin, B.L. (2008) 'Nation branding and public diplomacy: Challenges and opportunities', *The Fletcher Forum of World Affairs*, 32 (3), 19–34.

Smith, A.D. (1991) *National Identity*, London: Penguin Books.

Sumner, G.A. (1906) *Folk Ways*, New York: Ginn Custom Publishing.

Surowiec, P. (2017) *Nation Branding, Public Relations and Soft Power: Corporatising Poland*, New York: Routledge.

Takano, Y. and Osaka, E. (1999) 'An unsupported common view: Comparing Japan and the US on individualism/collectivism', *Asian Journal of Social Psychology*, 2 (3), 311–341.

Thompson, A. (2001) 'Nations, national identities and human agency: Putting people back into nations', *The Sociological Review*, 49, 18–32.

Tolz, V. (1998) 'Forging the nation: National identity and nation building in post-communist Russia', *Europe-Asia Studies*, 50 (6), 993–1022.

Torelli, C.J., Oh, W. and Stoner, J.L. (2021) 'Cultural equity: Knowledge and outcome aspects', *International Marketing Review*, 38 (1), 99–123.

Treanor, P. (1997) 'Structures of nationalism', *Sociological Research Online*, 2 (1), available at: http:www.socresonline.org.uk/socresonline/2/1/8.html (accessed 21/5/2001).

Tuck, J. (2003) 'The men in white', *International Review for the Sociology of Sport*, 38 (2), 177–199.

Usunier, J.-C. and Lee, J.A. (2005) *Marketing Across Cultures*, 4th edn, New York: FT Prentice Hall.

6 From country-of-origin and national identity to nation branding

Key points

- Common constructs in the fields of national identity and country-of-origin include national stereotypes, ethnocentrism, expressions of culture, individualism versus collectivism and the blurring of national identities and countries-of-origin in today's globalised world
- The category flow model of nation branding draws on the country-of-origin and national identity disciplines to present antecedents, properties and consequences of the nation branding construct
- Categories in the model comprise anticipation (stereotypes and personal experience), complexity (uncontrollability, the urban–rural dichotomy and managing diversity), encapsulation (redefinition, branding and zeitgeist), cultural expressiveness (heritage, landscape and the arts) and engagement (inclusiveness, exemplars)

DOI: 10.4324/9781003100249-8

Introduction

Country-of-origin and national identity are two related fields that underpin the concept of nation branding, yet rarely have the two fields been integrated. In this chapter we identify the areas of commonality between country-of-origin and national identity and relate them to the differentiating power of branding that forms the basis of nation brand development. A conceptual framework for nation branding is presented in the form of the category flow model, drawing upon key issues identified in the twin fields of country-of-origin and national identity. In this chapter, the first case discusses *essential* COSTA RICA as a place brand success story. The second case examines the intersection of the arts and politics in Venezuela's nation branding. Heather Skinner's academic perspective reflects on the role of culture and national identity in nation branding, whilst the practitioner insight by Malcom Allan focuses on aligning the practice of country branding with climate emergency mitigation.

National identity and country-of-origin: Areas of commonality

The national identity literature has rarely been drawn upon by country-of-origin researchers. This is surprising, in that many of the determinants of country-of-origin image perceptions are grounded in the cultural, social and political contexts that constitute national identity. Existing country-of-origin research has largely focused upon the effects of 'Made in' labels on consumer decision-making, without seeking to examine the cultural dimensions of national identity which contribute to country image. Papadopoulos and Heslop (2002) point out that the vast majority of product-country image studies have asked respondents to assess the *products* of various *countries*, equating the results with the countries' images – which, of course, they do not. Country image is determined by a far broader mix of factors than a country's products and services alone.

By taking into consideration determinants of national identity such as the invention of tradition, the role of education and sport, it is possible to provide a richer and more culturally informed basis from which to construct marketing strategies related to the branding of nations. In an increasingly globalised economy, nations which fail to plan the strategic management of their nation brand may struggle to compete with nations which take a more proactive approach to this challenge. Some of the common constructs to be found in the areas of national identity and country-of-origin are shown in Figure 6.1. These constructs play an important role in nation branding, influencing country image formation processes and providing the context within which nation brand strategy is developed.

The intersection of the common constructs between national identity and country-of-origin (Figure 6.1) can be located in the domain of culture. It will be helpful to consider how culture has been defined, in order to clarify how we may consider expressions of culture as a determinant of country image perceptions and as a significant component of a nation brand. Danesi and Perron (1999) define culture as 'a way of life based on a signifying order' passed along from generation to generation. The term *signifying order* referred

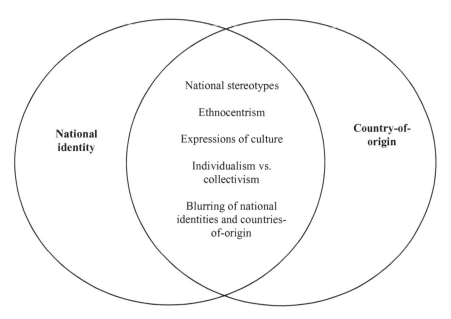

National identity

National stereotypes

Ethnocentrism

Expressions of culture

Individualism vs. collectivism

Blurring of national identities and countries-of-origin

Country-of-origin

Figure 6.1
Common constructs in national identity and country-of-origin

to by Danesi and Perron is the aggregate of the *signs* (words, gestures, visual symbols, etc.), *codes* (language, art, etc.) and *texts* (conversations, compositions, etc.) that a social group creates and uses in order to carry out its daily life routines and to plan its activities for the future. Other definitions of culture which have relevance to national identity and country-of-origin are provided by Goodenough (1971), who states that culture is a set of beliefs or standards, shared by a group of people, which help the individual decide what is, what can be, how to feel, what to do and how to go about doing it. A similar definition of culture is given by Child and Kieser (1977), whose definition is given in anthropological vocabulary but which could also be viewed in terms of marketing segmentation. Child and Kieser define culture as patterns of thought and manners which are widely shared. However, they also emphasise that the boundaries of the social collectivity within which this sharing takes place are problematic and therefore it may make as much sense to refer to a class or regional culture as to a national culture.

From these definitions of culture, it can be seen that many hitherto under-examined aspects of culture have direct relevance to the creation of nation branding strategy, in that a country's image is formed largely by its culture and not solely by consumer perceptions of a country's products or services. This view is largely echoed by Kotler and Gertner (2002) who contend that a country's image results from its geography, history, proclamations, art and music, famous citizens and other features.

In the context of organisations, Handy (1999) states that a culture cannot be precisely defined, for it is something that is perceived, something felt. According to Handy, factors that influence culture and structure for an organisation include history and ownership; size; technology; goals and objectives; the environment; and the people. There are implications for nation branding to be found in the organisational identity (OI) literature.

In their discussion of organisational identity in a diversified organisation, Barney and Stewart (2000) contend that the problem with diversified firms is that the values-based OI must be broad enough to signal convergent goals while clear enough to support a wide variety of knowledge-based means (i.e., core competencies) to achieve those goals. The authors' conclusion is that in order to generate the necessary breadth of values, highly diversified firms may have to create an OI that is defined in terms of moral philosophy – a statement about the right and wrong ways to behave in society and in a company. Managers can then take these moral imperatives and apply them in managing their particular subsidiary business. In terms of nation branding, a nation may be viewed as sharing some of the characteristics of a highly diversified organisation requiring a breadth of values as defined by Barney and Stewart.

Branding's differentiating power

Governments around the world are adopting branding techniques to differentiate their nations on the global stage and also to give themselves a competitive edge over rival countries with which they must compete in both international and domestic markets. Many scholars and practitioners have defined the nature and impact of branding. Keller (2003), for example, states that a brand is a product but one that adds other dimensions that differentiate it in some way from other products designed to satisfy the same need; these differences may be rational and tangible and related to product performance of the brand, or symbolic, emotional and intangible and related to what the brand represents. Aaker and Joachimsthaler (2000) also acknowledge the differentiating impact of branding and assert that the key to most strong brands is brilliant execution that bursts out of the competitive clutter, provides a boost to the brand, and creates a cumulative impact over time.

Kapferer (2004) echoes the notion of branding's cumulative impact over time by positing that along with research and development, a consumer orientation, an efficiency culture, employee involvement and the capacity to change and react quickly, brands are one of the very few strategic assets available to a company that can provide a sustainable competitive advantage. The CBBE perspective argues that a brand is something that resides in the minds of consumers (Kotler and Keller, 2006) and countries are taking an increasingly active approach to managing their nation brands, so that what resides in the minds of consumers is a more favourable set of perceptions than would be the case if governments left national reputation to externally imposed stereotype and cliché.

Nation branding conceptual framework

Based upon some of the key issues in branding, country-of-origin, and national identity discussed in chapters 1–5 and integrating these with the cases, academic perspectives and practitioner insights that appear throughout the chapters of this book, the conceptual framework embodied in the category flow model shown in Figure 6.2 proposes a network of relationships amongst nation branding antecedents, properties and consequences. As can be seen from Figure 6.2, the antecedents of the nation branding construct have been

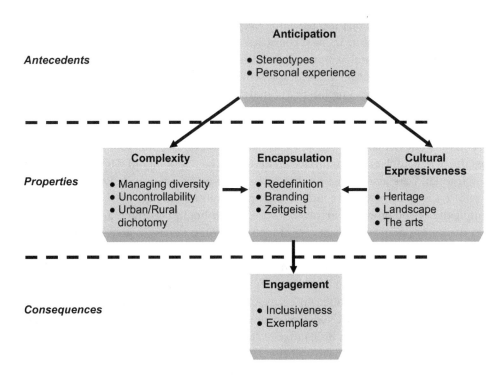

Figure 6.2
The category flow model of nation branding

grouped into the category of *anticipation*; the properties of the nation branding construct include the categories of *complexity*, *encapsulation* and *cultural expressiveness*; whilst the consequences of the construct are presented in the category of *engagement*.

The category flow model suggests a sequential flow from an initial category of anticipation to two further categories, complexity and cultural expressiveness. Complexity and cultural expressiveness comprise those elements of the nation brand construct which require encapsulation through the development of a nation brand strategy in order to achieve engagement, the ultimate stage in this conceptual framework for nation branding.

The category of anticipation represents the initial category in the model. This category derives from the existing consumer perceptions of the nation, prior to any attempts to consciously create a nation brand. These perceptions must be analysed and understood as an initial step in the nation branding process in order to gain an awareness of the stereotypes and personal experience which individuals draw on in forming their perceptions of the nation. The antecedents of anticipation may be based on superficial stereotyping, misinformation or isolated personal experience, none of which may truly reflect the essence of the nation brand. Therefore two further categories have been conceptualised in order to reflect the multifaceted nature of nation branding, lifting the construct above the facile stereotypes that can blight perceptions of a country's image.

The category of complexity acknowledges the uncontrollability of many of the factors that impact upon the nation brand, such as political events, war, natural disasters, the behaviour of prominent citizens, the performance of national sports teams and so on.

This category also contains the related concepts of managing diversity and the urban/rural dichotomy that exists in most countries.

The category of cultural expressiveness encompasses cultural elements such as the arts, language and history as well as landscape, which can play a significant role in the formation of national identity. A nation brand that did not acknowledge and incorporate these cultural elements would be a shallow, overtly commercially driven artifice, unlikely to secure engagement from its stakeholders.

The categories of complexity and cultural expressiveness thus recognise and encompass the rich, complex, and multifaceted nature of the nation brand. These two categories flow into, and are assimilated by, the category of encapsulation. It is within the category of encapsulation that explicit branding techniques emerge. By acknowledging the complexity of the processes involved in the nation brand construct, and by integrating into the nation brand a high degree of cultural expressiveness, marketers can then seek to encapsulate the essence of the nation in a multifaceted yet coherent nation brand. Such encapsulation entails redefinition of the nation brand values in harmony with the prevailing zeitgeist. This demands a managerial skills set and a level of cultural awareness far exceeding that required in conventional product or corporate branding. Once encapsulation has been achieved, from this should flow the final category, engagement. Without engagement from a wide range of stakeholders, little success can be expected for the nation brand. The relationship between encapsulation and engagement suggests a linkage between the effectiveness with which the nation brand redefines and brands itself in the context of the prevailing zeitgeist, and the subsequent level of engagement which may be achieved in support of the nation brand. Manifestations of such engagement may be perceived in the degree of stakeholder inclusiveness achieved by the nation brand, the existence of motivating exemplars, and a reasonable level of transparency in the development and management of the nation brand.

The categories of the model and their constituent elements are discussed in the following sections.

Anticipation: Stereotypes and personal experience

In terms of antecedents of the nation branding construct, the category of anticipation focuses on the expectations that consumers have of a nation, what is hoped for from the nation and what consumers are prepared for. Disconfirming such expectations is a risky strategy. However, if the existing stereotypes of a nation are negative, then the nation brand must be managed in such a way that these stereotypes can evolve in a more positive direction. Therefore an understanding of the concepts underpinning the category of anticipation is required.

The concepts of stereotypes and personal experience constitute the elements of the category of anticipation. The issue of stereotypes is one of the common constructs identified in both the country-of-origin and national identity literatures, whilst personal experience has recently attracted attention in the country-of-origin literature as one of the potential determinants of country image. Stereotypical perceptions tend to be of a negative nature. This can present a problem to nations attempting to enhance their reputations amongst external audiences. Effective nation brand management seeks to counter the potentially

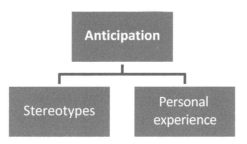

Figure 6.3
Anticipation category

damaging caricatures that national stereotypes can embody. Hackneyed stereotypes are insulting to those on the receiving end, tedious to more well-informed observers, and possibly detrimental to the nation's economic welfare. Therefore it is not surprising that governments are increasingly using branding techniques to overcome such stereotypes. Bolivia, for example, has long suffered from an image of misery and poverty which has obscured the richness of the country's culture and nature. A coordinated nation branding strategy represents a potential means to replace the old negative image with a more positive one (Aguirre and Renjel, 2008).

However, stereotyping is not always negative. The anticipated imagery associated with a nation can very often be positive. In terms of developing the nation brand, the conceptual issue centres upon how to harness the positive anticipated imagery without allowing the nation brand to become pigeon-holed by a narrow range of associations. Nation branding requires an acknowledgement, but then surpassing, of anticipated imagery.

The second concept within the category of anticipation, personal experience, represents an important aspect of the nation branding construct. Personal experience can range from visits by an individual to a particular country to personal interactions with citizens of other nations. Personal experience can also derive from the consumption of products or services from a particular country, which underlines the importance for export promotion agencies to support the international marketing activities of the country's exporters. Switzerland has taken an innovative approach in this regard. In response to research demonstrating that external audiences perceived Switzerland to be weak in terms of one particular attribute – 'Strong influence of citizens on political decisions' – the Swiss Confederation decided to finance Research Chairs on federalism in foreign universities to explain and promote the Swiss federal system (Pasquier, 2008). In this way, foreign students and academics may revise their previously held negative perceptions of one aspect of Switzerland's governance through the personal experience of interacting on a regular basis with academics explaining and promoting the Swiss federal system.

Complexity: Uncontrollability, the urban–rural dichotomy and managing diversity

The complex nature of nation branding presents a major challenge to policy makers wishing to develop a successful nation brand. The complexity of a nation brand is far greater than that of a product or corporate brand because of the multi-aceted character of the nation brand and also the multitude of stakeholders whose concerns and interests must be taken into consideration.

Managing diversity is a critical component of the nation brand construct. With increasing global integration there are now higher levels of migration across national boundaries, leading to far greater heterogeneity in many nations' populations than existed previously. Cultural and social diversity poses an important challenge to the application of branding techniques in developing a consistent message about the nation. Moreover, the diversity of organisations involved in nation branding activities represents a considerable managerial challenge in terms of achieving effective coordination and avoiding wasteful duplication of effort. Finally, the wide range of different audiences for the nation brand poses yet further challenges in managing diversity.

All nations have to contend with a diversity of internal stakeholders as well as a diversity of external audiences. In large, ethnically diverse nations the challenge of managing diversity assumes great proportions. In case of India, for example, it has been suggested that the country has succeeded in presenting a united front despite rivalries between different ethnic groups (Yan, 2008).

The concept of uncontrollability is related to that of managing diversity. The greater the diversity of the nation, the less controllable are its constituent elements and the more challenging it will be to develop a consistent, widely accepted nation brand. Brands in any sector of the economy are subject to the impacts of unexpected environmental factors. However, nations are subject to a far wider range of impacting factors than product or corporate brands, given that the behaviour and actions of every member of the nation's population are potentially a contributing factor to perceptions of the nation brand. Also, sudden events can erupt that can seriously damage a nation's image overnight. There are numerous uncontrollable factors that can impact upon nation branding activities. For example, Egypt's Business Image Unit identified the following factors as beyond its own control: corruption, customs clearance procedures, quality of products, sclerosis of politics and infrastructure (ZAD Group, 2008).

The urban/rural dichotomy refers to the gulf that can exist between urban and rural manifestations of the nation. Managing this dichotomy in such a way that the urban and rural appeal and imagery of the nation complement rather than contradict each other is

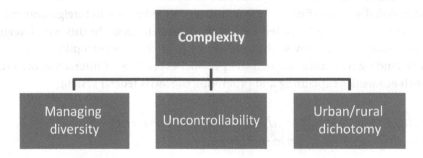

Figure 6.4
Complexity category

clearly a complex task. The presence of a nation branding coordinating body, for example, would help prevent the nation's image being dominated by traditional rural imagery as is often promoted by national tourism organisations, to the detriment of also positioning the nation as a desirable place for companies to invest (for which more suitable imagery would focus on modern infrastructure, cutting edge technology and so on rather than bucolic rural imagery).

A solution to the dilemmas posed here in terms of managing diversity and uncontrollability may be found in the development of a nation brand strategy that adopts and implements the basic marketing technique of segmentation. A crude, monolithic approach to branding the nation would fail because it would lack sensitivity to the specific needs and wants of clearly identified sectors. The bases for market segmentation that may be employed by the nation brand are diverse and limited only by the imagination of the marketers involved in managing the nation brand. Possible segmentation variables that have been identified in the country-of-origin literature include consumer ethnocentrism (Lantz and Loeb, 1996), gender (Heslop and Wall, 1985) and segmentation along cultural rather than geopolitical lines (Duany, 2000). Whichever segmentation variables are selected, it is important that the nation brand frames an appropriate appeal to the selected market. Ignoring this important consideration can lead to ineffective use of resources.

Cultural expressiveness: Heritage, landscape and the arts

Heritage, landscape and the arts are the constituent concepts of the category of cultural expressiveness.

Heritage as a concept encompasses a country's history, traditions and architecture. The challenge in this respect is to develop a modern nation brand, with resonance for contemporary audiences, without throwing away the heritage that has given rise to the current nation. The difficulties experienced by the 'Cool Britannia' campaign illustrate the risks of alienating sections of society by focusing too much on the new and too little on the old.

Landscape is treated in the present analysis as a concept rather than merely a physical presence. This is because of the extremely powerful emotional and symbolic value that is placed upon landscape by many people. This supports Gray's contention (1997) that landscape and geology play a defining role in the formation of national identity.

Figure 6.5
Cultural expressiveness category

However, there is a need to ensure that an exaggerated focus upon traditional rural imagery does not obscure the fact that a country can have tourist-attracting scenery as well as a vibrant modern economy that is also an attractive destination for inward investment.

The third and final concept in the category of cultural expressiveness is the arts. Several elements of the arts play an important role in the creation of national identity, for example, literature, music and other cultural artefacts. Literature and music are important elements of cultural expressiveness. Rodner and Kerrigan (2018) have discussed the relationship between art and the nation brand, whilst artist and art historian Lachlan Goudie has cautioned against unthinking acceptance of established iconography, specifically referring to Edwin Landseer's iconic painting *The Monarch of the Glen*, noting that 'Some today see it as an example of cultural colonialism, a myth imposed by an Englishman that obscures Scotland's authentic national identity' (Goudie, 2020, p. 187).

The individualistic, creative temperament normally associated with those active in the creative arts does not sit easily with structured marketing campaigns. Considerable hostility from writers and musicians can be expected if they perceive themselves as being dragooned into acting as cultural representatives of the nation. Therefore a challenge exists for those involved in developing the nation brand strategy with respect to how to integrate expressions of culture such as literature and music without doing so in a crude and manipulative manner. Japan's nation branding efforts provide an illustration of how a country's cultural assets – in this case, primarily music, movies and food culture – can be leveraged as part of an overall strategy to improve the country's image and reputation (Akutsu, 2008).

It is through organisations such as the British Council, the French Institute, the Goethe Institute and so on that nations incorporate cultural expressiveness into their nation brands. The activities of some such cultural organisations are summarised in Table 6.1.

Every nation has its own unique cultural expressions. In terms of nation brand management, these cultural expressions represent an important differentiator that decision-makers

Table 6.1 Organisations supporting cultural expressiveness

Nation	Arts organisation	Activities
France	French Institute	French language classes; programmes of French films; multimedia libraries; personal appearances by French cultural figures
Germany	Goethe Institute	Promotes the study of German abroad and encourages international cultural exchange; fosters knowledge about Germany by providing information on its culture, society and politics
United Kingdom	British Council	Connects people with learning opportunities and creative ideas from the United Kingdom to build lasting relationships around the world; emphasis on English language teaching and studying in the United Kingdom

need to incorporate into nation brand strategy development. State subsidy of the arts and the fostering of a healthy environment for the creative arts may be seen as a more effective manner of developing a nation brand's cultural expressiveness rather than crude attempts to present artistic figures as brand ambassadors for the nation. Organisations such as the French Institute, Goethe Institut and the British Council play a crucial role in promoting their nation's culture.

Encapsulation: Redefinition, branding and zeitgeist

Encapsulation is a crucial element in the nation brand construct. Given the diversity and multifaceted nature of nations, it is necessary to encapsulate an appropriate set of brand characteristics that can be communicated in a clear and consistent way to the target audience. Without a conscious process of encapsulation, there is a risk that an incoherent babble of contradictory messages could be sent out by the nation brand.

Redefinition of the nation, branding and integration and awareness of zeitgeist are the constituent concepts of the category of encapsulation. The category of encapsulation focuses on the requirement for a nation brand to compress and capture a diverse range of brand values, and at the same time to tap into the prevailing zeitgeist, which is one of the concepts underpinning this category. We have defined a nation brand as *the unique, multidimensional blend of elements that provide the nation with culturally grounded differentiation and relevance for all of its target audiences.* This definition acknowledges the multifaceted nature of the nation brand and the consequent challenge that exists for policy makers seeking to encapsulate this in a consistent, clearly differentiated way.

Redefinition, one of the concepts underpinning the category of encapsulation, refers to the efforts that can be made to actively redefine the ways in which the nation wishes to present itself to internal and external audiences. It focuses on the need for nations to consciously redefine their values and decide on which values they wish to project, both internally and externally. This is a central tenet of nation branding, the contention that if a nation does not actively define itself, then others will define the nation through stereotyping and myths that very often are negative and derogatory (Papadopoulos and Heslop, 2002).

The process of redefinition needs to be made manifest through branding, the second of the concepts underpinning the category of encapsulation. One could argue that the task of branding always concerns encapsulation of values, but when applied to such a rich and

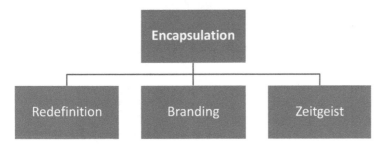

Figure 6.6
Encapsulation category

diverse entity as a nation, this represents a particularly difficult challenge. The identification of a set of positive attributes upon which to build a strong brand is an important first step.

The third concept in the category of encapsulation is zeitgeist, which is closely related to the first concept of redefinition in that the development of the nation brand is an ongoing process that must, as is the case with many product and corporate brands, adapt to global economic and political developments, evolving social trends and changing market conditions. Zeitgeist has been defined by the Concise Oxford Dictionary (1999) as 'the defining spirit or mood of a particular period of history'. Zeitgeist represents an essential concept in the nation brand construct owing to the fact that nation branding does not operate in a vacuum. The social trends and phenomena contributing to zeitgeist should be monitored and taken into consideration if the nation brand is to have resonance and relevance within society at large.

Certain countries may be better positioned than others to exploit the prevailing zeitgeist. For example, the consumer trend towards natural and organic food and drink chimes happily with the country-of-origin connotations possessed by nations which have a competitive advantage in those sectors. In this case, the implication for the development of a nation brand would be to incorporate the brand value of 'naturalness' into the overall nation brand. This would allow the nation brand to leverage the maximum potential from the prevailing zeitgeist in respect of the trend towards natural, pure products.

Engagement: Inclusiveness and exemplars

The concepts in the category of engagement are inclusiveness, exemplars and transparency. Engagement is as a major foundation of nation branding. Without engagement, no basis exists for nation branding and no resonance for the nation brand throughout the wider society beyond the limited confines of political decision-makers and those marketing and branding specialists employed to develop the nation brand.

The concept of inclusiveness refers to the need to establish a level of commitment to the nation brand from its full range of stakeholders. Commitment will not occur if some stakeholders feel excluded from the nation brand. There are, however, difficulties in this respect. It is problematic to try and include every stakeholder in the nation brand, and high levels of hostility can be expected from those who feel that the brand does not reflect their own values.

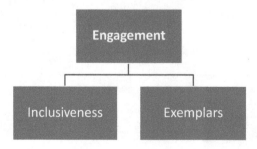

Figure 6.7
Engagement category

A further aspect of inclusiveness exists with regard to the nation's diaspora. Many nations possess large diasporas. Greece and Italy, for example, are two European nations with a large diaspora present in countries as geographically distant as the United States and Australia. Members of diaspora networks are often intensely patriotic, albeit at a distance, and well-disposed to helping the homeland in its economic development. There exists, therefore, considerable reputation-building capacity offered by the existence of ready-made diaspora networks that may be harnessed in strengthening the nation brand. The strategic development of diaspora networks may represent a more effective manner of building strong nation brands rather than glossy television advertising campaigns.

The concept of inclusiveness also needs to be refined in order to distinguish between an ideal state of full inclusiveness, and on the other hand an actual state of programme-specific inclusiveness. This important distinction is discussed in Chapter 8.

The second concept in the category of engagement is exemplars. Exemplars, in the form of examples of best practice or other types of success stories, are crucial to secure engagement for the nation brand in the face of apathy, cynicism or hostility. Any nation branding activity that is funded by public money will find itself under intense scrutiny from the media and therefore it is essential to provide examples of tangible benefits delivered from such branding activity. Also, in order to boost credibility, nations need to provide examples of success and testimonials from relevant sources to bolster the nation brand's credentials. For example, the New France campaign used testimonials from senior executives in top international corporations such as FedEx, Toyota, Xerox, GE and Sony in order to improve perceptions of France as an attractive proposition for inward investment (Favre, 2008).

The issue of transparency is closely related to the concept of inclusiveness. Strikingly divergent views may exist regarding the desirability of transparency in the nation branding process. The issue of transparency therefore represents a key challenge in the development of the nation brand. If governments or other agents involved in nation brand development operate in a transparent manner, openly communicating the aims and objectives of the nation brand strategy, will this achieve buy-in to the nation brand or will it have the opposite effect and unleash a cacophony of competing claims? Lack of transparency could result in few stakeholders buying in to the strategy. On the other hand, a less publicly visible approach to building the nation brand may be taken in order to avoid a storm of dissenting voices from derailing the nation brand strategy before the strategy can deliver its first benefits.

ACADEMIC PERSPECTIVE: THE ROLE OF CULTURE AND NATIONAL IDENTITY IN NATION BRANDING

Heather Skinner

The rise of the nation state in Europe has been traced to the Middle Ages, during which time some nations were formed as purely political entities without reference to any specific culture, while others were formed into geographically bounded entities containing individuals bound by similar strong cultural attachments (Cobban, 1969). These opposing perspectives can be seen in the two main schools of thought that arose in studies of nationhood and nationalism: the French school of thought equating the nation with the country as a political entity, and the German school considering nations almost exclusively from a cultural perspective. More contemporary views perceive the nation state as both a political and cultural entity (for a more in-depth discussion of these issues see Skinner and Kubacki, 2007).

Kotler and Levy's (1969) broadened concept proposed that marketing, and thus in turn branding, could be equally applied for the same purposes and to achieve the same outcomes as commercial products but in any non-business arena where 'producers' offer something of value to 'consumers'. From this perspective marketing could therefore be practiced in politics, education and other public services, campaigns for planned social change, and could apply also to entire nations. Nation branding should therefore seek to emulate the two main purposes of commercial product branding, namely: to create a positive identity in the perceptions of its target audiences, and to be distinctive from other competing nations' offerings (Govers, 2011). Hence nation branding, by creating a positive identity of the place can achieve a positive image and reputation for the place. This can then lead to the nation competing successfully with others to gain and grow economic development, increase exports, and be perceived as an attractive place for people to live, work, visit, and in which to invest (Skinner, 2021).

However, there is an opposing argument that the concepts of marketing and particularly branding should not be applied to places at all (Govers, 2020; Olins, 2002). Indeed, Morgan et al. (2002) claimed that the reason many academics may have shied away from dealing with the topic is because of the complexity of branding places. In order to resolve some of the confusion that remains regarding the application of the terms *marketing* and *branding* to places Skinner (2021, p. 176) has presented 'an original conceptualization derived from an understanding of the various approaches to locating place marketing and place branding within the extant literature' that justifies not only the position that place branding should fall within the practice of place marketing, but also that this marketing should fall within the overall management of a place. In this context, nation branding should be consistent with its overall strategic marketing, and its marketing should also align with the overall ambitions for the nation itself.

It must be recognised that national and cultural identity can change over time, yet some target markets outside the nation can retain outdated perceptions. One of the challenges of nation branding is therefore to communicate these changes to various external target markets. This leads Skinner and Kubacki (2007, p. 310) to 'recognise the importance of culture as knowledge, recognise the interconnectedness between the nation both as a cultural entity and as a political entity, and recognise the importance of cultural indictors in aiding both the internal and external construction and communication of a national identity'.

References

Cobban, A. (1969) *The Nation State and Self-Determination*, London: Fontana.

Govers, R. (2011). 'From place marketing to place branding and back', *Place Branding and Public Diplomacy*, 7 (4), 227–231.

Govers, R. (2020) 'Editorial: Imaginative communities and place branding', *Place Branding and Public Diplomacy*, 16 (1), 1–5.

Kotler, P. and Levy, S.J. (1969) 'Broadening the concept of marketing', *Journal of Marketing*, 33 (1), 10–15.

Morgan, N., Pritchard, A. and Pride, R. (2002) *Destination Branding: Creating the Unique Destination Proposition*, Oxford: Butterworth-Heinemann.

Olins, W. (2002) 'Branding the nation: The historical context', *Journal of Brand Management*, 9 (4–5), 241–248.

Skinner, H. (2021) 'Place branding – the challenges of getting it right: Coping with success and rebuilding from crises', *Tourism and Hospitality*, 2 (1), 173–189.

Skinner, H. and Kubacki, K. (2007). 'Unravelling the complex relationship between nationhood, national and cultural identity, and place branding', *Place Branding and Public Diplomacy*, 3 (4), 305–316.

PRACTITIONER INSIGHT: ALIGNING THE PRACTICE OF COUNTRY BRANDING WITH CLIMATE EMERGENCY MITIGATION

Malcolm Allan, President of Bloom Consulting

I believe that the greatest challenge facing country brand strategists and brand managers is to align their practice with action being taken to mitigate the challenges of the climate emergency. Why? Because the audiences and beneficiaries of our practice are increasingly concerned about the extent to which the places they live, work, study, run business, invest, or visit are building their resilience to meet those challenges, enabling them to remain in place or move to a more desirable one.

A defining example of a country and a country brand strategy that has addressed those challenges is Costa Rica and its country brand strategy, *eessential COSTA RICA*. This is not a recent initiative in response to the growing awareness of the potential impacts of the climate emergency. The central role of the brand strategy has developed over time, building on and combining a number of major policies and programs which have been linked by a central idea, a substantial and comprehensive commitment to sustainability typified by a range of 'on-brand' initiatives designed to increase the resilience of the country.

Thanks to groundbreaking decisions taken by the government over the past century, Costa Rica has become a world leader in social progress, environmental conservation, and sustainability. In 1948, the government officially abolished the country's standing army and allocated all associated funds to the development of robust education and universal healthcare systems. In 1970, the National Park System was created under the National System of Conservation Areas. Today, over 25 percent of land and marine territory is protected within 161 national parks, refuges, and conservation areas. New protected areas are added yearly through both private and public initiatives. What is more, 99 percent of the country's electricity is derived from renewable sources, supplying clean energy to nearly all the population.

Fully aligned with and now driven by its country brand strategy – *essential COSTA RICA* – a series of public policies promoting decarbonization have been developed and contribute to a nationwide plan to achieve zero emissions by 2050, not only for the benefit of the people of Costa Rica, but also making a meaningful contribution to reducing the level of global carbon emissions.

The *essential COSTA RICA* brand strategy has developed as a vehicle to promote and disseminate the nation's values of environmental and economic sustainability through education, health tourism, trade, and foreign direct investment programs, initiatives that now also seek solutions to mitigate the effects of climate change, to build the resilience of the country, an approach to country branding that remains true to the nationwide commitment to create a sustainable society for the benefit of future generations.

In conclusion, following decades of concerted successful efforts to protect the environment, *essential COSTA RICA* is now committed to carrying this forward to address climate emergency mitigation.

CASE: *ESSENTIAL* COSTA RICA – A PLACE BRAND SUCCESS STORY

Daniel Valverde Bagnarello, Costa Rica's Nation Brand Director

Beware of the place brand strategy killer: The short-term mindset

Unlike place marketing initiatives meant to deliver short-term rewards, place brand strategies – if done right – continue to deliver over time. They are also likely to engage a greater spectrum of productive sectors and foster opportunities that are not available through mere country-of-origin positioning strategies.

Ironically, most place branding projects struggle to succeed because they are born, funded, and managed within one government institution alone. All too often, their long-term strategic objectives fail to survive in a world of political agendas planned for the short term.

Evidence indicates that the life expectancy of many place brand strategies is closely related to presidential elections and not necessarily to the performance of the teams implementing them. In such cases, everything invested in the endeavor is lost twice. First, when the projects are either abandoned or shut down at the close of a political administration's term, and second, when the learnings and legacy are not passed on to the next team appointed for the task . . . that is, if there is one.

Several country brand teams are attempting to address this obvious but relentlessly ignored issue. Some will succeed, and some will not. The following paragraphs offer guidance on how Costa Rica's approach to overcoming short-term roadblocks in place brand implementation has been successful. It is the *essential COSTA RICA* nation brand governance structure.

How a little country made a big impact on the world

Most people think of Costa Rica as a land of beautiful beaches and rainforests to be explored on a family holiday. Beyond tourism, however, the country has equally impacted the international market through its agricultural export products like coffee, bananas, and pineapples.

Towards the end of the millennium, it first became clear that sticking to a place marketing effort focused only on tourism and a country-of-origin strategy with only a few agricultural products was shallow and unnecessarily risky for the Costa Rican economy.

There was more to be said and done to close the gap between what the world knew about Costa Rica and what the country was ready to offer. And so, due to a well-planned and executed export diversification strategy implemented in the early 1980s, the export sector expanded, and agricultural products currently represent only 10 percent of the country's offerings.

Through the in-country exportation of shared services operations and medical device manufacturing, the ever-growing exportations sector has grown exponentially and today represents approximately 30 percent of the national GDP.

Putting all your eggs in one basket may work for nation branding

Costa Rica passed a groundbreaking set of environment-protection laws during the 1970s and 1980s, which caught a lot of attention locally and internationally. For the first time in history, the little country stood out in the international arena as a champion of environmental conservation.

In fact, Costa Rica was among the first nations in the world to coin the term 'eco-tourism' in its promotion plans. And soon, it became the destination's primary value proposition. By the 1990s, positive brand image results started to show as the tourism industry blossomed. It was a real accomplishment at a time when the concept of 'sustainability' was a newcomer on the global stage and yet to be embraced by most nations as a value-added asset.

This head start at *going green* developed into one of Costa Rica's main positioning pillars – in addition to its dedication to peace, the abolition of its army, and a strong commitment to human rights and democracy. In fact, the government officially abolished the military in the late 1940s and reallocated its budget into what soon became a robust educational and healthcare system. Today, that combined revenue from the two sectors represents over 17 percent of the country's GDP.

The unified action of embracing environmental conservation and applying its democratic principles to health and education had the effect of skyrocketing Costa Rica's social progress performance, resulting in a balanced socioeconomic structure that was capable of distributing wealth evenly across the population and resulting in a national ethos of happiness and wellbeing. The following generations of highly skilled and environmentally conscious inhabitants are today at the core of the country's holistic value proposition.

The evolution from destination brand to country brand

Counting on its historical assets, in the early 2010s, the government decided to get a coordinated place brand strategy off the ground. A multisectoral team was appointed by the president to carry out the task. What resulted turned out to be an extensive, inclusive, detailed, and thoughtful process. From the start, every individual involved saw clearly how such an endeavor could succeed if built by leveraging the country's most promising 'golden egg': tourism.

Drawing from attributes like harboring close to 5 percent of the world's biodiversity in some 30 national parks in addition to toting a holistic and wellness-oriented culture, Costa Rica successfully leveraged a strong brand reputation. A reputation embodied in the all-encompassing national slogan, *Pura Vida* – meaning 'pure life' in English.

The powerful brand impact from tourism then served as the foundation upon which exports and direct foreign investment would build their narratives. The diversification of value-add markets gave the country an additional competitive advantage, both owned and earned.

What makes the *essential COSTA RICA* strategy different?

In September 2013, the *essential COSTA RICA* place brand strategy was officially launched. By recognizing that brand positioning is, and always will be, a moving target, the place branding team began by setting milestones for brand revision, analysis, and renewal.

Today, despite the fact that no country brand strategy is flawless, Costa Rica's model has proven to be a leader in both resilience and impact over time.

The following core elements are integral to the strategy's development:

1 Avoid the self-image bias

One fundamental component of the *essential COSTA RICA* campaign is to avoid the self-image bias by hiring outside professionals to research and analyze how key foreign populations and markets perceive the country and its assets, and to build upon it. If key investors (people interested in tourism, for example) have heard about the nation's eco-tourism industry but not the products available for exportation, then a campaign is launched to improve international awareness.

2 Address the gray area between place marketing and place branding

Like most successful and sophisticated enterprises, collaboration is critical among teams. Still, it is equally important to identify each group's responsibility and target goals and establish a clearly defined timeline of targets over time. Place branding, by nature, is inclusive of national attributes above and beyond what can be captured by a marketing campaign alone. These include national values, cultural ideologies, and the culmination of multisectoral efforts to advance the country.

3 Decentralize execution and budget

Unlike several countries that allocate their place branding responsibility to one government office, Costa Rica has been highly effective at assigning specific roles and responsibilities across several ministries. Ministry heads are then required to define a departmental strategy with clearly defined goals over time, present regular situation reports, and work in tandem with the country brand lead and the other ministries involved.

4 Private sector engagement

Private sector engagement has proven to be one of *essential COSTA RICA's* most effective assets. Businesses or services wishing to be identified with the *essential COSTA RICA's* brand standards of *Excellence, Sustainability, Innovation*, and *Social Progress* in their marketing must fulfill a rigorous licensing protocol established in the national strategy. The resulting 'army' of highly esteemed brands lends credibility and value to the country's image and attractiveness.

5 Build a governance structure resistant to political transition

Many national brand strategies are defunded when political administrations change hands. To ensure the effectiveness and sustainability of its place brand strategy, *essential COSTA RICA* established a

First Tier Committee with mandated long-term benchmarks that supersede transitional political agendas. Engagement with the private sector, as seen in step 4, further ensures that incoming governments are reluctant to eliminate strategy funding and displease national businesses, sector members, and stakeholders.

Similar to the challenges so many nation brands face, the *essential COSTA RICA* strategy has had its share of trials and tribulations. However, by remaining true to delivering the promise projected by its brand image, the global perception of Costa Rica has improved exponentially over time. A country of unadulterated nature, cultural values, and quality authentic products is what the nation preaches – and delivers.

The *essential COSTA RICA* country brand governance model demonstrates how nation branding is more than a marketing campaign. It is a tool for harnessing a country's international engagement potential, attract talent, and support the sustainability of its businesses and industries into the future.

CASE: NEGOTIATING AN IMAGE FOR THE NATION – EXAMINING THE INTERSECTION OF ARTS AND POLITICS IN THE CASE OF VENEZUELA

Dr Victoria Rodner, University of Edinburgh

As this third edition of *Nation Branding* testifies (Dinnie, 2007, 2015, 2021), the notion of a country projecting a brand image is now well accepted among scholarly circles. As a 'tool for communication between the country and the rest of the world' (Kerrigan et al., 2012, p. 319), nation branding initiatives should weave the country's political, historical, cultural and economic dimensions together in an effort to craft a reputable and marketable package (Olins, 2002).

Although it may be hard to weave a fully cohesive brand image for a nation, there is a drive to project a harmonious 'vision' for the nation through the collaboration of local government and private industry. Some exemplary cases of these multi-stakeholder branding tales include the 100% pure New Zealand campaign (Morgan et al., 2002), the romanticism of tribal qualities in the rebranding of the Middle East (Cooke, 2014) or the wave that put Korean popular culture firmly on the global map (Chen, 2016). In fact, destination marketing through cultural exports, can be an effective way of shaping our 'imaginaries' (Anderson, 2006) of a nation in a rich, seemingly organic and long-lasting way (Hankinson, 2004).

Although some would argue that organic images, that is, cultural expressions such as the visual arts, film, music, gastronomy and literature, should not be prescribed by a country's government (Leisen, 2001), it is clear that government policies have used the creative industries to shift or even 'correct' the perceived image of their nation. In the United Kingdom we saw how fashion, music and art were used in the 'Cool Britannia' campaign of the New Labour Government to refresh the country's image (Oakley, 2004). Similarly, in her review of a newly envisioned cultural identity in the Arab Gulf, Cooke (2014) highlights how government heritage initiatives aimed to strategically 'erase' the harsh realities of these desert nations' past whilst embellishing and modernising a nostalgic tribal quality. The image a nation projects through its cultural output can be a powerful one, whereby 'soft power' (Nye, 2004) can directly impact a country's reputation on the global playing field. Ali-Knight and Robertson (2009) have defined culture as the 'mechanism through which individuals, communities and nations define themselves' (p. 6), so that a nation's cultural image – promoted say through its creative industries to the rest of the world – will also help define how *others* see the country.

Well aware of this, national governments readily provide financial support in developing and sustaining the cultural field – museums, theatres, concert halls, the performing arts – as a means of disseminating a (favourable) cultural identity not only to local but also foreign audiences. Cultural institutions can be instrumental in setting the tone for the nation, as we see in the costly investments made in the Middle East with branded museums such as the Guggenheim and Louvre in Abu-Dhabi (Rodner et al., 2020a). In fact, these activities in the Gulf seek to replicate the 'Guggenheim effect' that branded museums may have on a city, clearly illustrated in the case of the Guggenheim Museum in Bilbao, Spain (Plaza, 2007). However, far from formulaic, investing in museums – including globally branded ones – does not necessarily translate into cultural clout for the nation (Rodner et al., 2020a). Alongside cultural urban development, there is a need to foster arts consumption among locals and visitors, meaning that nation rebranding through the arts should not be viewed as a quick-fix solution to redesigning a nation's image. Without an audience, museums as cultural institutions are little more than grandiose (and costly) mausoleums, which we can see in the case of the mushrooming of museums in China (Rodner and Preece, 2015). Museums – as potential (re)branding tools for a nation – should be culturally relevant, supporting the local art world, enculturating local audiences and creating an environment of arts consumption. These institutional spaces – and the legitimising work they do – carry a lot of weight in the cultural field and – as my own research has explored – in projecting (at times contested) imageries for the nation.

As well as investing in permanent physical structures such as museums, governments can also project a desirable image for the nation through temporary cultural venues, such as mega-art events like the Venice Biennale (Rodner et al., 2011). Alongside international participation at biennials, there exist government-led initiatives that support visual artists and commercial galleries to take part in international art fairs in North America, Western Europe or Asia. The Brazilian Trade and Investment Promotion Agency (APEX), for instance, provides financial support to private galleries and independent artists to participate at international art fairs across the globe. In fact, nation branding through the arts is particularly pertinent in the Global South, as emerging or newly emerged markets invest in culture to help build their reputation, accrue symbolic capital and position themselves on the global playing field (Rodner and Tjabbes, 2020). In line with arts marketing theories (Robertson, 2011), a country's cultural presence on the global art scene will in turn help strengthen its reputation in the arts and beyond. However, what sort of cultural image and how it is projected will directly impact the nation's brand.

As well as having to negotiate a multiplicity of national identities, say for instance in Kerrigan et al.'s (2012) account of the Incredible India campaign or Bouchon's (2014) critique of a 'truly' Malaysian identity, nation branders must also manage the conflicting needs and wants of a variety of stakeholders, who may well not be on the same 'nation-branding' page (Merrilees et al., 2012). Because of a country's differing ethnicities, cultural norms and belief systems, socio-economic distinctions and opposing political agendas, promoting a cohesive brand identity can be challenging.

My own research has examined how warring stakeholders, in the highly polarised context of the Venezuelan art market, projected conflicting images of the nation to local and international audiences (Rodner and Kerrigan, 2018; Rodner et al., 2020b), testifying that branding discourses are not always harmonious. With the arrival of the Socialist government in 1998, we saw in Venezuela how the arts were used as a 'mirror' for the nation to promote new socialist ideals and a newly branded identity for the country, one that centred on populism and collective action. In previous years, the Venezuelan art scene had been heavily influenced by a Modernist narrative, where the nation was branded – through its arts production – as a cutting-edge contemporary cultural centre (Rodner and Kerrigan, 2018). Taken to an extreme, institutional actors working in Venezuela's public and private sectors ended up promoting conflicting brand narratives for the country, effectively splitting the artworld into two halves, one pro-government populist based on socialism, the other anti-government, Western-oriented market economy (Rodner et al., 2020b). Although the socio-political polarisation of Venezuela may appear extreme, it helps us see how fraught nation brand images can in fact hinder a country's local industries and institutions, its distinctive positioning on the global market, and even confuse local and international audiences.

Venezuela's current cultural (and political) image it is projecting to the world is more acrimonious than harmonious, testifying that nation branding through the arts is no simple matter. Building on previous success stories, from the Korean wave (Chen, 2016) to the revitalisation of derelict cities like Bilbao (Plaza, 2007), we have seen how using the arts and culture as a nation branding tool can help stakeholders find common ground, negotiate their differences, and potentially craft a rich, positive and long-lasting reputation for the country.

References

Ali-Knight, J. and Robertson, M. (2009) 'Introduction to arts, culture and leisure', in Yeoman, I., Robertson, M., Ali-Knight, J., Drummond, S. and McMahon-Beattie, U. (eds.), *Festival and Events Management: An International Arts and Culture Perspective*, 3–13, London: Routledge.

Anderson, B. (2006) *Imagined Communities: Reflections on the Origin and Spread of Nationalism*, London: Verso.

Bouchon, F.A.L. (2014) '*Truly Asia* and global city? Branding strategies and contested identities in Kuala Lumpur', *Place Branding and Public Diplomacy*, 10, 6–18.

Chen, S. (2016) 'Cultural technology: A framework for marketing cultural exports – analysis of Hallyu (the Korean wave)', *International Marketing Review*, 33 (1), 25–50.

Cooke, M. (2014) *Tribal Modern: Branding New Nations in the Arab Gulf*, Berkeley, CA: University of California Press.

Dinnie, K. (2007) *Nation Branding: Concepts, Issues, Practice*, London: Routledge.

Dinnie, K. (2015) *Nation Branding: Concepts, Issues, Practice*, London: Routledge.

Dinnie, K. (2021) *Nation Branding: Concepts, Issues, Practice*, London: Routledge.

Goudie, L. (2020) *The Story of Scottish Art*, London: Thames & Hudson.

Hankinson, G. (2004) 'The Brand images of tourism destinations: A study of the saliency of organic images', *Journal of Product & Brand Management*, 13 (1), 6–14.

Kerrigan, F., Shivanandan, J. and Hede, A. (2012) 'Nation branding: A critical appraisal of incredible India', *Journal of Macromarketing*, 32 (3), 319–327.

Leisen, B. (2001) 'Image segmentation: The case of a tourism destination', *Journal of Services Marketing*, 15 (1), 49–58.

Merrilees, B., Miller, D. and Herington, C. (2012) 'Multiple stakeholder and multiple city brand meanings', *European Journal of Marketing*, 46 (7–8), 1032–1047.

Morgan, N., Pritchard, A. and Piggot, R. (2002) 'New Zealand, 100% pure: The creation of a powerful niche destination brand', *Journal of Brand Management*, 9, 335–354.

Nye, J.S. Jr. (2004) *Soft Power: The Means to Success in World Politics*, New York: Public Affairs.

Oakley, K. (2004) 'Not so cool britannia: The role of the creative industries in economic development', *International Journal of Cultural Studies*, 7 (1), 67–77.

Plaza, B. (2007) 'The Bilbao effect', *Museum News*, 86 (5), American Association of Museums.

Robertson, I. (2011) *A New Art from Emerging Markets*, London: Lund Humphries.

Rodner, V.L. and Kerrigan, F. (2018) 'From modernism to populism – art as a discursive mirror of the nation brand', *European Journal of Marketing*, 52 (3–4), 882–906.

Rodner, V.L., Omar, M. and Thomson, E. (2011) 'The brand-wagon: Emerging art markets and the Venice Biennale', *Marketing Intelligence and Planning*, 29 (3), 319–336.

Rodner, V.L. and Preece, C. (2015) 'Tainted museums: "Selling out" cultural institutions', *International Journal of Nonprofit and Voluntary Sector Marketing*, 20, 149–169.

Rodner, V.L., Preece, C. and Chang, Y.C. (2020a) 'Country branding through the arts – the role of museums in positioning a nation on the global market', in Eckström, K. (ed.), *Marketization of Museums: Cultural Institutions in the Neoliberal Era*, 170–187, London: Routledge.

Rodner, V.L., Roulet, T., Kerrigan, F. and vom Lehn, D. (2020b) 'Making space for art: A spatial perspective of disruptive and defensive institutional work in Venezuela's art world', *Academy of Management Journal*, 63 (4), 1054–1081.

Rodner, V.L. and Tjabbes, P. (2020) 'Institutionalising entrepreneurs: The case of Brazil's forum for cultural rights', in Fillis, I. and Telford, N. (eds.), *Handbook of Entrepreneurship and Marketing*, 320–337, Cheltenham: Elgar.

Summary

Although they have to a large extent been treated separately in the past, country-of-origin and national identity share many common constructs. These constructs infuse the concept and practice of nation branding. Whereas country-of-origin research has focused mainly on the effects of the 'Made in' label, national identity examines the essence of nations, their culture and character – those elements that constitute the reality of the nation and which must therefore form the basis of the nation brand. The category flow model offers a conceptual framework for understanding nation branding, based on a set of interlocking categories including anticipation, complexity, encapsulation, cultural expressiveness and engagement.

Discussion points

1   It has been argued that nations are too complex and uncontrollable to be treated as brands. To what extent do you agree?
2   Identify one country that you believe has successfully redefined itself. How did the country achieve its redefinition, and could that success be replicated by other countries?

References

Aaker, D.A. and Joachimsthaler, E. (2000) *Brand Leadership*, New York: Free Press.

Aguirre, X.A. and Renjel, X.S. (2008) 'Using nation branding to move beyond "trickle-down tourism": The case of Bolivia', in Dinnie, K. (ed.), *Nation Branding – Concepts, Issues, Practice*, 1st edn, 165–168, London: Butterworth-Heinemann.

Akutsu, S. (2008) 'The directions and the key elements of branding Japan', in Dinnie, K. (ed.), *Nation Branding – Concepts, Issues, Practice*, 1st edn, 211–219, London: Butterworth-Heinemann.

Barney, J.B. and Stewart, A.C. (2000) 'Organizational identity as moral philosophy: Competitive implications for diversified corporations', in Schultz, M., Hatch, M.J. and Larsen, M.H. (eds.), *The Expressive Organization: Linking Identity, Reputation, and the Corporate* Oxford: Oxford University Press.

Child, J. and Kieser, A. (1977) 'A contrast in British and West German management practices: Are recipes of success culture bound?', paper presented at the Conference on Cross-Cultural Studies on Organisational Functioning, Hawaii.

Concise Oxford Dictionary (1999) *Concise Oxford Dictionary*, 10th edn, Oxford: Oxford University Press.

Danesi, M. and Perron, P. (1999) *Analyzing Cultures: An Introduction & Handbook*, Bloomington: Indiana University Press.

Duany, J. (2000) 'Nation on the move: The construction of cultural identities in Puerto Rico and the diaspora', *American Ethnologist*, 27 (1), 5–26.

Favre, P. (2008) 'The new France – breaking through the perception barrier', in Dinnie, K. (ed.), *Nation Branding – Concepts, Issues, Practice*, 1st edn, 239–242, London: Butterworth-Heinemann.

Goodenough, W.H. (1971) *Culture, Language and Society*, 7, Reading, MA: Addison-Wesley Modular Publications.

Gray, A. (1997) *Why Scots Should Rule Scotland 1997*, Edinburgh: Canongate Books.

Handy, C. (1999) *Understanding Organizations*, London: Penguin Books.

Heslop, L.A. and Wall, M. (1985) 'Differences between men and women in the country of origin product images', Administrative Sciences of Canada Proceedings, Montreal, Canada, 148–158.

Kapferer, J.-N. (2004) *The New Strategic Brand Management: Creating and Sustaining Brand Equity Long Term*, London: Kogan Page.

Keller, K.L. (2003) *Strategic Brand Management: Building, Measuring, and Managing Brand Equity*, 2nd edn, New York: Prentice Hall.

Kotler, P. and Gertner, D. (2002) 'Country as brand, product, and beyond: A place marketing and brand management perspective', *Journal of Brand Management*, 9 (4–5), 249–261.

Kotler, P. and Keller, K.L. (2006) *Marketing Management*, 12th edn, New York: Pearson Prentice Hall.

Lantz, G. and Loeb, S. (1996) 'Country-of-origin and ethnocentrism: An analysis of Canadian and American preferences using social identity theory', *Advances in Consumer Research*, 23, 374–378.

Papadopoulos, N. and Heslop, L. (2002) 'Country equity and country branding: Problems and prospects', *Journal of Brand Management*, 9 (4–5), 294–314.

Pasquier, M. (2008) 'The image of Switzerland: Between clichés and realities', in Dinnie, K. (ed.), *Nation Branding – Concepts, Issues, Practice*, 1st edn, 79–84, London: Butterworth-Heinemann.

Yan, J. (2008) 'Smaller nations enter the global dialogue through nation branding', in Dinnie, K. (ed.), *Nation Branding – Concepts, Issues, Practice*, 1st edn, 170–172, London: Butterworth-Heinemann.

ZAD Group (2008) 'Egypt – an aspiring modern state', in Dinnie, K. (ed.), *Nation Branding – Concepts, Issues, Practice*, 1st edn, 37–41, London: Butterworth-Heinemann.

PART 3

ETHICAL AND PRAGMATIC ISSUES IN NATION BRANDING

7 Ethical issues in nation branding

Key points

- The legitimacy of nation branding is contested
- The identification and selection of nation brand values has an ethical as well as a functional dimension
- Good performance in environmental stewardship represents one means for countries to enhance their reputations through maintaining high ethical standards

Introduction

Nation branding must address a number of ethical issues. Every citizen is a stakeholder in the nation brand and is therefore affected by activities connected to the nation brand. The fact that public funds will almost certainly be allocated to a country's nation branding strategy means that there will be a high level of critical scrutiny of the strategy. Ethical issues surrounding nation branding include the legitimacy of applying brand management techniques to nations rather than to mere product brands; deciding who has the

DOI: 10.4324/9781003100249-10

right to identify and select nation brand values; and ensuring that nation brand strategy contributes to the nation's sustainable development. The first case in this chapter discusses the branding of Scotland. The second case focuses on Bosnia-Herzegovina and the challenge of destination branding in a post-conflict society. The academic perspective by Rosemarijn Hoefte and Wouter Veenendaal considers the challenges of nation branding in Suriname, a multi-ethnic, post-colonial country, whilst Clare Dewhirst's practitioner insight discusses whether nation branding is an ethical practice.

The legitimacy of nation brand management

If nation branding is to become accepted by both governments and citizens, it needs to establish itself as a socially and politically acceptable activity. A key ethical question that must be answered centres on the following issue: if a nation is to be treated as a brand, who has the right to be the nation brand manager? The only individual who can claim the legitimacy of a democratic mandate to fulfil the role of nation brand manager is the elected head of state. However, few politicians possess the requisite business and marketing skills to perform a brand management role. On the other hand, professional marketers and brand managers possess (at least to some extent) the required skill set, but they do not possess the democratic mandate. Warren and Dinnie (2018) investigated the strategies used by place branding professionals to construct legitimacy for their work and for themselves; although situated in the context of city branding, the study findings also have relevance at a nation brand level.

A potential solution to the dilemma of legitimacy can be found in collaborative public–private sector structures and programmes wherein citizens' interests are represented by elected politicians and commercial interests are represented by industry associations and companies. The collaborative model reflects the reality that no single individual can realistically be considered to be the 'nation brand manager'. Instead, the infinitely wide scope of nation branding activity can only adequately be conducted through an inclusive stakeholder approach.

A further ethical imperative to be taken into consideration when debating the legitimacy of nation brand management resides in an issue that affects every citizen, namely, why should any nation tolerate the perpetuation of inaccurate, outdated and offensive stereotyping and caricature? If a nation itself does nothing to counter negative stereotypes then there is nothing to stop the enduring degrading effect that such stereotypes can have. Nations do not have the choice of being branded or not. On the contrary, nations can merely make a simple choice between allowing others to brand the nation – through negative stereotyping – or, alternatively, nations can embrace the challenge of projecting a truer, more accurate and more uplifting image of the nation to the rest of the world.

In recent years critical perspectives on nation branding have multiplied and questioned its legitimacy. The neoliberal, free market logic of branding and selling countries has been challenged by Aronczyk (2013), Fehimović and Ogden (2018), Kaneva (2021) and Varga (2013). Carillo (2018) has drawn attention to the manipulation of public perceptions associated with the case of 'It's Colombia, NOT Columbia'. Browning (2016) questions the ability of nation branding to contribute to poverty alleviation, whilst Kaur (2020) provides a critique of capitalist and nationalist influences on the branding of India. The ethical and practical challenges of branding multi-ethnic countries have been discussed by Hoefte and Veenendaal (2019). These critical perspectives illustrate the highly contested nature of nation branding theory and practice.

Identification and selection of nation brand values

Nation branding strategy needs to be guided by the identification and selection of a set of appropriate brand values. Who has the right to identify such values and then decide which values will be used as foundations of the nation brand strategy? In terms of values, nations do not start with a blank slate. Advertising agencies or branding consultants cannot be given a free rein to conjure up a set of values that do not reflect the cultural norms and expectations that prevail in the nation. The identification of nation brand values needs to be based upon extensive research, both qualitative and quantitative in nature, that takes an inclusive approach to all the nation's stakeholder groups.

Without extensive consultation on the values by which the nation brand should be driven, there may be little buy-in to the positioning and imagery derived from those values. Many countries already have a motto which encapsulates certain values embodied in the nation. This can provide a useful starting point for nations embarking on an exercise in identifying and selecting nation brand values. Some examples of nations and their existing mottos are given in Table 7.1.

Table 7.1 National mottos

Nation	Motto
Columbia	'Liberty and Order'
France	'Liberty, Equality, Fraternity'
Argentina	'In Union and Freedom'
Botswana	'Rain'
Scotland	'No one provokes me with impunity'
Pakistan	'Unity, Discipline, and Faith'
Tunisia	'Order, Liberty, Justice'
Australia	'Advance Australia Fair'
Cuba	'Homeland or Death'
Greece	'Freedom or Death'
Norway	'All for Norway'
Armenia	'One Nation, One Culture'
Senegal	'One People, One Goal, One Faith'

The identification and selection of nation brand values may be facilitated through inviting key stakeholders to surface their vision for the nation brand and then, through the use of the Delphic brand visioning technique, attempting to arrive at a consensus vision (de Chernatony, 2008).

Is 'brand' acceptable?

In some quarters there is a deep-seated hostility to the very idea of treating a nation as a brand. To some extent, the hostility towards the idea of branding a nation may be rooted in an aversion to the word 'brand', and if alternative terminology was used, for example to talk in terms of building a nation's 'reputation' rather than 'brand', then there would perhaps not be the same degree of scepticism towards the concept of nation branding. In recent years there has been a trend towards integrating ethical considerations into brand management, with many companies turning to ethical branding to gain differential advantage as consumers become more ethically conscious (Fan, 2005). Emphasis has also been placed on the power of branding to contribute to progress (Ind, 2003). In the context of nation branding, it has been argued that branding does not equate with the commercialisation of local culture, but with the protection and promotion of diversity (Freire, 2005). This view is not, however, shared by Levinson (2018), who argues that branding has adverse socio-economic effects that exacerbate divisions in society.

Sustainability and nation branding

In recent years concern has grown on a global level regarding the dire threat to the environment from pollution, greenhouse gases and other consequences of industrialisation. The world is now experiencing a climate emergency (UN Environment Programme, 2021). The need for countries to commit to sustainable development is now well established and the Sustainable Development Report 2021, a comprehensive report assessing the progress of all UN Member States towards achieving the United Nations Sustainable Development Goals, has been published (Sachs et al., 2021). When considering the environmental sustainability performance of countries, one should remain vigilant regarding the methodologies that countries use in calculating their own carbon footprints – as Berners-Lee (2020, p. 8) has pointed out,

> a magazine publisher might claim to have measured its carbon footprint, but in doing so looked only at its office and cars while ignoring the much greater emissions caused by the printing house that produces the magazines themselves. And countries do this, too, in their carbon calculations, often omitting to include the footprints of imported goods (from fashion goods to steel and cement) or whole sectors like aviation and shipping.'

There are many online resources available for assessing different countries' performance across a range of sustainability indicators. For example, the Global Carbon Atlas online platform provides up-to-date data on country-level CO_2 emissions from human activity (Global Carbon Atlas, 2021). With the availability of such data, countries can be held accountable for their carbon footprint. This may influence country perceptions with regard to how responsibly or irresponsibly countries are behaving in a period of climate emergency.

Environmental awareness has spread from the domain of conservation activism into the economic, social and political mainstream. For example, Dekhili and Achabou (2015) found that the mention of a country-of-origin with an unfavourable ecological image may negatively influence the product's evaluation. In the same way that corporate social responsibility (CSR) has focused public attention onto the ethical behaviour of commercial organisations, the heightened concern for good environmental stewardship represents an opportunity to spotlight the level of responsibility with which nations are managing their environmental resources. Which of the world's nations are behaving in an environmentally responsible way, and which are failing in their duty to engage in sustainable development?

Through the efforts of various organisations, there now exist various sustainability indexes that allow the ranking of individual countries with regard to the quality of their environmental stewardship. This chapter looks at one of these indexes in some detail – the Environmental Sustainability Index (ESI) – and briefly compares this index with alternative sustainability indexes. How well or how poorly a country performs in such indexes may impact upon that country's nation brand image. High-performing countries can expect to benefit from an enhanced nation brand image whereas poor-performing countries may see their image damaged. If the results of the sustainability indexes are effectively communicated to the general public and widely disseminated through the media, then policy makers may be encouraged to improve their sustainable development credentials.

The World Bank has contributed to the sustainable development agenda, particularly through the publication in 2005 of its report 'Where is the Wealth of Nations' (World Bank, 2005). The report argues that conventional indicators used to guide development decisions – national accounts figures, such as Gross Domestic Product (GDP) – ignore depletion of resources and damage to the environment. The World Bank proposes other measures of total wealth, including natural resources and the value of human skills and capabilities, which show that many of the poorest countries in the world are not on a sustainable path. Although the report's conclusions show a general lack of sustainability in many nations' development path, the World Bank offers some examples of countries that have successfully embraced sustainable development principles. Mauritania, for instance, is praised for enhancing its sustainable development trajectory through better management of its fishery resources, whilst Botswana also distinguishes itself through specific provision in its budget to ensure that mineral revenues are invested rather than consumed through government expenditures – a policy which can both finance future investments and also buffer the government budget from swings in diamond prices. Such achievements can be communicated by Mauritania and Botswana so that their respective nation brands receive due recognition for their commitment to sustainable development.

In a similar vein to the World Bank, the United Nations Environment Programme has also sought to encourage sustainable development by calling upon nations to make well-directed investments in the environment such as terracing agricultural land to slow erosion, which can have a payback rate of three dollars or more for every dollar invested (The Economist, 2005). The economic argument for good environmental stewardship is likely to carry more weight amongst national policy makers than purely ethical appeals. Nation branding can play a role in supporting implementation of the sustainable development agenda by enabling individual countries – whether emerging nations, established economic superpowers, or anywhere in between – to project and benefit from an enhanced positive country image if their national environmental stewardship has been good.

Environmental Sustainability Index

A well known country ranking list for sustainable development is the Environmental Sustainability Index (ESI), produced by a team of environmental experts at Yale and Columbia Universities (Environmental Sustainability Index, 2005). The ESI is an environmental scorecard that was launched at the World Economic Forum (WEF) in January 2005 in Davos, Switzerland. The Executive Summary to the full report explains how the ESI attempts to benchmark the ability of nations to protect the environment over future decades by permitting country-by-country comparison across five fundamental components of sustainability:

- Environmental Systems (air quality, biodiversity, land, water quality, water quantity)
- Reducing Environmental Stresses (reducing air pollution, reducing ecosystem stresses, reducing population growth, reducing waste and consumption pressures, reducing water stress, natural resource management)
- Reducing Human Vulnerability (environmental health, basic human sustenance, reducing environment-related natural disaster vulnerability)
- Social and Institutional Capacity (environmental governance, eco-efficiency, private sector responsiveness, science and technology)
- Global Stewardship (participation in international collaborative efforts, greenhouse gas emissions, reducing transboundary environmental pressures)

A comparison between the ESI and two other widely used sustainability indexes – the Ecological Footprint Index (EFI) and the Environmental Vulnerability Index (EVI) – is given in Table 7.2.

From the ESI analysis, several conclusions emerged relating to the benchmarking of nations' environmental stewardship. For instance, the report notes that whilst no country appears to be on a fully sustainable trajectory, at every level of development, some countries are managing their environmental challenges better than others. Also, measures of governance such as the rigour of regulation and the degree of cooperation with international policy efforts, correlate highly with overall environmental success. A further key conclusion, with significant political implications for the future of environmental sustainability, is that environmental protection need not come at the cost of competitiveness. Professor Daniel C. Esty of Yale University, and creator of the ESI, states that:

Table 7.2 Sustainability indexes

Sustainability index	Source	Scope
Environmental Sustainability Index (ESI)	Yale Center for Environmental Law and Policy, Yale University; Center for International Earth Science Information Network, Columbia University; in collaboration with World Economic Forum, Geneva, Switzerland and Joint Research Centre of the European Commission, Ispra, Italy	The ESI integrates 76 data sets – tracking natural resource endowments, past and present pollution levels, environmental management efforts and a society's capacity to improve its environmental performance – into 21 indicators of environmental sustainability. It aims to enable national governments to take a more data-driven and empirical approach to policymaking.
Ecological Footprint Index (EFI)	Same source as ESI	The EFI converts a country's total resource consumption into the equivalent of hectares of biologically productive land, and then divides this by population to obtain a final value of hectares per capita. High levels of resource consumption are not sustainable long-term; however, countries with small footprints are not necessarily sustainable either if their footprints are small because of a lack of economic activity and pervasive poverty.
Environmental Vulnerability Index (EVI)	South Pacific Applied Geoscience Commission in collaboration with the United Nations Environment Programme and others	The EVI aims to provide a sense of the environmental conditions that predispose a country to internal and external shocks that adversely impact its physical entities (people, buildings, ecosystems), economy and wellbeing. This includes susceptibility to natural hazards, sea-level rise, natural resource depletion, fragile ecosystems and geographical isolation. High environmental vulnerability creates a variety of impediments to sustainable development.

Adapted from Environmental Sustainability Index (2005)

The ESI provides a valuable policy tool, allowing benchmarking of environmental performance country-by-country and issue-by-issue. By highlighting the leaders and laggards, which governments are wary of doing, the ESI creates pressure for improved results.

(Esty, 2005)

This increased pressure for improved results should help drive the sustainable development agenda at a global level. The leaders referred to by Professor Esty should

Table 7.3 Top 20 nations in Environmental Sustainability Index and Nation Brands Index

Top 20 country ranking	Environmental Sustainability Index	Nation Brands Index
1	Finland	Australia
2	Norway	Canada
3	Uruguay	Switzerland
4	Sweden	United Kingdom
5	Iceland	Sweden
6	Canada	Italy
7	Switzerland	Germany
8	Guyana	Netherlands
9	Argentina	France
10	Austria	New Zealand
11	Brazil	United States
12	Gabon	Spain
13	Australia	Ireland
14	New Zealand	Japan
15	Latvia	Brazil
16	Peru	Mexico
17	Paraguay	Egypt
18	Costa Rica	India
19	Croatia	Poland
20	Bolivia	South Korea

Adapted from Environmental Sustainability Index (2005) and GMI Poll (2005)

maximise the positive halo effect that good environmental stewardship may bestow upon their nation brand, whereas the laggards should improve their performance in order to avoid degradation of their nation brand with the associated negative consequences of lower global esteem. In this respect, it is interesting to compare the top 20 countries in the ESI with the top 20 countries in the Anholt-GMI Nation Brands Index (GMI Poll Press Release, 2005). By making this comparison, the potential for the future integration of environmental sustainability into nation branding may be identified.

There is a striking divergence between the top 20 country rankings of the ESI ranking on the one hand and the NBI ranking on the other. Before drawing conclusions from a comparison of the two rankings, it is important to note that whereas the ESI covered a total of 146 countries, the NBI covered only 25 countries, which places a limitation on comparative analysis of the two rankings. However, some pertinent observations can still be made based on the respective top 20 lists from both indexes.

From the perspective of smaller, less developed or emerging nations, it can be seen that a high ranking on the ESI is more achievable than on the NBI. Given that countries such as Bolivia do not currently possess the necessary recognition levels to make an impact on the NBI, such countries may benefit more than most from highlighting their impressive ranking on the ESI. In an era which has seen the rise of the ethical consumer, countries such as Bolivia can aspire to use their ESI ranking to enhance country image perceptions which in turn could generate increased tourism from environmentally conscious consumers, as well as increase willingness to buy Bolivian products on the part of ethical consumers. Good performance in environmental sustainability could contribute to a generalised positive halo effect around the country's nation brand. For less developed and emerging countries which do not have the financial resources to fund expensive image-building advertising campaigns, committing to the sustainable development agenda and communicating this commitment to the rest of the world represents perhaps a unique opportunity to build a strong nation brand.

Remote countries may benefit from committing to environmental sustainability as a means of overcoming their lack of proximity to large markets. Such a policy has been advocated, for example, in the case of Armenia whose products may have more chance of succeeding in international markets if they highlight their environmental credentials (Pant, 2005).

An Environmental Performance Index (EPI) has been created as a complement to the Environmental Sustainability Index (ESI) in order to show whether a country is getting closer to certain defined sustainability benchmarks rather than showing only how a country performs relative to other countries (Socioeconomic Data and Applications Center, 2021). The EPI ranks 180 countries on environmental health and sustainability using 32 performance indicators. One of the key aims of the EPI is to provide a scorecard highlighting good performance in environmental performance that may be useful for countries that wish to improve their own performance in achieving a sustainable future (Environmental Performance Index, 2021). The EPI thus represents a useful tool for nation branding policy makers in formulating future strategy that recognises the critical importance of environmental performance.

Ethical benchmarks in governance and human development

Good performance in governance and human development can also contribute to the formation of a respected nation brand. One available benchmark for assessing quality of governance is the Ibrahim Index of African Governance (IIAG). The IIAG is designed to encourage better governance and evaluates African countries' performance across the following dimensions: security and rule of law; participation, rights and inclusion; foundations for economic opportunity; and human development. In the 2020 version of the index, the top ranked five countries were Mauritius, Cabo Verde, Seychelles, Tunisia and Botswana (Ibrahim Index of African Governance, 2020).

A further benchmark for evaluating the ethical performance of a country is the United Nations Development Programme (UNDP) Human Development Index. The components of the Human Development Index are life expectancy at birth; mean years of schooling; expected years of schooling; and gross national income per capita. In the 2013 iteration of the index the top ranked five countries were Norway, Australia, Switzerland, Netherlands and the United States (United Nations Development Programme, 2014).

The need for countries to earn a good reputation through their actions rather than merely through brand communications has been emphasised by leading figures in the field such as Anholt (2020) and Govers (2018). This reflects the scale of the nation branding challenge – it cannot be outsourced to marketing agencies, it needs to be established upon solid foundations such as the good governance indicators provided by the Ibrahim Index of African Governance referred to here. In terms of human development and inclusiveness, gender equality is another foundation upon which nation branding can be based (Larsen et al., 2021).

ACADEMIC PERSPECTIVE: THE CHALLENGES OF NATION BRANDING IN SURINAME, A MULTI-ETHNIC, POST-COLONIAL COUNTRY

Rosemarijn Hoefte, Professor of the History of Suriname since 1873, University of Amsterdam/senior researcher KITLV/Royal Netherlands Institute of Southeast Asian and Caribbean Studies, Leiden

Wouter Veenendaal, Associate Professor, Institute of Political Science, Leiden University

Have you ever heard of Suriname and can you locate it on a globe? Maybe not, as Suriname is fairly unknown, except in the former colonizer the Netherlands. Since 2000 this small country north of Brazil has made attempts to change this by trying to put itself on the map as a dynamic, multi-ethnic country welcoming trade, foreign investment, and tourists, while mitigating its complex, heterogeneous socio-cultural and political identity. It is our contention that these commercial attempts at nation branding are intertwined with nation building, that is the way in which national identity and belonging are traditionally constructed and communicated (see also Hoefte and Veenendaal, 2019).

Domestically, governments can employ branding as a nation building strategy to stimulate the formation of a nationally shared identity, enhance pride in the nation, and thus promote social cohesion. At the same time, they can use nation branding to suppress domestic criticism and inequalities and undermine political opponents by equating government policies to national identities and commercial interests (Aronczyk, 2007, 2013; Jansen, 2012).

Suriname was built under European domination by enslaved Africans and Asian indentured labourers and their descendants. Exploitation of plantations and natural resources and (forced) labour migration determined the colonial hierarchy and consequently the development of ethnic and class relations. Rootedness, economic contributions, (past) experiences of oppression and neglect, as well as loyalty are arguments to support claims on the nation by different groups. As in many post-colonial societies, nation building in multi-ethnic Suriname is a complex and ongoing process. Yet, when Suriname became independent in 1975, nation building was not high on the political agenda, as it was considered an 'automatic' outcome of independence (Marshall, 2003, p. 267). Various rather short-lived government attempts at nation building produced mixed results at best.

Suriname slowly but surely has adopted an 'accommodationalist' approach to nation building. In return for loyalty to the republic and the law, the state authorizes schools, places of worship, socio-cultural associations, and holidays of the various ethnic groups. As a result, cultural diversity and harmony have become the main source of national identity and pride.

It is this element that features prominently in Suriname's nation branding strategies. With the slogan 'unity in diversity' Suriname presents itself as a harmonious mix of different but seemingly equal cultures. The most visible output is by the Suriname Tourism Foundation, a government–private partnership founded in 1996. It is in charge of tourism promotion and development by creating 'an attractive image' and by 'branding Suriname as a tourist destination' (Suriname, 'A colorful experience', n.d.). It lauds Suriname as 'a large melting pot of different cultures where the roots from their own soil are mixed with those from far away, which have merged to become the harmonious people of Suriname. Indigenous, African, Indian, Chinese, Indonesian and European descendants all live together in peaceful harmony' (Suriname, 'The Green Caribbean', 2012).

However, these commercial messages shroud a clearly discernible ethnic hierarchy in which some groups occupy a more marginal position than others. The Maroons and Native inhabitants in the interior, for example, tend to be viewed as separate peoples that are not fully part of the nation. They are exoticized as 'unique pre-modern tribes' living in the 'unspoiled' Suriname jungle. Within Suriname, such 'pre-modern' groups are classified below the urbanized population groups or when these underprivileged groups move to the capital of Paramaribo they are often ranked as less 'civilized'. Also excluded are recent immigrants from countries such as Haiti, Brazil, and China.

Moreover, the notion of 'unity in diversity' cloaks persistent problems regarding economic development, crime, corruption, or nepotism and clientelism. An ever increasing income inequality also undermines solidarity and loyalty, including within ethnic groups, thus complicating prospects of nation building and branding even further.[1] Summing up, civic and commercial processes – building and branding – cannot be separated when discussing the case of Suriname. The optimistic spirit of the branding campaigns presents a picture that many Surinamese will only partially recognize. In the ongoing and complex discussion of who belongs to the nation, commercial elements have now been added to the mix. In the attempts to attract foreign interest, harmony has become the key word.

References

Aronczyk, M. (2007) 'New and improved nations: Branding national identity', in Calhoun, C. and Sennett, R. (eds.), *Practicing Culture*, 105–128, London: Routledge.

Aronczyk, M. (2013) *Branding the Nation: The Global Business of National Identity*, New York: Oxford University Press.

Hoefte, R. and Veenendaal, W. (2019) 'The challenges of nation-building and nation-branding in multi-ethnic Suriname', *Nationalism and Ethnic Politics*, 25 (2), 173–190.

Jansen, S.C. (2012) 'Redesigning a nation: Welcome to E-stonia, 2001–2008', in Kaneva, N. (ed.), *Branding Post-Communist Nations: Marketizing National Identities in the 'New' Europe*, 79–98, New York: Routledge.

Marshall, E. (2003) *Ontstaan en ontwikkeling van het Surinaams nationalisme: Natievorming als opgave [Origin and Development of Surinamese Nationalism: Nation Building as an Assignment]*. Delft, the Netherlands: Eburon.

Suriname (2012) *'The Green Caribbean': The Official Tourist Destination Guide*, Paramaribo: Tourism Foundation Suriname.

Suriname (n.d.) *'A Colorful Experience . . . Exotic Beyond Words': The Official Tourist Destination Guide*, Paramaribo: Tourism Foundation Suriname.

PRACTITIONER INSIGHT: IS NATION BRANDING AN ETHICAL PRACTICE?

Clare Dewhirst, Founder and Director, City Nation Place

I understand why some early practitioners sought to distance themselves from the phrase 'nation branding' for a while, when international communications agencies were happy to approach national governments with strategies for presenting their country in its best light – regardless of its true colours. Throwing taxpayers' money at a new logo or a PR or advertising campaign without a real understanding of the nation brand is not an ethical practice.

However, as the marketing world has become more sophisticated in its understanding of branding, so too has the understanding of the complex nature of nation brands deepened. Advertising and PR has been subverted by digital media, with social platforms giving citizens an immediate platform for response, and since we launched City Nation Place in 2015, it has been interesting to see how a more ethical practice in place branding, and in nation branding in particular, has developed.

Then, the simple message was that nation branding is not the same as destination marketing. A nation brand is the sum of many parts – reputation, physical assets, people, skills, and ambitions for trade and economic development, including tourism development. The challenge of bringing together all the key stakeholders in a place to understand the brand and collaborate in a strategy to deliver on objectives continues to be the core focus of discussion. A central nation brand strategy enables more effective brand storytelling – and more effective destination marketing to attract visitors, talent, or investment.

Since 2015, there has been a growing recognition of the need to engage citizens in your place brand. If your citizens are not involved in the process of exploring what the nation stands for, and in developing the storytelling approach to communicate that, then they will reject your strategy and doom your marketing efforts from the start. Engaging your citizens in the process should also, of course, ensure that your strategy is geared towards delivering more equitable economic benefits – something we hear most about at the city or regional brand level but also, of course, relevant to nations.

The process of digging into your place brand story to understand how you are perceived by citizens and by the rest of the world forces nations to take a hard look in the mirror. Those countries who understand that this process is essential before any nation brand marketing takes place also understand that values are at the heart of any place brand – values your citizens believe are at the core of their identity, values that are reflected in governance and law making.

The synergistic relationship between what you should do to make a place brand strategy effective, and how that drives better behaviour and better outcomes is increasingly evident in the case studies and discussions amongst the City Nation Place community.

Nations recognise that taking the lead on strategies to protect the environment will deliver real value to their own citizens and the rest of the world and provide a strong platform for building the country's global reputation.

Covid-19 has highlighted which countries have effective and equitable healthcare strategies and good governance and those nations looking to rebuild global reputations will need to address those policies before they can rebuild confidence through marketing.

In general, city brands are more proactive in developing values-based strategies focused on diversity and inclusion. Although there are exceptions to this, nations find the issue of sexuality, religious expression, immigration, and race more politically sensitive, particularly when your brief as a nation branding team is to build global trade relationships with partners who may have different cultural values.

And that is the crux of it really: as more countries recognise the inextricable connection between a nation's values and the successful nation brand, it requires political commitment to 'live' the brand rather than try to sell a country through marketing spin. When the brand's values sit at the heart of policy, then ethical nation branding has succeeded.

CASE: THE 'SCOTLAND IS NOW' MOVEMENT – BRAND SCOTLAND

Cat Leaver, Director Brand Scotland

Background

With a product as iconic as Scotland, you could be excused for thinking that the marketing takes care of itself. But, in 2016/17, research suggested that Scotland was not as well recognised internationally as other nations relative to its size. What is more, Scotland's image was diluted by many narratives and relatively one-dimensional, most commonly recognised for its historic icons and sweeping landscapes, but not also for the wealth of progressive and pioneering innovation, research, talent and education. You could say it had a bit of an identity crisis, one which was a little bit stuck in the past and failed to truly communicate the breadth and rich mix of its people, places and experiences.

With separate agencies focusing on building Scotland's international profile and growth across particular economic pillars, there was a clear opportunity to come together and create a single, bold new narrative that clearly told the world who Scotland was and what it had to offer. And, in an increasingly connected and challenging international landscape, with nations competing for talent, trade, investment, and tourists, the need for this clear and consistent identity was more evident than ever.

Facing into this challenge, in 2018, the Scottish Government, VisitScotland, Scottish Development International (the international arm of our economic agency Scottish Enterprise) and Universities Scotland combined significant proportions of their international marketing spend, expertise and resource to form Brand Scotland and back a unified marketing initiative called 'Scotland is Now'. This aimed to focus on the holistic brand identity of Scotland and support pillar-specific activity, in essence endorsing why Scotland was a choice destination in which to live, work, study, do business and visit.

This new movement focused on a shift from just tactical, performance-based pillar marketing to brand marketing; long-term marketing centred on a clear values proposition which reflects the nation: welcoming, determined, creative, pioneering and generous of spirit. People films were put at the heart of a digital-first strategy, which aimed to provide shareable, authentic insights into Scotland's character and to drive all important advocacy.

Targets:

- **International awareness**

  To raise the profile of Scotland in key international markets.

- **International reputation**

  To improve Scotland's international reputation as a place to live, work, study, visit and do business.

- **Collaboration**

  To build strategic partnerships that create efficiencies and drive greater impact.

- **Consistency**

  To deliver a consistent brand identity and narrative for Scotland behind which others can galvanise.

With a clear new narrative 'Scotland is Now' behind which to rally advocacy, a streamlined digital infrastructure offering a 'gateway' into Scotland and shareable content, campaign activity focused on capturing the zeitgeist and ensuring that when Scotland had something unique or world-leading to share, it was communicated effectively.

Data-led strategy, monitoring and evaluation are core principles of Brand Scotland, seeking to constantly drive return on investment (ROI) and efficiencies for partners. By year two, the programme had delivered record levels of collaboration, some of the best-performing campaign activity to date and:

- Contributed to stability (and slight growth) in biennial AnholtIpsos Nation Brand Index performance, our key metric of brand awareness and international reputation.
- Achieved over 84 million views of Scotland Is Now videos.
- Achieved over 4.5 million brand keyword searches (actual behaviour) in 2018/19 against a target of just 2 million.
- Delivered Year on Year (YoY) growth in web traffic of 28.5% (2019 vs 2018) against a target of 20%.

- Delivered YoY increase in referrals to partner websites of 26% (quality traffic growth) against a target of 20%.
- Delivered more than 1.5 million uses of the #ScotlandIsNow hashtag in the year, equivalent to over 2K average uses per day (double the performance of year 1).

The time to tell the world that 'Scotland Is Open'

By 2019, the biggest challenge facing Scotland's value proposition was Brexit. By mid-February, Brexit uncertainty had become a significant risk to Scottish businesses and communities and it was influencing external perceptions of the nation. Prime Minister Theresa May's deal had twice been rejected by Parliament. And the Article 50 countdown was rapidly running out, with the UK scheduled to leave the EU on 29 March; with or without a deal.

Brand Scotland was inspired to take action to ensure Scotland's message was heard; Scotland values its relationship with Europe, no matter what. The ambition was to reach out to people in Europe who might otherwise be put off from living, working, studying, visiting, or doing business with us; sending the message that Scotland remains an open, welcoming, inclusive and compassionate nation.

The 'Scotland is Open' campaign set out ambitious objectives to achieve 10% campaign recognition amongst audience groups in key markets by mid-April, achieve 30% agreement that Scotland is an open and welcoming nation, and achieve 3% claimed action as a result of seeing the campaign.

This required multiple organisations to rapidly create a pan-European campaign in just 30 working days, with no way of predicting what the Brexit scenario would look like come launch day. But the message was simple, one based on the most authentic of human emotions – love; 'Europe, let's continue our love affair'.

With an integrated strategy combining organic, paid media, display, print and out of home, the campaign exceeded all objectives:

- Campaign recognition – 78 million people reached in just five days, that is 39% of the entire population of key markets, against a target of 10%.
- 70% agreement that Scotland is an open country and 76% agreement that Scotland is a welcoming country, against a target of 30% for both.
- 25 million completed video views with a further 8.8 million campaign engagements and over 90% positive sentiment.
- 82% claimed action as a result of seeing the campaign against a target of just 3%.

On 31 January 2020, the UK finally exited the EU. And though 'Scotland is Open' was crafted for a particular moment in time, it was decided to run a second phase of the campaign.

The result was overwhelming. The impact was even greater than the results in phase 1. In fact, one, single, organic Facebook post of the campaign film generated 2.64 million reach, 15.5k shares, 17.3k reactions, and just under a million video views.

That one organic post can produce this scale of impact, suggests the power of values-based international marketing.

It was a bold statement that unequivocally let EU citizens know how much Scotland values our relationship with them. It demonstrated that we are a country that is open, welcoming, inclusive and compassionate. And across the world, people engaged in huge numbers with our message.

Despite still being in its infancy, the Scotland Is Now movement shows us what is possible when separate organisations align behind a common vision.

Key lessons

- You need to be always on – listening, learning and responding to the world around you is at the heart of effective place branding and marketing.
- Expect the best – promoting a place is a passionate endeavour, expectations are high, and errors are not easily forgiven, so attention to detail and quality are critical.
- Collaboration is key – a shared vision behind which partners, industry, ministers and citizens can rally behind is central.
- Talent is the driving force – in an environment where budgets fluctuate, having the right team around you enables great results.
- Be bold – sometimes we need to be brave together to drive tangible change and impact.

CASE: DESTINATION BRANDING IN A POST-CONFLICT SOCIETY: BOSNIA-HERZEGOVINA

Tom Buncle, Managing Director, Yellow Railroad

Introduction

This is a Cinderella story: about a war-torn 'country' blossoming into an exciting new destination. It is also a story about searching for a needle in a haystack: of finding a way to distinguish a destination from its neighbours, which, to the international visitor's superficial eye, all seem very similar to each other. And it is a story about overcoming adversity: uniting people behind a destination brand, whose differences had recently been the source of the deadliest conflict in Europe since the Second World War.

That 'country' is Bosnia-Herzegovina. The scene is set 12 years after the end of the Bosnian War, in 2007.

Historic and strategic context

Peace does not always mean harmony

The Dayton Peace Accords had been signed in 1995, bringing an end to the 1992–1995 Bosnian War, which followed the breakup of Yugoslavia. The impression given in David Halberstam's *War in a Time of Peace: Bush, Clinton and the Generals*,[2] is that the signing of the Dayton Peace Accords was driven more by President Clinton's desire for re-election in the USA than for a lasting peace in the Balkans. Certainly, whatever the rights or wrongs of this account, it fits the narrative I heard so often in Bosnia-Herzegovina (BiH) that the war was never over; only a peace agreement had been signed. By this, my informants meant the issues that fuelled the conflict had not been sufficiently addressed to secure a unified approach to moving forward. They were still festering under the surface. 'You see', they would say, 'nobody ever won.' Consequently, both sides felt the quarrel to be merely on hold and honour to be unsatisfied. No victor meant no moral authority for the new status quo enshrined in the Dayton Peace Accords. This political impasse fomented the continuation of a certain level of discord, which stymied recovery efforts and frustrated economic progress. Failure to reach closure fostered a deep-seated sense of grievance on all sides. It seemed all that was holding back a return to arms was the horror of those three-and-a-half years, conflict fatigue, and the visceral fear of a resumption of violence.

I paint this picture of the context in which a destination brand was about to be developed for Bosnia-Herzegovina, not to make any political point or comment on who was wrong, right, innocent, or guilty, but to explain the complex background to this challenge: to develop a brand for a 'country' that neither saw itself as united nor described itself as a country.

You say 'country', we say 'state'

Despite Bosnia-Herzegovina competing as a country in recent years in the Eurovision Song Contest, I was corrected in those earlier days whenever I referred to it as a 'country'. It was a combination of two culturally, ethnically, religiously, and politically very different 'entities', the Federation of Bosnia-Herzegovina and Republika Srpska, plus the District of Brcko, which had aligned itself politically with neither side. The nearest acceptable description in English of this conglomeration of geographic-political constructs was the term 'state'. 'State' meant an overarching system of government administration (in certain matters only), whereas 'country' signified a more culturally cohesive geographical area with a shared sense of nationhood. Hence the distinction between these concepts and need for sensitivity and diplomacy when describing the bigger, overarching geographical area for which a destination brand was to be developed – the 'state'.

This was the background to the aid-funded tourism development project we were about to embark on: a constitutional Gordian Knot we were expected to help loosen with destination branding tactics.

Underpinning peace through economic development

There was widespread understanding a lasting peace would depend on growing prosperity. Tourism offered a significant opportunity to kickstart economic development throughout Bosnia-Herzegovina. It transcended both geographical and political boundaries. Of all sectors, tourism required least investment to develop, offered relatively quick returns, and was politically uncontroversial in that it favoured no particular community over another. Nevertheless, the impetus for change came strongly from the private sector. Enthusiasm at a political level was more muted.

The objective was to change Bosnia-Herzegovina's image from war-ravaged country to a destination worth visiting.

Main challenges and solutions

The main challenges in developing a brand for Bosnia-Herzegovina fell into four categories: political-diplomatic, infrastructural, strategic, and commercial, as follows:

- *Political-Diplomatic*

Challenges:

- Developing a destination brand for a 'state' that did not consider itself a 'country', and had no sense of shared nationhood or passionate commitment to projecting itself as a unified geographic entity, was a significant and ever-present challenge.
- Finding core values that could underpin the way in which this place might project itself on the international stage was never going to be easy when many of its senior representatives did not see themselves as belonging to the same place.
- Passion and pride, which are so often fundamental to uniting local stakeholders behind a brand for their home nation, existed politically to some extent at a geographically lower, 'entity' level, but not at the 'state' level. This risked derailing, rather than enhancing, the prospect of unity at a 'state' level, as it was exactly this passion for what each 'entity' now represented that had led to conflict in the first place.
- With no truly functioning 'state', there was no 'national'-level policy support structure for tourism planning or development, behind which a reviving tourism industry eager to progress could coalesce.
- At all times we were walking on linguistic eggshells to ensure the branding baby was not thrown out with the lexical bathwater as a consequence of antagonising political interests. Inadvertently using inappropriate terminology, such as 'nation' instead of 'state', or 'country' rather than 'entity', could torpedo progress.

Solutions:

- An unwavering focus on the economic argument was important. A robust brand would underpin effective marketing, which would lead to tourism growth at 'entity', 'district', and 'state' level, as well as for individual businesses. This would create jobs across the entire 'state'.
- It was important to convince political stakeholders in all administrations that a bigger destination offer (covering what looked like a 'country' to outsiders) would be more persuasive in attracting potential visitors' attention than the smaller, lesser-known 'entities'.
- Unexpectedly but fortuitously, a tourism advert for BiH running internationally on CNN caught the attention of several government ministers from both 'entities' while they were travelling in Europe. Apparently, the way their 'state' was being presented internationally evoked a sense of pride in ministers from both 'entities'. Whether this had any effect in advancing high-level political commitment to a 'state'-level destination brand was never clear.
- Fortunately, political delegates aside, the majority of workshop participants were commercial tourism operators, whose focus was on economic growth, not politics. They were the drivers of change. They endorsed the concept of a 'state' brand. Defining the brand and helping them understand how to communicate it was the priority.

- Critically, the local project teams in both Sarajevo (Federation of Bosnia-Herzegovina) and Banja Luka (Republika Srpska) were highly professional, committed to the objective of a 'state' brand, and expert at maintaining constructive momentum in every debate.
- *Infrastructural*

Challenges:

- Although civic infrastructure was being rebuilt after the devastation of war, BiH's tourism infrastructure was still quite limited. Few foreign investors had yet plucked up the commercial courage to invest in hotels or other tourism developments since the war. Attractions, such as the recently restored Trebevic cable car, which now whisks visitors high above Sarajevo, were still in ruins, having been destroyed during the war. Most investment in tourism infrastructure, therefore, tended to be local or regional, and not always up to the standards required to attract higher-spending international visitors.
- Nevertheless, BiH did attract the 2005 European Whitewater Rafting Championship, adding to its outdoor sporting reputation acquired by hosting the 1984 Winter Olympics.

Solutions:

- This history of sporting events offered a clue to how BiH might position itself in the aftermath of conflict, before mainstream tourism was ready to return: target younger, more adventurous, intrepid travellers, who are less concerned with a destination's security reputation and tend to be the pioneers of a resurgence in travel to countries that have suffered conflict, terrorism or natural disasters.
- Investment confidence would come with time. In the meantime, public relations activity focused on 'normalising' the destination experience in BiH. This meant a concerted effort to shift the international media narrative and associated imagery from a war-torn country to an exciting, scenic visitor destination.
- Initially, targets were younger, resilient, adventurous travellers, as well as markets closer to home, who had a more balanced understanding of the regional post-war political context. A PR campaign focused on specialist outdoor activity publications, through media releases and hosting journalists' visits, so they could see the 'normality' of Bosnian adrenalin activities for themselves.
- *Strategic*

Challenges:

- Communicating the role and value of a destination brand internally to stakeholders is seldom easy in any country. It can feel too whimsical and risky to political decision-makers and funders, who seek quick wins. And it can appear too long-term and unfocused to tourism businesses, who live or die by this month's sales. BiH's political context compounded this communications task.
- Destination differentiation was subtle, almost imperceptible. The Bosnian landscape shares many similarities with its Balkan neighbours – from Slovenia to Serbia, Croatia to Montenegro: scenic mountains, fast-flowing rivers, extensive forests. While there are local variations, regionally the cuisine tends to comprise more similarities than differences. Culturally, the variety of traditions, heritage, architecture, and beliefs amongst different communities is fascinating; but few of these characteristics

are unique to Bosnia-Herzegovina. And, as for wildlife, migrating birds spread throughout most Balkan countries, while most of Bosnia's bears allegedly fled north through Croatia to Slovenia during the war. Even the much-visited religious pilgrimage site of Medjugore received most of its sightseeing tourists, as opposed to religiously motivated visitors, on day trips from the Croatian coast, with the consequence that many believed it to be in Croatia rather than Bosnia-Herzegovina.

- Consequently, for a destination brand detective, there were few immediately obvious clues that dramatically differentiated Bosnia-Herzegovina from its neighbours (and future competitors). Finding a distinctive competitive identity for BiH was going to be more about nuance than in-your-face attributes.

- The ability to differentiate BiH from its relatively similar neighbours (superficially at least) would be the key to its economic transformation through tourism. If this challenge could not be met, and met convincingly, the risk was that BiH would remain mired in the media narrative of a war-ravaged country for years to come.

Solutions:

- Finding a way to make the BiH brand stand out and endow the destination with a truly competitive identity meant exploring the finer distinctions between what otherwise, to an international traveller, might seem universal Balkan traits.

- This meant, first, identifying what made BiH potentially appealing to visitors.

- Second, it meant excavating the nuances that made BiH different, including:

  - Identifying subtle differences between Bosnian, Slovenian, Serbian, and Montenegrin natural environments;

  - Unearthing cultural characteristics that might seem regionally ubiquitous, but which were peculiar to BiH;

  - Exploring how adventure might feel 'more adventurous' in BiH;

  - Uncovering symbols of uniquely Bosnian hospitality, which would distinguish the Bosnian tradition of welcoming strangers from the ubiquitous claims by countries worldwide to be 'friendly and welcoming'.

- Finally, it meant articulating all these elements to devise a brand essence, personality, and positioning statement, whose expression could provide an internationally distinctive competitive identity for BiH. These are summarised in the following BiH Brand Pyramid section.

- *Commercial*

Challenges:

- Commercial relationships between inbound tourism businesses in BiH and outbound tour operators in international markets were still few and far between – a result partly of limited exposure and partly lack of demand, post-war.

Solutions:

- Activity operators, particularly one or two hiking and river-rafting operators, were pioneers. By attending selected international trade shows, they began to inspire confidence amongst international tour operators to package BiH tourism products and put the destination back on the international travellers' map.

Building the brand

Main steps

A rigorous brand development process was pursued, which included:

- **Destination audit:** A picture of BiH's tourism infrastructure was developed through field visits and stakeholder interviews. This included existing tourism products and experiences and former ones, which had been destroyed or fallen into disrepair as a result of the war, but which might stand a chance of being resurrected. These were assessed according to their appeal to domestic and regional visitors and those that might attract international visitors.
- **Stakeholder consultation:** Key stakeholders in both public and private sectors were consulted at 'state' level, 'entity' level (Federation of Bosnia and Herzegovina; Republika Srpska) and 'district' level (Brcko) to establish a unified view of BiH's tourism assets and to secure stakeholder buy-in to the project.
- **Tour operator interviews:** Tour operators were interviewed in several international markets. A picture was built up of BiH's strengths and weaknesses as a tourism destination in the eyes of its main potential markets. This reflected tour operators' own views, as well as, by proxy, those of their previous clients, as cost and the tourism hiatus caused by the war had thwarted the possibility of interviewing recent visitors.
- **Stakeholder workshops:** Workshops were held with key stakeholders from across the 'state': from all levels of government, tourism operators, and academics. The aim was to seek validation on emerging ideas, refine them into a brand hypothesis, and establish consensus on BiH's core brand values. But, perhaps most importantly, it was also to ensure major stakeholders were involved from the outset as participants in developing the brand. This was their home and it was essential they felt committed to the way it would ultimately be projected on the international stage. To develop a brand without their participation would have been unthinkable, discourteous, and doomed to failure.
- **Brand toolkit:** A set of brand guidelines was prepared to explain to BiH stakeholders how to apply the brand in their own marketing communications.

The BiH Brand Pyramid

Using Yellow Railroad's Brand Pyramid model, core elements of the BiH brand were defined. This was a 5-step process, building up the brand from rational benefits to brand essence, as shown in Figures 7.1 and 7.2.

Results

- Consensus was achieved between private and public sectors, and all levels of government throughout the 'state', on BiH's brand strengths.

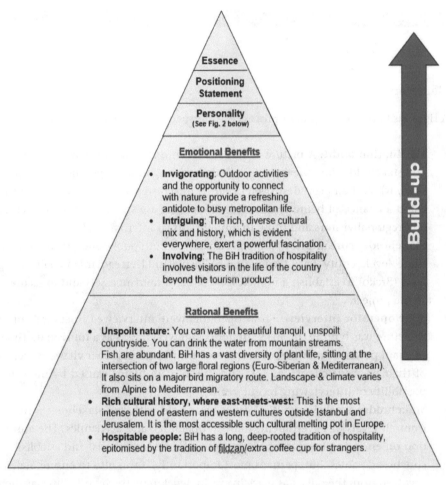

Figure 7.1
Bosnia-Herzegovina Brand Pyramid: Rational & emotional benefits

- Despite their universal presence in the branding arsenal of countries worldwide, distinctive competitive brand strengths were identified for BiH within the following areas:

  - nature
  - culture
  - heritage
  - adventure
  - hospitality

- A clear brand platform was established for the future promotion of BiH, based on external customer perceptions (using tour operators as a proxy for consumers) and internal stakeholder consensus.

- Bosnia-Herzegovina began its long journey back to economic growth, with tourism playing an increasing role in attracting foreign exchange.

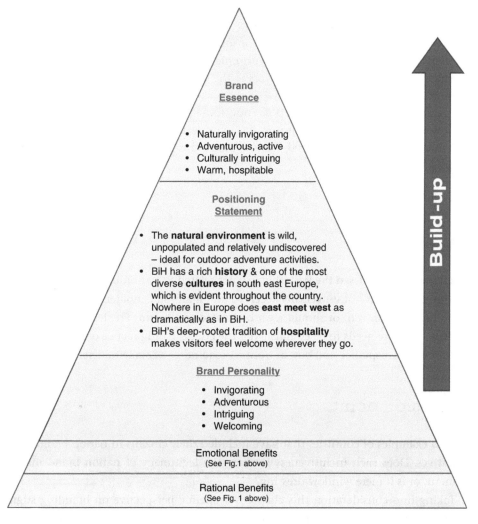

Figure 7.2
Bosnia-Herzegovina Brand Pyramid: Brand personality, positioning statement and brand essence

- Gradually, the international media narrative changed from war-torn country to exciting new destination.
- Investment in tourism infrastructure has boomed throughout BiH, with several international hotel chains now represented across the 'state'.
- BiH now receives over 1 million visitors a year.[3]
- BiH has firmly established its reputation as an adventure sports destination with its hosting of the European White Water Rafting Championships in both 2005 and 2015, the World Rafting Championships in 2009 and again in 2022, and the European Youth Olympic Winter Festival in 2019. The number of rafting operators has multiplied ten-fold, from approximately ten to now around one hundred.
- Perhaps the greatest endorsement of the 'normalisation' of BiH's media image is its consistent presence in the Eurovision Song Contest in recent years.

No one would claim the development of tourism was single-handedly responsible for Bosnia-Herzegovina's post-war economic growth or for consolidating the peace. But it seems likely it played a role, particularly in kick-starting 'state'-wide economic development in the early days, when investor confidence had not yet returned to other sectors to the extent required to create widespread jobs growth.

Like so many formerly war-ravaged countries, BiH has now joined the international tourism league as a mainstream, but quite special, destination. It now has what seemed unattainable back in those darker post-war days: the 'luxury' of being judged, like anywhere else, on no more than its ability to deliver a great visitor experience.

And it does.

Summary

This chapter has discussed the key ethical issues related to nation branding. The concept of nation branding is not universally accepted and many stakeholders remain sceptical as to whether a nation can, or should, ever be treated as a brand. The legitimacy of nation branding therefore needs to be established if the concept and practice of nation branding is to find wide acceptance and buy-in from a broad range of stakeholders.

Discussion points

1   Find examples of countries that have included their citizens in nation branding initiatives. Does such inclusiveness increase the legitimacy of nation brand management, or is it mere window-dressing?

2   Taking into consideration this chapter's academic perspective on branding stigmatised nations, to what extent do you believe that nation branding can improve perceptions of stigmatised nations?

Notes

1   In the UNDP development index Suriname is ranked 100th out of 187 countries with a Gini coefficient of 52.9, available at: http://hdr.undp.org/en/content/income-gini-coefficient (accessed 4/3/2019).

2   David Halberstam (2003) *War in a Time of Peace: Bush, Clinton and the Generals*, London: Bloomsbury Publishing.

3   United Nations World Tourism Organisation (UNWTO) figures for 2018 and 2019: UNWTO Tourism Highlights 2018 Edition, available at: www.e-unwto.org/doi/pdf/10.18111/97892 84419876 (accessed 25/6/2021) and UNWTO International Tourism Highlights 2019 Edition, available at: www.e-unwto.org/doi/pdf/10.18111/9789284421152 (accessed 25/6/2021).

References

Anholt, S. (2020) *Good Country Equation: How We Can Repair the World in One Generation*, San Francisco: Berrett-Koehler Publishers.

Aronczyk, M. (2013) *Branding the Nation: The Global Business of National Identity*, Oxford: Oxford University Press.

Berners-Lee, M. (2020) *How Bad are Bananas? The Carbon Footprint of Everything*, rev. edn, London: Profile Books.

Browning, C. (2016) 'Nation branding and development: Poverty panacea or business as usual?', *Journal of International Relations and Development*, 19 (1), 50–75.

Carillo, P.G. (2018) 'Covert nation branding and the neoliberal subject: The case of "it's Colombia, NOT Columbia" ', in Fehimović, D. and Ogden, R. (eds.), *Branding Latin America: Strategies, Aims, Resistance*, 95–116, New York: Lexington Books.

de Chernatony, L. (2008) 'Adapting brand theory to the context of nation branding', in Dinnie, K. (ed.), *Nation Branding – Concepts, Issues, Practice*, 16–17, London: Butterworth-Heinemann.

Dekhili, S. and Achabou, M.A. (2015) 'The influence of the country-of-origin ecological image on ecolabelled product evaluation: An experimental approach to the case of the European ecolabel', *Journal of Business Ethics*, 131, 89–106.

The Economist (2005) 'Greening the books', 17 September, 96.

Environmental Performance Index (2021) 'About the EPI', available at: https://epi.yale.edu/ (accessed 5/7/2021).

Environmental Sustainability Index (2005) available at: www.yale.edu/esi.

Esty, D.C. (2005) 'Finland tops environmental scorecard at world economic forum in Davos', *Yale News Release*, 26 January, available at: www.yale.edu/opa/news.

Fan, Y. (2005) 'Ethical branding and corporate reputation', *Corporate Communications*, 10 (4), 341–350.

Fehimović, D. and Ogden, R. (2018) *Branding Latin America: Strategies, Aims, Resistance*, New York: Lexington Books.

Freire, J.R. (2005) 'Geo-branding, are we talking nonsense? A theoretical reflection on brands applied to places', *Place Branding*, 1 (4), 347–362.

Global Carbon Atlas (2021) 'A platform to explore and visualize the most up-to-date data on carbon fluxes resulting from human activities and natural processes', available at: www.globalcarbonatlas.org/en/CO2-emissions (accessed 10/7/2021).

GMI Poll Press Release (2005) 'Australia is the world's favorite nation brand', 1 August, available at: www.gmi-mr.com/gmipoll/release.

Govers, R. (2018) *Imaginative Communities: Admired Cities, Regions and Countries*, Antwerp: Reputo Press.

Hoefte, R. and Veenendaal, W. (2019) 'The challenges of nation-building and nation branding in multi-ethnic Suriname', *Nationalism and Ethnic Politics*, 25 (2), 173–190.

Ibrahim Index of African Governance (2020) available at: https://mo.ibrahim.foundation/iiag/downloads (accessed 16/7/2021).

Ind, N. (2003) 'A brand of enlightenment', in Ind, N., Macrae, C., Gad, T. and Caswell, J. (eds.), *Beyond Branding*, London: Kogan Page.

Kaneva, N. (2021) 'Nation branding in the post-communist world: Assessing the field of critical research', *Nationalities Papers*, First View, 1–11.

Kaur, R. (2020) *Brand New Nation: Capitalist Dreams and Nationalist Designs in Twenty-First-Century India*, Stanford: Stanford University Press.

Larsen, E., Moss, S.M. and Skjelsbæk, I. (eds.) (2021) *Gender Equality and Nation Branding in the Nordic Region*, London: Routledge.

Levinson, B. (2018) 'Branding, sense, and their threats', in Fehimović, D. and Ogden, R. (eds.), *Branding Latin America: Strategies, Aims, Resistance*, 199–212, London: Lexington Books.

Pant, D. (2005) 'A place brand strategy for the Republic of Armenia: "Quality of context" and "sustainability" as competitive advantage', *Place Branding*, 1 (3), 273–282.

Sachs, J.D., Kroll, C., Lafortune, G., Fuller, G. and Woelm, F. (2021) 'Sustainable development report 2021', available at: https://s3.amazonaws.com/sustainabledevelopment.report/2021/2021-sustainable-development-report.pdf (accessed 5/7/2021).

Socioeconomic Data and Applications Center (2021) 'Environmental performance index', available at: https://sedac.uservoice.com/knowledgebase/articles/54669-what-is-the-reason-that-an-epi-was-established-as (accessed 5/7/2021).

UN Environment Programme (2021) 'Facts about the climate emergency', available at: www.unep.org/explore-topics/climate-change/facts-about-climate-emergency (accessed 5/7/2021).

United Nations Development Programme (2014) 'Human development index and its components', available at: http://hdr.undp.org/en/content/table-1-human-development-index (accessed 27/12/2014).

Varga, S. (2013) 'The politics of nation branding: Collective identity and public sphere in the neoliberal state', *Philosophy and Social Criticism*, 39 (8), 825–845.

Warren, G. and Dinnie, K. (2018) 'Cultural intermediaries in place branding: Who are they and how do they construct legitimacy for their work and for themselves?', *Tourism Management*, 66 (1), 302–314.

World Bank (2005) 'Where is the wealth of nations?', 15 September, available at: www.web.worldbank.org.

8 Pragmatic challenges to the nation branding concept

Key points

- Deciding on the appropriate extent of stakeholder participation is a major challenge in developing and implementing nation brand strategy
- The coordination of nation brand touchpoints is a daunting task, given the infinite number and variety of such touchpoints
- The optimal nation brand architecture needs to be developed and implemented
- Nation branding is a highly politicised activity

Introduction

This chapter describes how, from a managerial perspective, there are several pragmatic challenges to the nation branding concept. The extent of stakeholder participation is one such challenge. Further challenges relate to the coordination of nation brand touchpoints,

DOI: 10.4324/9781003100249-11

the need to develop a coherent nation brand architecture, and the highly politicised nature of nation branding. The first case in this chapter examines the role of digital asset management (DAM) in the branding of the island of Ireland. The second case focuses on the brand positioning of Nevis. The academic perspective by João Ricardo Freire suggests that in place branding the means are the end, whilst Theresa Regli's practitioner insight provides insights into the relevance of digital asset management for nation brands.

Who needs to be involved?

The wide-ranging nature of nation branding necessitates the involvement of many parties in the formulation and implementation of nation brand strategy. The principle of inclusiveness implies that all the relevant stakeholders need to be involved in strategy development. However, the inclusiveness concept is moderated by the unique set of circumstances prevailing within individual nations. Therefore it is useful to distinguish between two forms of inclusiveness: first, the ideal state, or fully inclusive approach, and second, the actual state, embodied in programme-specific inclusiveness.

Stakeholder theory

Stakeholder theory in the context of place branding suggests that multiple stakeholders must be involved in any project's planning and implementation (Currie et al., 2009; Donner and Fort, 2018; Helmi et al., 2020; Kavaratzis and Kalandides, 2015). Public participation should take a collaborative and partnering form (González and Lester, 2018; Martin and Capelli, 2018; Saraniemi and Komppula, 2019) and avoid being merely tokenistic (Lane, 2005). In a study of the nation branding of Cyprus, Dinnie and Fola (2009) present a conceptual framework for the identification and salience of stakeholders at the level of branding a nation as a destination. The benefits of a collaborative stakeholder approach are also demonstrated by Naipaul et al. (2009), who advocate the formation of partnerships among neighbouring destinations for regional destination marketing.

Ideal state: Fully inclusive approach

The benefits of an inclusive approach to strategy include motivating employees, generating buy-in and commitment, stimulating creativity and aligning stakeholders behind the corporate vision. Such issues have been well documented in the internal/employer branding literature (Ind, 2003; Barrow and Mosley, 2005). Key stakeholders in the nation brand include representatives from government, business, not-for-profit organisations, the media and civil society.

Applying the principle of inclusiveness to the context of nation branding, the fully inclusive stakeholder approach shown in Figure 8.1 provides a framework indicative of the range of potential stakeholders in the nation brand. The framework is not exhaustive, as every nation has its own specific set of stakeholders. However, the framework offers a

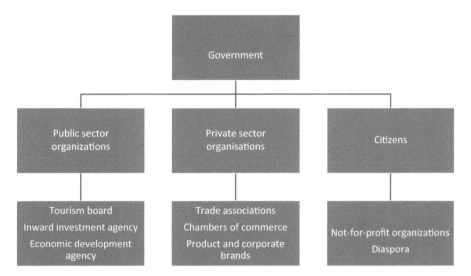

Figure 8.1
The fully inclusive stakeholder approach

basis for analysing the diversity of stakeholders that should be consulted in the development of the nation brand.

The fully inclusive stakeholder approach represents an ideal state rather than an actual state regarding levels of stakeholder inclusiveness in the development of nation branding strategy. It is a truism that nations truly come together only as a defensive impulse in response to an external threat such as imminent invasion or attack, and that once such a threat passes, nations return to their old political and social divides. It is therefore unrealistic to expect every stakeholder to be equally committed to supporting a country's brand strategy.

It can be seen from the fully inclusive stakeholder approach framework that government is the key actor that can realistically aspire to coordinate nation brand strategy encompassing the full range of stakeholders. The establishment of a coordinating body is essential in order to avoid fragmentation and duplication of activity by the different stakeholders. The coordinating body needs to possess a degree of political independence so that nation brand strategy, which is a long-term undertaking, does not veer off-course or shudder to a halt every time a new minister is appointed. Nation branding is a highly politicised activity and efforts need to be made to minimise disruption of nation branding strategy due to the waxing and waning of individual politicians' careers.

Public sector organisations are key stakeholders in the fully inclusive stakeholder approach. Tourism boards, inward investment agencies, and economic development agencies all have their own agendas and goals. There is increasing evidence that many nations are successfully coordinating the activities of such organisations in order to achieve important economic goals.

Public sector organisations frequently work closely with private sector organisations – export promotion agencies, for example, have close links with the nation's key export companies – yet there is less evidence of countries within which representatives of civil society are included in the development of nation branding strategy. Given that much of the funding of nation branding activities comes from the taxpayer, governments need to give more consideration to the ways in which the nation's citizens can be included in the development of nation brand strategy.

Actual state: Programme-specific inclusiveness

Rather than aspiring to an elusive fully inclusive approach, a more realistic goal is to achieve good levels of programme-specific inclusiveness in nation branding strategy. This has been achieved by various nations, and therefore we consider programme-specific inclusiveness as an *actual* state rather than an *ideal* state. This does not imply that all nations have achieved an actual state of programme-specific inclusiveness. On the contrary, many nations may find their nation branding efforts stymied by political corruption, power struggles or a lack of strategic vision on the part of the country's ruling elites. Even in such unpromising circumstances it should still be possible for countries to initiate nation branding strategy that embodies a modicum of programme-specific inclusiveness.

In this section we look at three campaigns that illustrate the concept of programme-specific inclusiveness: 'Brazil IT', 'Iceland Naturally' and 'The New France'. The stakeholder participants in each of these three campaigns are summarised in Table 8.1.

Although Brazil, Iceland and France are very different nations and face different nation branding challenges, each of the three campaigns summarised in Table 8.1 demonstrates the importance of fostering programme-specific inclusiveness for nations of any size, regardless of their stage of economic development or position in the global economy. In terms of campaign objectives, two of the campaigns – 'Brazil IT' and 'The New France' – illustrate how it is possible for a clearly defined strategy to remedy a country image deficit. In the case of 'Brazil IT', before the campaign was launched there was little awareness or recognition of Brazil as a provider of IT services and products. Brazil benefits from tremendously positive associations in other respects, such as football, music and other hedonic appeals, yet these associations conferred no country-of-origin advantage onto Brazilian IT providers. A different type of country image deficit was identified in the case of 'The New France' campaign, whose key objective was to improve foreign investor opinions of France in order to attract new business and increase inward investment. Pre-campaign, the image of France as a nation was dominated by highly positive perceptions in terms of the country as an attractive tourism destination and a country with fine food and drink. However, perceptions of France as a business destination were much weaker. 'The New France' campaign was launched to remedy this country image deficit. The 'Iceland Naturally' campaign differs notably from the 'Brazil IT' and 'The New France' campaigns in that for Iceland the challenge was not to overcome pre-existing dominant associations, but rather to develop an effective awareness-raising programme that would communicate to targeted markets the closeness of the fit between Icelandic products and the country's overall image of purity and naturalness.

All three campaigns follow the marketing principles of segmentation, targeting and positioning. 'Brazil IT' primarily targeted the United States market, 'Iceland Naturally' also targeted the North American market before expanding to include Europe, whilst

Table 8.1 Stakeholder participants in nation branding campaigns

Campaign	Brazil IT	Iceland Naturally	The New France
Key objectives	– To gain global recognition for the Brazilian IT industry as a capable producer of IT services and products, particularly in the United States, the world's largest consumer of IT products	– To increase demand for Icelandic products in the North American market – To promote the purity of Icelandic products – To encourage travel to the country	– To raise France's economic profile among five leading target investment countries: the United States, the United Kingdom, Germany, Japan and China – To improve foreign investor opinions of France to attract new business and increase inward investment – To create solid relationships with foreign investors for long-term dialogue
Stakeholder participants	– Brazilian government through Brazil's export promotion agency, APEX Brasil – Several IT clusters throughout Brazil – Individual IT companies – Brazil Information Center, a non-profit trade organisation based in the US which promotes Brazil to American opinion-makers and consumers	– Icelandic government through the Ministry of Foreign Affairs and Ministry of Communication – Icelandic Foreign Service (Overseas Business Services) – Iceland Tourist Board – Eight leading Icelandic companies and associations: Iceland Group plc, Icelandair, Icelandic Agriculture, Iceland Spring Natural Water, Leifur Eiriksson Air Terminal, 66° North, Blue Lagoon, Glitnir Bank	– Campaign developed and run by the Invest in France Agency, a government organisation – UBIFrance, international business development agency – Maison de la France, the national tourist office – Information Service Department – Ministry of Foreign Affairs – French Economic Mission – Sopexa, the national agricultural marketing and communication consultant – EDUFrance, the education promotion agency – Treasury Directorate – French State Council – Pierre Dauzier, communications expert and ex-President of advertising company Havas

Source: adapted from Sanches and Sekles, 2008; Palsdottir, 2008; Favre, 2008

'The New France' targeted five key investment countries: the United States, the United Kingdom, Germany, Japan and China. The clear strategic focus of each campaign was an important condition for establishing the wide-ranging stakeholder participation that each campaign achieved.

Government involvement in all three campaigns and commitment to achieving the campaign objectives are essential in order to sustain the participation of all the necessary stakeholders, although the degree of government involvement may be contingent upon the nature and stage of each individual campaign. Government involvement could be most active in the initial stages, in order to kick-start the campaign and galvanise stakeholder participation, and then government involvement may become more hands-off as private sector companies engage more actively in the campaign's development. 'Brazil IT', 'Iceland Naturally' and 'The New France' demonstrate the different types of public sector bodies that can be involved in specific campaigns. These campaigns also show that there is no rigid blueprint for nation branding campaigns, whose diversity defies easy categorisation. The appropriate range of participating stakeholders will vary according to each campaign's specific strategic objectives.

Nations should benefit from a cumulative effect in terms of stakeholder participation in specific campaigns. Participation in a campaign facilitates the formation of social networks that can usefully endure beyond the shelf-life of the campaign in question and underpin future campaigns. Social network theory in the context of the firm offers some interesting perspectives for those involved in nation branding campaigns. It has been argued, for example, that firms can draw on their unique social networks of relations to make a difference to their strategies rather than accepting strategy as merely a function of the market or of internally driven forces; and moreover, managers need to identify and develop network structures that are 'resourceful, rare and inimitable' (Hung, 2002). For nation branding strategy, such network structures are embodied in the range of stakeholder participants actively engaged in the three campaigns analysed here. An additional network at the disposal of nations is their diaspora, and governments are beginning to appreciate the potential benefits of engaging with their diaspora networks as key participants in developing a powerful nation brand.

Coordinating nation brand touchpoints

Brand touchpoints exist whenever and wherever the brand is experienced by any of its stakeholders or audiences. Brand touchpoints occur most obviously during consumption of the brand, although touchpoints also exist pre-consumption and post-consumption through multiple channels and occasions. Touchpoints consist of planned, controllable brand-building activities such as advertising, promotion, public relations and customer service, as well as unplanned touchpoints beyond the control of brand managers. Unplanned touchpoints include blogs, online discussion boards and the personal behaviour of individuals associated with the brand. For a product or service brand, there exists a multiplicity of brand touchpoints. For complex and multifaceted nation brands, with their vast range of internal and external stakeholders and audiences, the number of brand touchpoints assumes almost infinite proportions. The reason that brand touchpoints matter is that they can all contribute to, or detract from, brand equity in terms of the positive or negative perceptions that occur in audience's minds due to the assessments they make of how satisfying the brand touchpoint experience has been. The full range of brand touchpoints cannot be controlled but they can be managed, based on ongoing research that identifies and evaluates brand touchpoints as and when they occur. Brand expert Ian Ryder has noted that in place branding the acceptance or management of the brand depends upon knowing where the touchpoints are (Brand Strategy, 2007). Nation brand touchpoints can be bewilderingly diverse, from the potentially harmful effects on Iceland's country image due to that nation's resumption of whaling, to the potentially positive reputational effects of improved business formalities on perceptions of Egypt as a business destination. In the context of Brand Estonia, Interbrand consultancy point out that 'as well as the more obvious communication points that a new brand needs to touch, public infrastructure and public services are the most noticeable and memorable national symbols for visitors and those who come to work in a country' (Interbrand, 2008, p. 235).

In many respects there are similarities between corporate branding and nation branding. Both types of branding involve more complexity than is the case with product brands. The added complexity of corporate and nation branding lies in the wider range of stakeholders that such brands have, the multiplicity of communications channels that need to be used in order to reach those audiences, the difficulty of encapsulating a multifaceted entity into the distilled essence of a brand, and the unlimited number of uncontrollable factors that can affect perceptions of the brand.

Hankinson (2007) proposes five guiding principles for the management of destination brands based on an adaptation of corporate branding theory. Whilst a destination brand could be a single town, city, resort or other relatively limited entity, it could also be a whole nation and many destination branding campaigns are run at a national level. Hankinson's five guiding principles may therefore be considered as having potential application at a nation branding level. His five principles are as follows: first, strong, visionary leadership; second, a brand-oriented organizational culture; third, departmental coordination and process alignment; fourth, consistent communications across a wide range of stakeholders; and fifth, strong, compatible partnerships. The need for consistent communications across a wide range of stakeholders alluded to by Hankinson is illustrated in the case of South Africa, where there was a realisation that the country was suffering from certain perceptions that needed to be changed, but the uncoordinated proliferation of messages emanating from the country was not helping to challenge the problem. Johnston (2008, p. 5) describes how 'there were many messages entering the international arena, and these messages were as varied as the sources and did very little to change the perceptions. They added to the confusion.'

In order to address the multiple audiences that a nation brand possesses, the principles of integrated marketing communications (IMC) need to be applied. The emergence of IMC has been driven by the proliferation of new media channels in the digital age as well as by the fragmentation of previously homogeneous audience 'blocks' into smaller and more numerous discrete groups. IMC entails sending target audiences a consistent message across all marketing communications tools (Burnett and Moriarty, 1998). The marketing communication tools that are available to brands include traditional media advertising such as television, radio, newspapers and magazines; online advertising; event marketing; publicity; trade journal advertising; and conferences and expos. Nation brands can utilise such marketing communications tools to pursue their objectives in the same way that product or corporate brands have used such tools. For example, an illustration of the use of IMC in nation branding is provided by 'The New France' campaign, which used the following communications options: print advertisements in top economic news publications such as the *Financial Times*, *Wall Street Journal*, *Handelsblatt* and Nikkei; billboard advertisements in major airports in the United States, United Kingdom, Japan, China and France; sector videos; a book available in five languages entitled *France Means Business*, with 10,000 copies distributed in 60 different countries; a microsite www.thenewfrance.

com containing testimonials and information on doing business in France; and face-to-face meetings with economic leaders and potential investors at high-profile events such as the World Economic Forum in Davos, the Forbes CEO Conference, the BusinessWeek Leadership Forum and the Fortune Innovation Forum (Favre, 2008).

Iceland and Brazil have also implemented IMC principles in their nation branding activities, unifying their marketing communication tools in order to send their target audiences a consistent, persuasive message. The 'Iceland Naturally' programme, for example, created a logo for the campaign and used a variety of marketing tools including events, advertising in leading travel and lifestyle publications, a website, monthly newsletters, sweepstakes and other promotional techniques (Palsdottir, 2008). The 'Brazil IT' campaign also created a new logo and trademarked the brand in the United States, and then drew upon a range of communication tools such as video, the www.brazil-it.com website, traditional print media and consistent trade show participation (Sanches and Sekles, 2008).

The visual coordination of nation brand touchpoints is relatively straightforward compared to the management of the many uncontrollable touchpoints that every nation brand has. New Zealand, for example, has for many years used its silver fern logo to unify the visual aspect of its sport, education, trade and tourism promotions. Origin devices such as the fern can have a deep connection between a country's tradition, culture and people (Dooley and Bowie, 2005).

The coordination of nation brand touchpoints is a complex, challenging and necessary undertaking. A report by the Oxford Said Business School on developing a brand for Latvia, for example, states that the coordinating role in the nation brand should be played by a Brand Steward whose activities should be enabling rather than directive (Frasher et al., 2003).

Nation brand architecture

A further pragmatic challenge in nation branding is the question of deciding upon a suitable brand architecture. Brand architecture is a key concept in brand theory (Dinnie, 2018). It has been conceptualised as the specification of brand roles within an overall brand portfolio (Aaker and Joachimsthaler, 2000). Temporal (2002) suggests that brand architecture may be the most difficult area in brand management, given the lack of rules and the wide array of options available. Yvonne Johnston, CEO of the International Marketing Council of South Africa, has described how that country has developed a brand architecture that defines the relationship between the mother-brand and the various sub-brands that comprise Brand South Africa (Johnston, 2008). At a regional rather than national level, Datzira-Masip and Poluzzi (2014) have shown the concepts of brand architecture have been applied in four tourist destinations in Catalonia.

One of the clearest and most useful descriptions of brand architecture is given by Olins (1989), who distinguishes between three basic brand portfolio structures: monolithic, endorsed and branded. In the monolithic structure there is a single dominant corporate umbrella brand. In the endorsed structure, individual brands have their own brand names and identity but are clearly endorsed by the parent brand. Finally, in the branded structure each individual brand stands alone with its own identity and the parent brand is not visible. Examples of a monolithic brand structure can be seen with companies such as Canon (where the umbrella brand covers printers, fax machines, cameras, etc.) or Mitsubishi (financial services, cars, domestic appliances). An endorsed brand structure is used by General Motors (Chevrolet, Buick and so on). Finally, a branded structure is used by Johnnie Walker Red Label, where the parent brand (Diageo) is not visible to the consumer and the individual brand stands alone. Within these three basic structures there can be many permutations and variations, yet Olins' monolithic-endorsed-branded perspective remains a robust framework for brand architecture analysis and development.

Why do companies use different brand architectures, and how can they decide upon the most appropriate brand architecture for their own unique brand portfolios and markets? The rationale for a monolithic brand structure derives from the ability of a monolithic brand to create a unified, powerful and consistent image across different markets. Corporate brands such as Yamaha are so strong that they can enter sectors as disparate as motor bikes and guitars, and many other product categories in between. A risk with the monolithic structure, however, is that if one sub-brand receives bad publicity or performs poorly, this may taint the other brands in the portfolio.

The rationale for an endorsed structure is that an endorsed brand can enjoy the best of both worlds. An endorsed brand benefits from the power of the parent or umbrella brand whilst simultaneously establishing its own individual brand identity. A drawback of the endorsed structure is that the sub-brand's freedom to position itself in its target markets is restrained by the need to conform to the parent brand's positioning.

The rationale for a branded structure is that it allows maximum potential to develop a clearly differentiated brand that can stand alone and prosper without being associated with the parent brand. The branded structure is commonly used in the spirits drinks sector, where quirky, heritage-focused, or in other ways highly individualistic brands would gain no benefit – and in fact would certainly lose brand equity – if they were associated with the faceless multinational corporations that own them. However, a weakness of the branded structure is that there may be a failure to benefit from the positive associations of a powerful parent brand.

Douglas et al. (2001) contend that establishing a coherent international brand architecture is an important element of a firm's international marketing strategy because it provides a structure that enables the firm to leverage strong brands into other markets, and to integrate strategy across markets. Transposing the concept of brand architecture to the specific case of South Africa's nation branding, Dooley and Bowie (2005) show how South Africa has developed a 'nation umbrella brand' whose purpose, like that of a corporate umbrella brand, is to link together individual sub-brands. The 'sub-brands' in this case are South Africa's regions, cities and areas such as tourism, exports and foreign direct investment.

Although no fixed rules exist regarding brand architecture decisions, as a basic step managers must analyse the existing corporate and sub-brand equities of their portfolios in light of the markets they operate within and those markets they are contemplating entering. These equities must be evaluated in terms of what value the umbrella brand and the sub-brands are currently contributing, and the potential value that they could deliver in the future. In nation branding terms, the corporate or umbrella brand is the nation.

The nation's 'sub-brands' include its cities, regions and landmarks; product and corporate brands from all sectors; tourism, FDI and export promotion agencies; sporting teams, at both national and club level; cultural and political figures, and so on. The purpose of the brand architecture concept is to instil some order and structure on this otherwise sprawling and disjointed mass of sub-brands, in order to achieve synergistic benefits and to advance the overarching nation brand. The NBAR (nation-brand architecture) model in Figure 8.2 shows a framework for nation brand architecture that introduces strategic coordination and direction to the nation brand and its sub-brands.

In the NBAR model, the nation brand represents the 'umbrella brand'. At the next level down can be found 'endorsed brands' such as the nation's tourism, exports, inward investment, talent attraction and sports. The third level comprises a mix of 'endorsed' and 'standalone' brands.

The strategic purpose of nation brand architecture is to fully leverage the overarching, umbrella nation brand and all the 'sub-brands' of the nation in order to achieve maximum synergy on a long-term basis. It requires a creative and concerted effort to overcome the silo mentality that afflicts many large corporations. Whereas corporations need to foster cross-functional collaboration between marketing, research and development, operations, finance and so on, nations on the other hand must address a similar challenge in facilitating fertile collaboration between distinct bodies such as national tourism organisations, inward investment agencies, tertiary education providers, export promotion agencies and others.

The NBAR model proposes a brand architecture that encompasses the umbrella, endorsed and branded structures. The model is intended to stimulate the creative development of synergistic linkages between different sub-brands, for example between tourism and talent attraction, or between exports and sports. It is also designed to prevent the proliferation of uncoordinated visual branding systems that could cause confusion in target audiences and reduce potential synergies. Under the umbrella nation brand, an endorsed structure is suggested for the main agencies, sections and dimensions of the nation brand such as tourism, exports, inward investment, talent attraction, sports and cultural and political figures. However, this endorsed structure comes with an important caveat – the visual expression of endorsement by the umbrella brand should be merely the name of the nation brand, accompanied by a logo, for example, the New Zealand fern. It is challenging to try and boil down the essence of a nation to a single-phrase

Figure 8.2
The nation brand architecture (NBAR) model

slogan, as such a slogan would have to be so broad and all-encompassing that it would run the risk of being vacuous. It is at the endorsed, sub-brand level that each sub-brand should produce a slogan appropriate to its own specific target markets.

Different positioning strategies will be required for the branding of specific sectors. For example, in June 2011 the Australian Government launched Future Unlimited, a new brand for the international promotion of Australian education. Rather than focusing on the familiar lifestyle and tourism iconography of Australia's nation brand, the Future Unlimited brand downplays the hedonic aspects of the nation brand and instead emphasises the quality of the country's educational institutions and programmes. This approach illustrates the need to adopt a brand architecture approach that is appropriately balanced between the umbrella nation brand and a sectoral brand such as education.

A highly politicised activity

Nation branding is a highly politicised activity. Governments are assumed to represent the people of a nation and therefore governments must play a key role in nation branding strategy. Private sector organisations do not, on their own, possess the legitimacy to lead the direction of nation brand strategy. However, as Yan (2008, p. 171) has noted, 'governments are voted for very short terms, much shorter than what a branding campaign necessitates. . . . In addition, governments have not always been stellar exhibitors of promotion.' Eggeling (2020) has examined the politics of nation branding in the contexts of Kazakhstan and Qatar, whilst Fehimović and Ogden (2018) provide a wide-ranging, critical account of nation branding in Latin America from a more political perspective than is usually the case with studies of nation branding. A domestic politics perspective on Canada's nation branding is provided by Nimijean and Carment (2019). Saunders (2018) adopts a geopolitical perspective to analyse nation branding in the post-Soviet realm.

ACADEMIC PERSPECTIVE: IN PLACE BRANDING THE MEANS ARE THE END

João Ricardo Freire

The idea of promoting and selling a place is not new and has been around for more than a century. In the nineteenth century, places in the United States started using marketing tools intended to attract settlers to new lands in the West. Likewise in Europe, by the beginning of the twentieth century, French and British beach resorts started to use rudimentary marketing tools with a strong selling approach based on advertisements to attract visitors. The early tools adopted more of an operational and tactical approach, rather than a strategic one. Today these techniques are considered outdated; nonetheless, it highlights the first time that places put an importance on designing appropriate measures to attract people.

Notably, the relevance of the promotion of a place is not limited to the attraction of resources. A positive image of a place may have a direct impact on the sale of products manufactured in a specific location.

There is consensus among marketers and researchers that images of a country can influence the perceptions of certain products and brands. The relationship between place and product is called the country-of-origin (COO) effect. This effect illustrates that the goal of promoting a place should also include improving its image in order to increase the sale of its products and brands in international markets.

The concept of selling a place has evolved over time. The increased competition among places has forced place managers to think about how they act. It is in the context of this highly competitive environment that place managers have realized they must promote their places using a strategic focus instead of a tactical one. This realization has triggered the use of place marketing within a management framework and the development of a structure to operate in the marketplace, which is the basis for the development and creation of place brands. Place branding has now become one of the key strategic concepts when it comes to creating wealth for places.

Why is place branding often seen as an efficient way to create wealth? One reason is that to be successful and develop a meaningful branding strategy, there is a need to involve different stakeholders from the community. Stakeholders can be defined as citizens, private companies, non-governmental organizations (NGOs), local state agencies, central government, and others. To have a consistent and meaningful branding strategy, all of these stakeholders must be involved. The methodology used to develop the place brand strategy should take into account the needs and wishes of all stakeholders.

The involvement of different stakeholders is also relevant to collectively define the objectives for the place, the brand value proposition, positioning and the identification of target markets. It is only through the involvement of representatives from all of the stakeholders that a sustainable long-term branding strategy can be successfully implemented. The process of developing a place brand is an opportunity for democratic participation from the people. A place brand involving representatives from all of the different stakeholders is built with the people of the place. It is not imposed on the people of the place.

Therefore, one of the most important aspects of place branding is not the value proposition or the positioning of the brand, it is the way that the concepts are created, agreed on and accepted by all of the stakeholders. The methodology used to design the strategy is essential to creating a more cohesive place brand. One can argue that the most important aspect of place branding is the methodology or the means to an end. It can even be argued that in place branding the means are the end.

Destination branding kills place branding

Involving all of the stakeholders is how a place brand should be built, however, this is often not the case. Place brands are frequently developed involving only a few stakeholders representing a small part of society while excluding other stakeholders. This is also true for destination branding, which is place branding within a tourism context.

The tourism industry is an extremely organized industry with the means to develop strategies that best fit their interests. It is also a highly competitive and dynamic industry that has a strong need to constantly communicate its product to different target audiences.

Due to its need for continuous communication and that it is a relevant industry for job creation, governments tend to create organizations that support this industry. These organizations often have a significant marketing budget, directly supported by public funds, and are influenced by private stakeholders who operate in the tourism industry.

In many cases, the fact is that the destination brand becomes the place brand. When this happens the strategy of a place is created by the players in the tourism industry and developed for the tourism industry, without any involvement from the other stakeholders. In these situations, equitable forces are not applied and the destination branding becomes a mechanism that imposes its industry on all of the other industries and the local communities. The process of place branding, which should be a mechanism for democratic involvement and wealth creation for the entire society, does not occur and, in fact, the destination brand ends up killing the place brand.

PRACTITIONER INSIGHT: DIGITAL ASSET MANAGEMENT AND NATION BRANDS

Theresa Regli

'Brand' is a 21st-century watchword, inescapable across the consumer and media landscapes. Brands are more than just logos: they tell stories, provoke loyalty, spur emotions. Powerful brands convert to big revenues. This is why brand management technology has proliferated since the turn of the century.

Brand management is one use case of the broader technology category known as Digital Asset Management, or DAM. Digital Asset Management is not just a technology, but a practice: the management of digital media throughout its lifetime. When managing a brand, the discipline of DAM goes well beyond the logo: it includes images, video, audio, as well as supporting processes and metadata (data about the asset). As both a practice and a technology, DAM is concerned with delivering the right content to the right people, on all devices, and in the appropriate format, at the most appropriate time. DAM technology also offers the ability to track and measure digital asset engagement and global reach – which can be particularly important for nations wanting to draw business, investments, and tourism.

In my DAM consultancy practice, I have worked with several geographically diverse entities to manage their brands: a Canadian city, an island nation, a regional government in the USA. In every case, the principles of brand management mastered by corporations like Nike, Unilever, and Coca-Cola were equally applicable to these non-corporate entities, and DAM technology was instrumental in realising their strategy. Towns, cities, states, and nations can and should manage their digital assets as any commercial brand does. DAM technology is one of the elements that makes this possible.

In the DAM industry, we don't use the term 'asset' lightly. It's more than just a file. An asset has intrinsic or acquired value, as metadata is also managed alongside the file. Thus files can be distributed more usefully – for example, with GPS or landmark information, identifying what is in the photograph. Software, not just people, can thus find and use the asset in more targeted ways. DAM technology can manage a master file and then create derivations in multiple digital or physical forms: a website banner ad, or a massive subway poster. Creating these marketing assets from a single source of truth boosts efficiency and ensures consistency.

Digital assets serve to promote a brand, build brand loyalty, and thus brand value. In addition to these intangibles, DAM systems also provide the potential to realise hard financial ROI: reducing costs, as well as generating new revenue opportunities. DAM systems enable organisations – brands and nations alike – to do more with what they have. It takes drive and collaboration to make this happen, but when DAM programmes are done right, they have tremendous impact.

Nations and other jurisdictions – as well as the entities that promote them – will inevitably grow their collections of digital assets in the coming years. DAM systems will be instrumental to managing these assets effectively, and taking nation branding to the next level of impact and effectiveness.

CASE: THE ROLE OF DIGITAL ASSET MANAGEMENT (DAM) IN THE BRANDING OF THE ISLAND OF IRELAND: TOURISM IRELAND'S JOURNEY INTO DAMS

Patrick Lennon, Content Coordinator, Tourism Ireland

Introduction to Tourism Ireland

Tourism Ireland is the marketing body for tourism to the island of Ireland and was set up in 2002 with two goals:

1   Increase tourism to the island of Ireland
2   Support Northern Ireland to realise its tourism potential

In simple terms Tourism Ireland's remit is to market the island of Ireland overseas and attract more visitors to book a holiday, stay longer and spend more money.

Tourism Ireland does not sell a product or a service but an experience that is unique when someone pays a visit to the island of Ireland on holiday, vacation, business travel or to visit family or friends.

The Ireland Brand(s)

Tourism Brand Ireland in the form of a shamrock with the name Ireland in bold characters provides the platform for engagement with our audiences. Marketing the island of Ireland was not a new concept with the former Bord Fáilte and Northern Ireland Tourist Board cooperating on joint marketing ventures overseas. However, the concept of a 'Brand Ireland' was new and Tourism Ireland was set up to specifically market to the overseas audience.

In recent years Tourism Ireland has employed advertising campaigns with call to actions including 'Jump into Ireland' and the current campaign of 'Fill Your Heart With Ireland' with the Ireland brand to the fore. Each 17th March for the last 10 years Tourism Ireland has also used the 'Greenings' campaign to raise the profile of Ireland. Iconic buildings and attractions around the world go green for St Patrick's Day, with the help of the Department of Foreign Affairs, the Irish Diaspora and anyone who feels Irish.

Tourism Ireland also works closely with our sister agencies on the island of Ireland to promote regional brand experiences. Fáilte Irelands' *Wild Atlantic Way*, a coastal route that runs 2500km Irelands' western seaboard is a great example of this work. Fáilte Ireland has also developed *Ireland's*

Ireland 🍀

Figure 8.3
Tourism Brand Ireland logo

Ancient East focusing on the rich 5000 year history of the eastern part of the island. With Tourism Northern Ireland the *Embrace a Giant Spirit* brand encapsulates the landscape and spirit of Northern Ireland. In cooperation with our sister agencies the opportunities have been exploited to jointly commission content to reflect both these experiences and the Ireland brand.

Since 2013 at the heart of these commissions and marketing efforts lies the DAM known as Ireland's Content Pool which houses and gives access to all the digital marketing materials that are used to inform campaign communications.

What is a DAM?

'The management of digital media throughout its lifetime is the general domain of digital asset management.' *Theresa Regli*[1]

The digital media that Tourism Ireland uses across the communication channels include images, video, infographics, logos, music and copy documents such as touring itineraries. Collectively these digital media are called 'content'. These content digital media files are stored and distributed in various formats and MIME types to allow as wide a use as possible across all the marketing communications channels both online and off-line and to enable our partners at home and overseas to access content they can use in their promotions, and the world's media to reflect positive stories about the island of Ireland.

Simply put Tourism Ireland engages in content marketing and the goal is to create and market content that both inspires and informs.

'Content marketing is a strategic marketing approach focused on creating and distributing, valuable, relevant and consistent content to attract and retain a clearly defined audience – and, ultimately, to drive profitable consumer actions.' *Content Marketing Institute*[2]

Why a DAM?

Why did Tourism Ireland choose a DAM system over the image banks previously adopted or the historic mechanisms used to distribute imagery, video and logos? The reasons are simple:

- Process improvements – leading to efficiencies in workflow and reductions in costs
- Storing master files that are downloadable in multiple forms
- Value asset realisation via metadata
- Consistency of brand – a 'one stop shop' for all approved content
- Reduction in time to market – 'real time marketing' through social media communications

- Curation of content from external sources (influencers, trade, creatives, industry)
- Increase in use of video in the wider marketing communications mix – not just for advertising broadcast but increasingly in Facebook and Twitter posts.

DAM as a brand

DAM for marketing is not just a place to host content assets but a means of marketing the island of Ireland to the wider tourism trade overseas, to brand champions and to the world's media. In this respect, Ireland's Content Pool has become known as the source of quality digital marketing content for the island of Ireland and is a recognised brand in its own right. So much so, that when Tourism Ireland and its sister agencies moved to a new DAM supplier in 2020, a decision was taken not to change the name of Ireland's Content Pool but retain it, the logo and even the look and feel of the old DAM into the new portal mirroring the user experience or UX. Ireland's Content Pool has in many ways become a sub-brand of Brand Ireland.

History of adoption

The evolution of digital media over the lifetime of Tourism Ireland has prompted the changes that have been made in the nature and distribution of marketing assets. In 2002, Tourism Ireland did not have a stock of marketing assets but relied on those available from our sister agencies Fáilte Ireland and the Northern Ireland Tourist Board. After commissioning our own content that reflected the Ireland brand and our campaign communications, the need for a repository to host this content was required. Imagery and video assets were held on floppy discs, zip discs, on PC hard drives, VHS cassettes and film reels in different departments and in different locations on the island of Ireland, and in offices overseas. No one person in Tourism Ireland knew the totality of the content available nor where to put their hands on it.

The year 2003 saw the first justification for a dedicated 'data bank' to host digital assets and led to the creation of the Tourism Ireland Image Bank and thence the development of a mini-website to host brand assets such as logos, fonts and guidelines. In 2011, the need for a system that could manage higher resolution assets including video was required and in 2013 Tourism Ireland tendered for and contracted a DAM system in partnership with our sister agency Fáilte Ireland.

How does Tourism Ireland harness 'content'?

Tourism Ireland through our commissioning programmes and in cooperation with our sister agencies, the tourism industry, our trade partners, the Irish diaspora, media contacts and champions uses the DAM to provide inspiring, relevant and useful content to our prospective customers or target audience to encourage them to pay a visit to the island of Ireland.

Tourism Ireland deploys advertising campaigns across TV, Radio, Out of Home (OOH) and across social media platforms. Historically, Tourism Ireland has also worked with trade partners overseas for cooperative marketing campaigns based on tactical strategies – presenting real time travel or stay offers. Publicity teams have also worked closely with journalists in traditional and online media, including social media influencers, to create positive stories about great experiences to be enjoyed when visiting the island of Ireland.

Break out

Tourism Ireland's digital communication mix includes: the ireland.com website, Facebook, Twitter, Instagram, and YouTube, amongst others.

Increasingly Tourism Ireland is engaging with 'journey management' through building up a personalisation of digital communications with each customer. This strategy allows Tourism Ireland to know the propensity or likelihood of individual customers to travel to the island of Ireland and determine the next best communication to help them take the decision to travel.

Tourism Ireland employs this strategy through creating impactful personalised marketing communications with the Ireland brand at the heart of the message. These personalised communications are made possible via marketing technology – MarTech. The marketing digital media content used to create these communications starts with the DAM acting as the content hub for Tourism Ireland's marketing communications into the future.

To give the reader an insight into the level of usage of Ireland's Content Pool DAM system, in the period from 2016 to 2019 over **471,000** assets were downloaded. During that same period an average of 3000 new users per year from the travel trade and media around the world signed up to and used assets from Ireland's Content Pool DAM.

Usage figures from 2016–2019

3,600	new users of the Content Pool in 2019
21,400	total users (accessing the Content Pool in the previous 24 months)
52,000	log-ins
352,000	keyword searches
387,400	assets viewed

Conclusion

Ireland's Content Pool DAM allows for a visualisation of marketing assets employed through the full range of communication channels to assure and reassure the prospective visitor that it is worthwhile to make the purchase of a holiday to the island of Ireland. Great content supported by the DAM and allied with inspiring communications allows Tourism Ireland to project the Ireland Brand to the world.

CASE: NEVIS: THE MONACO OF THE CARIBBEAN?

Elsa G. Wilkin-Armbrister, Minister Counsellor, St Kitts
and Nevis High Commission, London

Nation branding refers to how a country positions and promotes itself to attract tourists, investments, and talent (Fan, 2010). Volcic and Andrejevic (2011) suggest that nation branding is a powerful political tool to strengthen a country's economic position, image, identity, and its ability to influence the opinions of foreign governments.

Branding Nevis

Nevis is a small island developing state, a part of the Federation of St Kitts and Nevis located in the Caribbean Sea. Both islands share a federal government arrangement like that of Scotland and the United Kingdom, and like Scotland and the United Kingdom they have separate tourism brands. 'Nevis Naturally' focuses on Nevis's natural unspoiled beauty whereas St Kitts has a separate brand to promote the island's festivals and appeals to a younger demographics of tourists. This concept of creating and promoting different tourist brands enables Nevis to brand itself independently of its sister island St Kitts. The challenge for Nevis would be which sector to use as its main point of focus in the nation branding process. There are several possible angles through which the island could be branded.

Mr Eustace Wallace (personal communication, 28/9/2020), Counsellor at the St Kitts and Nevis High Commission in Ottawa, Canada, argues that 'Nevis should be branded using its unique history, just as Greece did with its mythology, just as Monaco does with its royal aura'. He sees Nevis – popularly known as the 'Queen of the Caribees' – as a high-end destination for mega yachts, financial services and luxury travel, a progressive nation brand steeped in history and wonder. 'Nevis could be the Monaco of the Caribbean', he suggests. Mr Sheldon Henry (personal communication, 29/9/2020), Second Secretary at the St Kitts and Nevis Permanent Mission to the United Nations in New York, asserts, 'Nevis should use its unique and rich history to shape its nation brand concept. Thinking of the past, it's our history that fascinated tourists visiting the island. Thinking long-term the world is changing and a new brand we could push is the exclusivity of Nevis, more millennials are looking to escape where it's not over-crowded and where a lot of people haven't wandered.'

Traditionally, Nevis' main economic resource generators have been tourism and financial services sectors. Nevis has the potential to be branded using a single sector or a combination of sectors. Within the last five years, Nevis' profile was raised significantly when the musical *Hamilton* was released on Broadway in the United States. The story of the life of Alexander Hamilton is told in the musical, his contribution to the United States economic framework but it also highlighted that Hamilton's birthplace was Nevis, a tiny island in the Caribbean. In the last year a new sector has emerged in Nevis as a location where film companies come to film movies and documentaries. This new economic driver could also be used as a key angle in the branding of this small island state.

The Nevis Island Administration has at its finger tips the potential to re-shape and enhance Nevis' image to international audiences. Whilst the island has not officially been branded, Nevis is considered a high-end tourism destination as it one of the only islands in the region to have a five-diamond hotel, the Four Seasons Resort Nevis. Anholt (2007) argues that countries which do not engage in the nation branding process run the risk of being branded by others with an image that is not a true reflection of the country or one that the country does not identify with. Therefore, Nevis should create a nation branding strategy which it can identify with and be proud to articulate.

Having stated earlier that Nevis could be branded with a single focus or a combination of sectors, a public diplomacy approach should be considered. Public diplomacy involves communicating and engaging with foreign publics. The Nevis Island Administration should consider using its various social media platforms and its news channels to engage with foreign publics and nationals in the diaspora regarding its views, mandates, and policies.

Whereas Nevis has a rich history and heritage, a unique culture and is now emerging as a film location, it lacks the budget to embark on large-scale nation branding campaigns. Therefore, the government should seriously embrace the concept of branding Nevis using a public diplomacy approach. The current leader of Nevis, Premier Mark Brantley, is also the Foreign Minister at the Federal level of Government. The Honourable Brantley is in a unique position to advance the brand Nevis campaign. He has started to brand Nevis as he is quite active on several social media platforms promoting all things Nevis: from tourism, to agriculture, film industry, Nevis financial services sector and culture. Premier Brantley has the power, intellectual and diplomatic currency to brand Nevis using public diplomacy as the key strategy.

Conclusion

Nevis has the potential to be branded through different sectors, however, the challenge is which one should headline the nation branding process? Could Nevis be branded as the Monaco of the Caribbean? Specializing in financial services with strong legislation to protect its clients, a high-end tourism destination, a destination where movies are filmed or unique historical and cultural festivals? Diplomats Wallace and Henry are strong advocates of the idea of branding Nevis. They both argue that Nevis' history should be used to tell its story and assist in shaping the narrative for the nation brand. In this way, Nevis can be branded using public diplomacy as the main tool to promote its history, tourism, and financial service sectors to brand itself and reshape international public opinion of this small island – the Monaco of the Caribbean.

References

Anholt, S. (2007) *Competitive Identity: The New Brand Management for Nations, Cities and Regions*, Houndsmills: Palgrave Macmillan.

Fan, Y. (2010) 'Branding the nation: Towards a better understanding', *Place Branding and Public Diplomacy*, 6 (2), 97–108.

Volcic, Z. and Andrejevic, M. (2011) 'Nation branding in the era of commercial nationalism', *International Journal of Communication*, 5, 598–618.

Summary

In this chapter we have looked at the pragmatic challenges to the nation branding concept. In terms of inclusiveness, nation brands may aspire to a fully inclusive approach whereby all the nation brand's stakeholders are involved in the country's nation branding strategy. A more realistic goal may be to adopt a programme-specific approach, as in the case of campaigns such as 'Brazil IT', 'Iceland Naturally' and 'The New France'. The concept of brand architecture has been discussed and related to the concept of the nation brand. Nation branding is a highly politicised activity, which requires the active commitment of government if the nation brand's goals are to be achieved.

Discussion points

1   Is a fully inclusive approach to nation branding ever possible? Identify countries that have attempted to take an inclusive approach to their nation brand strategy, and discuss the effectiveness of such approaches.
2   How much attention do countries pay to the brand architecture concept? Provide examples to illustrate your answer.

Notes

1   Digital and Marketing Asset Management, Theresa Regli, 2016 Rosenfeld Media / Real Story Group.
2   Content Marketing Institute, available at: https://contentmarketinginstitute.com/what-is-content-marketing/.

References

Aaker, D.A. and Joachimsthaler, E. (2000) *Brand Leadership*, New York: The Free Press.
Barrow, S. and Mosley, R. (2005) *The Employer Brand: Bringing the Best of Brand Management to People at Work*, London: John Wiley & Sons.
Brand Strategy (2007) 'Roundtable: Russian reputation', *Brand Strategy*, February, 44–47.
Burnett, J. and Moriarty, S. (1998) *Introduction to Marketing Communications: An Integrated Approach*, New York: Prentice Hall.
Currie, R.R., Seaton, S. and Wesley, F. (2009) 'Determining stakeholders for feasibility analysis', *Annals of Tourism Research*, 36 (1), 41–63.
Datzira-Masip, J. and Poluzzi, A. (2014) 'Brand architecture management: The case of four tourist destinations in Catalonia', *Journal of Destination Marketing & Management*, 3, 48–58.
Dinnie, K. (2018) 'Contingent self-definition and amorphous regions: A dynamic approach to place brand architecture', *Marketing Theory*, 18 (1), 31–53.
Dinnie, K. and Fola, M. (2009) 'Branding cyprus – a stakeholder identification perspective', 7th International Conference on Marketing, Athens Institute for Education and Research (ATINER), Athens, Greece, 6–9 July.
Donner, M. and Fort, F. (2018) 'Stakeholder value-based place brand building', *Journal of Product & Brand Management*, 27 (7), 807–818.
Dooley, G. and Bowie, D. (2005) 'Place brand architecture: Strategic management of the brand portfolio', *Place Branding*, 1 (4), 402–419.
Douglas, S.P., Craig, C.S. and Nijssen, E.J. (2001) 'Integrating branding strategy across markets: Building international brand architecture', *Journal of International Marketing*, 9 (2), 97–114.
Eggeling, K. (2020) *Nation-Branding in Practice: The Politics of Promoting Sports, Cities and Universities in Kazakhstan and Qatar*, New York: Routledge.
Favre, P. (2008) 'The new France – breaking through the perception barrier', in Dinnie, K. (ed.), *Nation Branding – Concepts, Issues, Practice*, 1st edn, 239–242, London: Butterworth-Heinemann.

Fehimović, D. and Ogden, R. (2018) *Branding Latin America: Strategies, Aims, Resistance*, New York: Lexington Books.

Frasher, S., Hall, M., Hildreth, J. and Sorgi, M. (2003) 'A brand for the nation of Latvia', *Oxford Said Business School*, available at: www.politika.lv.

González, L.R. and Lester, L. (2018) '"All for one, one for all": Communicative processes of co-creation of place brands through inclusive and horizontal stakeholder collaborative networks', *Communication & Society*, 31 (4), 59–78.

Hankinson, G. (2007) 'The management of destination brands: Five guiding principles based on recent developments in corporate branding theory', *Journal of Brand Management*, 14 (3), 240–254.

Helmi, J., Bridson, K. and Casidy, R. (2020) 'A typology of organisational stakeholder engagement with place brand identity', *Journal of Strategic Marketing*, 28 (7), 620–638.

Hung, S.-C. (2002) 'Mobilising networks to achieve strategic difference', *Long Range Planning*, 35 (6), 591–613.

Ind, N. (2003) *Living The Brand: How to Transform Every Member of Your Organization into a Brand Champion*, 2nd edn, London: Kogan Page.

Interbrand (2008) 'Country case insight – Estonia', in Dinnie, K. (ed.), *Nation Branding – Concepts, Issues, Practice*, 1st edn, 230–235, London: Butterworth-Heinemann.

Johnston, Y. (2008) 'Developing Brand South Africa', in Dinnie, K. (ed.), *Nation Branding – Concepts, Issues, Practice*, 1st edn, 5–13, London: Butterworth-Heinemann.

Kavaratzis, M. and Kalandides, A. (2015) 'Rethinking the place brand: The interactive formation of place brands and the role of participatory place branding', *Environment and Planning A*, 47 (1), 1368–1382.

Lane, M.L. (2005) 'Public participation in planning: An intellectual history', *Australian Geographer*, 36 (3), 283–299.

Martin, E. and Capelli, S. (2018) 'Place brand communities: From terminal to instrumental values', *Journal of Product & Brand Management*, 27 (7), 793–806.

Naipaul, S., Wang, Y. and Okumus, F. (2009) 'Regional destination marketing: A collaborative approach', *Journal of Travel & Tourism Marketing*, 26 (5), 462–481.

Nimijean, R. and Carment, D. (2019) *Canada, Nation Branding and Domestic Politics*, New York: Routledge.

Olins, W. (1989) *Corporate Identity*, London: Thames and Hudson.

Palsdottir, I.H. (2008) 'The case of "Iceland naturally" – establishing an umbrella brand to increase country image impact and coherence', in Dinnie, K. (ed.), *Nation Branding – Concepts, Issues, Practice*, 1st edn, 183–186, London: Butterworth-Heinemann.

Sanches, R. and Sekles, F. (2008) 'Brazil IT: Taking Brazil's successful domestic IT industry abroad', in Dinnie, K. (ed.), *Nation Branding – Concepts, Issues, Practice*, 1st edn, 133–136, London: Butterworth-Heinemann.

Saraniemi, S. and Komppula, R. (2019) 'The development of a destination brand identity: A story of stakeholder collaboration', *Current Issues in Tourism*, 22 (9), 1116–1132.

Saunders, R. (2018) *Popular Geopolitics and Nation Branding in the Post-Soviet Realm*, New York: Routledge.

Temporal, P. (2002) *Advanced Brand Management: From Vision to Valuation*, Asia: John Wiley & Sons.

Yan, J. (2008) 'Smaller nations enter the global dialogue through nation branding', in Dinnie, K. (ed.), *Nation Branding – Concepts, Issues, Practice*, 1st edn, 170–172, London: Butterworth-Heinemann.

PART 4

CURRENT PRACTICE AND FUTURE HORIZONS FOR NATION BRANDING

9 Elements of nation branding strategy

Key points

- Strategic planning for nation branding should be based upon internal and external analysis
- Elements of nation branding strategy include advertising, public relations, social media, brand ambassadors, diaspora mobilisation and nation days
- The effectiveness of nation branding strategy needs to be assessed on an ongoing basis

Introduction

There is no universal template for nation branding strategy. Some basic principles of strategy are considered in this chapter and related to the context of nation branding. Internal and external analysis, for example, are important bases for strategy formulation and this chapter outlines techniques and issues in this regard. Specific elements of nation branding strategy are also discussed, including advertising, customer and citizen relationship management, and diaspora mobilisation. The first case in this chapter focuses on the brand image of the Greek islands during the refugee crisis. The second case provides a

DOI: 10.4324/9781003100249-13

range of insights into the evolution of Brand Sweden. Nicholas J. Cull's academic perspective discusses the concept of reputational security in the context of public diplomacy and nation branding, whilst the practitioner insight by David Haigh addresses the challenge of how to maximise nation brand value.

Principles of strategy

The basic principles of strategy centre upon three key questions for the firm, or in our case, the nation. First, where are we now? Second, where do we want to go? Third, how do we get there? The formulation and implementation of strategy is a complex task, yet these three guiding questions provide a framework within which strategy can be developed. Strategy involves the long-term direction and scope of an organisation (Johnson et al., 2005). Nation brands, like companies, must decide on their long-term direction and scope. For nations, this will involve strategic decisions regarding the configuration of resources and competences to achieve goals in the areas of FDI, export promotion, tourism, talent attraction and so on. Nations will rarely be able to excel in all of these competitive domains, and therefore strategic decisions must be made regarding the nation brand's direction.

Where are we now? Strategic analysis

In order to assess the nation brand's current competitive position, it is necessary to conduct both internal and external analysis. The main objective of the internal analysis is to evaluate the nation brand's capabilities across a range of sector-specific indicators. External analysis, on the other hand, focuses on the nation brand's competitors and also on the wider environmental forces that affect the nation brand's activities.

Internal analysis

Internal analysis for the nation brand serves to evaluate the nation's capabilities across the different arenas within which it competes. The analysis needs to be conducted on a sectoral basis in order to identify existing capabilities, evaluate the strength of these capabilities and then derive appropriate action points based on the nation brand capability analysis. The main sectors that nation brands compete in include tourism, FDI, export promotion and talent attraction. The internal analysis required by nation brands competing in these sectors is outlined in the following text.

Tourism: Many nations are heavily dependent upon tourism. Remote, landlocked states in particular find it difficult to compete in the other arenas of nation brand strategy and therefore turn to tourism as a key component of economic development. Other nations, blessed with attractive climates and sights, but poor in other resources, also rely heavily on tourism as a reliable revenue stream. An indicative, though not exhaustive, range of key success factors for nation brands' performance in the tourism sector are shown in Figure 9.1.

Key success factors	Nation brand capability									
Customer service levels	1	2	3	4	5	6	7	8	9	10
Safety	1	2	3	4	5	6	7	8	9	10
Value for money	1	2	3	4	5	6	7	8	9	10
Accessibility	1	2	3	4	5	6	7	8	9	10

Figure 9.1
Nation brand internal analysis: Tourism

The key success factors in Figure 9.1 are beyond the control of national tourism organisations, yet tourism boards can and do take initiatives to try and drive up overall levels of customer service levels, for example. Amongst the other key success factors, reasonable levels of safety and law and order are a prerequisite for attracting mainstream tourism; value for money is an important attribute; whilst accessibility can represent a considerable obstacle for otherwise highly attractive destinations – Australia and New Zealand, for example, enjoy positive perceptions as a tourist destination amongst UK consumers yet the distance involved in travelling there is a considerable deterrent. For other countries, such as Iceland and other Nordic states, their remoteness may be more perceptual than real. In such a case, there is potential for effective nation branding communications to correct misperceptions of remoteness.

Foreign direct investment: Globalisation has sharpened the competition between nations to attract inward investment. In response to this, nations need to put in place a long-term strategy to ensure that their levels of FDI attraction make a significant contribution to the nation's economy. Some of the key success factors in attracting FDI are shown in Figure 9.2.

Without a stable economic and political environment, there is little likelihood of attracting FDI. Companies looking to make long-term investments in foreign nations will be put off by a volatile political situation or a mismanaged economy. A skilled workforce is attractive in that it minimises the need for companies to pay for the training of their workforces in foreign locations and offers the prospect of higher productivity than less skilled workforces in other nations. Administrative procedures can be so complex, bureaucratic and slow in some nations that companies will look elsewhere rather than submit to the uncertainty of a wait of several months for approval to do business in a nation whose business environment is strangled by cumbersome administrative processes. Finally, nations need to invest in efficient, modern infrastructure if they are to compete effectively for highly sought-after FDI.

Export promotion: A key objective of nation branding strategy is to boost the nation's level of export performance. The practitioner insight in Chapter 4, for example, gives an insight into how the 'Made in Russia' project was initiated in order to enhance the international success of Russian exporters.

An indicative range of key success factors for export promotion includes the need to build high-quality brands, establish effective country-of-origin positioning through

Key success factors	Nation brand capability									
Stable economic and political environment	1	2	3	4	5	6	7	8	9	10
Skilled workforce	1	2	3	4	5	6	7	8	9	10
Streamlined administrative procedures	1	2	3	4	5	6	7	8	9	10
Infrastructure	1	2	3	4	5	6	7	8	9	10

Figure 9.2
Nation brand internal analysis: Foreign direct investment

Key success factors	Nation brand capability									
High quality brands	1	2	3	4	5	6	7	8	9	10
Effective country of origin positioning	1	2	3	4	5	6	7	8	9	10
Strategic development of target markets	1	2	3	4	5	6	7	8	9	10
Innovation	1	2	3	4	5	6	7	8	9	10

Figure 9.3
Nation brand internal analysis: Export promotion

Key success factors	Nation brand capability									
Favourable residency criteria (for visa, passport, etc.)	1	2	3	4	5	6	7	8	9	10
Attractive lifestyle	1	2	3	4	5	6	7	8	9	10
Opportunity for career progression	1	2	3	4	5	6	7	8	9	10
Reputation for higher education	1	2	3	4	5	6	7	8	9	10

Figure 9.4
Nation brand internal analysis: Talent attraction

sound management of country image perceptions, the strategic development of target markets and high levels of innovation.

Talent attraction: The two major objectives of talent attraction are to attract skilled workers and to attract foreign students to the country's higher education system.

The attraction of skilled workers will depend upon various criteria, including favourable visa and residency regulations, opportunity for career progression and an attractive lifestyle. The widespread pivot to remote working induced by the Covid-19 pandemic has led to countries making explicit appeals to attract digital nomads, skilled workers for whom the place they live matters as much as the work they do. For example, in order to broaden its image away from being perceived only as a tourist leisure destination, in Croatia a digital nomad residency contest was introduced in order to position Dubrovnik as a desirable location for remote workers (Lin, 2021). Talent attraction is emerging as an increasingly important objective of nation branding for many countries (Silvanto and Ryan, 2018).

For potential students, the country's reputation for higher education plays an important role, particularly in the highly competitive market for master's and MBA students.

External analysis

External analysis takes two main forms – *competitor* analysis and *environmental* analysis.

Competitor analysis focuses on a number of key questions, which have been identified as follows: Who are our competitors? What are their strengths and weaknesses? What are their strategic objectives and thrust? What are their strategies? What are their response patterns? (Jobber, 2004). Nation brands need to conduct this type of competitor analysis for each of the arenas within which they are competing. This can encompass tourism, FDI, export promotion, talent attraction and any further nation branding domains. The competitor set will vary according to which competitive arena is under analysis – a nation that is a key competitor in the tourism sector may barely figure at all as a competitor for FDI, for example. The nation brand competitor analysis matrix provides a tool for analysing the nation brand's competitive set across the key dimensions of nation branding activity such as tourism, FDI, export promotion and talent attraction.

	Strengths	Weaknesses	Strategic goals	Current strategies
Tourism				
Country A	Customer service	Distance from key markets		
Country B				
Foreign direct investment				
Country C	Highly developed infrastructure			
Country D				
Export promotion				
Country E				Promotion of 'Made in' label
Country F				
Talent attraction				
Country G	Good reputation for higher education	Visa requirements		
Country H				

Figure 9.5
Nation brand competitor analysis matrix (with hypothetical sample entries)

The nation brand competitor analysis matrix allows for the concise presentation of a large number of complex variables. It can be used not only for analysis of the nation brand's key competitors, but also as a basis for strategy development.

Where do we want to go? Strategic planning

Strategic planning involves setting specific, measurable goals and targets. For companies, this will encompass multiple objectives including market share, profitability, sales growth and others (Wilson and Gilligan, 2005). Likewise, nations will pursue multiple objectives and these objectives should underpin strategy formulation. One of the most widely used tools in strategic planning is Ansoff's matrix, which identifies potential directions for the development of strategy based on permutations of existing or new products and existing or new markets (Ansoff, 1988). In the context of nation branding, Ansoff's matrix can be used to identify strategic directions across the full range of nation brand activities.

How do we get there? Strategic implementation

After the preceding stages of analysis and strategic planning, the final and crucial stage in strategy lies in the implementation of the chosen strategy. Key challenges in strategy implementation include ensuring control, managing knowledge, coping with change, designing appropriate structures and processes and managing internal and external relationships (Johnson et al., 2005). It is perhaps in the area of implementation that nation branding faces its biggest challenge, given that the nation brand stakeholders may not be as easily structured and managed as the various business units of a commercial organisation. Switzerland is one country that has addressed the challenge of strategic implementation through establishing a coordinating body, Presence Switzerland, which performs many of the strategy implementation roles outlined earlier, for example, managing knowledge, coping with change and managing internal and external relationships (Pasquier, 2008).

Having provided an overview of the fundamental issues in strategic analysis, planning and implementation, we shall now focus on some of the specific elements that nation branding strategy may encompass.

Nation brand advertising

Nation branding does not consist merely of running advertising campaigns. Advertising can obviously be a powerful tool but it is only one element of a nation brand's overall strategy. In fact, if a nation has severely limited financial resources it would probably be better off activating its diaspora rather than placing its hope in an advertising campaign. However, if the funds are available then advertising should be used as part of an integrated strategy to achieve specific, clearly stated goals.

Advertising can deliver numerous benefits to brands. It can generate new markets for a brand; revitalise a declining brand; change consumer behaviour; and generate rapid sales increases (IPA Effectiveness Awards, 1998). There are, however, a number of common mistakes in advertising that nation brands need to be aware of before handing over significant resources to advertising agencies. Such mistakes include mistaken assumptions about consumer knowledge; failure to break through the advertising clutter; distracting, overpowering creative in ads; under-branded ads; failure to use supporting media; changing campaigns too frequently; and, substituting ad frequency for ad quality (Keller, 2003).

If advertising is going to be bought as part of a country's overall nation brand strategy, those involved in procuring the advertising need to have at least a basic knowledge of the advertising industry and the way that advertising agencies work. Without a basic level of advertising literacy, precious resources could be wasted through failing to develop a mutually beneficial relationship with the advertising agency selected to produce the campaign. Individuals in the nation brand team need to be familiar with what is meant by a client brief, creative teams and the concept of brand positioning. Individuals with a background or qualification in marketing will be familiar with such issues. But it cannot be assumed that individuals with non-marketing backgrounds, government officials or other stakeholders will be equally knowledgeable in this area. The concept of brand positioning has already been covered (see Chapter 2), so we will focus here on the other key advertising-related issues.

The *client brief* is issued by the client to the advertising agencies it is inviting to pitch for its business, in the form of a written brief which details the client's requirements. After an advertising agency has been appointed, the brief will normally be refined in order to establish clear lines of communication and accountability between client and agency (Hackley, 2005). The creative team within the advertising agency will normally comprise an art director and a copywriter, whose role is to produce creative work that will grab the target audience's attention and deliver the campaign's specified goals. The art director will be responsible for the visual element of the advertisement, whilst the copywriter will provide any text that the advertisement will use.

On a day-to-day basis, however, the client will not normally be in contact with the agency's creative team. Rather, the agency will communicate with the client via an account manager whose role is to ensure a smooth relationship between client and agency throughout the duration of the planning and implementation process. The quality of the work produced by the agency is therefore dependent not only on the agency's own creativity, but also on the client's ability to clearly communicate its needs to the agency. Clients can influence the creativity of their advertising agency in the following ways: by 'setting direction' through their initial brief to the agency, as they interact with the agency during the advertising planning process, and also by 'resource allocation' in terms of providing the advertising agency with access to the client's top management in order to provide strategic insights to the campaign, and by providing access to previously conducted consumer research data (Koslow et al., 2006).

Whereas the client brief will detail the strategic objectives to be met by the advertising campaign, the client will also need to produce a *creative brief* that focuses more closely on exactly what the advertisement is going to say, to whom and the tone that is going to be used. It is important to ensure that an appropriate tone is used in the advertisement's message. If the wrong tone is used, the audience may feel alienated or even offended. The advertising campaign promoting Australian tourism which used the tagline 'Where the bloody hell are you?' clearly runs the risk of offending its audience, who may find the slogan rude and aggressive. A different type of nation branding advertising, aimed at attracting FDI rather than tourists, was carried out by 'The New France' campaign, which launched in 2004 and followed up the first wave of advertising with a second wave in 2005, with 77 advertisements appearing in 19 publications. The effect of this campaign was evaluated based on a survey of the target audience – company managers in four of the target countries – and taking into consideration the survey results, the advertising approach in one of the target countries was switched to focus on sector-based magazines rather than financial publications (Favre, 2008). This illustrates the importance of evaluating the effectiveness of an advertising campaign and then fine-tuning the campaign based on the results of the evaluation.

A full-service advertising agency will not only produce the advertising for the client, but will also buy the media space within which the advertising will appear. However, there are dedicated media buying agencies that exist independently of the creative advertising agencies, and in some cases it may be cost-effective to hire the services of such a specialised media buying agency. It is a complex task to evaluate the numerous different media channels and vehicles available for any one advertising campaign. Media channels include television, newspapers and magazines, internet, radio, outdoor and so on. Media vehicles include the different options that exist within each media. For example, within newspapers as a media channel, the available vehicles are represented by the individual newspaper brands within that sector such as the *Financial Times*, *Wall Street Journal*, and so on. Full-service advertising agencies or specialised media buying agencies will normally use media planning software to determine the optimum mix of advertising media in order to achieve the campaign's stated goals. Media planning software works in the following way: first, the user develops a media database of possible advertising vehicles, specifying their ratings and cost; second, the user selects the criterion for schedule optimisation, e.g., reach, frequency; third, the user specifies constraints such as a budget constraint for the media planning period; and finally, the software algorithm seeks out the optimum media schedule according to the specified objectives and constraints (Shimp, 2003).

The structure of the advertising industry has been in flux over recent years and clients will usually have a choice between opting for a full-service agency or specialised creative agencies and media buying agencies. It has been argued, for example, by the head of WPP's media network, Mindshare, that the media agency is best placed to orchestrate a brand's communication efforts (Marquis, 2007).

Public relations

Public relations agencies are frequently hired by governments in an attempt to manage a country's international perceptions amongst not only the general public but also amongst other target audiences such as policy makers and journalists. The issue of public relations has been studied in the context of both public diplomacy (Rasmussen and Merkelsen, 2012; Yun and Toth, 2009) and nation branding (Szondi, 2010). The public relations component of nation branding strategy should be integrated with other elements of the strategy, rather than merely being resorted to as a crisis management tool.

Online nation branding

Online branding is an integral part of most businesses in the digital age. The internet has become recognised as a great equaliser, allowing any brand, however small, to become global simply by having a website and a social media presence. Pursuing nation branding objectives, Saudi Arabia and other countries have exploited the possibilities of online nation branding by tapping into the phenomenon of influencers to help shape their country's image (Hickman, 2019). Kenya's nation branding strategy includes an initiative led by the Kenya Export Promotion and Branding Agency (KEPROBA) to develop an e-commerce platform linking the country's exporters to international buyers (Mwita, 2020). El Banna et al. (2017) and Paniagua et al. (2017) have illustrated the role that online promotion can play in FDI attraction. Public diplomacy has also embraced the digital age (Cull, 2019), with digital diplomacy now recognised as an essential means to enhance countries' soft power (Digital Diplomacy Hub, 2021).

Chris Anderson, former Editor-in-Chief at *Wired* magazine and author of *The Long Tail* (Anderson, 2006), has described how the internet allows niche brands to build a market that is even greater than that of the big, blockbuster brands and even though word-of-mouth marketing may be the only marketing available to these niche brands, the tools are now available to enable this to happen (Mortimer, 2006). This is an encouraging observation for smaller, emerging or less developed nations that cannot realistically hope to compete with the global economic superpowers in terms of financial firepower to fund their nation branding. Online branding offers such nations the opportunity to establish themselves as niche brands in a way that would not be possible through using more conventional branding techniques such as extensive TV advertising, for example, whose cost puts it beyond the budget of many less wealthy nations. Online branding can stimulate positive word-of-mouth through techniques such as seeding trials, viral advertising, brand advocacy programmes and influencer outreach initiatives (Kirby and Marsden, 2005). Digital technologies now enable the emergence of the 'virtual state', a phenomenon studied by Tammpuu and Masso (2018) in their investigation of the nation branding implications of the virtual state and virtual residency in the context of Estonia.

Social media usage for place branding purposes varies widely from one country to another (Hays et al., 2012). Digital and social media storytelling are becoming increasingly prominent in place branding practice (Hudak, 2019; Lund et al., 2018)

There are virtual worlds such as Second Life, for example, in which some nations have established a presence. Sweden opened a virtual embassy in Second Life in 2007, inaugurated by the avatar of then Swedish Minister of Foreign Affairs Carl Bildt (Bengtsson, 2011). The open and participative nature of social media also offers scope for citizen-driven nation brand initiatives such as Turkayfe.org, a social networking site born from the desire of four entrepreneurs to counter the perceived negative portrayal of Turkey in American mass media (Sevin and White, 2011).

The most high-profile social media options that can play a part in nation brand strategy include Facebook, Twitter and YouTube. Countries such as Mexico and Brazil have implemented strategies to communicate a clear brand personality via Facebook (de Moya and Jain, 2013), whilst Sweden has led the way in embracing the nation brand-building potential of Twitter through the @Sweden project (also known as Curators of Sweden) in which the country's official Twitter account is handed over to a different citizen every week (Christensen, 2013). Diplomats from many countries now use Twitter. However, it is important for such individuals to realise that using Twitter to speak to foreign audiences is not enough; diplomats should also listen to what their audience is saying, and avoid having a Twitter feed where the owner is following no one (Cull, 2012).

Mobile applications can play an important role in nation branding, particularly in terms of harnessing consumer-generated content. The Canadian Tourism Commission, for example, has launched an app 'Explore Canada like a local' (ECLAL) that collates travel recommendations from members of the public and makes these searchable in categories such as Arts & Culture, City breaks, Culinary, Luxury and Outdoors. In 2012, Denmark's Minister for Trade and Investment Pia Olsen Dyhr presented the launch of Denmark Stay Tuned, the world's first nation branding smartphone application targeted specifically at international media. The app focuses on areas such as new Nordic cuisine, green growth and Danish architecture, fashion and design and provides ready-to-use content for journalists in the form of editorial texts, images and videos. The potential of videos to go viral represents an opportunity for place brands to raise their awareness quickly and widely (Strandberg and Styvén, 2019).

Nation brand ambassadors

Companies in many sectors employ brand ambassadors in order to provide a human face to their activities. Currency exchange firm Travelex, for example, signed up England rugby star Jonny Wilkinson as a brand ambassador for a two-year period. Travelex had previously signed up Australian cricketer Adam Gilchrist as a brand ambassador in 2003 (Barrand, 2005). Other companies appoint brand ambassadors internally. These brand ambassadors are individuals imbued with a deep knowledge of their company and they also possess the ability to communicate the company's brand values effectively to targeted audiences.

Nations, on the other hand, traditionally employ ambassadors in a more discreet role, so discreet that few people outside of diplomatic circles will know much, if anything, about them. Famous sporting or cultural figures may perform an unplanned, unscripted form of nation brand ambassador role, without any official endorsement from their nation or any agreement by the individual concerned that they are in fact a type of ambassador for their nation. Likewise, the behaviour of individual citizens when abroad in foreign countries can be interpreted as being representative of their home nation. When this behaviour is bad, as in the case of English football hooliganism during the 1980s, it can tarnish the overall country image. It is clearly unrealistic to expect every citizen in a population of millions to act as a nation brand ambassador, yet it may be possible to identify certain individuals who are qualified and willing to play such a role. The power of ambassador networks to exert an influence on place branding is attracting increasing attention amongst both policy makers and researchers (Andersson and Ekman, 2009).

Internal brand management

Internal branding is one area in which governments have been slow to engage compared to other aspects of nation branding strategy. Internal nation branding will gain in importance as nations realise that the necessary behaviours for successful implementation of strategy result from the commitment levels that individuals exhibit towards the strategy in question. For nation branding, the two audiences for internal branding are on the one hand the stakeholder organisations and individuals involved in the development and implementation of nation branding strategy, and on the other hand, the domestic population, the entirety of the nation's citizens. The domestic impact of nation branding has, for example, been examined in the context of curbing political polarisation in Colombia (Vecchi et al., 2021). The use of media technologies to encourage citizen participation in the branding of Sweden could be observed in the case of the Swedish Number campaign (Pamment and Cassinger, 2018).

In the context of the firm, Burmann and Zeplin (2005) have identified three key levers for generating brand commitment: brand-centred human resources management, brand communication and brand leadership. In a nation branding context, responsibility for these three key levers needs to be allocated to specified individuals or agencies, the identity of which will depend upon the specific structure within which the nation brand has been developed. Some of the steps to effective internal branding used by companies such as Yahoo! can equally be applied to internal nation branding. For example, don't work in silos, think like a marketer and use powerful keywords that embody your brand promise (Sartain, 2005).

Customer relationship management (CRM) provides a potentially useful lens through which to view the challenge of internal nation brand management. CRM is a well-established practice in the business world. The application of the CRM concept to nation branding is a much more recent development, where the term 'citizen relationship management' has been used (Sheth, 2006). The concept of citizen relationship management suggests that governments need to engage with their citizens in a similar way in which companies do with their customers. Understanding citizens' needs and communicating with citizens in an appropriate manner at an appropriate frequency represent CRM principles that nation branding strategy may usefully adopt. CRM as a process that 'involves the application of technology to help manage interactions and transactions with customers, so that organisations can optimise their returns across their customer portfolio' (Buttle, 2008, p. 66) also has applicability to nation brands that have a 'customer portfolio' spread across sectors as diverse as tourism, FDI, export promotion and talent attraction.

Citizen relationship management may be seen in the case of Russia's 'Church diplomacy' project as well as in its social projects (Lebedenko, 2008) and in the nation branding efforts of Estonia, where it is hoped that the brand's aim of establishing broader international recognition will motivate Estonia's own citizens (Interbrand, 2008).

Diaspora mobilisation

Nations that fail to have a strategy for activating their diaspora network are squandering a unique and precious resource. The existence of diaspora networks spread across the globe represents a potentially immense asset for the nation, not only in terms of remittances sent by diaspora members but also in terms of stimulating FDI through interventions by well-placed senior executives in international firms. Furthermore, the reputation-building capacity of diaspora networks represents another key opportunity to enhance the nation brand.

Some observers remain unconvinced that remittances by migrants can have a significant impact on a nation's development, although they acknowledge that such remittances play an important role in poverty alleviation (Kuznetsov and Sabel, 2006). Rather than the financial flows inherent in remittances, it has been suggested that a more important role of diasporas is their knowledge and institution-building capacity (Kapur and McHale, 2005). Kuznetsov (2006) has described successful diaspora networks as combining three main features. First, networks bring together people with strong intrinsic motivation. Second, members play both direct roles (implementing projects in the home country) and indirect roles (serving as bridges and antennae for the development of projects in the home country). Third, successful initiatives move from discussions on how to get involved with the home country to transactions, i.e., tangible outcomes. There is wide variation in the impact that different nations' diasporas have had. The diasporas of China and India, for instance, have had a considerable positive impact on their home countries, whereas Armenia has failed to benefit from its wealthy diaspora (Kuznetsov and Sabel, 2006). This highlights the necessity of integrating diaspora networks into overall nation brand strategy.

Diaspora networks are not necessarily monolithic and homogeneous. For example, there are many diaspora networks that take the form of professional associations dedicated to helping members advance in their professional field. Such networks include the Association of Doctors of Armenian Origin in the United States, the Association of Engineers from Latin America or Indus Entrepreneurs (Kuznetsov and Sabel, 2006). South Africa has two diaspora networks, the South African Network of Skills Abroad, a network that links expatriate and South Africa-based academics, researchers and practitioners working in science and technology; and the South African Diaspora Network, which focuses on developing knowledge and entrepreneurial connections between South African firms and well-connected, strategically placed individuals in the United Kingdom (Marks, 2006). Government support for such networks should focus on achieving synergies between the different diaspora networks and simultaneously avoiding duplication of effort and activity by complementary networks.

World Expos

World Expos can play a part in nation branding by providing countries with an opportunity and a platform to present a narrative to a global audience. Wang (2020) suggests that visitors to World Expos can be exposed to hitherto unfamiliar aspects of a country's culture. Countries that have actively used World Expos to help build their nation brand include Japan (Sano, 2019), Algeria (Bensalem, 2019), Azerbaijan (Alakbarov, 2019), Malaysia (Yahaya, 2019) and Pakistan (Wani, 2019). Whilst many countries have enthusiastically embraced World Expos as a component of their nation branding strategy, a more critical perspective is provided by Pereira (2018), who argues that World Expos perpetuate images of countries as being central or peripheral, and more developed or less developed.

Nation days

The celebration of nation days represents another potential element of nation brand strategy, both internally as a means of generating interest and pride domestically from the nation's citizens and also externally as a focal point for events to promote the nation brand. The natural place to hold such nation day celebrations outside of the home country is in locations where there is a significant diaspora presence. Ireland and Scotland, for example, have done this through their respective nation day celebrations in New York, a city that is home to large numbers of Irish and Scottish diaspora. The Irish celebration is based on St. Patrick's Day, whilst the Scottish celebration is based on what started as Tartan Day but which has since expanded to Tartan Week. The Tartan Day and Tartan Week initiatives may be considered as examples of the concept of 'invented tradition' that has been widely debated in the field of national identity (see Chapter 5). Ireland has massively expanded its St Patrick Day's celebrations as a tool for nation branding through its greening of iconic landmarks around the world, including the Great Wall of China; the Moulin Rouge in Paris, France; Soldier Field Stadium in Chicago, United States; the Rhine Falls, Switzerland; Abbey Road, London, England; the Temple of Hercules in Amman, Jordan; and the Merlion Statue, Singapore, amongst many others (Linder, 2019). Ireland's greening of the world campaign was initiated by Tourism Ireland with the country's Department of Foreign Affairs and Trade.

The naming of nation brands

The case of Iceland (Palsdottir, 2008) illustrates the potential effect of a nation's name on its country image perceptions. Nations rarely tamper with their names and when they do so, it is often to signal a powerful symbolic event such as the birth of a nation gaining its freedom from a former colonial power. This can be seen in the case of many African states, for example, the name Ghana replacing Gold Coast when that country achieved independence from the United Kingdom. Sometimes there can be widespread misunderstanding of a nation's name. Many people considered the old Soviet Union to be 'Russia', for example (Lebedenko, 2008), and there is still a widespread misperception that the United Kingdom and England are interchangeable terms. A further dimension of the naming of nation brands is that some nations have two different names in use, for example, Greece/Hellas, and Holland/Netherlands. In order to avoid potential confusion, when nation brand architecture is being developed (see Chapter 8) there will need to be a strategic decision taken on which name is to be used as the 'umbrella brand'.

Performance measurement

The effectiveness of nation branding strategy needs to be assessed on an ongoing basis. Various types of tracking studies can be conducted, and there are numerous indexes available that can be used to determine different facets of nation brand performance. A widely publicised survey in the field of nation branding is the Anholt-GfK Roper Nations Brands Index, an analytical ranking of the world's nation brands that appears on a quarterly basis. Fetscherin (2010) developed a country brand strength index (CBSI) based on objective secondary data; this index produced results similar to the Anholt-GfK Roper Nations Brands Index. A modified version of the country brand strength index has been developed by Lahrech et al. (2020). In addition to these, there are various other nation brand indexes, each with different methodologies, such as the Bloom Consulting Country Brand Ranking (www.bloom-consulting.com/en/country-brand-ranking), the FutureBrand Country Index (www.futurebrand.com/futurebrand-country-index-2020) and the Brand Finance Nation Brands report (https://brandirectory.com/rankings/nation-brands/).

There are also other indexes available which, although not designed with nation branding in mind, represent useful indicators of national performance that nations could use to enhance their country image perceptions – on condition, of course, that the nation performs well in these indexes. One such index is the Environmental Sustainability Index, which measures the quality of nations' environmental stewardship (see Chapter 7); another index is the World Economic Forum's Global Competitiveness Index, which assesses a nation's competitiveness in terms of its institutions, infrastructure, macro-economy, health and primary education, higher education and training, market efficiency, technological readiness, business sophistication and innovation. If a nation scores highly on these criteria, then it should highlight and communicate its positive performance in order to achieve strategic objectives such as increasing FDI, and talent attraction. The World Economic Forum also produces a Travel & Tourism Competitiveness Report benchmarking the competitiveness of 140 economies across the following four major dimensions: Enabling Environment, T&T Policy and Enabling Conditions, Infrastructure and Natural and Cultural Resources. In the 2019 report, the top five ranked countries were Spain, France, Germany, Japan and the United States, in that order (World Economic Forum, 2019). In the field of investment attraction, the EY Attractiveness Survey is a well-established ranking of countries as investment destinations (EY Attractiveness Surveys, 2021).

Institutions involved in nation branding

As interest in the field of nation branding has grown over recent years, countries have established institutions of various kinds to manage their nation brand strategy. The Sultanate of Oman, for example, set up the Brand Oman Management Unit to implement Oman's brand initiatives. In Sweden, the Swedish Institute was set up with a remit to promote Sweden and Swedish issues globally. The Swedish Institute has offices in Stockholm, Visby and Paris, with approximately 140 employees. In South Africa, the International

Marketing Council is involved in the branding of the country's tourism, exports, culture and heritage and investment. A similarly comprehensive remit is allocated in Iceland to the Promote Iceland organisation, a public–private partnership tasked with stimulating economic growth through increased exports, promoting Iceland as a tourism destination, assisting in the promotion of Icelandic culture abroad and positioning Iceland as an attractive location for foreign direct investment.

ACADEMIC PERSPECTIVE: PUBLIC DIPLOMACY AND NATION BRANDS/BRANDING: THE ROAD TO REPUTATIONAL SECURITY

Nicholas J. Cull, Professor of Public Diplomacy, University of Southern California

The concept of public diplomacy – the way in which foreign policy is conducted through the engagement of foreign publics – is closely related to that of nation branding, as evidenced by the extension of the journal *Place Branding* to include Public Diplomacy. The concepts relate in two ways. As Eytan Gilboa noted (2008), in the early twenty-first century nation branding became one of the fifteen or so standard instruments of public diplomacy. A nation wishing to enhance its image in the world may invest in international broadcasting or cultural diplomacy or a generous aid programme or launch a branding campaign employing communication specialists to identify the country with positive images and connotations. It is not hard to find examples of such efforts. One might cite Switzerland's creation of *Presence Switzerland*. Israel attempted it as Gilboa (2020) has documented. Correlating such work at the national level with measurable results is, however, harder.

The second way of understanding nation branding within public diplomacy is to see it as a framework of analysis. This approach draws a distinction between the idea of a nation having a brand – in Anholt's original conception, a set of ideas associated with that place, its people and products (Anholt, 2020) – and the practice of branding: marketing strategies to reposition the meaning of a place in the public mind. The advantage of this approach is that it allows the scholar to readily apply both concepts where they are not explicitly articulated by the governments concerned, either because the government is not consciously applying a brand strategy or because the case comes from a period before the concept was current. Some of the best examples of branding in the history of public diplomacy fall in this second category: William the Silent's projection of the new Dutch Republic in the 1580s (a task greatly helped by the identification thanks to a fortunate pun of his princely house with the emotive color, orange) or the creation of positive connotations for German industry by the Deutsche Werkbund at the dawn of the twentieth century (Cull, 2019).

The cultivation of American public opinion by the British government of Winston Churchill leading up to United States entry into World War Two, looks very like a skilled nation branding campaign before the word. The British government used all manner of media including movies, visiting speakers, radio broadcasts and the cultivation of journalists to get a consistent story across: the old Britain of Empire and class division had fallen away and a new Britain had emerged committed to egalitarian principles and waging a people's war. America fell in love with the image and moved to aid the country in its struggle. But the case contains an important qualification. The British public actually lived up to their government's narrative: pulling together and building a better Britain even in the midst of war

(Cull, 1995). Public diplomats have learned that success requires delivering on promises and 'living the brand'.

The logical extension of acknowledging the benefit of a positive image for a country is to explicitly link that into the security of the state in a concept of reputational security (Cull, 2019). States with positive reputations are more secure if only because the global community objects when they are threatened. Conversely, states without well-developed images like Czechoslovakia in 1938 or Ukraine in 2014, or with negative images like Afghanistan in the 1990s have been left to the mercy of hostile neighbours or internal extremists. Recent years have seen explicit attacks on the image of states by hostile media. Gilboa (2020) has referred to this as Brandjacking. Targets have included countries with some of the most positive brand images such as the Nordics, which have been demonized in hostile media as morally corrupt and mired in child abuse. Countries or regions challenged in this way would do well to work to minimize the genuine negative aspects of their conduct. Ultimately, as Anholt (2020) has argued, there is no substitute for actually being a 'good country'.

References

Anholt, S. (2020) *The Good Country Equation: How We Can Repair the World in One Generation*, San Francisco: Berrett-Koehler.

Cull, N.J. (1995) *Selling War: The British Campaign Against American Neutrality in the Second World War*, New York: Oxford University Press.

Cull, N.J. (2019) *Public Diplomacy: Foundations for Global Engagement in the Digital Age*, Cambridge: Polity.

Gilboa, E. (2008) 'Searching for a theory of public diplomacy', *The Annals of the American Academy of Political and Social Science*, 616 (1), 55–77.

Gilboa, E. (2020) 'Israel: Countering brandjacking', in Snow, N. and Cull, N.J. (eds.), *Routledge Handbook of Public Diplomacy*, 2nd edn, chapter 33, 331–341, New York and London: Routledge.

PRACTITIONER INSIGHT: HOW TO MAXIMISE NATION BRAND VALUE

David Haigh, CEO of Brand Finance

In the last 25 years branding has become a mainstream discipline in many organisations and entities that never considered its benefits before, including at the nation level.

The purpose of branding is to simplify choice and persuade stakeholders to confer economic and other benefits on the organisation or entity because of compelling brand identity, image and positioning attributes. In behavioural economics terms it is about nudging stakeholders to take actions which benefit the subject nation.

All the political parties and even the government now see the benefits of branding and are creating policies to maximise nation brand strength and value.

In the case of the UK, the GREAT campaign sought to enhance 'Brand Britain' deploying a multi-million-pound budget across all branches of government. The campaign has been very successful, enhancing tourism, trade, talent acquisition and foreign direct investment into the UK.

Many other nations have taken the same path – China, Ireland, Switzerland, Singapore, Dubai, India, Turkey, Peru and New Zealand are all good examples of active nation brand management campaigns that benefit their respective economies.

But whereas in the old days these efforts were largely amateurish – and changed from administration to administration over time – now many countries have multiyear, cross-party support to build their nation brand.

Brand Finance has contributed to this process for over 16 years. In 2004 we first conducted nation brand valuations. These involve a Nation Brand Strength assessment considering Input, Intermediate and Output measures.

We measure amounts spent and activities undertaken on promotion and brand creation (Inputs), we measure the effects on behaviour and the economic results of changed behaviour (Outputs) and the intermediate measures which help to predict the outputs.

The Intermediate measures are perceptual. What perceptions, attitudes and behaviours are attached to particular nation brands, how have they changed over the years and how does this translate into policy achievement?

Brand Finance's analysis shows how the perceptions of different nation brands have shifted and how economic performance has changed as a result.

Take Ireland as an example. It used to be regarded as a fairly sleepy agricultural economy until accession to the EU in the 1970s. This carried on for some years but in the 2000s it became a tiger economy within the EU by focusing on developing knowledge-based and IP-rich products, goods and services. Its economy has boomed since then despite a setback in the global financial crisis of 2009.

This was a conscious policy decision backed up by a robust B2B campaign globally. In parallel with the 'gateway Ireland' drive to attract FDI it has promoted the personal Irish brand to demonstrate what a great place Ireland is to live. Ireland has been very focused and diligent in pursuing these Brand Ireland policies.

Brand Finance provides insight, intelligence and data to inform such brand campaigns and has done so in South Africa, Italy, Korea, Canada, the Middle East and South America.

Our structured approach to nation brand strengths and weaknesses, with a brand strength assessment by segment of the economy and a financial and economic appraisal, result in recommendations with the potential 'size of the prize' analysis and an indication of where the greatest results will accrue.

Our latest contribution is the Global Soft Power Index, the world's leading analysis of Nation Brand Attributes, Familiarity, Reputation and Influence. The attributes fall under seven pillars: Business and Trade, Governance, International Relations, Culture and Heritage, Media and Communications, Education and Science and People and Values. In 2020, we surveyed 55,000 respondents in 100 countries to ask their perceptions of the 60 top nation brands of the world against these attributes. In 2021, we repeated the research in more than 100 countries with 75,000 respondents and derived perceptions of the top 100 nation brands.

This powerful global nation brand research will feed straight into our nation brand valuation exercise to be published in October 2021 and which will be used by national policy makers and other decision makers worldwide.

This research study is a watershed. Nation brand valuation has gone from a subjective assessment for general interest to a highly scientific and granular understanding of perceptions, strengths and weaknesses to feed into the increasingly professionalised discipline of nation brand and nation policy formulation.

CASE: GREEK ISLANDS' BRAND IMAGE DURING THE REFUGEE CRISIS

Vana Dimitropoulou, tourism and hospitality marketing expert

Introduction

The ongoing refugee crisis is one of the most tragic events of recent years. It is an issue which affects not only the people who are coming from war zones but also the countries which the refugees enter in order to continue their journey to Europe. One of these countries is Greece, which since 2015 has received over a million refugees. This recent mass migration has created concerns over the shifting brand image that the nation is projecting to the world. In particular some of the islands in the Aegean Sea, like Samos and Kos which are key tourism destinations and therefore important sources of income for the country, have become entry points into Europe for many migrating refugees, given their strategic location between the Middle East and continental Europe. From the beginning of the crisis, the media have been reporting from the islands showing images of despair, pain and inhumanity.

Because of this situation, hotel and tourism agencies received hundreds of cancellations or even early departures from their facilities during 2015 and 2016 which made the owners sceptical of how the travel preferences of tourists would evolve in the years to come and if the image of their island has been changed in people's minds. Hoteliers and tourism business people were brought into a position from where they had to handle the situation by shifting the damaging imagery created by the media around the world and take action by using marketing and branding strategies they had never used before.

Brand Greece and crisis issues

Greece started building its brand promoting at first its historical and archaeological sites. Gradually the tourism campaigns started projecting other destinations within the country, the natural beauty and the entertainment. Nowadays, Brand Greece has evolved and sells itself' mainly as an island destination. Considering that the total contribution of travel and tourism was 37.6% to 45.2% of the total employment in Greece in 2019 and the contribution to the national GPD was 27.5% to 33.1% in 2019, tourism is one of the one of Greece's most important industries and sources of economic development (Ikkos and Koutsos, 2019).

Thus, in pursuit of a more holistic image of Brand Greece, it is important to assess the positive and negative imagery that is being projected by the media. Before the outburst of the refugee crisis the induced images of Greece used to be positive. They were easily accessible through promotional videos, the internet, social media and conventions organised by the national tourism board in which the hoteliers participate frequently. This is how the golden beaches, the crystal clear waters, the Greek folklore and the traditional villages are used to promote the islands' image to the world and create a good reputation while shaping a unique holiday destination worldwide. However, in recent years the press media have also created negative inorganic images of Greece connected with the ongoing refugee crisis. The media, having a particular agenda over the issue transmitted negative images which caused concerns to people, preventing them from considering Samos and Kos as vacation destinations.

The reactions which followed the images were significantly negative towards the islands and their touristic product. The potential visitors hesitated with concerns over the security of the destination and many of them cancelled their bookings. The images of Greece at the heart of the refugee crisis inevitably created concerns of a negative reputation being shaped for the islands which might in turn stigmatise their brand name in the long run and the peoples' holiday preferences for years to come. Even within the tourism industry mixed opinions were expressed regarding the continuity of the negative reputation they received because of the refugee crisis.

Subsequently, they hoteliers suffered from numerous reservation cancellations, which led to the decrease of profits. Moreover, the refugee crisis threatened the cooperation with the tour operators who were reluctant to sign contracts for the coming years based on safety and aesthetic issues. When 70% to 80% of the visitors book their holidays through tour operators that means that the islands are dependent on their thoughts and decisions over the issue.

Solutions

However, changing the negative images and perception is not impossible. Previous studies have shown that countries can be rebranded after negative issues but little research has explored how a country can rebrand itself from a sudden refugee crisis, which has recently affected many of the Mediterranean countries including Greece.

When the refugee crisis started the government and the local communities were in shock and they did not have a certain plan on how to deal with this issue. Although Greeks are aware of the issue, limited efforts were made to effectively rebrand the nation during this period of crisis. In the following months, the local government did not provide them with any feasible action plan to cope with the problem, which gave way to further concerns. Even though there are applied frameworks for similar situations like Faulkner's (2001)) tourism disaster management framework with direct application for the recovery of a nation brand within six phases (preparation, response during the event, emergency activities immediately following the event, initial recovery, long-term recovery, including infrastructure repair and environmental rehabilitation and re-establishment as a tourist destination) the measures taken by the government were insufficient. Actions such as the stable value added tax (VAT) helped in some cases in order to maintain the profit of the businesses but it was not enough to alleviate the cancelations or change the negative images.

The government actions were confined to the relocation of the refugees in hotspots away from touristic areas (Pappas and Papatheodorou, 2017). In that case, the negative images projected by the media disappeared soon after the creation of the accommodation centres which are especially designed for facilitating the refugees but no branding strategies were set in action.

Consequently, the hoteliers realised that they had to take action to support a viable and positive touristic season despite the problems caused by the refugee crisis. Without following a specific action plan but using their instinct and professional knowledge they used rebranding techniques and activities to revitalise the touristic season and the islands' brand image. As yet, there are no action plans suggested by the government. However, looking through the recovery, rebuilding and re-imagining framework introduced by Volcic et al. (2014) it is noticeable that the hoteliers unconsciously took these steps throughout their rebranding actions. Thus, the image will pass through phases to build the country's brand stronger and more viable.

Understanding the need to manage the nation brand image, the private and public sectors collaborated on a structured plan. Advertising campaigns were created by professionals promoting the real images of the islands encouraging people to visit them. Moreover, the hoteliers tried to take the situation into their own hands and reassured the tour operators that the islands were safe and worked with them to promote the islands with offers in order to overcome the profit loss of the first two years, rebuild their relationship with the visitors and show that they still provide high standard services and touristic product.

Based on that, it is worth mentioning that the most affective images of a country are the ones that the visitors gain during their vacation. When visiting Samos and Kos, these complex images seem to meet the expectations that the organic and inorganic images have created. Thus, the complex images are more realistic and reflect on the experiences and the satisfaction of the tourists at the end of their visit (Özdemir and Şimşek, 2015). The same applies in the case of the refugee crisis. The people who visited the islands during the refugee crisis realised the misleading information of the media. Many of them did not see refugees during their stay at all. Even those visitors that did see evidence of the refugee crisis – especially visitors who were staying close to the islands' ports – did not actually feel disappointed by their holiday experience.

Eventually, the hoteliers started to re-imagine the branding of their islands and realised the importance of having a strong brand name, especially during a crisis. They became investment-oriented as they considered the significance of improving the existing services or adding new ones. They focused on the construction of new facilities, the expansion of their services and the enhancement of their knowledge regarding branding applications following the modern trends to create a touristic identity.

Conclusion

In conclusion, the refugee crisis was clearly a factor which impacted the organic and inorganic images as well as the attitudes of the visitors and the potential visitors of Samos and Kos. Interestingly the complex images worked positively for the reputation of the islands and gave an insight of the real image of the situation. Within this context the importance of having visitors who defied any negative images proved to be one of the most important tools against the negative media coverage and the significant amount of reservation cancelations. Without a certain action plan, the hoteliers took their own measures in order to attract visitors and transform the temporarily negative reputation to a positive one. They reimagined their brand name and grew it stronger in order to be able to overcome this kind of situation more efficiently in the future.

Since 2017 the tourist flows have bounced back and the hoteliers have done their best to integrate the touristic product of their islands. The visitors appear to have already forgotten the crisis and continue to choose the islands for their holidays.

References

Faulkner, B. (2001) 'Towards a framework for tourism disaster management', *Tourism Management*, 22 (2), 135–147.

Ikkos, A. and Koutsos, S. (2019) *Η συμβολή του τουρισμού στην Ελληνική οικονομία το 2019* (*The contribution of tourism to the Greek ecomony for 2019*), 4, Athens: INSETE Intelligence, available at: https://insete.gr/wp-content/uploads/2020/09/20_09_Tourism_and_Greek_Economy_2018-2019.pdf (accessed 1/10/2020).

Özdemir, G. and Şimşek, Ö.F. (2015) 'The antecedents of complex destination image', *Procedia – Social and Behavioral Sciences*, 175, 503–510.

Pappas, N. and Papatheodorou, A. (2017) 'Tourism and the refugee crisis in Greece: Perceptions and decision-making of accommodation providers', *Tourism Management*, 63, 31–41.

Volcic, Z., Peak, M. and Erjavec, K. (2014) 'Branding post-war Sarajevo: Journalism, memories, and dark tourism', *Journalism Studies*, 15 (6), 726–742.

CASE: BRAND SWEDEN

James Pamment, PhD, Associate Professor, Lund University Sweden;
Non-Resident fellow, Carnegie Endowment for International Peace

For decades, Swedes have agonised over how the rest of the world perceives their country. Embassies would report back selections of clippings from international broadsheets to show what the world was saying about Sweden, which the Foreign Ministry would share with stakeholders in annual reports. In the early 2000s, these activities were swept up in the new trends of nation branding and public diplomacy, leading to a period of creativity and modernisation that has intimately associated the country of Sweden with the concept of the nation brand. By the early 2020s, this work has become intensely analytical, with a strong emphasis on what Cull (2019) terms 'reputational security'.

Keeping up with the Joneses

While Swedes have always been fascinated by how the rest of the world views their country, a significant portion of the impetus for the creation of Brand Sweden originated with branding experts in the

United Kingdom. In the early-2000s, the Swedish Institute first invited British consultants to help shape their outward image. The formal adoption of this new nation branding practice was seemingly about keeping up with the competition. The Swedish Institute worked with the consultants behind the Nation Brand Index to ensure a compliant brand strategy and hence, generous results on the all-important ranking. Combining British expertise with the creativity of Swedish public relations bureaus proved to be an effective formula, albeit one which couldn't quite shake off traditional stereotypes of the blonde-haired, blue-eyed left-of-centre Swede.

Sweden formally launched its nation brand in 2007, defining itself as a 'progressive, open country . . . that balances development with people's needs and environmental considerations' (Swedish Institute, 2008, p. 6). A key institutional reorganisation saw cultural relations body the Swedish Institute produce much of Sweden's promotional outputs and image management. It would define itself as acting 'within the framework of public diplomacy' (Swedish Institute, 2009, p. 8). Public diplomacy and nation branding were by-and-large used interchangeably, though it would soon become apparent that the ability to influence diplomatic outcomes through public engagement was significantly less well developed than the ability to promote a coherent national image.

Since the launch of Brand Sweden, Swedish nation branding has involved telling *the story of its nation branding*; in effect making the ability to promote a coherent national image a key part of the national image. Such was the persuasiveness of this circular argument that it was not until Carl Bildt became foreign minister that the cracks started to show. Having famously exchanged the first emails between world leaders with President Clinton while Prime Minister in 1994, Bildt was fascinated by technology and wanted to know why, as of 2013, many Swedish embassies were not yet on social media. Upon closer inspection, it became clear that some of the bluster of Sweden's globally leading role in nation branding and public diplomacy had not been fully delivered upon.

The following years witnessed a period of introspection in which many of the capabilities promised since the birth of Brand Sweden were gradually implemented. A number of initiatives were piloted, often blurring distinctions between nation branding, public diplomacy, international development, and economic promotion. Data analysis was part of the process from the very beginning. Promotional actors captured activities and worked to evaluate the impact of branding efforts, giving the impression – to those sitting in Stockholm at least! – of a degree of control over the brand image. By the early 2020s, this developed into a significant analysis capability focused on traditional and social media, which is used to inform decision-makers as well as the public on how significant audiences around the world perceive Sweden. In 2021, Brand Sweden is more modest in its scope and intent and more honest in what it delivers.

The interplay between governmental and corporate actors

The brand platform has therefore been aimed at domestic stakeholders as much as it has targeted foreigners. The branding attempted to neatly summarise Swedish qualities and create consensus around them, so that Swedish promotional actors can align themselves around a set of shared values. Corporations such as Ikea, Volvo, H&M and Spotify were conscious of obvious overlaps between Brand Sweden and their own marketing. Ikea, for example, drapes its warehouses in the blue and yellow of Sweden's flag, while its handbooks for new employees explain the core values developed by the Swedish Institute as a way of introducing staff to Swedish national values. Given the gulf in advertising, marketing and branding expenditure by corporate brands, it could be argued that Brand Sweden is shaped far more by the activities of corporations than by government promotional actors.

An innovative example of how nongovernmental actors have engaged with the brand may be seen in the Swedish Telephone Number campaign. Launched by the Swedish Tourist Association in 2016, some 30,000 Swedish members of the association signed up to act as brand ambassadors to field questions from curious foreigners who dialed the 'official' telephone number to Sweden: +46771793336. The campaign cleverly drew upon values and tropes established by Brand Sweden but was an independent promotional activity by an association of hotels and destinations trying to drive tourism (Pamment and Cassinger, 2018).

Cohesion during the permanent image crisis

The value-based brand keywords of *progressive*, *open*, *authentic*, *caring* and *innovation*·are well established as the cornerstone of the outward face of Sweden. Much of the focus of Sweden's formal nation branding strategy, as in other countries, has therefore been on crystallising this kind of nationalistic storytelling. Initially, the emphasis was on encouraging citizens to actively represent its core values; by the early 2020s, in the face of increased populism and social polarization, the emphasis is more on ensuring that government institutions coordinate properly as reputational crises hit. The 2015–16 migration crisis and 2020–21 coronavirus pandemic are two examples where Swedish national policies created groundswells of resistance that contributed to reputational crises.

The displacement of 5 million Syrians in 2015 led to a humanitarian crisis in which 75% of European asylum applications were registered in five member states: Germany, Hungary, Sweden, Austria and Italy (European Commission, 2016). Sweden took a moral stand and accepted the highest number of refugees per capita, but followed with a political U-turn that saw the country close its borders. The idea of Open Sweden met with criticism on both sides: from those who felt that the Swedish policy was too generous, and those who felt it was not generous enough (Pamment et al., 2017). Similarly, Sweden's divergent policy toward coronavirus – being the only country in the region not to enforce various restrictions – made it a target for reputational attacks (Vetenskapsradion/Ekot, 2021).

More generally, Brand Sweden has found itself challenged by a key political trend: the rise of far-right populism in the form of the Sweden Democrats party (SD). Back when the Brand was created in 2006, SD polled at around 3%, gradually rising to 10% in 2014. Since the migration crisis, however, SD has consistently polled at around 20%, which has fundamentally changed the dynamics of Swedish politics. In tandem with these new political currents, adversarial narratives targeting Sweden's international reputation have taken root. The suggestion that parts of Sweden have adopted Sharia law, that it has become unsafe for Europeans, that Malmö is the rape capital of the world, and that Sweden is a society on the brink of collapse, have been widely promoted by a select group of alt-right and pro-Kremlin international media (EUvsDisinfo, 2018).

With the decline of domestic political consensus, the weaknesses of Brand Sweden are exposed. As of 2019, approximately 20% of the Swedish population was born in another country (Migrationsinfo, 2021). Hence the image of the blonde-haired, blue-eyed Swedish identity has changed rapidly, if it was ever more than a stereotype to begin with. SD's growth demonstrates a persistent resistance to centrist consensus politics but may also harken back to a more traditional image based on comfortable stereotypes. Now, and for the foreseeable future, Brand Sweden will struggle to represent plurality while battling the image of a country in permanent crisis. As an exporting country dependent on a positive reputation for its goods and services, and in light of the deteriorating security situation in the Baltic and problematic relationship with China, Brand Sweden is increasingly drawn into questions of reputational security, in the sense that adversarial narratives provide a compelling threat to the country's prosperity.

Prospects: Toward genuine plurality?

Brand Sweden has persisted for a decade and a half and is likely to remain a central fixture of the working relationship between government bodies charged with national promotional overseas. Exporting businesses and nongovernmental organisations will also retain a stake in the brand. However, the 2020s are likely to see a number of trends. These include 1) the gradual rollback of the brand from being the whole of Sweden's national brand to assets for targeted national promotion; 2) the introduction of security-related concepts and objectives to brand strategy; 3) increased tensions around activities designed to counter misconceptions, in tandem with the foothold far-right politics is likely to gain in upcoming elections; and 4) a need to revisit the core values of the brand to represent pluralism both with changing demographics and changing political currents. In sum, the heyday of Brand Sweden is over.

References

Cull, N.J. (2019) *Public Diplomacy: Foundations for Global Engagement in the Digital Age*, New York: John Wiley & Sons.

European Commission (2016) 'The EU and the refugee crisis (July 2016), European Commission, Brussels', available at: http://publications.europa.eu/webpub/com/factsheets/refugee-crisis/en/.

EUvsDisinfo (2018) 'In Sweden, resilience is key to combatting disinformation', available at: https://euvsdisinfo.eu/in-sweden-resilience-is-key-to-combatting-disinformation/?highlight=sweden.

Migrationsinfo (2021) 'Hur många i Sverige är födda i ett annat land?', available at: www.migrationsinfo.se/fragor-och-svar/hur-manga-utrikes-fodda-sverige/.

Pamment, J. and Cassinger, C. (2018) 'Nation branding and the social imaginary of participation: An exploratory study of the Swedish number campaign'. *European Journal of Cultural Studies*, 21 (5), 561–574.

Pamment, J., Olofsson, A. and Hjorth-Jensen, R. (2017) 'The response of Swedish and Norwegian public diplomacy & nation branding actors to the refugee crisis', *Journal of Communication Management*, 21 (4), 326–341.

Swedish Institute (2008) *Sverigebilden 2.0: Vägen till en uppdaterad Sverigebild* [*Sweden's Image 2.0: The Way to an Updated Image*], Stockholm: Svenska Institutet.

Swedish Institute (2009) *Årsredovisning 2008* [*Annual Report 2008*], Dnr 00511/2009, Stockholm: Svenska Institutet.

Vetenskapsradion/Ekot (2021) *Private Facebook Group Attempts to Influence Swedish Interests Abroad*. Stockholm: Swedish Radio, available at: https://sverigesradio.se/artikel/private-facebook-group-attempts-to-influence-swedish-interests-abroad.

Summary

Nation branding strategy is a complex undertaking. The principles of strategic analysis, planning and implementation apply to nations as they do to companies, although the specific elements of nation branding strategy will differ considerably from those encountered by commercial organisations. Nation brands need to conduct internal and external analysis in order to assess their current competitive position, from which they can formulate and implement strategy in an appropriate direction.

Discussion points

1 Apply internal and external analysis to a country of your choice, and propose a suitable nation brand strategy based on that analysis.
2 How can a country's diaspora be mobilised in pursuit of nation branding objectives? Give examples of countries that have successfully engaged their diaspora for nation branding purposes.

References

Alakbarov, A. (2019) 'National image and the Expo Movement: The experience of Azerbaijan', *Bureau International des Expositions (BIE) Image of a Nation: Country Branding at World Expos*, 124–136.

Anderson, C. (2006) *The Long Tail: How Endless Choice Is Creating Unlimited Demand*, London: Random House Business Books.

Andersson, M. and Ekman, P. (2009) 'Ambassador networks and place branding', *Journal of Place Management and Development*, 2 (1), 41–51.

Ansoff, H. (1988) *Corporate Strategy*, London: Penguin.

Barrand, D. (2005) 'Travelex secures Jonny Wilkinson as ambassador', *Marketing*, 18 May, 4.

Bengtsson, S. (2011) 'Virtual nation branding: The Swedish embassy in second life', *Journal of Virtual Worlds Research*, 4 (1).

Bensalem, M. (2019) 'Algeria and the world of expos: A happy encounter', *Bureau International des Expositions (BIE) Image of a Nation: Country Branding at World Expos*, 123.

Burmann, C. and Zeplin, S. (2005) 'Building brand commitment: A behavioural approach to internal brand management', *Journal of Brand Management*, 12 (4), 279–300.

Buttle, F. (2008) 'A CRM perspective on nation branding', in Dinnie, K. (ed.), *Nation Branding – Concepts, Issues, Practice*, 1st edn, 66–67, London: Butterworth-Heinemann.

Christensen, C. (2013) '@Sweden: Curating a nation on Twitter', *Popular Communication: The International Journal of Media and Culture*, 11 (1), 30–46.

Cull, N.J. (2012) 'Listening for the hoof beats: Implications of the rise of soft power and public diplomacy', *Global Asia*, 7 (3), 8–12.

Cull, N.J. (2019) *Public Diplomacy: Foundations for Global Engagement in the Digital Age*, Cambridge: Polity.

de Moya, M. and Jain, R. (2013) 'When tourists are your "friends": Exploring the brand personality of Mexico and Brazil on Facebook', *Public Relations Review*, 39, 23–29.

Digital Diplomacy Hub (2021) 'Soft power 30', available at: https://digitaldiplomacy.soft power30.com/ (accessed 17/7/2021).

El Banna, A., Hamzaoui-Essoussi, L. and Papadopoulos, N. (2017) 'A comparative cross-national examination of online investment promotion', *Journal of Euromarketing*, 25, (3–4), 131–146.

EY Attractiveness Surveys (2021) 'Attractiveness surveys', available at: www.ey.com/en_uk/attractiveness (accessed 17/7/2021).

Favre, P. (2008) 'The new France – Breaking through the perception barrier', in Dinnie, K. (ed.), *Nation Branding – Concepts, Issues, Practice*, 1st edn, 239–242, London: Butterworth-Heinemann.

Fetscherin, M. (2010) 'The determinants and measurement of a country brand: The country brand strength index', *International Marketing Review*, 27 (4), 466–479.

Hackley, C. (2005) *Advertising and Promotion: Communicating Brands*, London: Sage Publications.

Hays, S., Page, S.J. and Buhalis, D. (2012) 'Socia media as a destination marketing tool: Its use by national tourism organisations', *Current Issues in Tourism*, 16 (3), 211–239.

Hickman, A. (2019) 'Saudi Arabia turns to influencers to give nation's image a makeover', *Campaign*, 16 October, available at: www.campaignlive.co.uk/article/saudi-arabia-turns-influencers-give-nations-image-makeover/1662726 (accessed 16/7/2021).

Hudak, K.C. (2019) 'Resident stories and digital storytelling for participatory place branding', *Place Branding and Public Diplomacy*, 15 (2), 97–108.

Interbrand (2008) 'Country case insight – Estonia', in Dinnie, K. (ed.), *Nation Branding – Concepts, Issues, Practice*, 1st edn, 230–235, London: Butterworth-Heinemann.

IPA Effectiveness Awards (1998) available at: www.ipa.co.uk.

Jobber, D. (2004) *Principles and Practice of Marketing*, 4th edn, London: McGraw-Hill.

Johnson, G., Scholes, K. and Whittington, R. (2005) *Exploring Corporate Strategy: Text and Cases*, 7th edn, Upper Saddle River, NJ: Prentice Hall.

Kapur, D. and McHale, J. (2005) *Give Us Your Best and Brightest: The Global Hunt for Talent and Its Impact on the Developing World*, Washington, DC: Center for Global Development.

Keller, K.L. (2003) *Strategic Brand Management: Building, Measuring, and Managing Brand Equity*, 2nd edn, Upper Saddle River, NJ: Prentice Hall.

Kirby, J. and Marsden, P. (eds.) (2005) *Connected Marketing: The Viral, Buzz and Word of Mouth Revolution*, London: Butterworth-Heinemann.

Koslow, S., Sasser, S.L. and Riordan, E.A. (2006) 'Do marketers get the advertising they need or the advertising they deserve?', *Journal of Advertising*, 35 (3), 81–101.

Kuznetsov, Y. (2006) 'Leveraging diasporas of talent: Towards a new policy agenda', in Kuznetsov, Y. (ed.), *Diaspora Networks and the International Migration of Skills: How Countries Can Draw on Their Talent Abroad*, 221–237, Washington, DC: WBI Development Studies, The World Bank.

Kuznetsov, Y. and Sabel, C. (2006) 'International migration of talent, diaspora networks, and development: Overview of main issues', in Kuznetsov, Y. (ed.), *Diaspora Networks and the International Migration of Skills: How Countries Can Draw on Their Talent Abroad*, 3–19, Washington, DC: WBI Development Studies, The World Bank.

Lahrech, A., Juusola, K. and Al Ansaari, M.E. (2020) 'Toward more rigorous country brand assessments: The modified country brand strength index', *International Marketing Review*, 37 (2), 319–344.

Lebedenko, V. (2008) 'On national identity and the building of Russia's image', in Dinnie, K. (ed.), *Nation Branding – Concepts, Issues, Practice*, 1st edn, 107–111, London: Butterworth-Heinemann.

Lin, C. (2021) 'Remote work made digital nomads possible: The pandemic made them essential', *Fast Company*, 13 May, available at: www.fastcompany.com/90631452/remote-work-made-digital-nomads-possible-the-pandemic-made-them-essential?utm_source=pocket-new-tab-global-en-GB (accessed 10/7/2021).

Linder, S. (2019) *Ireland's Greening of the World*, Dublin: The O'Brien Press.

Lund, N.F., Cohen, S.A. and Scarles, C. (2018) 'The power of social media storytelling in destination branding', *Journal of Destination Marketing and Management*, 8, 271–280.

Marks, J. (2006) 'South Africa: Evolving diaspora, promising initiatives', in Kuznetsov, Y. (ed.), *Diaspora Networks and the International Migration of Skills: How Countries Can Draw on Their Talent Abroad*, 171–186, Washington, DC: WBI Development Studies, The World Bank.

Marquis, S. (2007) 'Buyers storm the creatives' citadel', *The Guardian, MediaGuardian*, 23 April, 10.

Mortimer, R. (2006) 'Chris Anderson on smashing hits', *Brand Strategy*, March, 17.

Mwita, M. (2020) 'KEPROBA targets 6.5% exports growth on eCommerce', *The Star*, 27 November, available at: www.the-star.co.ke/business/kenya/2020-11-27-keproba-targets-65-exports-growth-on-ecommerce/ (accessed 17/7/2021).

Palsdottir, I.H. (2008) 'The case of "Iceland naturally" – establishing an umbrella brand to increase country image impact and coherence', in Dinnie, K. (ed.), *Nation Branding – Concepts, Issues, Practice*, 1st edn, 183–186, London: Butterworth-Heinemann.

Pamment, J. and Cassinger, C. (2018) 'Nation branding and the social imaginary of participation: An exploratory study of the Swedish Number campaign', *European Journal of Cultural Studies*, 21 (5), 561–574.

Paniagua, J., Korzynski, P. and Mas-Tur, A. (2017) 'Crossing borders with social media: Online social networks and FDI', *European Management Journal*, 35 (3), 314–326.

Pasquier, M. (2008) 'The image of Switzerland: Between clichés and realities', in Dinnie, K. (ed.), *Nation Branding – Concepts, Issues, Practice*, 1st edn, 79–84, London: Butterworth-Heinemann.

Pereira, A.P.C. (2018) 'Promotion before nation branding: Chile at the world exhibitions', in Fehimović, D. and Ogden, R. (eds.), *Branding Latin America: Strategies, Aims, Resistance*, chapter 1, 35–57, Lanham, MD: Lexington Books.

Rasmussen, R.K. and Merkelsen, H. (2012) 'The new PR of states: How nation branding practices affect the security function of public diplomacy', *Public Relations Review*, 38, 810–818.

Sano, M. (2019) 'Nothing but nation building: Promoting Japan's national image at early expos', *Bureau International des Expositions (BIE) Image of a Nation: Country Branding at World Expos*, 90–110.

Sartain, L. (2005) 'Branding from the inside out at Yahoo!: HR's role as brand builder', *Human Resource Management*, 44 (1), 89–93.

Sevin, E. and White, G.S. (2011) 'Turkayfe.org: Share your Türksperience', *Journal of Place Management and Development*, 4 (1), 80–92.

Sheth, J. (2006) 'Keynote speech', Academy of Marketing 2006 Annual Conference, 4–6 July, Middlesex University Business School, London.

Shimp, T.A. (2003) *Advertising, Promotion, & Supplemental Aspects of Integrated Marketing Communications*, 6th edn, Mason, OH: Thomson South-Western.

Silvanto, S. and Ryan, J. (2018) 'An investigation into the core appeals for nation branding to attract and retain talent to enhance a country's competitiveness', *Competitiveness Review: An International Business Journal*, 28 (5), 584–604.

Strandberg, C. and Styvén, M.E. (2019) 'What's love got to do with it? Place brand love and viral videos', *Internet Research*, 30 (1), 23–43.

Szondi, G. (2010) 'From image management to relationship building: A public relations approach to nation branding', *Place Branding and Public Diplomacy*, 6 (4), 333–343.

Tammpuu, P. and Masso, A. (2018) ' "Welcome to the virtual state": Estonian e-residency and the digitalised state as a commodity', *European Journal of Cultural Studies*, 21 (5), 543–560.

Vecchi, A., Silva, E.S and Angel, L.M. (2021) 'Nation branding, cultural identity and political polarization – an exploratory framework', *International Marketing Review*, 38 (1), 70–98.

Wang, J. (2020) 'The world expo and nation branding', in Snow, N. and Cull, N.J. (eds.), *Routledge Handbook of Public Diplomacy*, 2nd edn, chapter 22, 224–230, New York and London: Routledge.

Wani, M.U.D.A. (2019) 'Showcasing a rich and diverse nation: Pakistan at expos', *Bureau International des Expositions (BIE) Image of a Nation: Country Branding at World Expos*, 182–190.

Wilson, R.M.S. and Gilligan, C. (2005) *Strategic Marketing Management: Planning, Implementation & Control*, 3rd edn, London: Elsevier Butterworth-Heinemann.

World Economic Forum (2019) 'The travel & tourism competitiveness report 2019', available at: http://www3.weforum.org/docs/WEF_TTCR_2019.pdf (accessed 17/7/2021).

Yahaya, M.A.B.H. (2019) 'Malaysia: The confluence of heritage, diversity and progress', *Bureau International des Expositions (BIE) Image of a Nation: Country Branding at World Expos*, 152–166.

Yun, S.-H. and Toth, E.L. (2009) 'Future sociological public diplomacy and the role of public relations: Evolution of public diplomacy', *American Behavioral Scientist*, 53 (4), 493–503.

Future horizons for nation branding

Key points

- Future trends in nation branding may include a shift away from anglocentric paradigms, improved coordination of nation branding strategy, and a rising impact of citizen-generated media
- An alternative terminology for nation branding may emerge, less linked to the domains of marketing and business
- The ICON model of nation branding proposes an approach to nation branding that is integrated, contextualised, organic and new

Introduction

This chapter views the future horizons for nation branding, identifying a number of trends that could characterise nation branding in the coming years. These trends range from the increasing impact of citizen-generated media to the potential of nation branding to act as a catalyst for sustainable development. In this chapter, the first case outlines how

Brand Singapore's strengths will help in Covid-19 recovery. The second case discusses how Brand Canada may have experienced a shift from insecure identity crisis to smug superiority complex. The academic perspective by Luke Devereux provides insights into the relevance of complexity theory for nation brands, whilst Robert Govers' practitioner insight discusses the issue of naming conventions in nation branding.

Technology leadership

As the Covid-19 pandemic has accelerated the adoption of digital technologies across all areas of society, notably in the proliferation of remote working and online service delivery, countries will need to sharpen their focus on technology leadership as a core component of their nation branding efforts. The IMD World Digital Competitiveness Ranking provides an overview of the capacity of country economies to adopt digital technologies for economic and social transformation; in the 2020 ranking, the top four countries were the United States, Singapore, Denmark and Sweden (IMD World Competitiveness Center, 2021). Good performance in such rankings can be highlighted in nation brand campaigns in contexts where the objective is talent attraction, positioning countries as attractive destinations for highly skilled tech workers. Estonia's brand image, for example, is largely based on its positioning as a digital state (Cheregi and Bargaoanu, 2020).

Blockchain, though controversial and still widely viewed with suspicion, may play a future role in countries' nation branding. The soft power potential of embracing blockchain could lead countries to explore possible blockchain implementations. Werbach (2018, p. 123) has noted that China may decide to harness blockchain to increase its soft power:

> From all indications, Chinese leaders understand very well how economic soft power, embodied in mechanisms such as the Marshall Plan after World War II and Treasury Bills as the global reserve currency, helped make the U.S. the world's lone superpower. Tokenizing the Chinese renminbi before other major fiat currencies is one potential path toward similar soft power in the twenty-first century.

China is also well placed in the race with the United States to become the world's leading artificial intelligence (AI) superpower, with former Microsoft, Apple and Google China executive Kai-Fu Lee arguing that 'in the crucial realm of government support, China's techno-utilitarian political culture will pave the way for faster deployment of game-changing technologies' (Lee, 2018, pp. 82–83). Should Lee's prediction be realised, China's economic soft power would be significantly enhanced.

A shift away from anglocentric paradigms

As the twenty-first century unfolds, and the BRICS nations emerge as global economic superpowers, joined by other nations taking a more prominent place on the global stage, we can expect to see a shift away from existing anglocentric paradigms of brand management towards new paradigms that better reflect a diversity of views. This direction of travel mirrors the 'decolonising the curriculum' movement, which involves challenging and remaking current pedagogy that is rooted in colonial ideas about knowledge and learning (Batty, 2020).

What exact form the new paradigms take is yet to be seen. In the field of management studies, Barkema et al. (2015) have explored how non-Western concepts and contexts can enrich existing management theories, whilst in the nation branding discipline Jack Yan has predicted that 'by the second part of the twenty-first century, India will probably be the source from which the West will learn how to nation brand' (Yan, 2008, p. 171). Simon Anholt has described how his work, initially brand-focused, has evolved into building and training high-level teams of national decision-makers in the principles of competitive identity (Anholt, 2007). The immense scope of nation branding and the need for countries to compete effectively in a globalised economy make it unlikely that the fundamentally Western-based paradigm of brand management will remain dominant over the coming decades. Exciting new perspectives can be expected as more and more nations find original, context-specific solutions to their own unique challenges.

Improved coordination of nation branding strategy

The concepts and issues involved in nation branding are not difficult to grasp intellectually. The challenge is in delineating the areas of activity that the nation brand strategy needs to encompass and then ensuring that there is adequate coordination of the different organisations and individuals involved in the overall strategy's component parts. This challenge has been alluded to by Akutsu in the context of Japan's nation branding (Akutsu, 2008), whilst in the context of Singapore's nation branding Koh (2021a, pp. 234–5) has observed that 'The political and public sector have done much. Perhaps what remains is the adaptive challenge to unleash the full potential of its people and private sectors.'

Increasing adoption of brand management techniques

Although in the long term the emergence of alternative paradigms to the brand management paradigm may occur, in the short to medium term it is likely that nations will become more savvy with regard to using the tools and techniques of brand management in order to promote their nation's competitiveness in the global economy. Established principles such as brand identity, brand image and brand positioning are useful for clarifying the bases of nation brand strategy and for guiding the development and implementation of coordinated campaigns. Another branding concept for which nations may investigate potential applications is the practice of co-branding. Co-branding is commonly seen in business, where two brands owned by different companies join together in order to benefit from each other's existing brand equity. Co-branding can be seen in the domain of nation branding in the joint bids that two countries make to host high-profile sporting events, for example, the Austria-Switzerland bid to host the 2008 European Football Championship and the Poland-Ukraine bid to host the same tournament in 2012. Another example of co-branding being practised as an element of nation brand strategy can be seen in print magazine advertisements forming part of the 'Malaysia Truly Asia' campaign, where the participating 'brands' are Visit Malaysia 2007, Tourism Malaysia, Malaysia Airlines and, perhaps surprisingly, Manchester United FC.

In terms of basic marketing literacy, the marketing principles of segmentation and targeting of markets and audiences are useful – and easily understood – techniques for ensuring that resources are not wasted on poorly targeted activities and communications. Politicians, government officials and other public servants who are involved in nation branding strategy should also be trained to at least a basic level in the principles of branding, so that they can contribute effectively to the achievement of nation branding goals and also in order to ensure that public money is not squandered on hiring inept or under-performing advertising agencies or branding consultants.

It would also be useful for government and public agencies involved in nation branding to have some knowledge of marketing metrics, i.e., the ways in which marketing's return on investment can be measured. Tim Ambler, a Senior Fellow at London Business School, has stated that 'clear goals and metrics are what separate the professional from the amateur', and he goes on to suggest the following ten questions that companies should ask themselves about their marketing performance: 1) Does the senior executive team regularly and formally assess marketing performance? 2) What does the senior executive team understand by the term 'customer value'? 3) How much time does the senior executive team give to marketing issues? 4) Does the business/marketing plan show the non-financial corporate goals and link them to market goals? 5) Does the plan show the comparison of your marketing performance with competitors or the market as a whole? 6) What is your main marketing asset called? 7) Does the senior executive team's performance review involve a quantified view of the main marketing asset and how it has changed? 8) Has the senior executive team quantified what 'success' would look like five or ten years in the future? 9) Does your strategy have quantified milestones to indicate progress towards that success? 10) Are the marketing performance indicators that are seen by the senior executive team aligned with these quantified milestones? (Ambler, 2006). Although designed for senior executives in the corporate world, these metrics can also be applied to the marketing activities conducted for nation branding campaigns. If such metrics are not applied then there will be a lack of accountability that will hamper the effective evaluation of the marketing-specific elements of the nation brand strategy.

Being familiarised with marketing and branding techniques, even at a basic introductory level, will equip those involved in nation branding activities with the tools and insight to increase their personal and team effectiveness. However, these marketing and branding techniques should not be viewed as a means to gloss over unethical behaviour. The essence of nation branding should be to coordinate the nation's key stakeholders in pursuit of goals that will benefit the whole nation; it is not a public relations exercise for spinning away the nation's social, commercial, political or military faults. Nation branding aims to enhance a nation's image and reputation in order to allow benefits to flow in terms of boosting FDI, tourism, export promotion and so on. This can only occur if the nation's actions are respectable and well communicated. It has been suggested that the prerequisites for a strong reputation are to perform and explain reputable acts and to listen carefully (Stewart, 2006).

Rising impact of citizen-generated media

A key phenomenon in the digital age has been the emergence of consumer-generated media, which in the context of nation branding is more appropriately termed citizen-generated media. Such citizen-generated media can affect the brand associations and brand equity associated with places (Andéhn et al., 2014; Pamment and Cassinger, 2018; Skinner, 2018). The equalising nature of the internet has empowered consumers in terms of their ability to make their voice heard in comparison to previous eras when it was brand owners who had a near monopoly on communications. The business-to-consumer monologue has transformed into a dialogue in which the co-creation of brand value occurs through interaction between the brand and the consumer. This implies a willingness on the part of brand owners to reduce their control over the brand, for example by inviting consumers to suggest creative themes and executions for future advertising campaigns. There are probably few nations that would consider such a radical redistribution of brand influence away from the brand owner and towards the consumer. Yet there is potential for nation brands to emulate some of the brand value co-creation strategies currently employed by product and corporate brands. The @Sweden project on Twitter is one such example.

Companies are taking an increasing interest in the 'blogosphere' and nation brands can be expected to follow suit by devising strategies to engage with the ever increasing numbers of bloggers, many of whom are writing about issues that affect nation brands. The most obvious example is individuals who publish blogs on their experiences as a tourist visiting various nations. Koh (2021b, p. 13) has argued that 'citizens who aspire to make a mark in the world (as a YouTube musician, for example) always add to the brand value of the countries they represent, whether they intend to do so or not, and in however small a way'.

Sonic branding

Sonic branding is a relatively recent addition to the array of techniques available to brand managers. There are three components of sonic branding: voices, music and sound effects (Jackson, 2003). Sonic branding can take the form of a sonic logo that plays on every advertisement for a brand, or it can take on a wider application through the consistent use of sound and music across every aspect of the business, as is practised by companies such as Honda, Intel and Easyjet (Mortimer, 2005). Siemens, for example, has added a seventh element to its branding, with sound now joining logo, claim, typeface, colours, layout and style amongst the basic building blocks of its brand; the company is using sound through the creation of an audio signature, or sonic logo and also some mood sound (Treasure, 2007). It has been claimed that sonic branding implants a memory in the aural pathways of listeners' brains that is so powerful that it is virtually impossible to forget, and that sonic branding is now a key weapon in competition for market share (Arnold, 2005).

Although the strategic use of sound in branding has only recently been adopted by companies, the power of music to affect consumer behaviour has been widely researched for several years in the service sector, particularly in the retail and restaurant sectors (Alpert and Alpert, 1990; Herrington and Capella, 1996). Some studies have indicated that musical tempo can affect consumer behaviour – supermarket shoppers have shown increased purchase levels when slow-tempo music was being played compared to fast-tempo music (Milliman, 1982), whilst fast-tempo music significantly increased diner eating speed (Roballey et al., 1985) and fast-tempo renditions of piano tunes were found to increase drinking speed compared to slow tempo versions (McElrea and Standing, 1992). These studies usefully demonstrate the power of music to affect specific aspects of consumer behaviour, but of more direct relevance to nation branding is one of the best known studies in the area of the use of music in marketing, the so-called 'wine-aisle experiment'.

The 'wine-aisle experiment' (North et al., 1999) took place over a period of two weeks during which the music played in the wine section of a supermarket was alternated on a daily basis between French and German styles. The study's findings indicated that when French music was played the French wine would outsell its German counterpart and vice-versa, even though customers did not seem to be consciously aware of the music being played. Export promotion agencies and provenance brands should consider the implications of this study, and develop branding strategies that incorporate the use of appropriate music in the promotion of their products. Nations are uniquely well equipped to this, as they have centuries of musical heritage to draw upon. The 'wine-aisle experiment' demonstrates how the country-of-origin effect can be subtly yet effectively incorporated into marketing communications. Few, if any, of the numerous national wine promotional campaigns run by various nations over recent years have incorporated a sonic branding dimension. Future campaigns that do so can thus expect to gain first-mover advantage.

An alternative terminology for nation branding?

The words 'brand' and 'branding' generate mixed responses. For some, the words embody notions of manipulation, deceit and superficiality. For others, the words are innocuous descriptors of elements and practices of the commercial world, with nation branding considered as a tool at the disposal of all nations, but particularly smaller, poorer or otherwise struggling nations, to help them compete effectively on the world stage rather than being trampled upon by more powerful rivals. 'Nation branding' is an imperfect term, as the activities involved in nation branding transcend conventional views of branding as merely marketing hype for everyday products. The activation of diaspora networks, the coordination of diverse government agencies, and debate on national identity are all part of nation branding yet are far removed from the conventional view of branding's domain. Other terms that may at some point in the future supplant the term 'nation branding' include 'reputation management' and 'competitive identity'.

Nation branding as a driver of sustainable development

Branding can play a role in the regeneration, growth and sustainability of places (Maheshwari et al., 2011). Koh (2021c) has argued that Singaporean businesses can benefit by aligning better with that country's nation brand, specifically by aligning with Singapore's Green Plan 2030 to promote their own focus on sustainability. Steps to improve environmental management and accountability need to be taken in order to develop genuinely 'green' destination brands (Insch, 2011). Pant (2008), for example, has shown how a sustainable development agenda can form the foundation of a nation brand strategy, particularly for nations that are challenged by geographic remoteness or lack of access to foreign markets. By highlighting their performance on environmental stewardship indexes such as the Environmental Sustainability Index (ESI), countries can seek to leverage their nation brand through high levels of performance across a wide range of sustainability metrics. The practice of nation branding can thus help nations to achieve competitive parity in cases where they do not possess the resources or the favourable locations of competing nations.

The ICON model of nation branding

The ICON model presented in Figure 10.1 provides a framework for the development and implementation of nation brand strategy, reflecting the key issues and concerns covered throughout this book. The model proposes that good practice in nation branding is characterised by adopting an approach that is integrated, contextualised, organic and new.

An *integrated* approach to nation branding involves high levels of inter-agency collaboration, as well as collaborative public–private sector programmes. Residents should also play an active part, particularly in the context of nation branding for tourism promotion (Uchinaka et al., 2019). A natural setting for the encouragement of inter-agency collaboration lies in a country's network of embassies in foreign countries. An embassy can bring its country's representatives (in trade and investment, tourism, culture, security, and so on) together and initiate nation branding activities through its close contacts with relevant audiences in the host country. However, there is wide variation in the degree of commitment shown by embassies in this regard, and a wariness in some quarters towards the risk of 'institutionalising' coordination (Dinnie et al., 2010).

Nation branding must be *contextualised* rather than conducted according to an off-the-shelf template; strategy should respond both to stakeholder needs and capabilities and should also match the values of target audiences. This implies granting a reasonable degree of empowerment to professionals on the ground in foreign countries, such as diplomats and trade and investment officials, so that the nation brand is customised appropriately to the values of local populations and target audiences.

Policy makers should acknowledge that nation branding, like other forms of branding in the age of digitally empowered citizens, is not totally under the control of official authorities. There is an *organic* dimension to nation branding that should be welcomed

Figure 10.1
The ICON model of nation branding

rather than resented. A nation brand evolves not according to a tightly controlled master plan, but subject to a plethora of activities and incidents that may be planned or unplanned. Many of these unplanned elements will emerge organically from the country's identity and culture in the form of books, films, sporting performances, music and art that make an impact on perceptions of a country.

To be noteworthy and interesting for domestic and international audiences, a nation brand should deliver something that is *new*. This could take the form of innovative products, services and experiences or at a more abstract level the creation of new national and place-based narratives (Grenni et al., 2020; Rebelo et al., 2020). The election victory in January 2015 of the anti-austerity Syriza party, for example, offered Greece the opportunity to construct a more positive and hopeful national narrative to replace the narrative of economic and social suffering that had dominated media coverage of that country in previous years. The importance of understanding and framing national narratives can be seen in the development of the British Council's New Narratives programme, which 'aims to contribute to changing perceptions of the countries of Africa and the UK, to stimulate new understanding and unlock connections and collaborations for mutual benefit' (Curran, 2020, p. 12).

ACADEMIC PERSPECTIVE: THE RELEVANCE OF COMPLEXITY THEORY FOR NATION BRANDS

Luke Devereux, Middlesex University London

What exactly is it that makes up a nation brand? Is it the visual design? The citizens? The tourists? Decisions of a marketing team? Or is it an interaction of elements like these and many more? Nation brands could be considered as being diverse, non-linear and made of multiple interacting parts, and as such could be considered to be complex systems. In this respect, nation brands are not just complex on the surface level, but also in the 'complexity theory' sense as well. Complexity theory therefore has much to offer to nation brands, and those studying them.

What is complexity theory?

Before we discuss how nation brands can benefit from complexity, it is worth briefly discussing what is complexity theory? Complexity theory is the study of complex systems. And one part of this is complex adaptive systems (CAS). Complex adaptive systems are systems that are diverse, non-linear and made up of multiple interacting parts. Complex systems are also seen as systems whose behaviour is not predictable from the elements that constitute the systems (Wilensky and Rand, 2015). So taking this perspective we can view a nation brand as being a complex system. We can view it as being made of all kinds of elements and actors that interact. As that previous definition suggests, it is these interactions that give rise to emergent properties. This is what makes complex systems hard to predict. Complexity theory opposes the notion of reductionism, in that the systems cannot be broken down into their constituent parts to understand the system. It is how they all merge, combine and adapt together that makes the system. For example, in nation brands, could we understand a brand if we reduced a nation brand into all of its individual components? Or is it actually how these things interact with each other that creates the magic of a nation brand? And that by cutting it up, we would lose some of the essence of what we were looking at. This is how complexity theory can begin to help us explore, and understand, nation brands.

How does it apply to nation brands?

Future research could look at the relevance of complexity theory to nation brands from multiple levels. First, we can see a nation itself as a complex adaptive system, made up of its population, culture, history, and so on. And then a nation brand is merely an emergent property of this particular system (or nation). This is interesting as nation brands can be regarded as not belonging to any one particular organisation or marketing director, and this could be due to the fact that they are an emergent property of the system under study. The other way we can apply this viewpoint is by looking at the brand itself being a system in itself. And again made up of its interacting elements that make up the brand. Complexity theory has been applied to many areas related to marketing, such as the study of organisations, social media networks, and the economy. And in some respects nation brands fit perfectly in with this, with their large group of interacting elements. This idea of looking at nation brands through multiple levels raises the question: at what level do we stop looking at a system? We could look at nations, regions, towns, boroughs, houses, people, cells, atoms. What exactly is the level of elements that we are looking at? One could keep going down to a very small level, and part of the analysis would involve deciding what level one is choosing to focus on. Some levels may be more relevant than others.

So what does this mean for researchers looking into this area?

Acknowledging that nation brands are complex systems may inspire new ways of looking at nation brands. For example, do we take a bottom-up approach to nation brands or a more top-down approach? And should we adapt our research methods to reflect the complexity of the system that we are looking at? So whilst this brief contribution cannot give a full overview of complexity theory and its application, we hope it does offer an inspiration to look into these things further. The joy of studying how these parts interact can help us better understand nation brands, and how they come to be.

Reference

Wilensky, U. and Rand, W. (2015) *An Introduction to Agent-based Modeling: Modeling Natural, Social, and Engineered Complex Systems with NetLogo*, Cambridge, MA: The MIT Press.

PRACTITIONER INSIGHT: COUNTRIES MAKING NAMES FOR THEMSELVES

Robert Govers, Chairman, International Place Branding Association (IPBA)

Despite the fashionable logos and slogans, research has finally demonstrated beyond doubt what many have assumed for long, that places are primarily recognized by their name and build reputation by attaching meaning to that name (see Beritelli and Laesser, 2018; Kladou et al., 2017). That assessment seems to suggest that the usefulness of classic visual identity branding as applied in the commercial world has limited utility to places. What is more, most places have long established names and changing them is politically, technically and strategically problematic, contested and difficult. Yet, there are plenty examples of countries contemplating naming conventions; the complexity of which is often underestimated.

During a nation brand project in Kazakhstan, the idea of renaming it as the Kazakh Republic was discussed. This seemed to make sense, as retaining the reference to Kazakh would likely preserve accumulated brand equity while losing the negative "-stan effect" (by which Pakistan, Afghanistan, Turkmenistan, Tajikistan, Kyrgyzstan, Uzbekistan and Kazakhstan are all seen as war-torn and corrupt countries that are dealing with Islamic extremism, regardless of the achievements of individual communities). The renaming of Kazakhstan has not happened so far because of fear of ethnic tensions and the impact renaming has on the national institutions and the international community and its systems.

During a project in the Kingdom of the Netherlands heated discussions about the use of the name Holland as an alternative to the official name of the country resulted in an international media storm (Govers and Anholt, 2021). Some in the country argue that Holland is associated with sex and drugs and rock & roll, while The Netherlands sounds more prestigious. Hence, they argue, using the name Holland should be avoided. There is no proof that supports the claim that The Netherlands is the better 'brand name', but objectively, geographically and historically, it is indeed inaccurate to use the name Holland in English or Dutch. However, this ignores the fact that for the vast majority of the world's population this whole naming issue is irrelevant as the name of the country in for instance Mandarin, Arabic, French, Spanish or Portuguese – major international languages – has its own translation. In other words, in most parts of the world audiences might be wondering what all the fuss is about, considering that Holland has significant equity.

The United Arab Emirates has recently launched a logo in which it uses the name The Emirates in order to lose the "Arab"-reference and to make it easier for foreign audiences to pronounce and recognize the name of the country. An official renaming was discussed in nation brand projects, but has not materialized, probably to avoid unrest considering the political reality in the country. Incorporating an alternative name that rolls off the tongue – like Holland in the Netherlands – as part of the brand strategy, is potentially an attractive and clever alternative to an official name change, which often has serious consequences. For example, the renaming of Swaziland to eSwatini by Africa's last absolute monarch in 2018, has raised some eyebrows. The new name, eSwatini, means 'land of the Swazis' and therefore – locally – might seem like a small change from Swaziland. In addition, the king's belief that Swaziland was often confused with Switzerland might also be valid. However, it seems as though that with this move – as foreigners do not recognize the link between Swaziland and eSwatini – the Monarch might have thrown away quite a bit of accumulated brand equity; while not making any new friends inside the country as citizens believe the king should focus on more pressing issues such as the nation's sluggish economy.

So, when considering naming conventions, one better make sure to look at all the angles and options. Looking at the issue as part of a brand strategy and visual identity, as opposed to an official name change, might seem appealing, but success is never guaranteed. It requires careful consideration of local identities, sensitivities and politics; international awareness and perception; historical and geographical contexts; and potential consequences.

References

Beritelli, P. and Laesser, C. (2018) 'Destination logo recognition and implications for intentional destination branding by DMOs: A case for saving money', *Journal of Destination Marketing & Management*, 8, 1–13.

Govers, R. and Anholt, S. (2021) 'The Netherlands', in Freire, J.-R. (ed.), *Routledge Focus on Nation Branding: Nation Branding in Europe*, London: Routledge.

Kladou, S., Kavaratzis, M., Rigopoulou, I. and Salonika, E. (2017) 'The role of brand elements in destination branding', *Journal of Destination Marketing & Management*, 6 (4), 426–435.

CASE: BRAND SINGAPORE'S STRENGTHS WILL HELP IN COVID-19 RECOVERY

Koh Buck Song, Brand Adviser and author of Brand Singapore: Nation branding in a world disrupted by Covid-19, Third Edition

In tackling the spread of Covid-19, Singapore is one of a few countries that have managed comparatively well. The Republic's initial response in early 2020 was praised in a Harvard University epidemiology study as a 'gold standard' (Kuhori, 2020). However, an outbreak among migrant workers led to tens of thousands of cases later in 2020. But Singapore recovered well from this situation, drawing from its substantial national reserves and public health capabilities to dedicate healthcare and containment resources to keep the fatality rate among the world's lowest.

Now, as the globe is still reeling from the pandemic, the strengths of Singapore's country brand will help steer the city-state out of the treacherous currents of disruption, back into the smoother channels of a reconstituted global economy. Since independence in 1965, this tropical island with no natural resources has cemented for itself one of the world's strongest country reputations (Koh, 2021), especially on 'hard' indicators. Even this pandemic cannot shake the primary asset: an excellent geostrategic position at the tip of the Asian land mass, along the major trade routes between Asia and the world. Now, the Republic has enhanced its prowess as a trading and transshipment hub further, adapting to new patterns of global logistics and inventory backups, and reconfigured supply chains.

This former British colony, developing from Third World to First World status in a generation, always scored well on country brand rankings – often emerging top in Asia, or second only to Japan. Singapore's Bicentennial year commemoration in 2019, marking two centuries since the British arrived, reinforced Sir Stamford Raffles' vision of positioning Singapore as a trading hub open to the world. The nature of country branding is that 'hard' aspects such as the ease of doing business usually dominate questionnaires, and for most international businesses – and even tourists and voters, for that matter – a strong government is often preferred, seen as better able to meet the demands of various constituencies, or, if needed, to change direction.

In the last half-century, brand Singapore has impressed mainly because the brand delivery has been sound on 'bread-and-butter' aspects. Singapore compared well against other countries less able to deliver even on very basic aspects of quality of life, from crime-free streets to clear skies. The Lion City's infrastructure (the port, airport, legal system, etc.) was always efficient, even top-notch. Its pro-business environment featured an ability – peculiar to a far-sighted, pragmatic, business-oriented government – to keep tweaking economic policies to further facilitate foreign investment. All the more in a Covid-19 world – when, in some places, freedom can even mean revolting against wearing face masks – tourists, investors and migrants will gravitate towards places that are reliably safe and welcoming, like Singapore, with a pragmatic, responsive government and high public trust.

As Singapore renews its capacity to create jobs, it can build on some six decades of brand affinity built mainly on 'direct marketing' by government agencies such as the Economic Development Board. Singapore's value propositions are presented directly to captains of industry, and their lieutenants, in the most developed economies and sunrise industries – through its own officers in overseas centres knocking on corporate doors every day, or via targeted niche communication platforms. The jolt that Covid-19 sent to international businesses on 'not putting all eggs in one basket' is actually a boost to

Singapore's attractiveness as an alternative base from which to command business expansion and logistics across the region by multinational companies moving into Asia. At the same time, in the opposite direction growing out of Asia, Chinese enterprises, spurred by geopolitical tensions between China and the United States, head to a more globally connected Singapore as a traditionally dependable external launch pad to the rest of the world.

The result is that Singapore might be small – just over 720 square kilometres – but wields immense influence in many spheres of international life, out of all proportion to its land area. External trade is three times its gross domestic product (GDP). It is the world's fifth-largest recipient of foreign direct investment inflows, with China as its largest trading partner and the biggest base in Asia for US investments. Singapore, through its sovereign wealth funds, is a significant player in overseas investments. Singapore is always at, or near, the summit of global economic competitiveness indices such as that of the World Economic Forum. Dubbed the 'poster child of globalisation', Singapore continues to exercise leadership in regional groupings such as the Association of Southeast Asian Nations (ASEAN) with initiatives like a smart nation regional network, as well as in other fora such as the Forum of Small States (FOSS) at the United Nations, with over 100 member countries. Singapore has also led the way in progressive platforms such as the World Cities Summit, which brings together thought leaders from across the globe to build more liveable cities.

Meanwhile, the softer aspects of brand Singapore have grown in potency, in recent years. The 2018 Hollywood film *Crazy Rich Asians*, set in Singapore, garnered significant international mindshare for the Republic. For tourism, the Singapore Tourism Board's 'Passion Made Possible' concept, launched in 2017, is the best-ever, showcasing the authenticity of real-life citizen brand ambassadors. This has earned more emotive resonance and brand affinity, making Singapore the world's fifth-most visited city before the pandemic. Of the recent paradigm shifts in country branding, the most powerful are for stewardship of nature, demonstrating ways to overcome the constraints of high-rise urban living. As a 'Garden City' in the first four decades from 1965, Singapore was well-known internationally for its gardens, parks and street landscaping. It was a conscious policy to apply the attention to detail necessary for well-trimmed hedges and lawns as a signal to potential foreign investors that this country would take just as good care of manufacturing and services investments. Since the new millennium, becoming a 'City in a Garden' meant holistically nurturing the whole country's greenery first, and then, weaving in urban development. This included transplanting more flowering plants onto streetscapes and vertical greenery onto skyscrapers, as well as redeveloping coastal boardwalks and bringing back wildlife with even man-made bird's nests where needed. Now, in the 2020s, to lift Singapore's position higher still on liveability surveys, the new vision is to become a 'City in Nature', in which nature is reinstated into the urban fabric, such as converting concrete canals back into streams with grass banks.

International perceptions of Singapore have softened even further with significant investments such as the National Gallery, especially its unofficial role as a regional custodian and showcase for some of the best art of Southeast Asia, something actually quite rare in the usually nationally focused museum world. The arts calendar became so full that no-one could attend every main event anymore. Much ground had been gained in being seen to be loosening up and dispelling old, outdated negative perceptions such as being a 'cultural desert' or 'nanny state'. Globally, opinion has shifted towards embracing the 'good nanny' aspects of a state, such as national security and citizen welfare – two hygiene factors now more crucial when physical hygiene itself has become paramount. The reinvention called for to recover from Covid-19 might create room for such facets of a 'funkier', artistically freer Singapore, with a more sophisticated approach to key brand attributes of soft power such as openness to new ideas.

In the last few years, Singapore's socio-political milieu has evolved further, possibly irreversibly. The force of public opinion is more influential than ever, with the yearning for more diverse political representation expressed in the General Election of 2020, which saw a historic ten Parliament seats won by the opposition. Most importantly, multiculturalism remains the 'X factor' of brand Singapore, a reservoir of social capital built up by decades of unusually interventionist public policies and the people's cooperative participation in sustaining social cohesion. Ranked by the USA's Pew Research Center as 'the world's most religiously diverse', Singapore has a key brand attribute of being unusually welcoming to foreign talent – which has gained added value in a world beset by rising nativist, protectionist and even xenophobic sentiment in the second half of the 2010s. Anyone looking to study, work, invest or live long-term in Singapore can see how multiculturalism is clearly lived and signalled in a society that has a Muslim woman head of state (elected to the presidency in 2016, the first reserved for Malay candidates, albeit through a controversial process), an Indian Leader of the Opposition in Parliament and a Eurasian Olympic gold medallist.

Overall, as more companies and people relocate or visit here to recover their footing in a world turned upside-down by this pandemic, Singapore's foundation factors, on balance, look set to boost the island's geostrategic position as a firm basis for just as impactful a role as before in transnational business and international relations. Singapore's strengths as a nation and society should help in recovering a commanding position as one of the world's most vital nodes and a role model for country branding after the worst of Covid-19, and into the future.

References

Koh, B.S. (2021) *Brand Singapore: Nation Branding in a World Disrupted by Covid-19*, 3rd edn, Singapore: Marshall Cavendish Business.

Kuhori, R. (2020) 'Coronavirus detection in Singapore "gold standard" for case detection: Harvard study', *The Straits Times*, 18 February, available at: www.straitstimes.com/singapore/coronavirus-detection-in-singapore-gold-standard-for-case-detection-harvard-study (accessed 4/1/2021).

CASE: BRAND CANADA: FROM INSECURE IDENTITY CRISIS TO SMUG SUPERIORITY COMPLEX

Giannina Warren, PhD, Middlesex University London

Often, a nation brand is defined by that which it is *not*. When a nation is shadowed by more established and more recognised brands that surround it geographically, its own brand image might struggle for recognition. Such is the case of Canada – although enjoying frequent inclusion on dominant place branding indices as a top 10 nation. Canada's brand identity still operates as somewhat of an enigma. Positively viewed by most of the world as friendly, beautiful and benign, Canada enjoys a high level of respect internationally but there still exists a confusion and uncertainty about what Brand Canada actually is, as opposed to what it is not.

As a Canadian who has lived abroad for over a decade, I cannot count the number of times I have been asked 'What part of America are you from?' – only to be met with a dramatic level of embarrassment when I inform the enquirer of my national origin north of the 49th parallel. 'Oh I'm so sorry! I know how much you Canadians hate that! But it's basically the same thing, isn't it?' is a very common follow-up. More often than not, I am told that Canadians are supposed to be very nice people, and apparently the country is really beautiful, and that person would love to visit . . . maybe someday. Recent conversations usually veer at this point to a mention of our 'very attractive' Prime Minister, Justin Trudeau. And therein lies the extent of the brand recognition afforded to the country most recently ranked as number one in the world, nudging out the competition for quality of life, social purpose, lack of corruption, strong economic prospects, high levels of employment, literacy and a solid public education system, respect for human rights and commitment to social justice (US News & World Report, 2021).

In truth, Canada has struggled with a national identity crisis and a longstanding inferiority complex as America's humble neighbour to the north. Its vast land mass and low population density (39 million as compared to America's 333 million) has meant it could never quite compete economically. Brand Canada would always struggle to define itself on its own terms, largely overshadowed by the sheer power and international position that America occupied through much of the 20th century. The two countries' distinctly different historical development – America's independence hard fought and won through bloody revolution, Canada's emergence occurring slowly, peacefully via diplomatic evolution – set the nations apart in myriad ways. This historical divergence has resulted in a shift in values, identity and national pride amongst Canadians that, in the 21st century, has begun to solidify a brand proposition that might not always be defined in relation to America but which reflects the country's emergence as a progressive international player on its own merit as global shifts occur.

The historical settlement of Canada looked very different to that of the United States. While commonalities occurred in the horrific treatment of Indigenous Peoples and the struggles of establishing homesteads and new communities among difficult terrain and in challenging weather, the co-existence and the long history of conciliation between French and British settlers meant that the two new nations began their cultural divergence early. The War of 1812 was a watershed moment, as it became clear the US appetite for war and independence was not shared by Canadians. This lack of need to forcefully assert our independence and to let it evolve naturally over time has been embedded in the DNA of Canadians.

Instead of violently disassociating with British rule, the country established a long co-existence, maintaining comfort as a Commonwealth nation, adopting British parliamentary rule and keeping strong ties through a Governor General. A cultural allegiance to the Queen was maintained via ubiquitous imagery in government buildings, on currency and through tradition. Whilst Canada eventually emerged as an independent country in 1967 a lingering identity crisis prevailed, as the young country grappled with its place in a rapidly changing world.

Clear signs of its divergence from its neighbour began to emerge midway through the last century, as democratic socialist ideals began to take root in the western provinces, paving the way for nationalised initiatives such as universal healthcare, social welfare and a deeper trust in government to provide for its people. The large corporate and collective infrastructure based on the natural resource economy embedded a trust in large institutions, borne out of the Hudson's Bay Company and projects like the Canadian National Railway, two of Canada's largest employers for decades.

The race riots and civil rights movement in the US, the war in Vietnam and the American and British shift towards neo-liberalism in the 1980s instigated and solidified the divergent establishment of Canadian identity and values – although, along with the rest of the world, a deep intrinsic love for the culture, the innovation and economic might of the United States remained. The first wave of 'Trudeaumania' – for Justin's indomitable father, Pierre, captured the hearts and minds of the nation, as its first assertions of a multi-cultural, progressive and pluralistic approach accompanied huge waves of post-war immigration and economic growth. Pierre Trudeau famously declared that 'the state has no place in the bedrooms of the nation' (CBC Archives, 2021) and the 1982 Canadian Charter of Rights and Freedoms had a significant and permanent impact on the political landscape of Canada, shifting from a culture of deference and self-restraint to a bolder and influential assertion of identity (Morton, 1987).

At its heart, this identity continued to defy definition. A major issue in establishing a common and unifying brand for Canada is its intrinsic multi-culturalism. It is one very large country with two predominant cultures and official languages, a growing awareness of multiple original Indigenous foundations, and a pluralistic respect for hundreds of ancestral identities (it is very common for Canadians to refer to themselves as, for example, Italian-Canadian, Chinese-Canadian, Jamaican-Canadian) resulting in a dynamic fusion as the children of immigrants mix and form new cultural identities. Further, strong regional identities (East Coast vs West Coast, Quebec, Ontario, 'the west'), complete with unique cultural traditions, cuisines and speaking accents means that no one definition of a Canadian identity would resonate nationwide.

As the country emerged from the shadows of the United Kingdom and then the United States, throughout the last decades of the last century Canadians began to understand that they might actually have their own identity but also struggled with how to define that identity in positive terms. The 'I AM CANADIAN' Molson Canadian beer advertisement that ran in the late 1990s through 2005 set a new tone for national pride, igniting a movement and acting as a rallying cry for Canadians. It was a moment in time when we no longer felt insecure or ashamed of our pride, but instead revelled in it. The timing aligned with a further divergence in values illustrated by Canada's refusal to participate in the war in Iraq; by a distaste for cultural imperialism borne from globalisation; and finally, in a quiet pride in weathering the financial crisis (or lack thereof) in 2008, through a strongly established and trusted banking system. Something shifted in the psyche of Canadians around this time, as we began to see ourselves as no longer invisible, but actually standing for something distinctly not-American. It represented our coming of age as a nation – more than that, it solidified to ourselves and to the world that we definitely were not American, and that this was something worth shouting about.

The powers-that-be agreed. The official creation of 'Brand Canada' was an attempt to reflect the nation's new identity and create a clear unique brand positioning, attempting to appeal to the emotions of tourists by playing up the distinct experiential nature of being in the country (Hudson and Ritchie, 2009). This approach also appealed to Canadians, for whom being open, friendly and inviting to both visitors and migrants became markers of personal and national pride.

Canadians have always been hyper-aware of the inherent asymmetrical relationship with the US. This is a relationship where we know everything about our nearest neighbour, but they appear to know next to nothing about us (a fact illustrated by the countless comedic 'vox pops' on Canadian television asking Americans to describe what they know about Canada, and they invariably come up blank). This results in a hyper-sensitivity to American cultural forces and companies within our borders. Especially in the years since the 2008 financial crash, Canada's progressive politics, its open borders to immigration, universal healthcare, a stable economy and a relatively non-violent society have become defining points of pride. A prior inferiority complex has given way to a resistance to subordination – especially as we see markers for growth, quality of life and our values diverging so starkly with the US (particularly during the Trump years).

As such, Canadian national pride has, admittedly, taken on an air of smug superiority. Every Canadian is familiar with stories of American backpackers sewing Canadian flags on their luggage to curry favours from locals when traveling abroad, and most Canadians will ensure their own luggage is likewise adorned so as not to be mistaken for American (as negative connotations abound). The modern-day version of Trudeau-mania – this time for Justin, son of Pierre – is certainly not as manic as it once was, but still garners a degree of self-satisfaction, particularly when conversing with foreigners, and especially in light of and relation to the recent political landscape to the south. A country's celebrity leader frequently can, after all, serve as a *de facto* representation of brand identity in the crowded world of international politics (Dinnie, 2016).

As with all nation brands, the picture is not entirely rosy. Despite concerted efforts at reparations and reconciliations, Canada still struggles with Indigenous rights and correcting the historical atrocities and inequities that persist today. The country has been an international leader in acknowledging the history, culture and traditions of Indigenous peoples, with a very strong focus on education that begins in primary school and continues throughout the curriculum. Amends are being attempted at every level of government, and yet more could always be done. Whilst racial tensions might not be as profound (or as public) as that which occur in the US, some pockets of Canada still experience xenophobia and an unwelcoming atmosphere, particularly against new immigrants who are continuously drawn to Canada in relatively large numbers. There is also a rhetoric vs reality gap in major areas such as climate change and human rights, with the Trudeau government offering a loud commitment to environmentalism whilst failing to meet its emissions targets and prioritising natural resource extraction and pipelines; it also proclaims a proud political platform of equality and peacekeeping while continuing to defend the sale of military equipment to Saudi Arabia that contributes to fatalities in Yemen (Nimijean, 2018). Most recently the country struggled in the Covid-19 pandemic, as cracks in the healthcare infrastructure were revealed to have had significant capacity diminishment by subsequent governments who neglected to maintain investments in the system, resulting in higher morbidity numbers and a slower vaccination roll-out than other comparatively developed nations.

Still, it is early days for the global emergence of Brand Canada. Its higher latitude, vast undeveloped land mass, abundance of natural resources and a broader long-term commitment to sustainability has placed Canada among the top tier in countries that are poised to both survive and adapt to climate change. There is still ample room for economic growth as it becomes a beacon for the best and brightest migrants from the Global South and war-torn countries like Syria. Both finance and tech are driving the growth – a strongly regulated financial sector, along with a commitment to innovation fuelled through immigration and a relatively young population enjoying a high quality of life combined with a progressive, internationalist and multi-cultural outlook means that there is little standing in the way of Canada's ascendance as a top nation brand. In the eyes of the world, Canada might remain the sleepy

'Friendly Giant' – benign, welcoming, easy-going and amiable – but the coming decades could signify a major shift in its economic, cultural and social might – as the second and third generations of new Canadians assert themselves on the world's stage, comfortable and confident in the knowledge that their way of life is one most aspire to and will want to experience, as climate change, political upheaval and economic stagnation plague other parts of the world.

References

CBC Archives (2021) 'Pierre Trudeau: There's no place for the state in the bedrooms of the nation', available at: www.cbc.ca/player/play/1811727781 (accessed 25/6/2021).

Dinnie, K. (2016) *Nation Branding: Concepts, Issues, Practice*, 2nd edn, London: Routledge.

Hudson, S. and Ritchie, J.R.B. (2009) 'Branding a memorable destination experience: The case of "Brand Canada"', *International Journal of Tourism Research*, 11 (2), 217–228.

Morton, F.L. (1987) 'The political impact of the Canadian charter of rights and freedoms', *Canadian Journal of Political Science/Revue canadienne de science politique*, 20 (1), 31–55.

Nimijean, R. (2018) 'Introduction: Is Canada back? Brand Canada in a turbulent world', *Canadian Foreign Policy Journal*, 24 (2), 127–138.

US News & World Report (2021) 'Overall best countries ranking', available at: www.usnews.com/news/best-countries/overall-rankings (accessed 23/6/2021).

Summary

As more and more nations turn to the techniques of nation branding and as nation branding gains academic, practitioner and government recognition as an important phenomenon, a proliferation of new approaches, tactics and strategies is occurring. Policy makers at a national level still need to become more aware of the power of branding to help achieve country goals, and there will be increasing understanding of the need for nations to manage their reputations rather than passively endure the malign and humiliating effects of persistent, outdated national stereotypes. Perhaps the key lesson for nations to learn is the need to coordinate their nation branding efforts. Without such coordination, a country's nation branding strategy will stagnate and the nation's image will drift, likely in a negative direction.

Discussion points

1   Identify one country which appears to demonstrate a high level of coordination in its nation brand strategy. Describe the nature of this coordination, and its effects.
2   Apply the ICON model of nation branding to a country of your choice in order to identify possible new directions for that country's nation brand.

References

Akutsu, S. (2008) 'The directions and the key elements of branding Japan', in Dinnie, K. (ed.), *Nation Branding – Concepts, Issues, Practice*, 1st edn, 211–219, London: Butterworth-Heinemann.

Alpert, J.I. and Alpert, M.I. (1990) 'Music influences on mood and purchase intentions', *Psychology and Marketing*, 7 (2), 109–133.

Ambler, T. (2006) 'Mastering the metrics', *The Marketer*, 24, May, 22–23.

Andéhn, M., Kazeminia, A., Lucarelli, A. and Sevin, E. (2014) 'User-generated place brand equity on Twitter: The dynamics of brand associations in social media', *Place Branding and Public Diplomacy*, 10, 132–144.

Anholt, S. (2007) *Competitive Identity: The New Brand Management for Nations, Cities and Regions*, New York: Palgrave Macmillan.

Anholt, S. (2008) 'From *nation branding* to *competitive identity* – the role of brand management as a component of national policy', in Dinnie, K. (ed.), *Nation Branding – Concepts, Issues, Practice*, 1st edn, 22–23, London: Butterworth-Heinemann.

Arnold, S. (2005) 'That jingle is part of your brand', *Broadcasting & Cable*, 24 January, 78.

Barkema, H.G., Chen, X.-P., George, G., Luo, Y. and Tsui, A.S. (2015) 'West meets East: New concepts and theories', *Academy of Management Journal*, 58 (2), 460–479.

Batty, D. (2020) 'Only a fifth of UK universities say they are "decolonising" curriculum', *The Guardian*, 11 June.

Cheregi, B. and Bargaoanu, A. (2020) 'Branding Romania as a "Tech Country": Nation branding in times of digital disruption', Conference: Redefining Community in Intercultural Context, Cluj Napoca, May.

Curran, T. (2020) 'Our minds' eye, impact', *The Market Research Society*, 31, October, 12–13.

Dinnie, K., Melewar, T.C., Seidenfuss, K.-U. and Musa, G. (2010) 'Nation branding and integrated marketing communications – an ASEAN perspective', *International Marketing Review*, 27 (4), 388–403.

Grenni, S., Horlings, L.G. and Soini, K. (2020) 'Linking spatial planning and place branding strategies through cultural narratives in places', *European Planning Studies*, 28 (7), 1355–1374.

Herrington, J.D. and Capella, L.M. (1996) 'Effects of music in service environments: A field study', *Journal of Services Marketing*, 10 (2), 26–41.

IMD World Competitiveness Center (2021) 'World digital competitiveness ranking', available at: www.imd.org/centers/world-competitiveness-center/rankings/world-digital-competitiveness/ (accessed 18/7/2021).

Insch, A. (2011) 'Conceptualization and anatomy of green destination brands', *International Journal of Culture, Tourism and Hospitality Research*, 5 (3), 282–290.

Jackson, D.M. (2003) *Sonic Branding: An Introduction*, New York: Palgrave Macmillan.

Koh, B.S. (2021a) *Brand Singapore: Nation Branding in a World Disrupted by Covid-19*, 3rd edn, Singapore: Marshall Cavendish Business.

Koh, B.S. (2021b) *Brand Singapore: Nation Branding in a World Disrupted by Covid-19*, 3rd edn, Singapore: Marshall Cavendish Business.

Koh, B.S. (2021c) 'Businesses and brand Singapore in a post-Covid world', *The Business Times*, 11 June, available at: www.businesstimes.com.sg/opinion/businesses-and-brand-singapore-in-a-post-covid-world (accessed 16/7/2021).

Lee, K.-F. (2018) *AI Superpowers – China, Silicon Valley, and the New World Order*, Boston and New York: Houghton Mifflin Harcourt.

Maheshwari, V., Vandewalle, I. and Bamber, D. (2011) 'Place branding's role in sustainable development', *Journal of Place Management and Development*, 4 (2), 198–213.

McElrea, H. and Standing, L. (1992) 'Fast music causes fast drinking', *Perceptual and Motor Skills*, 75 (2), 362.

Milliman, R.E. (1982) 'Using background music to affect the behaviour of supermarket shoppers', *Journal of Marketing*, 46, Summer, 86–91.

Mortimer, R. (2005) 'Sonic branding: Branding the perfect pitch', *Brand Strategy*, February, 24.

North, A.C., Hargreaves, D.J. and McKendrick, J. (1999) 'The influence of in-store music on wine selections', *Journal of Applied Psychology*, 84 (2), 271–276.

Pamment, J. and Cassinger, C. (2018) 'Nation branding and the social imaginary of participation: An exploratory study of the Swedish number campaign', *European Journal of Cultural Studies*, 21 (5), 561–574.

Pant, D. (2008) 'Re-positioning Nepal in global public opinion and markets: Place-branding for sustainable economic development', in Dinnie, K. (ed.), *Nation Branding – Concepts, Issues, Practice*, 1st edn, 50–51, London: Butterworth-Heinemann.

Rebelo, C., Mehmood, A. and Marsden, T. (2020) 'Co-created visual narratives and inclusive place branding: A socially responsible approach to residents' participation and engagement', *Sustainability Science*, 15 (2), 423–435.

Roballey, T.C., McGreevy, C., Rongo, R.R., Schwantes, M.L., Steger, P.J., Wininger, M.A. and Gardner, E.B. (1985) 'The effect of music on eating behaviour', *Bulletin of the Psychonomic Society*, 23 (3), 221–222.

Skinner, H. (2018) 'Who really creates the place brand? Considering the role of user generated content in creating and communicating a place identity', *Communication & Society*, 31 (4), 9–25.

Stewart, G. (2006) 'Can reputations be "managed"?', *The Geneva Papers*, 31, 480–499.

Treasure, J. (2007) 'Sound: The uncharted territory', *Brand Strategy*, March, 32–33.

Uchinaka, S., Yoganathan, V. and Osburg, V. (2019) 'Classifying residents' roles as online place-ambassadors', *Tourism Management*, 71, 137–150.

Werbach, K. (2018) *The Blockchain and the New Architecture of Trust*, Cambridge, MA: The MIT Press.

Yan, J. (2008) 'Smaller nations enter the global dialogue through nation branding', in Dinnie, K. (ed.), *Nation Branding – Concepts, Issues, Practice*, 1st edn, 170–172, London: Butterworth-Heinemann.

Index

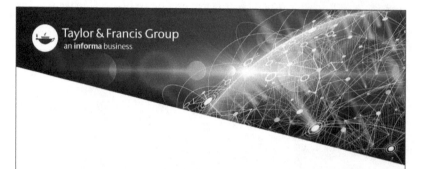